AIRCRAFT CARRIERS

Other Titles in ABC-CLIO's
WEAPONS AND WARFARE SERIES

AIRCRAFT CARRIERS

AN ILLUSTRATED HISTORY OF THEIR IMPACT

Paul Fontenoy

A B C  C L I O

Santa Barbara, California   Denver, Colorado   Oxford, England

Library of Congress Cataloging-in-Publication Data
Fontenoy, Paul E.
Aircraft carriers : an illustrated history of their impact / Paul Fontenoy.
p. cm. — (Weapons and warfare series)
Includes bibliographical references and index.
ISBN 1-85109-573-X (hardback : alk. paper) — ISBN 1-85109-578-0 (ebook)
1. Aircraft carriers—History. I. Title. II. Series.
V874F65 2006
359.9'4835—dc22
2006007471

06 07 08 09 / 10 9 8 7 6 5 4 3 2 1

This book is also available on the World Wide Web as an eBook.
Visit abc-clio.com for details.

ABC-CLIO, Inc.
130 Cremona Drive, P.O. Box 1911
Santa Barbara, California 93116-1911

Acquisitions Editor: Alicia Merritt
Media Editor: Ellen Rasmussen
Media Manager: Caroline Price
Production Editor: Cisca Louise Schreefel
Editorial Assistant: Alisha Martinez
Production Manager: Don Schmidt
Manufacturing Coordinator: George Smyser

This book is printed on acid-free paper. ∞
Manufactured in the United States of America

CONTENTS

INTRODUCTION TO
ENCYCLOPEDIAS OF WEAPONS
AND WARFARE SERIES

WEAPONS BOTH FASCINATE AND REPEL. They are used to kill and maim individuals and to destroy states and societies, and occasionally whole civilizations, and with these the greatest of man's cultural and artistic accomplishments. Throughout history, tools of war have been the instruments of conquest, invasion, and enslavement, but they have also been used to check evil and to maintain peace.

Weapons have evolved over time to become both more lethal and more complex. For the greater part of man's existence, combat was fought at the length of an arm or at such short range as to represent no real difference; battle was fought within line of sight and seldom lasted more than the hours of daylight of a single day. Thus, individual weapons that began with the rock and the club proceeded through the sling and boomerang, bow and arrow, sword and axe, to gunpowder weapons of the rifle and machine gun of the late nineteenth century. Study of the evolution of these weapons tells us much about human ingenuity, the technology of the time, and the societies that produced them. The greater part of technological development of weaponry has taken part in the last two centuries, especially the twentieth century. In this process, plowshares have been beaten into swords; the tank, for example, evolved from the agricultural caterpillar tractor. Occasionally the process is reversed and military technology has impacted society in a positive way. Thus modern civilian medicine has greatly benefitted from advances to save soldiers' lives, and weapons technology has impacted such areas as civilian transportation or atomic power.

Weapons can have a profound impact on society. Gunpowder weapons, for example, were an important factor in ending the era of the armed knight and the Feudal Age. They installed a kind of rough democracy on the battlefield, making "all men alike tall." We can only wonder what effect weapons of mass destruction (WMD) might have on our own time and civilization.

This series will trace the evolution of a variety of key weapons systems, describe the major changes that occurred in each, and illustrate and identify the key types. Each volume begins with a description of the particular weapons system and traces its evolution, while discussing its historical, social, and political contexts. This is followed by a heavily illustrated section that is arranged more or less along chronological lines that provides more precise information on at least 80 key variants of that particular weapons system. Each volume contains a glossary of terms, a bibliography of leading books on that particular subject, and an index.

Individual volumes in the series, each written by a specialist in that particular area of expertise, are as follows:

Ancient Weapons
Medieval Weapons
Pistols
Rifles
Machine Guns
Artillery
Tanks
Battleships
Cruisers and Battle Cruisers
Aircraft Carriers
Submarines
Military Aircraft, Origins to 1918
Military Aircraft, 1919–1945
Military Aircraft in the Jet Age
Helicopters
Ballistic Missiles
Air Defense
Destroyers

We hope that this series will be of wide interest to specialists, researchers, and even general readers.

Spencer C. Tucker
Series Editor

AIRCRAFT CARRIERS

CHAPTER ONE

Origins and Early Development of the Aircraft Carrier

WARSHIP DESIGN CHANGED RAPIDLY in the second half of the nineteenth century, driven by two major technological developments: steam power and advances in artillery. The challenges these novel vessels presented to fleet commanders were not just operational but extended more widely into tactics and strategy. Reconnaissance had always been a problem that the advent of steam vessels with their greater speed and mobility exacerbated. While steam made production of speedy scouting vessels possible, faster steam-powered enemy fleets independent of the wind were more difficult to locate. Speed also brought with it the possibility of surprise, both tactical and strategic. Naval artillery had changed little in its fundamentals for three centuries but in the mid-nineteenth century weapon design took a great leap forward. As guns grew in size warships could carry fewer weapons. Accurate gunfire consequently became more important. Furthermore, these larger weapons possessed greater range and, as the century progressed, battle ranges slowly extended, while the battle space became more obscured as it filled with the smoke from guns and furnaces. At the turn of the nineteenth century gunnery officers also came to appreciate the advantage of long-range heavy gunfire over the close-range battering effect of large weapons.

Both these technological developments encouraged efforts to discover means by which commanders might see beyond the smoke and confusion of the battle zone to discern the enemy's movements and direct long-range gunfire, and beyond the horizon to locate and shadow an opposing fleet. Consequently, admiralties and naval officers generally showed considerable receptiveness to the benefits of aviation at sea from shortly after practical aerial vehicles emerged. The successful development of the balloon led many navies to experiment with its use as a battlefield reconnaissance platform from the mid-nineteenth century onward. Some, most notably the United States Navy during the Civil War, deployed balloons operationally from converted or specially constructed vessels. When self-propelled aircraft, both heavier and lighter than air types, appeared around 1900, the world's major navies were quick to appreciate their potential for distant reconnaissance and battlefield observation. Both the German and British fleets moved quickly to acquire rigid airships from as early as 1908, even though these expensive vessels were still in the infancy of their development.

Heavier-than-air machines proved even more attractive. Prior to World War I several of the world's navies commissioned vessels as parent ships for seaplanes. Not surprisingly, given that the American Wright brothers were the first to make a successful controlled flight in a heavier-than-air machine, the United States Navy was the first to experiment. Captain Washington I. Chambers, appointed in 1910 to coordinate aviation matters for the Navy Department, arranged with the Curtiss Aeroplane Company to use one of the firm's aircraft and its chief test pilot, Eugene Ely, to conduct a pair of trials operating aircraft from warships. In the first, on November 14, 1910, Ely took off in a Curtiss pusher biplane from an inclined wooden platform, 83 feet long and 24 feet wide, erected over the forecastle of the cruiser *Birmingham* while it was anchored in Hampton Roads. In Chambers' second experiment, on January 18, 1911, in San Francisco Bay, Ely landed a Curtiss pusher on a platform constructed over the quarterdeck of the anchored armored cruiser *Pennsylvania*. The platform was 119 feet 4 inches long, 31 feet 6 inches wide, and fitted with a primitive arresting gear formed by twenty-two transverse ropes suspended just above it and weighted at each end with sandbags lying on the platform. The Curtiss was fitted with hooks on its landing gear axle to catch the ropes and there was a crash barrier, in the form of a deck awning stretched vertically at the forward end of the platform in case Ely missed the arresting gear. In the event, the hooks engaged the eleventh rope and halted the Curtiss 50 feet beyond the touchdown point. Shortly afterward, on February 17, 1911, Glenn Curtiss himself conducted a further experiment for the Navy. He flew a prototype seaplane out to the *Pennsylvania,* by then stripped of the landing platform, while the cruiser was anchored in San Diego harbor. The seaplane was hoisted aboard and, a while later, set back on the water for a return flight, demonstrating the practicality of operating seaplanes from surface ships.

The Royal Navy also undertook considerable experimental work before World War I began. On January 10, 1912, Lieutenant Charles R. Samson, one of the first four British naval officers to receive flight training during 1911, successfully flew a Short Brothers pusher biplane off an inclined track constructed over the forward turret and forecastle of the battleship *Africa* while it was anchored off Sheerness. Soon afterwards, the Navy erected a similar more horizontal track on the battleship's sister ship, the *Hibernia.* Two Shorts, one the original landplane and the other a new seaplane, were embarked for the naval review at Weymouth. Samson flew the landplane off the track while the *Hibernia* was underway at ten knots on May 2, 1912, the first such flight from a moving ship, and landed ashore. The following year the Navy equipped the protected cruiser *Hermes* as a seaplane carrier for the annual fleet maneuvers. The cruiser had a takeoff track over the forecastle, a canvas hanger for aircraft stowage on the quarterdeck, and a long derrick on the mainmast for handling seaplanes. A Short Folder Seaplane, fitted with Short's patented wing-folding mechanism that greatly eased accommodating aircraft aboard ships, and a René Caudron amphibian that had wheels projecting through the bottom of its floats, were embarked. The two aircraft made about thirty flights between July 5 and October 6, 1913, the Short using a wheeled trolley for taking off. On at least two occasions the aircraft took off while the *Hermes* was underway.

These experiments, especially the extended operations using the *Hermes,* greatly influenced the Royal Navy's approach to deploying aircraft at sea and laid the foundation for the fleet's aviation operations during World War I. They also led directly to the Admiralty's decision to commission a permanent aviation ship for the Royal Navy. This vessel, the *Ark Royal,* was a merchant ship purchased in May 1914 while still under construction at the Blyth Shipbuilding and Dry Docks Company. The Assistant Director of Naval Construction, John H. Narbeth, assisted by Constructor Charles J. W. Hopkins, so completely redesigned the ship that all that remained of its merchantman origins were the keel, framing, and shell plating. The machinery and superstructure were relocated at the stern of the ship, leaving the forward two-thirds of the hull available for aviation features. It had an enclosed hangar within the hull, specialized aircraft maintenance shops, fuel and lubricant stowage, and ordnance magazines. A large sliding hatch gave access for a pair of steam cranes to hoist aircraft from the hangar. The sheer was completely flat, allowing seaplanes to take off using wheeled trolleys from the clear foredeck, although there is no clear evidence this ever occurred. When the *Ark Royal* commissioned on December 10, 1914, it was a testament to the Admiralty's prewar commitment to naval aviation.

The *Ark Royal,* however, was not the first British design for an aviation ship for the Royal Navy. In December 1912 the shipbuilders William Beardmore & Company in Dalmuir submitted a proposal to the Admiralty for the construction of a "parent ship for naval aeroplanes and torpedo-boat destroyers." The design envisaged a 15,000-ton ship 450 feet long and 110 feet in the beam. It featured a flush deck from end to end, flanked amidships by two superstructures that each incorporated a stack, mast, and hangar accommodation for three seaplanes in separate bays. Seaplanes would take off on trolleys from the forward section of the flush deck and land on the aft deck. A bridge connected the superstructures over the flight deck and carried navigation and conning stations. The deck between the superstructures could be closed off at each end during bad weather and an internal hangar below the flight deck could accommodate ten disassembled seaplanes. The design also envisaged workshop facilities, aircrew accommodations, large magazines and fuel storage spaces, and a powerful wireless installation. For self-defense the ship would carry six 4-inch guns. The Admiralty gracefully declined the proposal on the grounds that "as sufficient experience had not yet been gained with hydroplanes working from a ship at sea to enable naval requirements to be definitely stated, it was considered inadvisable to proceed further with the matter at present." In fact, as later experience with carriers such as the *Furious* would demonstrate, the impact of furnace uptake gases and eddies created by the large superstructure on air flow over the after deck would have rendered landing on it extremely hazardous if not impossible, but the design demonstrated considerable appreciation of the requirements for the efficient operation of aircraft with the fleet.

France also was an early participant in experimental operation of aircraft with the fleet. In March 1912 the *Foudre,* originally constructed as a cruiser to carry and launch torpedo boats at sea and operated as an experimental balloon carrier during naval maneuvers in 1898 and 1901, was converted into an aircraft carrier with a large hangar abaft its stacks. From May 27, 1912, the *Foudre* operated seaplanes during the regular fleet maneuvers. In early 1914 a take-off platform was installed over the forecastle and, on May 8, René Caudron, a civilian pilot and notable aircraft designer, took off from it flying an amphibian of his own design (identical to the machine embarked on the British *Hermes* the previous year). Lieutenant de Vaisseau Jean de Laborde, one of the earliest French naval aviators, attempted the same feat on June 9, 1914, but this effort ended in a crash. The French Navy also began investigating the design of a flight-deck ship as early as May 1912, a process that was sufficiently advanced for at least semiofficial authorization of construction by the end of the year. It also proposed to purchase a British tanker, the *Fornebu,* for conversion into an aviation ship to replace the *Foudre,* which was regarded as capable of fulfilling the fleet's needs only temporarily. In any event, neither the flight-deck ship nor the conversion of the *Fornebu* proceeded further after the outbreak of war.

The Russian Navy undertook considerable experimental work operating balloons from warships around 1900, including converting the old German transatlantic liner *Lahn* into the specialized aviation ship *Russ,* designed to deploy up to nine balloons and incorporating hydrogen generators and compressors, balloon winches, a clear handling deck, aerial photographic equipment, and air-to-ship telephone communications. The ship, however, was worn out and, probably fortunately, was unable to accompany the Third Pacific Fleet on its epic voyage to destruction at the Battle of Tsushima in 1905. This early experience of specialized aviation requirements proved valuable during World War I.

Italy succeeded in deploying an aviation vessel in combat prior to World War I. The converted brigantine *Cavalmarino* briefly deployed its kite balloon to spot for the gunfire of the battleship *Re Umberto* and cruiser *Carlo Alberto* against Turkish shore positions around Tripoli before a storm wrecked the balloon on December 12, 1911. Nevertheless, the Italian fleet proceeded very slowly with shipboard aviation, even during World War I.

As important as all these experiments in operating aircraft from ships were, there were very rapid advances in the design of aircraft for naval use. The earliest American and British experiments were conducted using landplanes equipped with flotation bags in case of an emergency water landing. By the time of the *Hibernia* trials the Royal Navy was using seaplanes, which predominated in shipboard use thereafter until well into World War I. René Caudron and the Farman brothers in France, Glenn Curtiss in the United States, and the Short brothers in Britain all developed practical seaplanes by 1912. They quickly were joined by other designers, especially after the French industrialist Jacques Schneider established the valuable Coupe d'Aviation Maritime Jacques Schneider in December 1912 to encourage the development of seaplanes through international races to be held annually from 1913. Flying boats also developed rapidly, with very practical machines emerging from Curtiss, again, in the United States, Sopwith in Britain, the Franco-British Aviation Company in France, Lohner in Austria, and Oertz in Germany. Seaplanes, aircraft with float undercarriages, nevertheless predominated over flying boats, aircraft with boat-type fuselages, for shipboard operations.

Some further developments were very significant for the emergence of effective aircraft carriers. In 1913 the Short brothers patented their wing folding mechanism. This allowed them to reduce the stowed width of their seaplanes to as little as 12 feet and permitted rapid and trouble-free unfolding before flight, while maintaining structural strength for safe operation. This advance greatly increased the potential aircraft capacity of carriers, since the relative fragility of early machines required hangar stowage while at sea if they were to remain operational. In 1914, working very closely with Commander Charles R. Samson, in command of the Naval Wing of the Royal Flying Corps (usually known as the Royal Naval Air Service), and Captain Murray Sueter, head of the Royal Navy's Air Department, Short produced more powerful versions of its folder seaplanes that were equipped to carry and drop torpedoes or bombs. This enabled the Royal Naval Air Service to conduct experiments in using its aircraft offensively. The greater load-carrying capabilities of these seaplanes also permitted experiments with wireless telegraphy communications, long-distance navigation over water, and some early trials of night flying operations.

CARRIER DEVELOPMENTS
DURING WORLD WAR I

When World War I began Britain added mercantile aircraft carrier conversions to its fleet. The Royal Navy initially opted for simple conversions of three fast cross-Channel packets that could keep pace with the battle fleet. Their features owed much to experience with the *Hermes,* and initially included only canvas hangars fore and aft and additional derricks to handle seaplanes. Operations soon demonstrated the need for more sophistication, and the next conversion, the *Ben-my-Chree,* incorporated permanent enlarged hangars and takeoff platforms over the foredeck, features that also were very quickly added to the original group of aircraft carriers. The final four conversions were still more elaborate and were designed from the outset to operate both seaplanes for reconnaissance and strike missions and landplane single seat fighters for fleet air defense and interception operations against the German Navy's Zeppelins.

The Royal Navy quickly realized that the relatively small size of these carriers limited their capabilities for fleet operations, both because of their small aircraft capacities and their limitations in heavy weather. To support aviation operations with the Grand Fleet, the main battle force, the Admiralty purchased the old but fast Cunarder *Campania* for conversion into what was termed, even then, a "fleet carrier." The *Campania* was much larger than the packet conversions, endowing it with much improved sea-keeping qualities, greater aircraft capacity, and enhanced facilities for maintenance.

In May 1916 Admiral Sir John Jellicoe, commander of the Grand Fleet, requested that the Admiralty provide a special aviation ship to supplement or replace the collection of mercantile conversions operating with the various components of the fleet in the North Sea. Jellicoe was near obsessive about the threat of the German Navy's Zeppelins, and his main concern was for this ship to protect the fleet against the airship threat. In August the Admiralty decided to acquire the incomplete hulls of two Italian cargo liners whose construction by William Beardmore & Company at Dalmuir had halted with the outbreak of war. Ultimately, the Admiralty decided to proceed with just one vessel to be named *Argus.* The genesis of the design for this new carrier was a proposal from Lieutenant R. A. Holmes, RNVR, who had been an assistant naval architect with the Cunard Company prior to the war and had served aboard the converted carrier *Riviera* from the time of the ship's first commission. Holmes suggested a design whose principal features were a flight deck running unobstructed by any superstructure from bow to stern and long ducts running along the each side of the hangar to the stern for discharging furnace gases. This concept was taken up by John H. Narbeth, the Assistant Director of Naval Construction, and modified to a form that somewhat resembled the 1912 proposal from Beardmore, coincidentally the *Argus*'s builder, with two side superstructures but retaining the long ducts from Holmes's original suggestion. Tests of a wind tunnel model at the National Physical Laboratory in November 1916 demonstrated the operational hazards of this superstructure arrangement, so Narbeth cast about for some alternative. One arrangement considered was contained in an idea for a carrier put forward in September 1915 by Flight Commander Hugh Williamson. He had served aboard the *Ark Royal* until he was injured in a crash and then had been assigned to the design section of the Air Department. His design incorporated an island offset to one side that contained all the bridge structure, masts, and stacks, the superstructure arrangement that has prevailed in most carriers since the end of World War I. Narbeth seems to have considered the design too advanced to allow for the changes needed for an island structure and eventually incorporated a charthouse in the middle of the flight deck that could be retracted hydraulically during flight operations. As a result of these design issues, the *Argus* did not commission until September 14, 1918, and was too late for operations during the war.

Aircraft operations with the fleet showed the Royal Navy that a carrier required a very considerable excess of speed over that of the fleet. Flying off and recovering aircraft necessitated diverging from the axis of the fleet's advance or stopping to pick up seaplanes. The *Campania*'s speed was still insufficient, while its machinery was worn and unreliable. The advent of Admiral Sir David Beatty, an enthusiastic supporter of fleet aviation operations, as commander of the Grand Fleet in November 1916 also expedited an upgrade of the fleet's aircraft carrier capabilities. The Grand Fleet Aeronautical Committee, in May 1917, recommended the alteration of the incomplete large light cruiser *Furious* to a fast seaplane carrier. When the cruiser joined the fleet on July 4, 1917, its speed of over 31 knots represented a great advance over the *Campania*'s 24 knots (on a good day!). It also encouraged Squadron Commander E. H. Dunning, in command of the ship's aviation personnel, to experiment with landing aircraft onto the ship's flight deck forward since, when the ship was steaming at full speed into the wind, the air speed over the deck was not much below the landing speed of his Sopwith Pup single seater fighter. On August 2, 1917, Dunning flew his Pup up the port side of the *Furious* while it was steaming at full speed and side-slipped onto the deck where waiting officers seized toggles specially attached to the aircraft and held it to the deck, the first successful landing onto a moving ship. He repeated the feat on August 7 but was killed when his Pup slid over the side of the deck as he made another attempt the same afternoon. As a result of Dunning's experiments and further operational experience with the *Furious* in the North Sea the fleet recommended that it be altered to allow a

less risky means of recovering aircraft on board. The carrier underwent a further reconstruction from November 14, 1917, to March
15, 1918, gaining an additional hangar aft with a landing-on deck
above it equipped with fore-and-aft wire arresting gear and a crash
barrier at its forward end. This arrangement proved very hazardous
because of furnace gases and dangerous air eddies created by the
superstructure amidships (only three out of thirteen attempts to
land onto the after deck ended in success) and use of the deck for
landing aircraft was abandoned, although it proved useful for operating dirigible airships.

The Grand Fleet required a second fast carrier to work with the
Furious. The Admiralty selected the incomplete large new cruiser
Cavendish for conversion into an aircraft carrier very similar in layout to the *Furious*'s second state. Renamed the *Vindictive* in honor
of the old cruiser that had led the assault force during the Zee-
brugge raid on April 23, 1918, the new carrier commissioned on
October 1, 1918, just too late for wartime operations.

Early in the war the Royal Navy in the Canal Zone created two
carriers "in theater" from German merchantmen interned at Port
Said. Modifications to the *Anne* and the *Raven II* consisted of
adding a 12-pound low angle gun for self defense and erecting canvas screens to protect embarked aircraft. These vessels initially operated under the Red Ensign with mixed naval and civilian crews and
their first aircraft were up to six French Nieuport floatplanes apiece,
originally operated by the French seaplane carrier *Foudre*, flown by
French pilots with British observers, an extraordinary arrangement
that worked very well in practice. During the summer of 1915 they
were at last commissioned as Royal Navy vessels with naval crews
and served until the later half of 1917.

The French Navy too created a seaplane carrier locally at Port
Said in 1915 from a requisitioned French cargo liner, the *Campinas*.
This vessel was very similar to the two extemporized British vessels
and operated as many as ten Nieuport floatplanes. In home waters
the French Navy also created a pair of seaplane carriers from cross-
channel packets. The *Pas-de-Calais* and the *Nord* acquired two
hangers to accommodate two or three F.B.A. flying boats and were
lightly armed. Their main distinction was their propulsion system—
they were very unusual among aircraft carriers in being side-wheel
steamers.

Other navies also responded to the outbreak of war by adding aircraft carriers conversions to their fleets. Germany took over two
cargo passenger ships, the *Answald* and the larger *Santa Elena*, soon

after the war began. Both received hangars fore and aft of their midships superstructures to accommodate three to four aircraft apiece, and also armed with a pair of 88-millimeter antiaircraft guns. The initial conversions proved unsatisfactory and both were modified further, delaying their entry into service until the summer of 1915. They operated in the Baltic, where they joined another simpler mercantile conversion, the *Glyndwr,* which had entered service earlier, in January 1915. The naval commander there, Grossadmiral Prinz Heinrich of Prussia, was the Kaiser's younger brother and a qualified pilot who appreciated the possibilities of aircraft operations with the fleet. As early as November 1914 he embarked two seaplanes on the armored cruiser *Friedrich Karl* to provide distant reconnaissance for the fleet. He made good use of the *Glyndwr,* until the ship was mined and heavily damaged on June 4, 1915, and then of the *Santa Elena,* despite the disadvantage of their very low speed. They operated very actively with the German Baltic fleet along the coast of Kurland and in the Gulf of Riga, providing aerial reconnaissance and undertaking bombing missions. Prinz Heinrich also deployed seaplanes aboard the cruisers and destroyers of his fleet for several operations to compensate for the inability of his aircraft carriers to keep up.

In contrast, German carrier operations in the North Sea were far from aggressive (unlike those of the navy's shore-based seaplanes which earned and retained the healthy respect of Royal Navy airmen, surface sailors, and submariners throughout the war). They mainly involved cover of submarine, minelaying, and minesweeping operations, and intercepting enemy and neutral shipping. In early December 1917 the High Seas Fleet requested provision of a special aviation ship with sufficient speed to operate with the fleet, something the mercantile conversions were far too slow to accomplish. The Naval Office ruled out new construction as too time-consuming and instead explored either conversion of fast merchant ships or light cruisers. All the fast merchantmen candidates were eliminated as either too large or too small and the Naval Office also decided against light cruiser conversions on the grounds of their impact on front-line firepower. Nevertheless, the High Seas Fleet reiterated its urgent request on December 29, and the Naval Office approved conversion of the cruisers *Stettin* and *Stuttgart* on January 20, 1918. The *Stettin*'s alteration never occurred but work began on the *Stuttgart* in late January and it was commissioned as an aircraft carrier on May 16, the only German "fleet carrier" to complete in either world war. The *Stuttgart* served as the flagship of the officer commanding North Sea Aerial Forces and was a component of Admiral Franz von Hipper's reconnaissance force, providing air cover for minesweeping operations in the North Sea.

The Imperial Japanese Navy's first experience with operating aircraft at sea occurred during the annual fleet maneuvers in October and November 1913, when the transport *Wakamiya Maru* deployed with a couple of Farman seaplanes on board. The same ship recommissioned on August 17, 1914, as a seaplane carrier, fitted with two canvas hangars and carrying four Farman aircraft. It used them during the Japanese operations against the German base at Tsingtao, beginning on September 1. Although damaged by a mine on September 30, the *Wakamiya Maru* returned to operations before the fortress surrendered on November 7 and its aircraft also attempted unsuccessfully to bomb German and Austro-Hungarian ships that remained in Kiaochow Bay on November 27, the first such effort by carrier-based aircraft.

The Imperial Russian Navy created aircraft carriers by conversion in both its main operating areas, the Baltic and the Black seas. Only a single carrier operated in the Baltic. The *Orlitza* previously a cargo liner, was commissioned on February 2, 1915, and served primarily in the defense of the Gulf of Riga. The *Orlitza* had two canvas hangars fore and aft of the superstructure, was armed with eight 3-inch guns and two machine guns for antiaircraft defense, and could carry up to nine aircraft.

The main focus of Russian aircraft carrier operations was in the Black Sea. Russia converted two relatively fast modern cargo liners, the *Imperator Alexandr I* and the *Imperator Nikolai I,* and the small cruiser *Almaz* into very effective seaplane carriers for service there. The conversions were very simple and only involved clearing away superstructure to provide space for aircraft handling and adding armament to the merchantmen. Nevertheless, these three vessels demonstrated great efficiency in launching and recovering aircraft and proved to be very useful carriers during extensive operations against Turkish forces.

The United States Navy briefly deployed two aircraft aboard the battleship *Mississippi* during operations at Vera Cruz, Mexico, in April 1914. The Navy's experience there revived work to develop reliable catapults for launching aircraft that had been shelved after Captain Chambers left the Navy Department. The first shipboard tests took place in November 1915 aboard the armored cruiser *North Carolina* at Pensacola. An improved catapult was installed the following spring and testing began in the summer of 1916. The success of these tests led to two further armored cruisers, the *Hunting-ton* and the *Seattle,* receiving catapults during refits in early 1917. It was also planned to fit a catapult to the *Montana,* creating a complete catapult-equipped cruiser division, but this was abandoned. The three cruisers carried out tests during 1917 but all had the equipment removed by the fall of 1917, largely because it was unsuitable for their service as convoy escorts. Serious efforts by the United States Navy to take aircraft to sea as part of the fleet did not resume until after the end of World War I.

SHIPBOARD AIRCRAFT DEVELOPMENTS DURING WORLD WAR I

The furnace of war greatly accelerated the development of shipboard aircraft. The performance and capabilities of seaplanes, both floatplanes and flying boats, improved dramatically. Much of this advance came from more powerful engines—in 1914 few seaplanes were powered by engines greater than 200-horsepower but in 1918 shipboard seaplanes commonly used engines of 375-horsepower. This greater engine power translated into stronger airframes, greater load-carrying capacity, and longer range. The Royal Navy's new Short Type 166 floatplane in 1914, with a 200-horsepower Salmson engine, could carry a 14-inch torpedo but only at the price of operating with a pilot alone and fuel for a round trip of barely 40 miles. At the end of the war the Short Type 320 floatplane, with a 320-horsepower Sunbeam engine, could carry a pilot, observer/gunner, wireless equipment, and an 18-inch torpedo for a distance of just over 200 miles. Similar advances took place with shipboard flying boats, deployed extensively by the French and Russian navies on their seaplane carriers, and also employed on a limited scale by the Austro-Hungarian and Italian fleets aboard ships. There also was a widely produced family of small single-seater floatplanes derived from the winner of the 1914 Schneider Trophy race, the Sopwith Tabloid. Initial production examples, known as Sopwith Schneiders, were powered by 100-horsepower Gnome rotary engines and could carry a single machine gun and a 65-pound bomb at up to 87 miles per hour, with a total endurance of two and one-quarter hours. The final versions, know as Sopwith Babys, were powered by 130-horsepower Clerget rotary engines and could carry two 65-pound bombs at up to 100 miles per hour. They were used on almost all British seaplane carriers for scouting and interception missions, and also used by the French and Italian navies, with most of the latter machines produced under license by Macchi in Italy.

The greatest change, however, in the character of shipboard aircraft during the war, particularly in the Royal Navy, was the dominance of landplane types aboard major warships and fleet carriers by the later years of the conflict. As early as the spring of 1915, when planning began for the conversion of the *Vindex*, facilities for launching landplane fighter aircraft were incorporated in the design process. The forward flying-off platform on this and later "mixed carriers" was intended for launching both floatplanes (using trolleys) for reconnaissance and landplane fighters to intercept Zeppelins. The first landplanes embarked were Bristol Scouts, with 80-horsepower Gnome rotary engines, capable of 93 miles per hour at sea level and armed with a single machine gun. By 1918 British carriers embarked a specialized variant of the famous Sopwith Camel fitted with a 150-horsepower Bentley rotary engine, giving it a top speed of 117 miles per hour, and carrying two machine guns. It had a slightly smaller wingspan than the normal version and the rear fuselage of this Ship's Camel was detachable for stowage aboard ship. From mid-1917 most British fleet carriers landed their floatplanes and embarked two-seater Sopwith 1-1/2 Strutter landplanes for reconnaissance missions, and at the war's end a specialized landplane torpedo bomber, the Sopwith Cuckoo, was entering service in the strike role. This single-seater, with a 200-horsepower Sunbeam engine, could carry an 18-inch torpedo at a maximum speed of 100 miles per hour and had a range of some 240 miles.

CARRIER OPERATIONS DURING WORLD WAR I

Carrier aircraft undertook three broad roles during World War I: reconnaissance, offensive missions, and fleet defense. Before the war most opinion envisaged reconnaissance, in its broadest sense, as the likeliest contribution of carrier aircraft to naval warfare. Their primary roles, officers thought, would be spotting for naval guns in battle, extending the fleet's tactical range of vision in the approach to action, and strategically reconnoitering the enemy fleet's dispositions and activities in its bases. During World War I carrier aircraft undertook all these missions, though sometimes the outcomes were not what prewar opinion had expected.

The earliest use of carrier-based aircraft during the war was by the Imperial Japanese Navy. On September 1, 1914, the seaplane carrier *Wakamiya Maru,* embarking four Farman floatplanes, joined the Second Squadron for operations against the German fortress city of Tsingtao. The aircraft conducted reconnaissance missions over the target, made several bombing attacks on shipping, and searched for mines, not always successfully, since the carrier struck a mine on September 30 and had to return to Japan temporarily for repairs. In total the *Wakamiya Maru*'s floatplanes made forty-nine sorties in support of the assault and dropped 199 bombs (without sinking any of their targets). This single operation was the sole contribution of Japanese naval aviation to the war.

Fregattenkapitän Max Looff, commander of the German light cruiser *Königsberg,* captured the *City of Winchester,* the war's first British merchant ship casualty, in the Gulf of Aden and sank the small British cruiser *Pegasus* at Zanzibar before serious engine problems forced him to take refuge in the Rufiji Delta for repairs. The British sent a squadron of three modern light cruisers, led by Vice-Admiral Herbert King-Hall, to locate the *Königsberg.* On September 30, 1914, they found it, but the cruiser was out of range and their charts too poor to risk entering the delta. It was clear to King-Hall that destroying the *Königsberg* required aircraft to locate it but his requests to London for support were denied. Instead, he acquired the services of a privately-owned Curtiss flying boat and its civilian pilot, Dennis Cutler, who was hastily commissioned into the Royal Navy. Maintaining the Curtiss was a nightmare—almost all the parts of a second Curtiss were cannibalized to keep it flying and even then the radiator had to be replaced by one from a Ford car. Cutler located the cruiser on November 22 and maintained constant surveillance of the ship until he was shot down and captured on December 10. King-Hall appealed to London again, and the Admiralty dispatched the balloon ship *Manica* embarking a seaplane squadron, commanded by Flight Lieutenant J. T. Cull, which arrived on February 20, 1915. Although King-Hall was reinforced by the pre-dreadnought *Goliath* in March, even its 12-inch guns could not reach the *Königsberg.* Finally, two shallow-draft 6-inch gun monitors, the *Mersey* and the *Severn,* were towed from Malta. On July 6 they entered the delta. At first the *Königsberg*'s fire, directed by shore observers, was dangerous but it deteriorated after the shore stations were knocked out. The monitors used seaplanes to spot their fire but scored only a dozen hits after expending 600 rounds. A second attack began on July 11. The *Königsberg* lacked shore observers and the British spotters had learned from experience. Within twelve minutes the *Severn* scored a hit, and the two monitors knocked out all the *Königsberg*'s guns and wrecked the cruiser within two hours. Looff ordered the ship abandoned and scuttled.

The contribution of ship-borne aircraft to the defeat of a Turkish attempt against the Suez Canal in late 1914 also was very important. Not only did the aircrafts' work play a crucial role in this success but the entire operation was also a tribute to creative improvisation. The aircraft involved were two-seater Nieuport floatplanes assigned to the French carrier *Foudre*, which was sent to Port Said in December 1914, more as a means of getting the ship and its aircraft out of the way of the main French fleet than for any strategic objective. The officer commanding British forces defending the Suez Canal, Lieutenant-General Sir John Maxwell, quickly realized that deploying aircraft from ships would greatly extend the reach of his reconnaissance. The French aircraft initially were carried aboard British warships, the cruiser *Doris* operating off the Sinai Peninsular and the cruisers *Minerva* and *Diana* in the Gulf of Aqaba during December 1914. The cruisers, however, could only embark a single aircraft apiece, so Maxwell himself seems to have conceived the idea of extemporizing aircraft carriers from available merchant vessels at Port Said. Two German cargo liners, the *Aenne Rickmers* and the *Rabenfels* (later renamed the *Anne* and the *Raven II*) that had been seized at the outbreak of war, were selected. The conversions were minimal, simply fitting canvas screens to protect aircraft stowed on the cargo hatch covers. The carriers entered service in January 1915. They still flew the merchant service's Red Ensign, the ships' officers were from the British merchant marine, and most of their crews were Syrian and Greek seamen supplemented by a few Royal Navy and Royal Marines personnel. The Nieuport aircraft transferred from the *Foudre* were flown by French naval pilots, the observers were British officers, and operational command devolved on a British Army officer, Captain L. B. Waldron of the Dublin Fusiliers. By all normal standards, this motley assembly was a recipe for disaster, but it worked brilliantly. The aircrews succeeded in locating the unconventional Turkish advance, across the Sinai Desert rather than along the more usual coastal route, and tracked it with sufficient accuracy to allow British forces to anticipate closely the place and time of its arrival and have troops and warships for fire support in place to repel the assault on February 3, 1915.

The next Allied operation against the Turks involving carrier aircraft was far less successful. From the beginning of planning the effort to force the Dardanelles with an Allied fleet, both local commanders and planners at national headquarters saw the need for carrier aircraft for reconnaissance missions and gunfire spotting duties. Accordingly, the new British carrier *Ark Royal*, joined later by the *Foudre*, formed an important element of the fleet of sixteen pre-dreadnought battleships, the battlecruiser *Inflexible*, and the new super-dreadnought *Queen Elizabeth*, armed with 15-inch guns, all led by Vice-Admiral Sir Sackville Carden, that gathered at the islands of Tenedos and Lemnos for the assault. The performance of the *Ark Royal*'s aircraft as gunnery spotters proved disappointing. The aircraft, although new and of the latest available design, were plagued by engine problems and unreliable wireless sets. Their engines, when functioning properly, all too often produced too little power under local atmospheric and sea-state conditions to unstick the floatplanes or to overcome the weight of their airframes and equipment, especially the wireless sets, sufficiently to reach an adequate altitude for spotting. Worst of all, the crews lacked experience in the art of spotting for artillery, let alone for naval guns, and had to contend with the fact that their sets could transmit but not receive, so they had to improvise methods on the spot, with uncertain results. The unreliability of aerial spotting for the fleet's guns limited their efficacy, particularly against the mobile howitzer batteries deployed in the defenses. When the fleet, commanded by Vice-Admiral John de Robeck after Carden's health breakdown on March 17, pressed into the Narrows on March 18, the result was a debacle. Three old battleships were sunk by unswept mines, which also seriously damaged *Inflexible*, and two old battleships were heavily damaged by gunfire, which also drove away the now unsupported minesweepers. The effort to force the Dardanelles using warships alone was over.

During the dismal Gallipoli campaign that followed this failure, carrier aircraft played a less central role because the Royal Navy dispatched a larger force of landplanes to the theater that were based on the islands close off shore. Nevertheless, aircraft from the *Ark Royal* and later from the faster carrier *Ben-My-Chree* engaged in reconnaissance and gunnery spotting duties, supported by three balloon ships, the *Manica*, the *Hector*, and the *Canning*, that also embarked several floatplanes apiece in canvas hangars aft. The *Ben-My-Chree* also carried the new Short Type 184 torpedo planes and, in conjunction with the Navy's landplanes, at least seventy attacks were made on Turkish shipping engaged in supplying troops on the Gallipoli peninsula via the Black Sea. Several attacks used torpedoes for the first time and it is possible that they succeeded in sinking as many as three small Turkish merchantmen, although firm evidence of their destruction beyond the aircrews' reports is lacking.

After the Allied withdrawal from Gallipoli in January 1916 the Royal Navy moved the *Ben-My-Chree* to Port Said, where it joined the carrier *Empress*, newly arrived from home waters, and the ex-German merchantmen, now commissioned warships. Together they formed the East Indies and Egypt Seaplane Squadron, the Royal Navy's first carrier squadron. Initially, Squadron Commander Cecil L'Estrange led the unit, but he was replaced by Squadron Commander Charles Samson in May 1916.

Samson was one of the more remarkable characters in the Royal Naval Air Service. He was one of the first four naval officers selected for flight training in 1911 and the first to graduate. On January 10, 1912, he made the first takeoff from a British warship and on May 2 the same year the first flight from a ship underway. Before war came he undertook much experimental work, including bombing and torpedo-dropping trials and tests of early wireless telegraphy sets. At the beginning of the war he commanded the naval air station at Eastchurch and took its aircraft to Ostend in Belgium in support of the Royal Marines brigade based there. Even though the Marines were withdrawn only three days after he arrived, the flamboyant Samson contrived to have his squadron attached to French forces based in Dunkirk. The squadron began using automobiles in conjunction with aircraft for reconnaissance and raids, leading Samson to have them fitted with extemporized armor plating manufactured at the local shipyard. Using these vehicles, plus newly designed armored cars supplied by the Admiralty (and several trucks "liberated" from the British Army and fitted with armor and 6-pounder guns), Samson's squadron was very active in the defense of Antwerp and, after the Allies evacuated the city, the region around Dunkirk. Simultaneously, he also oversaw a series of long-distance air raids by Royal Naval Air Service landplanes against Zeppelin installations, culminating in the raid that destroyed the German Army airship *Z.IX* in its shed at Dusseldorf on October 9, 1914. In March 1915 the Eastchurch squadron was withdrawn from Flanders, equipped with new aircraft, and sent to Tenedos to provide air support for the Gallipoli operation. One measure of Samson's initiative was the establishment of a forward landing strip on the beaches within two days of the first landings, although the proximity of the strip to the Turkish front lines made its use hazardous—one Voisin based there was the target of no less than 127 shells in a day, all of which missed. During the nine months his squadron served at Gallipoli, it accumulated no less than 2,600 flying hours.

Samson took to his new mission with gusto. During the next two years the aircraft from his carriers operated all along the coast of the eastern Mediterranean from Salonika to the Libyan border, throughout the Red Sea, and even into the Indian Ocean while engaged in the search for the German raider *Wolf*. They conducted reconnaissance missions throughout the area, often far inland, spotted for the gunners aboard Allied ships off shore, and bombed port facilities and ships along with depots, troop concentrations, and supply lines. The squadron's aircraft made a concentrated effort to disrupt lines of communication by attacking bridges, railroad lines, and station facilities. They also provided air support for T. E. Lawrence's Arab irregulars, operating both in the Red Sea and off the Palestine coast.

The only surface fleet action in which carrier aircraft undertook the tactical reconnaissance role that prewar planners envisaged as their primary function was the Battle of Jutland. Two carriers then formed part of the Grand Fleet, the *Campania* attached to the battle-fleet itself and the *Engadine* providing air support for the Battle Cruiser Force. When Admiral Sir John Jellicoe took the Grand Fleet to sea on May 30, 1916, signals failures resulted in the *Campania* not receiving the order to depart. Although it sailed at midnight, Jellico decided to order the carrier back to Scapa Flow early in the morning of May 31 because he believed the ship could not catch up with his fleet and because of fears for its safety from submarine attack while unescorted. The *Engadine* formed part of the Battle Cruiser Force's scouting line. A Short Type 184 seaplane crewed by Flight Lieutenant F. J. Rutland and Assistant Paymaster G. S. Trewin was launched at 3:08 PM. They spotted the German battle cruiser's cruiser scouting screen, but signaling failures prevented the information from reaching Vice-Admiral Beatty on his flagship, HMS *Lion*.

Operations against German Zeppelins formed the major focus of Royal Navy carrier operations in the North Sea during World War I. In large part this was because of the perception of both the Admiralty and the Grand Fleet's commander, Sir John Jellicoe, of the danger Zeppelins posed to the fleet and these airships' effectiveness, even though at the outbreak of war, the German Navy possessed but a single operational unit and that number had risen to only four by the end of 1914. As the number of German airships grew and particularly after they began a bombing campaign against the British Isles, the pressure on the Royal Navy to take action increased. Given the limitations of carrier floatplanes versus airships—they were incapable of rising to the altitudes of the Zeppelins or of carrying weapons sufficient to destroy them in the air—the British solution was to strike at them in their bases. These operations became a major feature of the operations of the Harwich Force, led by Reginald Tyrwhitt, and its aircraft carriers during the first two years of the war. They also were seen as temptations to the High Seas Fleet, offered the opportunity to cut off and destroy a weak squadron of the Royal Navy, to come out and be trapped into facing the might of the Grand Fleet.

Cuxhaven was the target for the first attempts. The attack plan was for three seaplane carriers, each embarking three seaplanes, to enter the Heligoland Bight escorted by cruisers and destroyers from the Harwich Force. Once within range the carriers would launch their aircraft to attack the Cuxhaven Zeppelin sheds, then await their return. Tyrwhitt took Harwich Force to sea on October 24, 1914, but heavy weather forced its return. Bad weather aborted a further attempt in October and two in November. The next attack was scheduled for December 25, with Vice-Admiral Sir David Beatty's Battle Cruiser Force providing heavy cover. This time the weather cooperated and the seaplane carriers reached their launch point. Seven of the nine floatplanes succeeded in taking off, starting at 7:00 AM, and headed for Cuxhaven. Fog over the target proved to be the main impediment to British success. A case of mistaken identity caused by fog on the river earlier in the morning made the German fleet jittery. Fog caused the pilots to lose their way and forced them to descend to fix their positions, only to be driven off by antiaircraft fire. Low on fuel, the British pilots attacked whatever targets they could find, and then turned back toward the carriers. One pilot actually succeeded in dropping his bombs on the base at Cuxhaven, without causing any damage, but he most probably was lost and hit his target by accident. Only two floatplanes reached their parent ships, the others came down and were located and recovered by Harwich Force destroyers and submarines. Tyrwhitt ordered Harwich Force to retire at 11:45 AM, the submarines withdrew after nightfall, and the raid was over.

The Cuxhaven Raid completely failed in its objective. Nevertheless, it served as a model for a series of eight similar operations between March and July 1915, all of which failed, entirely due to the inadequacies of contemporary aircraft and available navigational equipment in the face of North Sea weather conditions. When Tyrwhitt resumed the campaign in January 1916 matters did not improve. Four operations up to May 4, 1916, resulted in but a single

Sopwith Baby reaching its objective, during the final raid on Tondern, where its two bombs missed their target. The Germans, however, did lose the Zeppelin *L7*, sent to locate Tyrwhitt's force, which was hit by gunfire from two of the Harwich Force's cruisers, brought down, and destroyed by the submarine *E31*'s deck gun. A hiatus followed in these operations until the arrival of the newly-reconstructed carrier *Furious* and, equally important, more reliable aircraft in the form of Sopwith Camels, encouraged planning for fresh attacks on Zeppelin bases. In June 1918 two attempts were made to use the *Furious* to attack the airship sheds at Tondern but both were aborted by weather conditions. The third mission departed Rosyth on July 17. The *Furious* was escorted by five light cruisers and an escort of destroyers, and the Grand Fleet provided cover with the five battleships of the 1st Battle Squadron with more cruisers and destroyers. The *Furious* embarked seven Sopwith Camels, which it launched in two flights starting at 3:00 AM on July 19. Six of the seven aircraft found the base (one had to abort due to engine failure) and bombed the sheds, destroying the airships *L54* and *L60*. Two of the attackers successfully returned to the fleet, three made forced landings in Denmark and were interned, and one drowned, presumably because he force landed in the sea. The base never became effective again and the attack was a spectacular demonstration of the potential of carrier aviation and its advances during the war.

The other great exponent of carrier aviation during World War I was the Imperial Russian Navy in the Black Sea. From early 1915 the Black Sea Fleet mounted a sustained interdiction campaign against Turkish sea communications. A particular target was the coal trade from Anatolia to Constantinople on which the Turkish-German fleet largely depended and that had to come by sea because there was no rail line and the road system was inadequate. According to Russian claims, their naval forces sank over 1,000 vessels during this campaign, in which the fleet's aircraft carriers played a central role and must have been directly responsible for an appreciable percentage of these successes. On more than one occasion the battle cruiser *Goeben* and the light cruiser *Breslau,* units technically transferred to the Ottoman Navy from the German fleet but actually commanded and manned by Germans, that formed the modern heart of Turkish naval forces were incapable of putting to sea on operations for lack of fuel reserves.

The three carriers converted in early 1915 were fast enough to maintain formation with the older battleships that initially formed the core of the fleet and could keep up with even the new dread-noughts that joined the fleet later. Consequently, there were few operations of any size in which the carriers were not tightly integrated and in several of those against the Anatolian and Bulgarian coast-lines, the carriers formed the principal striking force with the battle-ships relegated to support and distant cover roles. Russian carriers used Curtiss flying boats initially, which eventually were supplanted by excellent indigenous Grigorivich boats. The carriers carried large numbers of aircraft for the period and their crews were highly trained, so their launch rates were impressive. One American observer timed a carrier launching seven aircraft in fifteen minutes, compared with the Royal Navy's standard of twenty minutes to launch three aircraft (admittedly under North Sea conditions). After 1916, when Romania joined the war, the Black Sea Fleet's aircraft carrier strength increased when one Romanian auxiliary, the *Rominia*, joined the fleet as a full-time carrier and was supplemented periodically by four other auxiliary cruisers embarking aircraft as operationally necessary. The carriers' aircraft attacked Turkish and Bulgarian ports, their facilities, and ships at dock, conducted wide-spread reconnaissance missions, raided coastal shipping, bombed shore installations, spotted for the fleet's guns, and provided cover for mine-laying operations and convoys.

By the end of World War I, naval aviation had secured for itself an important place in operations. For the most part, however, naval air-craft were shore based. While operational experience had confirmed the potential value of carrier-based aviation, the technical and func-tional details necessary for success remained immature. Major navies accepted that aircraft carriers were an essential feature of fu-ture fleets but the shape, size, arrangements, facilities, and equip-ment all were uncertain and still required much experiment and testing.

CHAPTER TWO

The Aircraft Carrier Matures

BY THE END OF WORLD WAR I all major navies had concluded that aircraft carriers would play an important role in future operations. This conviction was ratified in the Washington Five-Power Naval Limitation Treaty, in which the only category of warship other than battleships subject to limits of both size and total tonnage was the aircraft carrier. Nevertheless, many concentrated discussions of concepts, expensive experimentation, and drawn-out trials were required before fully effective warships emerged. The twenty years between the two world wars encompassed this development, filled with blind alleys and triumphs as designers and operators struggled with the challenge of exploiting the potential of aircraft at sea.

The qualitative and quantitative restrictions imposed by naval arms limitation treaties dominated carrier design during the period between the two world wars. The provisions of the Five-Power Naval Limitation Treaty signed at Washington on February 6, 1922, restricted the total tonnage of capital ships (battleships and aircraft carriers) within the British and United States navies to 525,000 tons each, within the Japanese fleet to 315,000 tons, and within the French and Italian navies to 175,000 tons apiece. It also imposed an upper limit of 35,000 tons on the size of individual capital ships and established a 10-year moratorium on the construction of any vessel over 10,000 tons armed with anything larger than 8-inch guns. Warships of 10,000 tons or less, provided they were armed with a maximum of 8-inch guns, were not subject to quantitative limitations.

The provisions of the Washington Treaty were scheduled to remain in force until 1936, when a new conference was to be held to review the naval armaments situation. It soon became clear that the agreement was not very effective in limiting worldwide naval competition. An abortive meeting at Geneva in 1927 was followed by a more successful conference at London in 1930. At this meeting, representatives from Britain, Japan, and the United States extended quantitative limitations to encompass cruisers, destroyers, and submarines, and imposed new qualitative restrictions on cruisers and destroyers, but neither France nor Italy would adhere to the terms of the London Conference. A further inconclusive meeting at London from December 1935 to March 1936 witnessed the Japanese abrogation of the entire treaty regimen. Nevertheless, the terms of the various limitation agreements profoundly affected the design of the majority of the carriers that were to serve during World War II.

BRITISH CARRIER DEVELOPMENTS
BETWEEN THE WORLD WARS

British operational and design experience exerted substantial influence on the early post–World War I carriers of all nations. In July 1917 the Admiralty ordered the *Hermes,* the Royal Navy's first carrier designed as such from the outset, and followed by purchasing the incomplete Chilean battleship *Almirante Cochrane* for conversion into the carrier *Eagle.* Naval attachés from France, Japan, and the United States eagerly monitored the progress of both vessels and also closely observed the Royal Navy's operational carrier practices with its existing vessels, especially the *Furious.* The two new British carriers, destined to be completed well after the end of World War I, were still semi-experimental vessels that also crystallized the Royal Navy's hard-won experience of aircraft carrier operations during four years of war.

The *Hermes* was designed as a scouting carrier to work with the fleet's cruisers and deploy its aircraft to increase their range of reconnaissance. The *Hermes*'s size, structure, machinery, speed, protection, and defensive armament emulated those of contemporary light cruisers. The initial design featured a flush flight deck flanked on either side by small island structures accommodating the furnace uptakes and conning and flying control facilities. The flight deck formed the upper flange of the hull girder and side passages enclosed the hangar, which was also closed forward. These design features were standard British design practice thereafter. The hangar was open aft to admit seaplanes landing on a special slip extending over the stern. Forward there was a rotating catapult so that aircraft could be launched without having to turn the ship into the wind. A Grand Fleet officers' conference reviewed the design on January 8, 1918. It objected to the seaplane slipway and forward catapult, both of which were then eliminated and the flight deck widened forward. The outcome of trials with the *Furious* after reconstruction highlighted problems with the dual island arrangement and the design was changed to a single large island structure to starboard, an alteration that created its own major problems requiring the addition of 500 tons of fuel to port to correct the heeling movement and necessitating water ballast in the port bulge as fuel was consumed. Trim problems were to be a permanent feature of the ship's career, especially as modifications added weight, so that even the specific gravity of fuel oil became a significant factor in determining the ship's stability.

When the Admiralty decided to take up the incomplete Chilean battleship *Almirante Cochrane* for conversion into an aircraft carrier, the ship's construction had been suspended since the outbreak of war. The hull was almost complete but no armor had been installed, although it had been manufactured and delivered. The design initially prepared featured a flush deck from bow to stern flanked by islands staggered lengthwise on either side and connected by heavy cross bracing, leaving a clear passage between them 68 feet wide with 20 feet overhead clearance. To increase the ship's speed the designers proposed to greatly reduce the original battleship scale of armor protection and also to modify the furnaces to burn both coal and oil while at cruising speed but oil only when the ship was operated at high speed, thus boosting output from 37,000 shaft horsepower to 55,000 shaft horsepower. After the completion of the carrier *Furious* it became clear that the superstructure arrangement proposed for the *Eagle* posed an unacceptable hazard to aircraft operations. Alternative arrangements were explored, including hinging or telescoping stacks, exhausting furnace gases through the side of the ship, and making the islands and stacks very narrow, but ultimately the best arrangement was a single island to starboard that incorporated two stacks and all navigation, conning, and aircraft and gunnery control facilities. The only substantive change required was to offset the forward elevator to port and slightly reduce hangar overhead clearance in the vicinity of the flue trunking. At the same time, because of the concerns of the Air Department about the corrosive impact of coal firing on aircraft longevity, and the desire to endow the new carrier with the highest possible speed in the most economical way, the previous mixed fuel furnace arrangements were replaced by an exclusively oil-burning system. It was in this form that the *Eagle* was finally completed, after a very extensive series of arresting gear trials that delayed completion but provided valuable data.

At the end of World War I the Royal Navy accepted that the *Furious*, in its existing state, was effectively useless as a carrier. A major reconstruction would be necessary to fit it for service. This was an attractive option since its cost would be about one-third the cost of constructing a new carrier from the keel up. In July 1920 design work began. Wartime experience demonstrated that a flush deck was essential but the major problem for a ship of such power was to determine an effective means of combining this feature with disposing of the smoke from the carrier's furnaces. John Narbeth, by now the Department of Naval Construction's expert on aircraft carrier design, proposed to trunk the furnace uptakes along the side of the hangar and to offset the loss of stowage by adding another hangar below it. The design Narbeth produced incorporated two hangars, each with 15 feet of overhead clearance; a long flush flight deck, which was also a strength deck and thus reduced hull stresses substantially, that terminated well short of the bow; and a shorter flying-off deck accessed directly from the front of the upper hangar. Two elevators served both hangars and the deck arrangements (theoretically, at least) allowed the carrier to launch two aircraft from the upper flight deck and another from the forward flying-off deck simultaneously. Navigation and flying control stations were set on either side of the flight deck at deck level and there was a retractable central charthouse. Large bulges improved the ship's stability and helped maintain a reasonable draft. The one feature of the *Furious*'s design that always proved unsatisfactory was the arrangement of the furnace ducts. The spaces surrounding them could be unbearably hot and smoke low down around the stern could cause landing problems. Ultimately, as aircraft grew in size, the forward flying-off deck became too short for safe takeoffs, and the limitations of the relatively short flight deck became more serious.

The Naval Staff concluded in 1920 that the postwar Royal Navy would require five carriers to provide adequate aircraft for its needs. Accordingly, it was decided to convert one of the two remaining large light cruisers, half-sisters to the *Furious*, into a similar carrier.

While planning for the latter's conversion was still underway, the provisions of the Washington Treaty forced a reevaluation of plans for the future carrier force. In particular, the impending additions to the American and Japanese fleets of a pair of very large fast carriers apiece, converted from incomplete capital ship hulls, made it important to add another large fast carrier to the British fleet. The Admiralty therefore decided to convert both the *Courageous* and the *Glorious* into vessels similar to the *Furious*. The design, as a result of initial experience with the *Furious*, was modified, primarily by fitting more conventional furnace uptakes to starboard incorporated into a small island. This change eliminated the problems encountered in the *Furious* with the long horizontal ducts, enlarged hangar space, and also reduced topweight, allowing the hangar height to be increased to 16 feet for the two hangars. The two new carriers also marked a break with previous defensive armament concepts since they carried no low-angle guns but relied on a powerful antiaircraft battery to fend of air attack and the guns of escorting vessels to defend them against surface attack. Neither the *Courageous* nor the *Glorious* were fitted with arresting gear until their pre–World War II refits.

The first British carrier designed as such from the keel up since the *Hermes* was the *Ark Royal*, which entered service just before World War II began. The design had an extended gestation, having its origins in studies begun in 1931. It included the double hangars of its immediate precursors but eliminated the forward flight deck, since larger and faster aircraft had rendered this feature obsolete. Aerodynamic considerations necessitated long round downs fore and aft. To compensate for their impact, the flight deck extended considerably beyond the stern. From the outset an island structure was envisaged and the final design compensated for its weight to starboard through an asymmetric hull. The three elevators were of a new design. They had two levels, so that on each upward trip the upper level transported an aircraft from the upper hangar to the flight deck while the lower level simultaneously brought a machine from the lower hangar to the upper. This shorter travel distance translated into simpler lifting machinery (a single hydraulic ram rather than cables and balance weights) and a fast 20-second cycle of operation. The final design also incorporated transverse-wire arresting gear, a crash barrier, and two catapults from the outset, although the principle of a deck park was not accepted. The antiaircraft armament also was changed late in the design process, when the guns were raised to gallery deck level, thus increasing sky arcs.

The *Ark Royal*'s loss to torpedo damage at the end of 1941 was in part a result of the impact of policies and limitations on its design. To save weight and keep vital equipment within the smallest possible armor box it had only steam-powered generators, which were located inside the machinery compartments, and no backup diesel units. The furnace uptakes were led below the main deck armor to keep down weight and also avoid encroaching on the lower hangar space—features resulting from arms limitation treaty restrictions (that limited tonnage) and British carrier operational practice (which eschewed a deck park). Ultimately, its loss owed more to less-than-optimal damage control practices, which were corrected rapidly.

The final British carriers designed before World War II represented a major departure from earlier types. They were a response to two clear problems: protecting the carrier's greatest vulnerability—the hangar and its explosive and inflammable contents—against aerial attack, and preserving the reconnaissance and strike aircraft vital to its mission against the same attack threat. During preparation of various design studies for the new class, planners had to wrestle with the outcome of many fleet exercises demonstrating that defending fighters could never intercept all incoming aircraft in time to prevent an attack. In this scenario, passive defense gained in importance, while that of defending interceptors diminished, especially as exercises also inflated the efficacy of the fleet's antiaircraft batteries. Rear-Admiral R. G. H. Henderson, the Third Sea Lord (and therefore responsible for overseeing new construction), was also the Royal Navy's most experienced carrier commander, and his opinions on the vulnerability of carriers and the importance of striking an enemy fleet hard carried great weight. The final outcome was the decision to construct carriers that, within the upper tonnage limit of 23,000 tons imposed by the recently-signed London Treaty, sacrificed hangar capacity for protection against air attack in the form of flight deck and hangar side armor sufficient to defeat a 500-pound bomb.

The central feature of the *Illustrious* class design was its armor protection. The flight deck over the hangar and the hangar deck received 3-inch armor, the hangar sides and ends and the deep side belt that extended from the hangar deck to nine feet below the waterline were all 4-1/2 inches thick, and there were 2-1/2-inch armor bulkheads enclosing the magazines and machinery spaces. Weight limitations prevented applying armor to the elevators, but the wells were isolated using 4-1/2-inch thick vertical shutters. As a result of

the scale of armor protection, the double hangar that was a prominent design feature of British interwar carriers was reduced to a single hangar 458 feet long and 62 feet wide with 16 feet of overhead
clearance. Aircraft capacity therefore fell to only thirty-six machines
but, to avoid alerting foreign observers to the radical change in design, the air group published (as required by the London Treaty) was
fifty-four aircraft including a notional deck park, though there was
no intention of adopting such an element operationally. Other features of the design strongly resembled those of *Ark Royal*, but the
machinery rooms were more widely spaced and all auxiliary machinery was located outside the main machinery compartments. The design reverted to a symmetrical hull, compensating for the offset
weight of the island by widening the port oil fuel tanks (which also
formed part of the anti-torpedo protection system) and including
400 tons of fixed ballast. As in all interwar British carriers, the designers paid considerable attention to aerodynamic features in this
class. The flight deck incorporated long round downs both fore and
aft and streamlining of the island and stack was carried further than
in previous designs. The main antiaircraft battery remained eight
twin 4.5-inch mountings, but these now were fully enclosed and
power operated. Only a single, more powerful catapult was fitted to
port on the flight deck, a further concession to topweight limitations. The design was so tightly constrained by treaty tonnage requirements that at one point the designers suggested expanding the
number of noncommissioned aircrew and pilots at the expense of
commissioned officers so that accommodation demands could be
reduced, and the problem of overcrowding only increased as
wartime additions and modifications impacted the class.

Two elements dominated the characteristics of British interwar
carrier designs. The first was the focus on aviation qualities in the
structures of the ships themselves. This showed itself externally in
an emphasis on the aerodynamics of the hull, flight deck, and superstructures, all of which were optimized to ease aircraft operation. It
also was apparent in the central need for stowage of aircraft within
the hangars while they were not flying—carriers had to accommodate all their air group within the hangar which, in turn, imposed a
significant upper limit on the size of the air group. The second was a
focus on survivability, manifested in the isolation of hangar spaces
by surrounding the hangar with flash-tight bulkheads, voids, and
ventilation systems built within the hull structure and, most prominently, by the eventual adoption of armor protection for the hangar
and flight deck.

FRENCH CARRIER DEVELOPMENTS
BETWEEN THE WORLD WARS

During World War I, the French Navy devoted relatively limited resources to carrier aviation, in keeping with the national concentration on the land war on the Western Front. French naval officers,
however, maintained a close interest in British carrier developments
and this continued in the years immediately following the war. In
1919 a French naval mission was sent to the United Kingdom to
study these developments more formally and examined both the design studies for the *Hermes* and the *Eagle* and the existing flush-
decked carrier *Argus*. The mission's January 1920 report recommended the addition of a flush decked carrier to the fleet, and
suggested the conversion of the incomplete hull of one of the *Normandie* class battleships, whose construction had been suspended
on the outbreak of war. The design for this carrier owed much to the
commission's observations of the *Argus*. It envisaged a hangar 325
feet long and 98 feet wide surmounted by a 490-foot long flight
deck, with two large elevators linking them. It would have 6-inch
guns and torpedo tubes for defense against surface vessels. The
bridge was to be suspended beneath the forward edge of the flight
deck and the furnace uptakes would be trunked to exhaust at the
stern as far as possible below the level of the flight deck. The Conseil Supérieur approved this project and selected the *Béarn*, the
member of the class in the least advanced stage of construction, for
conversion. The hull was launched in April 1920. During the summer it was equipped with a temporary wooden flight deck carrying
twelve wires weighted with sandbags for arresting gear. A series of
deck-landing trials by Lieutenant de Vaisseau Paul Teste concluded
in October and prompted funding for a full conversion. There was
much debate about the decision to proceed with a conversion rather
than design and construct a new vessel from the keel up. Ultimately,
the possibility of completing a conversion within two years at a
much lower cost than new construction (which would take five
years) prevailed.

Even though there was a concern that the ship might be rendered
obsolete by rapid advances in carrier design, construction proceeded
at a relatively leisurely pace and did not begin until August 1923.
The vessel as completed differed appreciably from the original 1920
proposal. The *Béarn* originally was to have used turbines on all four
shafts but was reengined with the machinery intended originally for
the *Normandie*—two turbines on the center shafts and four-cylinder

triple expansion engines on the outer shafts for use while cruising. This plant also required fewer boilers but the result was a reduction in power from 45,000 shaft horsepower to 37,500 shaft horsepower, limiting the carrier's maximum speed to 21.5 knots. The *Béarn* as completed also had a longer flight deck than originally envisaged, much improved workshop and overhaul spaces, an additional elevator for a total of three, and a prominent island enclosing a large conventional vertical stack on the starboard side in place of the long trucked vents in the 1920 design. This island featured very elaborate arrangements for air cooling the furnace gases prior to their discharge in an effort to limit their impact on air flow over and behind the flight deck. The *Béarn* also received a sophisticated transverse-wire arresting gear produced by Schneider-Fieux that used friction drums to control run-out and featured an effective reset mechanism. Schneider-Fieux sold a similar system to Japan to replace the original longitudinal system, derived from early British practice, aboard the *Hosho* and the *Akagi*.

The French Navy considered the *Béarn* a semi-experimental vessel to be replaced by new construction as soon as was practicable. Between 1930 and 1932 seven design studies were prepared (PA 1 through PA 7) for carriers in the range 15,000 tons to 18,000 tons standard, armed with 6-inch guns, and capable of accommodating twenty to thirty aircraft. Four further designs (PA 8 through PA 11) were considered thereafter, between 1932 and 1935. They were of similar size but emphasized speed (the designers sought between 32 and 35 knots) in vessels of 14,000 tons to 19,000 tons standard, protected on a light cruiser scale, and armed with antiaircraft weapons only. In 1936 the Conseil Supérieur again emphasized the need for new carriers and put forward the idea of converting France's first Washington Treaty heavy cruisers, the *Duquesne* and the *Tourville,* into carriers. Two studies retained one 8-inch gun turret, the other two eliminated the main battery entirely. The displacement would rise to 12,000 tons standard and the ships could carry twelve to fourteen aircraft. This idea too was dropped in favor of new construction. After the Conseil Supérieur completed yet another series of four studies (PA 12 through PA 15), an acceptable design (PA 16) emerged and funding was authorized to construct two new carriers.

Displacement: 18,000 tons (standard), 20,000 tons (normal)
Dimensions: 774'0" (oa) x 80'6" x 21'6" (mean)
Flight deck: 656'2" x 91'10"

Machinery: Parsons geared turbines, 8 Indret boilers, 2 shafts.
120,000 shp = 33 knots
Bunkerage & range: 7,000 nm @ 20 knots
Aircraft: 40
Armament: 4 x twin 5.1" AA, 4 x twin 37mm AA, 6 x quadruple
13.2mm AA
Complement: 1,250

The design incorporated a number of unusual features. There was a very long island to starboard that accommodated not only the navigation and flying control spaces and the stack but also all the principal armament. To counterbalance its weight the flight deck was offset to port, which also served to eliminate the encroachment of the island on the flight deck and limited narrowing of the hangars. There were two hangars, one above the other. The upper hangar was 521 feet 7 inches long and 68 feet 3 inches wide, the lower was 259 feet 2 inches long and 51 feet 2 inches wide and they were connected to the flight deck by two large elevators. The flight deck carried transverse-wire arresting gear but, unlike many of their foreign contemporaries, no catapults were fitted. The *Joffre* and the *Painlevé* were ordered from Chantiers de l'Atlantique (Penhoët-Loire) at St. Nazaire in 1938. At the outbreak of World War II the *Joffre* was about 25 percent complete and the *Painlevé* only just started. Both hulls were dismantled on the slip after the fall of France in June 1940.

JAPANESE CARRIER DEVELOPMENTS BETWEEN THE WORLD WARS

During World War I the Imperial Japanese Navy's direct involvement with carrier aviation was limited to the brief deployment of the *Wakamiya Maru* during the operations against Tsingtao in 1914. Of much greater import for future indigenous carrier developments were the observations and analyses of the Royal Navy's experience with aircraft at sea and carrier operations by Japanese naval officers attached to the Grand Fleet. Their recommendations led to the inclusion of an aircraft carrier in the 1918 "8–6 Fleet Expansion Program" as one of six auxiliary vessels proposed (the other five were oilers, which has led to a common misconception that this first Japanese carrier was a conversion rather than designed as such from the outset). The *Hosho* was the world's second carrier designed as such from the keel up and the first to complete. The *Hosho*'s small size and simple design, plus considerable assistance from the British Aviation Mission to the Imperial Japanese Navy led by Colonel the Master of Semphill, resulted in its completion within just over three years from keel-laying, compared with well over five years required to construct the *Hermes,* the first carrier laid down as such.

The design for the *Hosho*'s hull and machinery owed much to those of contemporary light cruisers for the fleet, though with reduced power. The aircraft stowage arrangements were unusual. There were two separate hangars. One was amidships 225 feet long, 30 feet wide, with overhead clearance of 13 feet. At the stern there was a two-level hangar the full width of the hull. The upper level was 150 feet long and had 18 feet overhead clearance, the lower level was 90 feet long and 15 feet high. Two elevators linked the hangars to the flight deck, the after elevator serving both levels of that hangar. Japanese designers consulted the British Aviation Mission on the design of the flight deck and its arrangements. As a result, it featured the forward downward slope and longitudinal arresting gear of contemporary British practice. As completed, the *Hosho* carried a small island with a large tripod mast to starboard but these were removed very shortly after commissioning since they interfered too much with operations and also caused stability problems, and the ship was conned thereafter from a bridge at the front of the forward hangar beneath the flight deck.

The provisions of the Five-Power Naval Limitation Treaty signed at Washington on February 6, 1922, allowed Japan to convert the incomplete hulls of two large warships scheduled for disposal under the treaty's terms into large aircraft carriers. Two 40-percent complete battle cruisers, the *Akagi* and the *Amagi,* were selected for conversion and design work began, led by Constructor Captain Fujimoto Kikuo. Before construction work could begin, however, the *Amagi*'s hull was irreparably damaged by the great Kanto Earthquake on September 1, 1923, and the incomplete hull of the battleship *Kaga,* another vessel schedule for scrapping, took its place. The two aircraft carriers that resulted were based on the same design but there were significant differences between them, due largely to the different hull forms on which they were based.

The common design featured two long hangars built on top of the original hull's upper deck with a short shallow hangar built into the hull itself at the after end of the main hangars to accommodate spare dismantled aircraft. A long flight deck stretched from the extreme stern to the front of the main hangars, stopping about one-quarter of the ship's length short of the bow. A pair of flying-off decks projected forward of each hangar, staggered so that there was clearance for aircraft to take off from both decks simultaneously (while other aircraft flew off or landed on the main flight deck at the same time), and the arrangement also obviated the need to raise aircraft to the flight deck with the elevators from the hangars below. The design also featured very heavy antiship armament in the form of ten 8-inch guns disposed in two twin turrets and six single casemates, along with twelve 4.7-inch antiaircraft guns in twin mountings.

The *Akagi* and the *Kaga* differed in some important respects. The *Akagi's* flight deck, at 624 feet overall, was some 65 feet longer than that of the *Kaga*. It sloped slightly down toward bow and stern from a point about 325 feet from the after end to improve the airflow over the deck. The *Akagi* also was fitted with British-style longitudinal arresting gear that occupied almost the whole of the after sloping section. The *Kaga's* flight deck was flat and fitted from the outset with Schneider-Fieux transverse wire arresting gear purchased from France. The two carriers also differed in their arrangements for exhausting furnace gases. The *Kaga* used very long flues trunked to the stern along the side of the upper hangar, while the *Akagi* used a large stack that vented downward on the starboard side, supplemented by a smaller vertical stack abaft it.

In service the unusual triple deck arrangement on these carriers proved much less useful than anticipated, especially as aircraft increased in size and weight and thus required longer takeoff runs. Aircraft growth also emphasized the disadvantages of the short main flight decks. Japan therefore reconstructed the two carriers, expanding their hangars, removing the auxiliary decks and extending the main flight decks from bow to stern, fitting islands, improving smoke disposal, upgrading their antiaircraft defenses, and, in the case of the *Kaga*, replacing the machinery and lengthening the hull in a not very successful effort to raise the ship's speed. These changes increased aircraft capacity by 50 percent and greatly increased their operational capabilities. Since the carriers were expected to operate together as a *koku-sentai* (carrier division), the *Akagi's* island was fitted amidships to port. The Imperial Japanese Navy's practice for landing operations was for aircraft to orbit to one side of the carrier, peeling off and landing as ordered by the air operations officer. When a *koku-sentai* operated in formation, the carriers were abreast one another, each carrier's aircraft were orbiting outboard of the formation, and it was considered advantageous to locate the islands to suit. In practice, this island location proved to have serious disadvantages: it limited the landing space, caused excess air turbulence over the flight deck, and obstructed the normal path for aborted landings. Consequently, by the time the carriers of the *Shokaku* class were fitting out for service, this island arrangement was abandoned in favor of the conventional position forward of amidships on the starboard side.

The provisions of the Washington Treaty greatly influenced planning for new aircraft carrier construction by the signatories (Britain, France, Italy, Japan, and the United States) throughout the period before World War II. Nowhere was this more obvious than in Japan, where planners found the combination of both qualitative and quantitative limitations on the size and composition of the navy's carrier fleet to be major obstacles to the creation and maintenance of a balanced powerful force, especially in view of its treaty-imposed inferiority to its likeliest opponent, the United States. Because the *Hosho* was under construction in 1922, it was classed as experimental and its tonnage did not count within Japan's total. The carriers *Akagi* and *Kaga*, however, consumed two-thirds of Japan's allocation of 81,000 tons, leaving only 27,200 tons for further construction, barely more than the maximum tonnage permitted for a single carrier. The *Ryujo*, Japan's first new carrier subject to the treaty restrictions, therefore was also designed so that its tonnage was not counted against Japan's total allocation, taking advantage of the treaty's definition of an aircraft carrier as a vessel with a displacement in excess of 10,000 tons standard by constructing a vessel under that size.

The *Ryujo*'s initial design envisaged a cruiser-type flush-decked hull carrying a long single hangar over the midships three-quarters of its length, topped by a flush flight deck that terminated at the forward end of the hangar. The limitation this concept imposed on the size of the carrier's air group soon was realized and the design was recast very rapidly by adding a second hangar level, thus doubling the aircraft capacity. The furnace uptakes were trunked to the starboard side and vented through downward inclined stacks; the bridge was located immediately below the forward edge of the flight deck; and the main antiaircraft battery carried in twin mounts sponsoned to just below flight deck level, which gave these weapons excellent sky arcs. The combination of changes, however, had a drastic impact. The design's tonnage increased substantially, and most of the added weight was high in the ship, especially as all armor protection was eliminated to restrict growth. Within eighteen months of commissioning, the *Ryujo* had to be modified to compensate for its inherent problems and in reaction to a fleet-wide concern about the stability of vessels constructed under the limitations of the Washington Treaty. The changes (bulges, hull strengthening, and topweight reduction) largely succeeded in correcting its deficiencies, but only at the cost of increasing tonnage by over 25 percent and cutting antiaircraft armament by a third.

The Washington Treaty limited both the maximum size and each nation's total tonnage of aircraft carriers. The *Ryujo*'s design was an effort to circumvent the tonnage restriction. The provisions of the later London Five-Power Naval Limitation Treaty, signed on April 22, 1930, extended the total tonnage limitations to cover cruisers and eliminated the loophole exploited by the *Ryujo*. It also included a clause allowing up to 25 percent of a nation's cruiser tonnage to be made up of ships with flight decks. This provision prompted Japanese designers to investigate the possibilities of creating "cruiser-carriers," vessels with both powerful gun batteries and useful aircraft capabilities. In the summer of 1932 design "G6" proposed a vessel similar to a scaled down *Akagi* minus the forward flying-off decks and with three superimposed twin 8-inch gun turrets in their place on the foredeck. The double hangars were 420 feet long and 60 feet wide under a 625-foot long flight deck. Aircraft capacity was similar to that of the *Ryujo* at forty-eight machines. The designers, however, failed completely to accomplish this project within the 10,000-ton size limitation applicable to cruisers—the design would actually displace some 17,500 tons. A second effort, "G8," followed the next year. The designers reduced the gun armament to five 6.1-inch weapons in a twin and a triple turret on the forecastle, moved the hangars forward, extended the flight deck to cover the full length of the ship and included a very large overhang at the stern to bring its total length to 850 feet, and proposed a large vertical stack for the furnace gases, for the first time in Japanese carrier design. This project, too, greatly exceeded the permissible individual cruiser tonnage, and also was abandoned, although it became the basis for work leading to the pure carrier design constructed as the *Soryu*.

The *Soryu* and the *Hiryu* were half-sisters and the models for all subsequent fleet carriers. The *Soryu* design evolved from the earlier cruiser-carrier studies but rejected all the larger caliber weapons featured in those designs in favor of six twin 5-inch dual-purpose mounts. The hull was very long and narrow and the powerful cruiser-type machinery made the new design exceptionally fast. The double hangars that characterized earlier Japanese fleet carriers also featured in this design, although this was not apparent externally, since the lower hangar was constructed within the hull itself. Hangars were 65 feet wide and the lower hangar was about 100 feet shorter than the 520 feet of the upper hangar, due to the narrowing of the hull forward. Three elevators linked the hangars to the full length flight deck. The *Soryu* had very light passive armor protection, only 1.8 inches thick on the sides and 1 inch on the deck over the machinery spaces, with 2.2 inches of deck armor over the magazines. The heavy antiaircraft weapons were supplemented by fourteen twin 25mm mountings for close-in defense and the small island was to starboard.

By the time the *Hiryu* was ordered, Japan decided to abrogate the Washington Treaty. The *Soryu's* design was modified to increase the beam and widen the flight deck, raise the forecastle by one deck to improve sea-keeping, and strengthen the hull structure, all probably as a result of the lessons learned from the storm damage suffered by the Fourth Fleet during maneuvers in September 1935. The designers took advantage of the lack of tonnage restrictions to enhance side armor protection substantially. Belt armor rose to 3.5 inches with 5.9 inches abreast the magazines. The *Hiryu*, like the *Akagi* after its major modernization, carried its island amidships on the port side for the same reason—to facilitate operation within a *koku-sentai* with the *Soryu*.

In the design of its interwar carriers the Imperial Japanese Navy placed a premium on high speed, long range, and large aircraft capacity (measured by stowage within the hangar). Its carriers had fine lines, light structure, capacious bunkers, powerful machinery, and capacious hangars. With the exception of the *Akagi* and the *Kaga*, armor protection was limited to save weight. All Japanese carriers proved very vulnerable to action damage since their designs featured enclosed hangars with very limited flash protection or ventilation combined with wooden flight decks that offered little resistance to bombs. While the navy was very cognizant of the importance of quickly launching large numbers of aircraft, enclosed hangars, the lack of facilities for arming or fuelling aircraft on flight decks, and the almost complete absence of catapults on Japanese carriers potentially inhibited this goal. Equally anomalous is the fact that relatively few Japanese carrier aircraft incorporated folding wings that could maximize hangar stowage, despite the imperative for the largest possible embarked air group.

UNITED STATES CARRIER DEVELOPMENT
BETWEEN THE WORLD WARS

Prior to the entry of the United States into World War I, the United States Navy's interest in shipboard aviation centered on catapult-launched floatplanes and flying boats, although individual officers, such as Lieutenant Commander Henry C. Mustin, had envisaged the potential of specialized aircraft carrying vessels from as early as 1914. It took the experience of operating with the Royal Navy during the war to generate official interest in the design and acquisition of aircraft carriers. The secondment of the British naval constructor Stanley V. Goodall to the Bureau of Construction and Repair in late 1917 proved important in translating the advocacy of sea officers, most notably Admiral William S. Sims, into concrete designs, for he brought with him plans of many of the newer British warships, including the *Hermes,* and summaries of the Royal Navy's war experience. A preliminary sketch, owing much to Goodall's recommendations, appeared in October 1918 and, modified somewhat the following spring, became the basis for the first American carrier design, intended for carriers requested in 1920 and again in 1921. Congress, however, turned down both requests and instead authorized only the conversion of the new collier *Jupiter.*

The new aircraft carrier, renamed the *Langley,* was a very simple conversion that clearly was intended to be no more than experimental and essentially added little more than a flight deck, aircraft handling gantry crane, and elevator on top of the collier's original structure, placed stowage for aircraft, fuel, munitions, and spares in the former coal holds, and modified arrangements for smoke disposal. There was no hanger; aircraft were stowed disassembled in the holds, moved to the lowered elevator platform for assembly, and raised to the flight deck. Striking down aircraft required reversing the procedure. Initially, the *Langley*'s flight deck carried British style longitudinal wire arresting gear and a single catapult. The latter was soon replaced by a pair of compressed air powered units that became irrelevant to flight operations as procedures improved and were subsequently removed entirely. Transverse wires were added to the original arresting gear in 1926 and completely replaced the original system late in the following year. Although the work of Captain Joseph M. Reeves (promoted to rear-admiral in 1927) as Commander Aircraft Squadrons, Battle Fleet transformed the *Langley* from an experimental vessel into a fully operational aircraft carrier, although its limited speed severely restricted its utility, especially after more capable ships entered service.

The navy continued work on designs for large carriers, culminating in a vessel of some 39,000 tons (normal). The General Board requested the priority construction of three such carriers in July 1921. The similarity of this design's dimensions to those of the battle cruisers under construction and the prospect of these ships' cancellation as a result of the upcoming international conference on naval arms limitations led to consideration of converting incomplete battle cruisers into aircraft carriers instead. When the terms of the Washington Treaty demanded the cancellation of all six battle cruisers, the United States negotiated an exception to the restriction on the 27,000-ton limit of the size of individual aircraft carriers to permit vessels converted from existing capital ships to displace up to 33,000 tons standard. This allowed the conversion of two battle cruisers into the carriers *Lexington* and *Saratoga,* although it still required the use of 3,000 tons for notional upgrades to protect against air and submarine attack (permitted by the treaty to modernize existing ships) in order to avoid a drastic reduction in machinery output.

The design of these huge converted ships incorporated much of the British practice derived from the Royal Navy's experience late in the war and immediately thereafter. The hangar was a fully enclosed integral part of the hull structure, the flight deck was the hull's strength deck, its arresting gear took the form of longitudinal wires intended to engage hooks on the axles of landing aircraft to prevent their deviation from the deck's axis, and the ships carried powerful antisurface guns in addition to a strong antiaircraft battery. None of these features reappeared in subsequent American carrier designs until after World War II. The large size of these vessels was controversial at first, especially as they consumed a hefty proportion of the navy's limited carrier tonnage permitted by the Washington Treaty. The enclosed hangar, of necessity smaller than an equivalent open structure, was a particular target for criticism. Until Reeves demonstrated the overwhelming value of the deck-load strike, with these carriers,, and therefore the importance of large flight decks, in the 1929 Fleet Problem, critics equated aircraft capacity with hangar accommodation. By that standard the big carriers were deficient compared with later keel-up designs with open hangars. The enclosed hangar design indeed limited the capabilities of these carriers, not by reducing their aircraft capacity but by preventing aircraft from warming up their engines in the hangar and therefore increasing the time required to prepare a massed strike. The placement of the heavy antisurface guns in turrets to starboard incurred the penalty of ballast to offset the instability it caused, while the weapons themselves also proved of dubious value relative to their space, weight, and crew requirements. Nevertheless, the sheer size of the *Lexington* and the *Saratoga* conferred great flexibility and enabled the United States Navy to develop particularly effective operational carrier doctrines during the 1930s. Their speed allowed them to operate with the battle fleet and their size and aircraft capacity gave commanders invaluable opportunities to appreciate the importance of efficient deck-handling procedures, rapid aircraft launch and recovery, and concentrated mass attacks; all elements that served the navy well during World War II.

The major issue confronting United States Navy planners after the decision to complete the *Lexington* and the *Saratoga* as large aircraft carriers was to determine the size of future vessels, given the strict limits on individual size and overall tonnage available under the terms of the Washington Treaty. When planning began for new carriers only the *Langley* was in service and the British had terminated communication of their operational experience. Experience from war games simulations at the Naval War College therefore played a central role in determining the best composition of the future carrier force. The 69,000 tons that remained unused would permit the construction of five carriers of 13,800 tons, four of 17,250 tons, or three of 23,000 tons. War games indicated that the ability to launch large numbers of aircraft quickly was crucial and that carriers were extremely vulnerable to air attack. Both factors pointed toward constructing a larger number of smaller carriers, since deploying more carriers lessened the risk of losing all of them and increased overall aircraft capacity, especially as this was viewed as a function of hangar space at this time. A long series of studies emerged between 1922 and the final design for the United States Navy's first carrier constructed as such from the keel up.

The *Ranger* was designed as a relatively slow flush-decked 13,800-ton vessel. The carrier was envisaged as the first of five new vessels of similar size permitted within treaty limits. The *Ranger's* lower speed resulted from the General Board's desire for the largest possible air group which, combined with the Bureau of Aeronautics insistence on a flush deck, required limiting power to minimize machinery space and reduce the problems of smoke disposal absent a more conventional stack arrangement. The *Ranger* introduced several features characteristic of subsequent American carriers that entered service before the mid-1950s. The hangar deck formed the main strength deck of the hull and the hangar and flight deck made up the ship's superstructure. It was the first American carrier to feature an open hangar, which allowed aircraft to warm up in the hangar before being lifted to the flight deck for takeoff and simplified access for reprovisioning and resupply. The *Ranger* was also the first to eschew a large-caliber single purpose armament intended to combat enemy surface vessels—its design instead incorporated a large antiaircraft battery for the period (eight 5-inch antiaircraft guns plus forty heavy machine guns). The design also introduced the flight deck gallery decks, prominent in later designs, which eased access fore and aft and provided additional crew space. Weight limitations, however, prevented installation of any of the four catapults originally envisaged or the provision of any armor protection, and led to the elimination of torpedo stowage. Operational experience with the *Langley*'s enlarged air group, plus the demonstrated advantages of the island structures aboard the *Lexington* and the *Saratoga* also led to the addition of an island to the design in December 1931.

Even before the *Ranger*'s completion there was concern that the design sacrificed too much capability in order to limit displacement and, therefore, maximize the number of carriers. From the outset, designers focused their attention on designs displacing either 18,400 tons, which would allow construction of three identical vessels, or 20,700 tons, which would produce two vessels and leave 13,800 tons to build a smaller carrier compatible with the *Ranger*. The main objectives were to increase speed, incorporate both antitorpedo and armor protection, enhance aircraft operations with an enlarged hangar, more and better arranged elevators, and possibly a second flight deck (or hangar deck catapults), and expand the antiaircraft battery. Further refinement of preliminary sketches demonstrated that the 18,400-ton design was a poor compromise and, in September 1931, it was decided to proceed with the construction of two larger 20,000-ton carriers and enlarge the smaller vessel to 15,200 tons, using the 1,400 tons thus saved. Design work, however, veered away from the direct line of development as designers responded to the request of Secretary of the Navy Charles F. Adams that they investigate the possibilities of constructing "cruiser-carrier" type vessels instead, motivated by the fleet's liking for the 8-inch guns of the *Lexington* class and the concept of independent carrier operations that might require carriers to embark heavier armament in order to defend themselves while away from the main fleet. A series of design studies quickly demonstrated the aviation costs—two 25,000-ton cruiser-carriers together would barely carry half the combined aircraft of the proposed three pure carriers. Adams, in December 1931, promptly approved proceeding with the original plan, but construction was delayed further by the vicissitudes of the Great Depression and it was not until the passage of the National Industrial Recovery Act on June 16, 1933, that funding was authorized for the two 20,000-ton carriers *Yorktown* and *Enterprise*. A third unit, the *Hornet*, was ordered in 1939 after the Washington Treaty expired. To speed the ship's entry into service, this carrier used the same design with only minor modifications that added some 200 tons to its displacement.

The *Yorktown* class proved very successful. They were fast, long-ranged, and could accommodate and operate a powerful and balanced air group. The deep girders beneath the flight deck that connected the gallery decks provided space to stow large numbers of spare aircraft—theoretically sufficient to replace up to half the air group. They also reintroduced catapults into fleet carriers. The four catapults, two on the flight deck and two fitted athwartships on the hangar deck, could launch aircraft of up to 7,000 pounds at 70 mile per hour. In fact these catapults were used very infrequently until late in World War II. The hangar deck catapults, in particular, were hardly ever used (the *Enterprise*, for example, used its 19 times in 1939 and 3 times in 1940) and they were removed in June 1942 from the two vessels then still in service. The class's main deficiency was the vulnerability of its machinery arrangements to underwater attack, since a single torpedo that penetrated the relatively weak side protection could knock out the entire power plant, a weakness that contributed greatly to the *Hornet*'s loss.

The *Wasp* was the final prewar carrier for the United States Navy. Its design proceeded in parallel with that of the *Yorktown* class and used up the last remaining carrier tonnage available under the Washington Treaty. The reduction in tonnage from the 20,000 tons of the *Yorktown* to the 14,500 tons of the *Wasp* (modifications to the *Ranger* had absorbed 700 tons) entailed the elimination of almost all armor and any substantive anti-torpedo protection, a much reduced power plant that cut speed to 29-1/2 knots, a smaller air group that excluded torpedo bombers and their heavy weapons, very limited accommodation for spare aircraft, and an appreciably shorter hull and flight deck. The *Wasp* was unusual in having an asymmetric hull to balance the island structure without requiring added ballast. Despite all these efforts to save weight, the ship as completed substantially exceeded its design displacement, which caused concerns for its stability. The *Wasp*, like the *Yorktown* class, carried four catapults (two on the hanger deck). It also introduced an important feature of later carriers, the deck-edge elevator in place of a conventional elevator amidships. In the *Wasp's* case this was a T-shaped structure rather than a full platform, no doubt to save weight in a tight design, but its value in improving the flow of traffic on the hangar and flight decks led to the adoption of this feature on all subsequent large American carriers.

CARRIER AIRCRAFT DEVELOPMENT BETWEEN THE WORLD WARS

It is commonly accepted that conflict greatly accelerates technological advance. While that may have been true of the impact of World War I on aviation development, the advances in aircraft design in the twenty-year period between the two world wars tend to belie this truism. At the end of World War I shipboard aircraft were almost exclusively fabric-covered wire-braced wooden biplane airframes. Engine outputs were between 150 and 320 horsepower, top speeds were between 90 and 120 miles per hour, and few aircraft were endowed with ranges in excess of 200 miles. Twenty years later the majority of front-line carrier aircraft were all-metal low-wing monoplanes, often of stressed-skin construction. Their engines produced between 700 and 900 horsepower, giving fighters top speeds in excess of 300 miles per hour and strike aircraft top speeds of over 200 miles per hour. The operational ranges of these aircraft were between 700 and 1,000 miles. These advances took place within an environment of very limited aircraft production, tight military budgets, and largely without the spur of combat operations.

Experience from World War I generated four principal roles for carrier-borne aircraft: reconnaissance, gunfire observation, strike, and fleet air defense. During the twenty years before World War II carrier-operating navies developed a wide range of aircraft and operational practices, within the constraints of flight deck and hangar dimensions and vessel size, to fulfill these missions effectively in accordance with each fleet's priorities.

Navies placed considerable emphasis on the reconnaissance and gunfire observation missions from the outset. The Royal Navy's first such aircraft was the Parnall Panther, whose design originated late in World War I as a dedicated carrier machine. It featured a wooden monococque fuselage that folded for stowage. Powered by a 230-horsepower Bentley B.R.2 rotary engine, it attained a top speed of 108 miles per hour and had a maximum range of 350 miles. British carriers then embarked a series of three-seater biplanes from the Fairey Aviation Company, derived from a successful medium-size floatplane design that saw limited service during World War I. The first of the series, the Fairey IIID, was a sturdy wooden machine powered by either a 375-horsepower Rolls-Royce Eagle or a 450-horsepower Napier Lion engine, giving it a top speed of 106 to 118 miles per hour and a range of 550 miles. During the production run of its more streamlined successor, the Fairey IIIF, the type made the transition from an all-wood to an all-metal structure. Thanks to a more powerful Napier Lion engine of 570 horsepower, top speed rose to 128 miles per hour and range increased to 750 miles. The final development was the Fairey Seal, first deployed in 1933, which introduced a 600-horsepower Armstrong-Siddeley Tiger radial engine. Speed rose to 140 miles per hour and range increased to 850 miles. The Fairey Swordfish began replacing the Seal from 1936, its arrival signaling the end of the Royal Navy's commitment to single-purpose carrier-borne reconnaissance types.

Unlike other fleets, the Royal Navy also briefly deployed highly specialized gunnery observation aircraft equipped with facilities intended to maximize their effectiveness in this limited role. The first was the Westland Walrus, a much-modified variant of the Airco D.H.9A light bomber featuring an observation cupola below the fuselage to accommodate the gunfire spotter. Powered by a 450-horsepower Napier Lion engine, it reached a top speed of 124 miles per hour and had a range of 350 miles. Its successors were the Avro Bison and Blackburn Blackburn. Both aircraft featured large cabins with good observation facilities to accommodate gunnery spotters and their equipment. Their Napier Lion engines gave them top speeds of 105 and 122 miles per hour respectively, while their maximum ranges were 360 and 440 miles. By 1931 the Royal Navy determined that the performance penalties of their accommodations and the burden of incorporating such specialized aircraft within the limited size of carrier air groups made further development of this category unnecessary, and the mission devolved on the fleet's regular reconnaissance aircraft.

The French Navy too introduced dual-purpose observation and reconnaissance aircraft in 1928, when the Levasseur PL.4 entered service aboard the *Béarn*. This three-seater biplane, with an all-metal structure, was powered by a 450-horsepower Lorraine 12eb engine, giving it a top speed of 111 miles per hour and a range of 560 miles. Its successor, the Levasseur PL.10, entered service in 1932. Its 600-horsepower Hispano-Suiza 12Lb engine gave it a maximum speed of 137 miles per hour but its range fell to 450 miles.

The Imperial Japanese Navy gave up deploying carrier-based reconnaissance aircraft when the Mitsubishi C1M left front-line service in 1931. This aircraft was introduced in 1922 as the Type 10 Carrier Reconnaissance Plane, one of a trio of designs by Herbert Smith who came to Mitsubishi from the defunct Sopwith Aviation Company and created the navy's first machines specifically designed for carrier service. It had a 300-horsepower Mitsubishi Type Hi engine giving it a top speed of 127 miles per hour and a range of 350 miles. Thereafter, until well into World War II, Japanese carriers relied on dedicated reconnaissance support from aircraft deployed on accompanying heavy cruisers and, to a lesser extent, on missions flown by their own attack aircraft.

Dedicated carrier reconnaissance types fared considerably better in the United States Navy. The Chance Vought Corporation produced a series of two-seater biplanes, derived from the successful VE-7 advanced trainer, that formed the backbone of the fleet's carrier observation aircraft from 1922 until 1934. These machines started as all-wooden airframes and switched to steel tube fuselages in 1927. The original engine was a 200-horsepower Wright J-3 radial that gave the OU-1 a top speed of 124 miles per hour and a range of 400 miles. The improved O2U, powered by a 450-horsepower Pratt & Whitney Wasp radial engine, could reach 150 miles per hour and had a range of 600 miles, while the final SU-4, with a 600-horsepower Pratt & Whitney Hornet radial engine, had a top speed of 167 miles per hour and a range of 680 miles. An early Grumman Aircraft Engineering Corporation product, the SF-1, briefly supplemented these Vought types until 1936. This biplane aircraft, with an all-metal structure and powered by a 700-horsepower Wright Cyclone, featured a retractable undercarriage and could reach 207 miles per hour with a range of 920 miles. The real replacement for the Vought observation aircraft, however, was a series of scout-bombers, introduced in late 1935, that combined the scouting role with the dive bombing mission.

At the end of World War I, naval officers all generally agreed that torpedoes offered the best prospects for successful aircraft attacks against ships. The Royal Navy's first dedicated carrier-based torpedo bomber, the Sopwith Cuckoo, entered service just before the Armistice. It was followed by a series of rugged designs from the Blackburn Aeroplane Company. First of the series was the Dart. Like the Cuckoo, it was a single-seater, to conserve weight and allow it to lift an 18-inch torpedo. The Dart was a biplane of mixed metal and wooden construction. Powered by a 450-horsepower Napier Lion engine, it attained 107 miles per hour and had a range of 285 miles. Its successors all were two-seaters. The Ripon had a 570-horsepower Lion engine giving it a top speed of 126 miles per hour and a range of 450 miles. The Baffin introduced a 565-horsepower Bristol Pegasus radial engine, whose lighter weight raised the top speed to 136 miles per hour. The final Blackburn torpedo bomber was the Shark, which entered service late in 1934. It introduced a monocoque fuselage and all-metal structure. Speed rose to 152 miles per hour and range to 625 miles, thanks to a 760-horsepower Armstrong-Siddeley Tiger radial engine. It was replaced in service by probably the most famous British naval aircraft of the period, the Fairey Swordfish, a biplane designed to combine the torpedo strike and reconnaissance roles in a single airframe in order to offset the limited space available in the Royal Navy's carriers' hangars. In many ways the Swordfish was a less advanced design than its precursor, but its reliability and flight deck handling characteristics compensated for a somewhat lesser performance. Powered by a 690-horsepower Bristol Pegasus radial engine, the Swordfish reached 139 miles per hour and had a range of 546 miles.

France's first carrier-based torpedo bomber was the Levasseur PL.2, which entered service in 1926. A three-seater biplane with mixed wooden and metal structure, the PL.2 was powered by an unreliable 580-horsepower Renault 12Ma engine, giving it a top speed of 90 miles per hour and a range of 440 miles. The similar Levasseur PL.7, with a very reliable 600-horsepower Hispano-Suiza 12Lbr engine, quickly replaced it in 1929. Its speed remained the same but range increased to 600 miles. The French Navy developed a number of prototypes of aircraft intended to replace the PL.7 in service, including the ambitious twin-engined all-metal stressed skin construction monoplane Dewoitine D.750 and SNCAO CAO.600 torpedo bombers intended to deploy on the *Foch* and the *Joffre*, but no production machines emerged before the outbreak of World War II, leaving the obsolete PL.7 to soldier on.

The Mitsubishi Aircraft Company's British designer, Herbert Smith, was responsible for the Imperial Japanese Navy's first two carrier-based torpedo bombers models. The first, the Type 10 Carrier Torpedo Bomber, was a very unusual single-seater triplane with an all-wooden structure. Smith adopted the triplane arrangement to provide the additional lift to enable his design to carry an 18-inch torpedo. The machine had a top speed of 130 miles per hour and a range of 250 miles. Although it was well-received by its pilots, the aircraft's height made it hard to handle on deck. A new Herbert Smith design, the Type 13 Carrier Attack Bomber (also known as the B1M), quickly replaced it. This similarly-powered conventional two-seater biplane's performance at first closely matched that of the Type 10. Later models changed to the indigenous 450-horsepower Mitsubishi Type Hi engine and added a third crew member. This cut the top speed to 121 miles per hour but greater engine efficiency extended the range to 400 miles, enabling the B1M to supplant the navy's dedicated reconnaissance aircraft from 1930. Mitsubishi also produced the next Japanese torpedo bomber model, contracting the design from the Blackburn Aeroplane Company in Britain. The new three-seater Type 89 Carrier Attack Bomber (also known as the B2M) had an all-metal structure and was powered by a 650-horsepower Mitsubishi Type Hi engine, giving it a top speed of 142 miles per hour and a maximum range of 1,100 miles. The uprated Type Hi engine proved somewhat unreliable, so the B2M never totally replaced its precursor.

The navy was disappointed with the B2M design so it turned to its own resources in designing a replacement. The First Naval Air Technical Arsenal's engineers, led by Suzuki Tamefumi, designed the three-seater biplane Type 92 Carrier Attack Bomber (also known as the B3Y1) that entered service in 1933. Wing structure was of wood and the fuselage structure of welded steel tube. Powered by a 750-horespower Type 91 water-cooled engine, the B3Y1 had a top speed of 136 miles per hour and a range of 500 miles. This model's engine also proved unreliable and the performance, especially in range, was unsatisfactory, so a new design was prepared by Kawasaki Sanae at the First Naval Air Technical Arsenal that entered service in early 1937 as the Type 96 Carrier Attack Bomber (or B4Y1). The new design married the wings of the successful E7K1 shipboard floatplane to a new fuselage and tail unit to produce a three-seater biplane with all-metal structure. Powered by an 840-horsepower Nakajima Hikari radial engine, it had a maximum speed of 173 miles per hour and a range of 978 miles, both markedly superior to any of its precursors or any similar machine in service, although this superiority was cut short by the introduction of Douglas's monoplane TBD-1 later in 1937.

The navy viewed the B4Y1 as a stopgap type pending the introduction of a more modern machine. This took the form of the Nakajima Type 97 Carrier Attack bomber (or B5N1), designed by Nakamura Katsuji in 1936. This three-seater all-metal monoplane of stressed-skin construction featured folding wings to enable it to fit standard carrier elevators, flaps to keep down landing speeds, and a retractable undercarriage to boost performance. Powered by an 840-horsepower Nakajima Hikari radial engine driving a variable-pitch propeller, it had a maximum speed of 229 miles per hour and an extreme range of 1,400 miles. When the B5N1 entered front-line service in early 1938 it was the best torpedo bomber in service with any of the world's navies by a substantial margin.

Torpedo-bomber development for carrier deployment in the United States Navy generally followed a similar pattern as in other fleets, although a small number of very large Douglas T2D twin-engine aircraft briefly operated from the *Langley* in 1927 before they were fitted with floats and redesignated patrol types to avoid political conflict with the Army Air Corps. American carriers used essentially a single design from 1925 until 1937. The initial version, the Martin T3M-2, was a three-seater biplane powered by a 770-horsepower Packard 3A-2500 water-cooled engine that gave it a maximum speed of 109 miles per hour and a range of 630 miles. Subsequent versions, introduced from 1928, used radial engines, either the 525-horsepower Pratt & Whitney Hornet or the 620-horsepower Wright Cyclone, which gave the final version, the Great Lakes TG-2, a maximum performance of 127 miles per hour and a range of 330 miles. The Douglas TBD-1 re-equipped the fleet's torpedo squadrons in 1937 and 1938, marking a great advance in capabilities. This all-metal low-wing monoplane of stressed-skin construction also introduced flaps to aid slow-speed handling, a retractable undercarriage, and power-operated wing folding. Powered by a 900-horsepower Pratt & Whitney Twin Wasp radial engine driving a variable-pitch propeller, the TBD-1 had a maximum speed of 206 miles per hour and a range of 716 miles, both vastly superior to the performance of its precursors.

Fighters for fleet defense against air attack formed the third component of carrier aircraft complements at the end of World War I. The Royal Navy replaced its Sopwith Camels with Nieuport Nightjars in 1922. This variant of the Royal Air Force's Nieuport Nighthawk was powered by a 230-horsepower Bentley B.R.2 rotary engine that gave it a maximum speed of 120 miles per hour and a range of 200 miles. It was soon replaced by the Fairey Flycatcher, a very sturdy and nimble machine with excellent flight deck characteristics, thanks to its Fairey patented camber-changing mechanism. The Flycatcher's 410-horsepower Armstrong-Siddeley Jaguar radial engine gave it a top speed of 133 miles per hour and a range of 310 miles. In 1932 the Hawker Nimrod entered service. It featured all-metal structure and was powered by a 590-horsepower Rolls-Royce Kestrel liquid-cooled engine that gave it a top speed of 195 miles per hour and a range of 225 miles. The urgent need for a Nimrod replacement led the Admiralty to adopt a navalized version of a biplane Royal Air Force fighter as the Gloster Sea Gladiator in 1938. Its 840-horsepower Bristol Mercury engine gave it a speed of 245 miles per hour and a range of 380 miles. The Royal Navy also adopted two-seater fighter-reconnaissance aircraft in the 1930s. The Hawker Osprey, a version of the fast Hawker Hart biplane light bomber, entered fleet service in 1932. It had a top speed of 176 miles per hour and a range of 225 miles, courtesy of its 640-horsepower Rolls-Royce Kestrel engine.

Development of carrier fighters for the French Navy followed a very distinctive course. The first type embarked on the *Béarn* in early 1928 was the Lévy-Biche LB2. This wooden biplane had a detachable undercarriage, a boat-shaped lower fuselage, and small floats under the lower wings to allow it safely to alight on water in an emergency. Its 300-horsepower Hispano-Suiza 8Se engine gave it a top speed of 135 miles per hour. It was replaced late in 1928 by the Dewoitine D.1, a parasol-winged monoplane with an all-metal structure and a monocoque fuselage. With an engine similar to that powering the LB2, it attained 140 miles per hour and had a range of 250 miles. In 1931 another parasol-winged all-metal monoplane replaced the D.1. The Wibault 74's corrugated metal stressed skin produced a strong, light, and relatively durable structure. Using a 420-horsepower Gnôme-Rhone 9Ady radial engine, its performance was almost identical to its precursor's, but had the advantage of a much superior rate of climb and greater structural strength. The final French carrier fighter to enter service before World War II was yet another parasol-winged design. L'Aeronavale accepted two versions of Dewoitine's D.37 fighter, the D.373 with fixed wings and the D.376 with folding wings, in 1938. These aircraft were of all-metal stressed-skin construction, and their powerful 930-horsepower Gnôme-Rhone 14Kfs radial engines gave them a top speed of 255 miles per hour and a range of 560 miles. Their engines, however, were unreliable and low-wing monoplanes clearly offered greater performance potential. Consequently, the French Navy ordered an export version of Grumman's F4F-3 to replace its Dewoitines, but these Grumman Model G-36A aircraft were not delivered before France fell in June 1940 and instead served with the Royal Navy.

Carrier fighter development for the Imperial Japanese Navy followed a more conventional path. Its first carrier fighters were export versions of the Royal Navy's Nightjar. Mitsubishi's Herbert Smith then produced a fighter design that entered operational service as the Type 10 Carrier Fighter in 1923. It was powered by a 300-horsepower Mitsubishi Type Hi engine, giving it a top speed of 147 miles per hour and a range of 200 miles. In 1929 it was replaced by the Nakajima Type 3 Carrier Fighter (also known as the A1N) that was a modified version of the Gloster Gambet. Performance with a 450-horsepower Nakajima Kotobuki radial engine was not much better than the earlier Mitsubishi type, but it was much sturdier and more maneuverable. Nakajima's engineers then designed a replacement fighter with an all-metal structure that incorporated many features of contemporary Boeing F2B and Bristol Bulldog fighters. This entered service as the Type 90 Carrier Fighter (A2N1) in 1932. Its Nakajima Kotobuki radial engine now developed 580 horsepower, giving the new fighter a top speed of 182 miles per hour and a range of 310 miles. The company took advantage of the availability of more powerful radial engines to improve its biplane fighter design. The new aircraft, the Type 95 Carrier fighter (A4N1), entered service in 1936. It had a top speed of 220 miles per hour and a range of 525 miles, thanks to its 730-horsepower Nakajima Hikari engine. Nevertheless, the day of the biplane carrier fighter in Japanese service was soon over, for Nakajima's rival, Mitsubishi, had developed a remarkable new aircraft. Designed by Horikoshi Jiro, it was an all-metal low-wing fighter of stressed-skin construction. The first version of the Type 96 Carrier Fighter (A5M) had a 600-horsepower Nakajima Kotobuki engine. With this lower power output it attained a maximum speed of 252 miles per hour and had a range of 550 miles, while later models, with 785-horsepower engines, reached 270 miles per hour and increased their range to 750 miles, thanks to the use of drop tanks.

The first fighters to serve aboard United States Navy carriers were variants of existing U.S. Army fighters. Both the Curtiss F6C-3 and Boeing FB-5 were powered by 435-horsepower Curtiss D-12 water-cooled engines that gave them virtually identical performances: a top speed of 155 miles per hour and a range of 360 miles. They also were the last American carrier aircraft powered by liquid-cooled engines, since the navy decided to use only air-cooled radial engines because of their lighter weight and greater reliability. Curtiss responded with its F6C-4, powered by a 410-horsepower Pratt & Whitney Wasp, whose performance matched its precursor. Boeing produced two new designs, the F2B-1 and F3B-1, with very similar performances and succeeded in netting orders for over 100 examples delivered between January and December 1928. Less than a year later the company delivered the first examples of the very successful Boeing F4B series that formed the backbone of the navy's carrier fighter strength until 1936. Early models had a top speed of 176 miles per hour and a range of 370 miles using a 450-horsepower Wasp engine, later models could reach 188 miles per hour, thanks to an additional 100 horsepower from improved Wasp radials. Boeing's dominance was brought to an end by the new Grumman Aircraft Engineering Corporation, whose tubby biplanes, with retractable undercarriages, all-metal structure, and monocoque fuselages, constituted almost all the navy's fighter force prior to the outbreak of World War II in Europe. The F2F-1 was powered by a 700-horsepower Twin Wasp engine and had a top speed of 231 miles per hour, while the ultimate F3F-3 used a 950-horsepower Wright Cyclone that endowed it with a top speed of 264 miles per hour while maintaining a range of 980 miles. As war loomed in Europe, the navy also received its first monoplane fighter aircraft in the form of Brewster F2A-1s. With the same Cyclone engine as the F3F-3 Brewster's barrel-like fighter had a top speed of 311 miles per hour and a range of 1,545 miles, an indication of the still greater increases in performance to come.

In several navies during the 1920s fighter pilots discovered the efficacy of diving attacks on moving warships but only in the United States Navy was this technique systematically explored and quickly incorporated into operational carrier practice and organization. Initially the navy continued to use existing fighters, redesignating certain squadrons as bombing squadrons instead of fighting squadrons. It then ordered modified versions of fighters for use as dive bombers, epitomized by its two only moderately successful Curtiss Hawk variants, the BFC-2 (with a fixed undercarriage) and the BF2C-1, whose undercarriage retracted. The best solution, though, was to develop purpose-built dive bombers. The Martin BM-1 biplane entered service in 1932. Powered by a 625-horsepower Pratt & Whitney Hornet, it had a top speed of 146 miles per hour and had a range of 413 miles carrying a 1,000-pound bomb. The more powerful 750-horsepower Twin Wasp of Great Lake's BG-1 raised its speed to 188 miles per hour and increased its range to 549 miles. The introduction of the all-metal stressed skin monoplane Northrop BT-1 in 1938 marked a dramatic increase in performance. Top speed rose to 222 miles per hour and range increased to 1,150 miles, even though its Twin Wasp only offered an additional 75 horsepower.

Even before Northrop's BT-1 entered service, the navy had concluded that it would be more effective to combine the scouting and dive-bombing missions into a single more effective airframe, differentiating between the two missions through specialized training of scouting or bombing squadron crews. Vought and Curtiss produced biplane scout-bombers, the SBU and the SBC, both powered by 700-horsepower Pratt & Whitney Twin Wasp radial engines. The SBU, despite its fixed undercarriage, could reach a top speed of 205 miles per hour and had a range of 550 miles, while the SBC-3, with a retractable undercarriage, attained 220 miles per hour and had a range of 635 miles, both with a 500-pound bomb; again, a low-wing monoplane replaced these last biplanes. Vought's SB2U, which entered service in late 1937, had an all-metal structure but both the wings and the after half of the fuselage were still fabric-covered. A more powerful 825-horsepower Twin Wasp gave it a top speed of 243 miles per hour and increased the range to 1,120 miles with a 500-pound bomb.

The Imperial Japanese Navy observed the effectiveness of dive bombing and introduced its own dive bombers into service in 1934. The Aichi Watch and Electrical Equipment Company imported an example of Ernst Heinkel's He 66 dive bomber from Germany and modified it to suit the navy's needs. Powered by a 580-horsepower Nakajima Kotobuki 2 engine, Aichi's Type 94 Carrier Bomber (D1A1) had a top speed of 174 miles per hour and a range of 656 miles with a 550-pound bomb. The improved Type 96 Carrier Bomber (D1A2) took advantage of the 730 horsepower available from its Nakajima Hikari engine to raise its speed to 192 miles per hour but at the cost of a reduction in range to 576 miles. This version gained notoriety by sinking the United States Navy gunboat *Panay* on the Yangtse River on December 12, 1937.

In 1934 the British Admiralty issued a specification for the design of a dive bomber for the Royal Navy, which entered service in October 1938 as the Blackburn Skua. This all-metal low-wing monoplane of stressed-skin construction was also required to operate as a fleet fighter, due to the chronic shortage of aircraft stowage space aboard British carriers. As a fighter it was far too slow, but it was an effective dive bomber, with a top speed of 225 miles per hour and a range of 720 miles carrying a 500-pound bomb. The French Navy also came to appreciate the potential of dive bombing. Unsuccessful trials of the prototype Loire-Nieuport LN.140 in 1936 delayed adoption of dive bombers until just after war had begun in Europe, when the same firm's LN.40 entered service, albeit operating from land bases as the *Béarn* was occupied in transporting aircraft from the United States. It had a 690-horsepower Hispano-Suiza 12Xcrs liquid-cooled engine, giving it a top speed of 238 miles per hour and a range of 750 miles with a 550-pound bomb. As a stopgap the French Navy turned to Vought's successful SB2U instead. The Vought V-156-F, differentiated mainly from United States Navy equivalent models by its dive brakes, was just entering service as World War II began.

NAVAL AVIATORS BETWEEN THE WORLD WARS

At the end of World War I the vast majority of naval pilots were commissioned naval officers, as were most observers, while the majority of radio operators and air gunners were enlisted men. (Although the British air services combined to form the Royal Air Force as a separate service on April 1, 1918, its members still retained the right to revert to their original service arm without loss of rank or privilege). Thereafter, each carrier-operating navy followed its own diverging path for training and manning its aircraft and aviation units.

The French Navy after World War I maintained a dozen or more front-line land-based aviation units in metropolitan France and North Africa, seaplane units spread throughout the French Empire, and embarked aircraft aboard battleships, cruisers, seaplane carriers, and its sole aircraft carrier, the *Béarn*. The majority of its pilots and observers were commissioned officers, graduates of the Naval Academy at Brest, who received flight training and anticipated professional naval careers. Aspiring enlisted aircrew also received specialized training. In general, aircrew tended to remain within their specialized fields (fighters, reconnaissance, etc.) throughout their flying careers. There were some uncertainties, since naval aviation was a relatively small part of the navy and its survival was always subject to political influences.

Naval aviators, both officers and enlisted men, underwent initial flying orientation prior to beginning specialized training at the *base d'aéronautique navale* (BAN) Rochefort. Successful graduates then proceeded to basic flying training, officers to BAN Fréjus-Saint-

Raphaël (1919–1922), then to BAN Istres or BAN Rochefort (1923–1930), and enlisted pilots to BAN Istres. All those who successfully completed basic flying training and who opted for carrier service then completed advanced training at BAN Fréjus-Saint-Raphaël. Other aircrew (non-pilots) underwent training at BAN Hourtin as observers, bombardiers, or air-gunners. In 1931 the navy merged its training system with that of l'Aviation Militaire (which became l'Armée de l'Air in 1933). Basic flying orientation took place at Versailles, with flying training at either Villacoublay or Avord, though non-pilots continued to train at BAN Hourtin. In 1933 the government transferred the bulk of the navy's land-based units, both aircraft and personnel, to l'Armée de l'Air. Consequently, these units retained a strong naval flavor for some years afterwards and some of their members reverted to naval service when the navy was able to reestablish shore-based units in 1938. Furthermore, the French Navy never established a clear career path for its aviation officers.

The United States Navy followed a slightly different path. The bulk of its pilots immediately after World War I were commissioned officers who had graduated from the Naval Academy at Annapolis and who volunteered for flight duties. In 1917, the navy also began training limited numbers of enlisted men, usually petty officers, to qualify as Naval Aviation Pilots, though relatively few continued to serve in the peacetime fleet. The establishment of the Bureau of Aeronautics in 1921 gave naval aviation an institutional base within the navy. This led the Naval Academy to add courses in naval aviation to the syllabus in 1925 and also offer midshipmen limited flying experience. The following year Congress passed the Naval Aircraft Act in response to the recommendations of the Morrow Board. It authorized the addition of 1,000 aircraft to the fleet's inventory and restricted command of aircraft carriers, seaplane tenders, and naval air stations to naval aviators or naval aviation observers, thus opening a clear path for career advancement and offering the prospect of flag rank. In response to concerns that the appetite of naval aviation for commissioned officers, especially with the imminent entry into service of the two very large carriers Lexington and Saratoga, could excessively deplete the officer corps, the act also required the navy to expand the number of enlisted Naval Aviation Pilots to 30 percent of the number of commissioned pilots.

Until 1935 the navy drew all its officer pilots from the ranks of Naval Academy graduates. After their first two-year tour at sea, ensigns were eligible to apply for flight training. Basic training lasted one year, followed by seven months of advanced training, during which they familiarized themselves with all categories of aircraft the navy operated. Finally, the new pilots underwent operational training with fleet squadrons at shore bases. Because pilots did not specialize in a single aircraft category, most of them had very varied flying careers. A pilot might well serve successively with a battleship's floatplane observation unit, with a carrier-based fighter squadron, and with flying boats from a seaplane tender.

When the navy began expanding after the Depression it became clear that its needs for pilots far exceeded the capacity of the Naval Academy to graduate ensigns. Congress passed the Aviation Cadet Act in 1934, authorizing the navy to recruit mainly college graduates for flight training. Those found suitable underwent one year of basic training and spent three years on active duty as aviation cadets, following which they were commissioned as reserve ensigns in inactive status. The program succeeded in recruiting pilots but the navy found it challenging to retain them since, as aviation cadets, their flight operational prospects were restricted, pay was low, and prospects for advancement in the reserves were minimal. Consequently, the number of naval aviation pilots (including members of the Marine Corps) only increased from about 1,200 in 1935 to 1,800 in 1939.

The provisions of the Naval Aircraft Act led to a modest increase in the numbers of Naval Aviation Pilots in the fleet, manifest most publicly by the formation of Fighting Squadron Two, composed entirely of enlisted pilots except for flight leaders and the squadron commander. Naval Aviation Pilots followed the same training schedule as Naval Academy graduates and had similar flying career paths, although they were barred from commanding flights within squadrons. In 1931 the navy abandoned recruiting enlisted pilots, citing a shortage of funding for training that made it difficult to train sufficient numbers of officer pilots. When naval aviation began expanding the navy resumed recruiting enlisted pilots in 1935 but the total number still fell very far short of the 30 percent mandated by Congress and was closer to 10 percent at the end of 1939.

When the Imperial Japanese Navy began to build up a large carrier force it took a very different tack from other fleets in providing naval airmen. It was unique among the world's navies in its reliance on enlisted men to provide the vast bulk of its aircrews; only about 10 percent of its pilots were officers. Initially the navy's intake of enlisted aircrew came from transfers of suitable candidates from the fleet. Established in May 1920 as the *hikojutsu renshusei* (flying technique training program) and renamed the *sohju renshusei* (pilot trainee program) in June 1930, it accepted both enlisted seamen and noncommissioned officers. Standards were very high; anecdotal evidence indicates that only about 5 percent of applicants were accepted for training, while only about 40 percent of each class graduated. In 1930 the navy introduced the *hikoyoka renshusei* (flight reserve enlisted trainee program), a direct-entry program for civilians, while still retaining the intake from the fleet. This three-year program took suitable young men straight out of primary school (boys between fifteen and seventeen years of age educated to the equivalent of the second year of American middle school), gave them a basic naval education and put them through flight school. In 1937 the navy introduced a second direct-entry program, the *koshu hikoyoka renshusei* (Class-A flight reserve enlisted trainee program) which drew from young men aged between sixteen and nineteen who had completed three and one-half years of middle school education (equivalent to the middle of the first year of an American high school education), resulting in qualification of these trainees in a two and one-half year period. (The original program simultaneously was redesignated the *otsushu hikoyoka renshusei* (Class-B flight reserve enlisted trainee program).

Aircrew officers were almost all graduates of the Naval Academy at Eta Jima who had first served a year at sea before volunteering for flight training. Despite its early development of a coherent and effective command structure for naval air operations, the Imperial Japanese Navy never established a career path for its flying officers outside the aviation branch. The navy did not require its carrier captains, *kokutai* commanders, or flag officers in command of larger aviation units to be qualified naval aviators themselves, so there was little incentive for more senior officers to learn to fly. As the need for larger numbers of commissioned aviators became more apparent, a direct entry program for university graduates was introduced in 1934. The *koku yobi gakusen* (air reserve student program) drew from members of the Japan Student Aviation League. Its numbers never were very large because of resistance from Naval Academy graduates to what they perceived as dilution of the ranks of commissioned officers.

Training emphasized quality over quantity. Primary training, which lasted for six months, was very intensive and designed to weed out the less suitable candidates. Intermediate training took a further four to six months and was followed by three months of operational training in one of the various specialties. The pilots then were posted to an operational unit, by which time officers generally had logged some 400 flying hours, enlisted men about 250 hours. Operational units considered that pilots required a further year of extensive training within the unit before they were ready for combat operations. Starting in 1928 aircrew specialized in one of the various operational types: fighters, carrier attack or bombers, seaplanes, or land-based long-range bombers. In general, they remained in their specialty throughout their flying careers.

The Royal Navy's situation was completely different from that of other fleets, since it did not directly control either its aircraft or its aircrew and squadron personnel after the formation of the Royal Air Force on April 1, 1918. Initially all aircrew were Royal Air Force personnel, but the navy soon determined that this was unworkable, since pilots and observers rotated in and out of the Fleet Air Arm too rapidly to maintain competence and efficiency. In 1921 the Admiralty therefore created a specialist Observer Branch in the Royal Navy that would provide suitable officers for spotter-reconnaissance units serving on carriers. The interim report of the committee, led by the Marquess of Salisbury from March to June 1923 to examine the manner in which Royal Air force operations should be integrated with those of the Army and Royal Navy, also led to further changes. The need for continuity resulted in the Royal Air Force agreeing that 70 percent of all naval pilots and all naval observers would be commissioned officers in the Royal Navy who would hold parallel commissions in the RAF, a situation that could be fraught with confusion.

Naval officers volunteered for aircrew training after spending one year at sea. Observer candidates attended either the Naval Observers Course or the RAF Fleet Observers Course (held only during 1922 and 1923) for six months, after which they joined the fleet for further operational training with a front-line unit. Pilot candidates attended the Naval Pilots Course for basic flying training lasting seven to nine months. Successful graduates then took an advanced training program for a further five months, after which they were posted to a front-line unit. Most of this training took place at RAF facilities but naval officers made up the entire class. In 1922 the Admiralty also initiated a six-month training course for enlisted aircrew (Telegraphist Air Gunners). The need for additional aircrew as the carrier fleet expanded led to the addition of Observers Mates courses in 1935 and Ratings Pilots courses in May 1939, both drawing on enlisted volunteers.

Royal Air Force officers serving with the Fleet Air Arm followed a similar pattern of training, joining their naval colleagues for advanced training in carrier operations after nine to twelve months of basic flying training. In general, RAF officers rarely spent more than four years of their careers serving with the Fleet Air Arm, since longer service limited their prospects for professional advancement within their own arms of service. Naval officers who became naval aviators also found their flying careers could inhibit their long-term prospects, since no track toward senior rank existed that accommodated aviation service. Consequently, the Royal Navy suffered from a dearth of senior officers with direct aviation experience due to wastage among the more junior ranks.

The return of control of aircraft and aircrews to the Admiralty in 1937 did not materially change the situation before World War II began, since the navy had to set up its own infrastructure to generate replacements for RAF aircrew and squadron personnel. Some technical ranks among ground crews aboard carriers were still filled by RAF personnel to the end of the war.

CARRIER OPERATIONS BETWEEN THE WORLD WARS

Carrier-borne naval aviation was a radically new weapons system that presented great challenges to its users. Navies that deployed carriers learned they had to invest heavily in experiments, exercises, training, tactical studies, and new equipment in order to exploit its strengths and compensate for its pitfalls. Most carrier operations in this period concentrated on the practical development of effective procedures and techniques. Only the Imperial Japanese Navy, whose carriers intensively participated in the conflict in China, engaged in significant combat operations prior to the outbreak of World War II.

Determining the most effective deck-handling techniques and procedures required much experiment. From the earliest trials of landing aircraft onto the after deck of the *Furious,* the Royal Navy experimented until late in 1920 with arresting gear. Unlike later arresting gears, the objective of these British systems was not to slow down the aircraft after it had landed but rather to catch the aircraft from the moment it touched down and prevent it from being blown over the side. In large part this preoccupation arose from the fact that the Royal Navy was a pioneer in deck landing and its aircraft therefore were small and light and, thus, very susceptible to the effects of eddies and crosscurrents of air. The first system laid the foundation for later arrangements and used a series of longitudinal wires spaced about 9 inches apart and suspended some 15 inches above the deck between a pair of ramps. The aircraft landed within the confines of the wires and was held to the deck by hooks on the undercarriage engaging the wires. First installed on the *Furious,* the same system was fitted to the *Argus* from the outset and was the subject of a whole series of tests to determine the best form. Ultimately, the wires on the *Argus* were raised pneumatically and a shallow recess was fitted across the deck into which the aircraft wheels dropped as they ran along the deck. Further trials aboard the *Eagle* in 1920 demonstrated the efficacy of the system, which was lengthened and lowered so the wires were about 9 inches above the deck and supported by hinged flaps that fell as the aircraft ran into them. The American and Japanese navies both installed very similar systems on their first carriers, influenced by British practice (the *Langley* also carried an early transverse wire arresting gear system derived from a 1918 design by British naval constructor, W. A. D. Forbes). Nevertheless, the longitudinal arresting system had some serious failings, not least that it made a second attempt at landing very risky, since the pilot could not know if the hooks had engaged, and also because it was all too easy to catch wing tips under adjacent wires. After 1926, Royal Navy carriers were stripped of the longitudinal wires and operated without any arresting gear whatsoever until later in the 1930s. The *Langley*'s longitudinal wire system was removed in 1927, leaving only the transverse wires, and the Japanese replaced the *Akagi*'s longitudinal arresting gear with transverse wire gear in 1931.

The British conducted experiments with transverse wire arresting gear aboard the *Furious* and the *Vindictive* at the end of World War I but preferred the longitudinal system. The *Langley*'s transverse wire gear was designed to stop a landing aircraft and used friction brakes to modulate run-out. By the time the *Lexington* and the *Saratoga* fitted out for service, the United States Navy developed a hydraulically damped braking system for its arresting gear that remained unchanged in principle until after World War II. France used a transverse system from the outset, installing a sophisticated transverse-wire arresting gear produced by Schneider-Fieux that used friction drums to control run-out and featured an effective reset mechanism. Schneider-Fieux sold a similar system to Japan to replace the original longitudinal system, derived from early British practice, aboard the *Hosho* and the *Akagi.* The Japanese navy further improved this equipment by substituting hydraulic damping and used this version on all its later carriers. In Britain, trials began of friction-braked transverse-wire arresting gear in 1931, also drawing on W. A. D. Forbes's 1918 design. Although these were satisfactory, an improved hydraulically-damped system finally was adopted from 1932, because it offered smoother operation.

Arresting gear had a major impact on carrier aircraft operational cycles. With the longitudinal system, which was designed to slow down landing aircraft and prevent them from sliding sideways off the deck, each aircraft had to be struck down to the hangar below before the next plane could land, since otherwise there was a serious danger of an aircraft crashing into a machine that had landed but was still on the flight deck. This requirement greatly slowed aircraft operations and also limited aircraft capacity strictly to the number that could be stowed in the hangar. All navies initially adopted this procedure (in France, this was more a consequence of the complex, slow operating cycle of the *Béarn*'s elevators than of the type of arresting gear). When Captain Joseph M. Reeves, then the United States Navy's leading battleship gunnery expert, took command of Aircraft Squadrons, Battle Fleet aboard the *Langley* in October 1925 he found this slow operating cycle incapable of meeting the fleet's aviation requirements and began working with the ship's complement and aircrews to change it.

The replacement of the *Langley*'s original longitudinal arresting gear with transverse wires, the installation of a crash barrier, the training and deployment of Landing Signals Officers, the creation of specialized deck handling crews, the development of the deck park, and replenishing aircraft on the flight deck all served to transform operations. Previously, early carriers had barriers at the forward end of the flight deck to prevent aircraft from going over the bow. The new crash barrier prevented aircraft from running into machines parked forward on the deck. After each plane landed the barrier was lowered, the plane moved forward into a safe zone, and the barrier reerected. This procedure greatly increased the rate at which aircraft could land on the carrier. A shorter landing zone, the great importance of catching an arresting wire, and the faster tempo of landings required taking away the decisions about their approaches from the pilots and giving them to the Landing Signals Officer, a specially trained pilot who could observe and control their approaches from his vantage point on the carrier flight deck. The faster tempo also required creating specialized crews to handle the various aspects of deck operations. Once it became standard practice to park landed aircraft ahead of the barrier, it quickly became clear that respotting them aft for their next flight was much faster than striking them below to the hangar. Keeping aircraft on deck rather than in the hangar in turn required making arrangements to refuel and rearm them on the flight deck. The transformation wrought by these changes in practice was dramatic. In 1925 the *Langley* was hard pressed to keep more than six aircraft in the air at any one time (because of the time needed for their recovery). By the end of 1927 the *Langley* could launch a 42-plane strike and Reeves believed he could raise that number to 48. American carriers subsequently standardized these procedures to maximize their striking power.

Other navies did not adopt these procedures in their entirety, even though all appreciated the importance of launching the maximum number of aircraft in the shortest possible time, and the urgency of minimizing turnaround between missions. The Royal Navy's carriers, in particular, embarked much smaller air groups than comparable contemporary American vessels. British naval aviators, fleet commanders, and ship designers were aware of the potential of the American procedures in the early 1930s but were hamstrung by the Royal Air Force's lock on personnel, both aircrew and maintenance staff, that inhibited expanding air groups and thus diminished the urgency of changing operating practices. The Royal Navy introduced Deck Landing Control Officers (better known in the fleet as batsmen) in 1937 and simultaneously began development of a crash barrier, but operational barriers did not go to sea until the *Ark Royal* began operations in 1939. Although all the components for their use were in place, the Royal Navy was not to adopt deck parks and thus larger air groups until well into World War II.

Japanese carriers, by the 1930s, used a landing cycle similar to American practice but did not adopt the deck park. Instead, the aircraft parked forward of the crash barrier and usually were struck below to the hangars for refueling and rearming after the entire landing cycle was complete, then brought back to the flight deck for the next mission, so the tempo of operations was somewhat slower than on American carriers. Instead of a Landing Signals Officer, Japanese pilots relied on arrays of colored lights, adjustable to suit the various aircraft types, positioned one on either side of the flight deck. If a pilot could see a green light immediately above a red light, he was exactly on the path to land safely. Other light combinations indicated he was either too low or too high and needed to correct his approach. A steam jet forward gave wind direction and a flag signal indicated wind speed. The carrier's air operations officer and the *seibiin* (a crewman under his command) stationed aft signaled to "wave off" a pilot. Japanese carriers were fully equipped for night flying operations—white lights outlined the deck and its centerline, red lights indicated the crash barrier and aft end of the deck, and a trio of colored lights signaled wind speed and direction.

The *Langley* carried catapults, primarily for launching seaplanes rather than for faster deployment of its air group. These were essentially identical to the catapults, powered by compressed air, that earlier were fitted to some armored cruisers, and saw very little service. The *Lexington* and the *Saratoga* also carried a catapult apiece, an unusual type powered by a flywheel and designed by the same Carl Norden who later was responsible for developing high-altitude bomb sights. Subsequent American carrier catapults installed on the *Yorktown* and later classes were hydraulically powered. The H2 model available before World War II could launch a 5,500-pound aircraft at 65 miles per hour in a distance of 55 feet. Catapults were rarely used until well into World War II because it was faster to launch aircraft under their own power.

Catapult development for British aircraft carriers also began in the early 1930s. Interestingly enough, the same naval constructor, W. A. D. Forbes, who had designed the transverse wire arresting gear in 1918 that was later revived and developed into the hydraulically-braked system used on British carriers, was the designer of the British catapults too. His design used the ship's hydraulic system to power a flush-deck catapult that, even in its initial form installed on the *Courageous,* the *Glorious,* and the *Ark Royal,* accelerated a 7,000-pound aircraft to 56 knots. This had considerable impact on British flight operations, even though the preference remained to launch aircraft under their own power, since it allowed carriers equipped with catapults to launch fighters while in harbor and even while under weigh from within its protective screen, thus obviating the need to turn into the wind to provide air cover for a force at sea.

From the early 1930s the principal focus of American and Japanese carriers became conducting strike missions, as the composition of their air groups demonstrated. Attack aircraft formed at least 50 percent of an American carrier's air group from the outset, and this rose to 75 percent with the introduction of the scout-bomber category. Fighter aircraft always made up 30 percent or less of a Japanese carrier's complement. The Royal Navy remained wedded to the observation mission longer than the other two fleets, though it too accepted the primacy of strike operations in the later 1930s.

Torpedo attack initially ruled over bombing and retained its primacy in the British and French navies throughout the period between the two world wars. The *Langley*'s aviators showed the efficacy of dive-bombing at San Diego in 1926 and this success, followed by later spectacular demonstrations by aircraft from the *Lexington* and the *Saratoga*, led the United States Navy to concentrate on this technique and pay less attention to torpedo attack. Japanese aviators took note of dive-bombing and, while fully embracing it, developed very effective attack techniques that combined it with low-level torpedo attacks to overwhelm the target. Just before World War II broke out, both Britain and France also incorporated dive-bombing into their arsenals, developing indigenous aircraft for the mission and also, in the case of France, purchasing suitable American types.

The most important proving grounds for testing tactics were the regular unit, squadron, and fleet-level exercises that all the carrier-operating navies conducted. Such exercises allowed naval aviators to explore new ideas and validated their concepts to squadron and fleet commanders so that the tactical possibilities offered by improved aircraft and weaponry could be incorporated into operational doctrine. In these venues carrier aircraft units demonstrated the efficacy of coordinated torpedo attack, dive bombing against fast-moving warships, tactical search missions, strike operations against shore targets, and distant reconnaissance. They also enabled fleet and squadron commanders to evolve effective combinations of carriers and escorting surface warships, and to develop concepts to integrate fast-moving carrier forces with battle fleet operations. These exercises also revealed the limitations of aviation: the vulnerability of carriers to tactical surprise brought on by deficiencies in search, the impact of weather, and, above all, the magnitude of the task of maintaining an effective defense against an enemy air attack. Navies discovered that it was very difficult to provide adequate fighter cover, since the warning time of an incoming attack was more often than not too short to allow quick launch of defending fighters while it was impossible to maintain a large enough standing covering force without crowding out attack aircraft from the carrier's air group. This problem would not be solved until the advent of radar and accounts for the emphasis navies placed on striking fast and first with the most aircraft possible, the attendant diminution of fighter strength in favor of attack aircraft, and even the adoption of armored carriers by the Royal Navy.

Beyond the annual routine of exercises, carriers also engaged in the usual flag-showing operations of peacetime navies, provided assistance in times of emergency, and supported imperial policing (in the case of the British and French fleets). Royal Navy carriers stationed in Chinese waters, for example, regularly found themselves engaged in antipiracy patrols and strikes.

Japan's carrier force alone saw combat in the period before World War II. The 1st *Koku-sentai* (the *Hosho* and the *Kaga*) deployed off Shanghai on February 1, 1932, to support Japanese troops during the Shanghai Incident. Chinese fighter aircraft engaged Japanese bombers and escorting fighters sporadically throughout the month, including one well-known action on February 22 during which an American pilot, Robert Short, who was flying for the Chinese, was shot down in his Boeing 218 and killed in combat with three Japanese Type 3 fighters. Japanese carriers withdrew after a cease-fire was negotiated on March 3.

Much more significant was the deployment of Japanese carriers during the war in China that erupted after the Marco Polo Bridge incident on July 7, 1937. The *Kaga* deployed off Shanghai on July 15 and was joined by the *Hosho* and the *Ryujo* the following day. Japanese carriers thereafter engaged in offensive operations against Chinese land targets from Shanghai to Canton almost continuously until the end of November 1939. Their aviators learned very valuable lessons from these combat operations, most important the value of long range aircraft, strong fighter escort for attack aircraft, formation flying for coordinated self-defense, and effective unit fighter tactics. Consequently, when the world war came, Japan's naval aviators collectively were probably the best trained and most effective in the world. On the other hand, it is remarkable that the Imperial Japanese Navy, despite its experience of the drain from combat losses, did not accelerate or even seriously explore options for training larger numbers of naval aviators that would be needed in a global conflict.

NAVAL AVIATION IN 1939

Before the end of World War I the Royal Navy, on the basis of its operational experience, had accepted that ship-borne aircraft were an essential component of the main fleet's strength, vital both for defense against enemy aerial search and attack and for its own reconnaissance. The United States Navy had come to a similar conclusion as a result of extensive war-gaming at the Naval War College and from observing British practice. During the period between the two world wars, all major navies came to the same realization, and added two further missions: gunnery observation and antiship strike attack. Effective aircraft carriers joined the American, British, French, and Japanese fleets, and by 1939 carrier aviation was no longer experimental but an integral part of the arsenal of the world's major navies.

Fleet commanders were well aware of the importance of carrier aviation in future combat operations, not as an ancillary but in a central role. Carrier reconnaissance, strike, and observation missions all were accepted as essential components of any future major fleet action. Some ardent carrier advocates, especially in Japan and the United States, proclaimed the primacy of naval aviation. Some Japanese officers envisaged superior naval aviation as capable of nullifying the United States' numerical advantage in battleships and other surface warships. Some American officers came to see carrier aviation, capable of long-range flexible assaults, as the most effective platform for enabling the United States Navy's drive across the Pacific that formed the center of its strategic planning. Nevertheless, the vast majority of officers in all navies still were not convinced that aircraft could displace the battleship's heavy guns in a fleet action. While accepting the importance and potential of carrier aviation, they doubted that aircraft alone could destroy modern battleships on the high seas.

CHAPTER THREE

Capital Ships

WHEN WAR BROKE OUT AGAIN in Europe in September 1939 between Britain and France allied against Germany, all navies understood that aircraft could strongly influence the outcome of naval operations. Those fleets with distant oceanic commitments had developed over the previous twenty years an organic aviation component, based on aircraft carriers, to support their operations. The importance of aircraft carriers in defending naval forces, searching out and locating their enemies, and projecting naval power beyond the horizon was widely accepted. Aircraft carriers had become a vital support element in the arsenal of oceanic navies.

During the 1930s more senior naval officers began advocating a larger role for carriers. They envisaged carrier aircraft forming the first line of the fleet's defense and dominating its offensive operations, with battleships and auxiliary warships operating in support of the carriers. Over the course of the six years of World War II, their vision became reality, as aircraft carriers supplanted battleships, becoming the new capital ship of the world's fleets.

BRITISH CARRIER DEVELOPMENT
DURING WORLD WAR II

When design work began for the two carriers *Implacable* and *Indefatigable* of the 1938 program, the Admiralty decided to reassess the armored carrier design. The principal objective was greater aircraft capacity, since the limited air group of the armored carriers seemed too great a price to pay for their enhanced protection. By reducing the hangar height to 14 feet it proved possible to incorporate a 208-foot long lower hangar aft, which increased the stowed aircraft capacity to fifty-four. Hangar side armor was reduced to 1-1/2 inches, while the elevators and catapult were upgraded to accommodate aircraft up to 20,000 pounds in weight. These vessels gained enhanced survivability from an improved four-shaft power plant, arranged in the unit system, which also increased their speed.

Many of the changes featured in the 1938 carrier design were applied to the final unit of the *Illustrious* class, the *Indomitable*. It had its hangar reduced to 14 feet in height and the hangar side armor limited to 1-1/2 inches, which allowed the construction of a 168-foot long lower hangar and increased aircraft capacity to forty-eight machines. The *Indomitable* also carried the uprated elevators and catapult of the *Implacable* class.

These three vessels, together with the three *Illustrious* class ships from the 1936 and 1937 construction programs, were the only large carriers to join the Royal Navy during World War II. All were of prewar design. The Royal Navy's overwhelming need to construct and commission warships for antisubmarine warfare diverted scarce resources from carrier construction until late in the war. Consequently, the only large carriers laid down during the war, the *Eagle* and the *Ark Royal*, did not commission until the 1950s. Orders were placed for the four very large carriers of the *Malta* class that incorporated the fruits of British operational experience. Their characteristics were:

> Displacement: 46,900 tons (standard), 56,800 tons (full load)
> Dimensions: 916'6" (oa) x 115'9" x 29'6" (mean), 34'6" (full load)
> Flight deck: 900'0" x 146'0"
> Machinery: Parsons geared turbines, 8 Admiralty 3-drum boilers, 4 shafts, 200,000 shp = 33 knots
> Bunkerage: 6,000 tons
> Aircraft: 80
> Armament: 8 x twin 4.5" DP, 8 x 6-barrel 40mm AA, 3 x single 40mm AA
> Complement: 3,520

The *Malta* class design represented a substantial shift in British thinking. It included a single-level open hangar, as in American carriers, which allowed aircraft to run up their engines before rising to the flight deck, although the presence of side plating up to the flight deck in the bow and along much of the side obscured this. The hangar deck formed the strength deck, for the first time in a British design. Four elevators were included, two along the centerline and two on the port side. Two catapults were included on the flight deck. All four ships of the class, however, were cancelled by January 1946 before any were laid down.

Concern about the slow pace of fleet carrier construction led the Admiralty to explore other options for more rapidly expanding the carrier fleet. It considered conversions of cruisers or fast passenger liners, but both categories were important for the war effort and in short supply. Ultimately a new design was selected for a light fleet carrier that was based on mercantile scantlings to allow construction in merchant shipyards and thus not disrupt warship deliveries. The new design dispensed with all armor protection and heavy anti-aircraft weapons in favor of better subdivision and a large light anti-aircraft battery. Two elevators linked the single-level hangar to the flight deck, which carried full arresting gear, crash barriers, and a single catapult forward. Sixteen vessels of this type were ordered, although it was decided to use a revised design for the final six ships that incorporated a strengthened flight deck to accommodate faster, heavier aircraft. Only the first four ships of the *Colossus* class commissioned before the end of World War II, although too late for combat operations, but the light fleet carriers became the mainstay of British carrier operations in the years immediately after the war.

Two of the *Colossus* class, the *Perseus* and the *Pioneer,* completed as maintenance carriers before the war's end and joined the purpose-built *Unicorn* in this unique category. The type was intended to support carrier squadrons by undertaking major aircraft overhauls and transporting replacement machines. Unlike the two later vessels, the *Unicorn* was fully capable of combat operations, although appreciably slower than contemporary fleet carriers. The Royal Navy, therefore, relied primarily on escort carriers to fulfill much of the maintenance carrier role, although all three vessels remained operational into the 1950s.

Like both the Imperial Japanese and United States navies, during the 1930s the Royal Navy explored conversion of suitable merchant ships into aircraft carriers in the event of war. Unlike its contemporaries, however, the Royal Navy's interest was exclusively in conversions for service as trade protection carriers. When war broke out in September 1939 the Admiralty's interest in trade protection carriers revived and designs were prepared for mercantile conversions with three distinct levels of capability.

Escort Carrier Type A
Maximum speed: 20 knots
Endurance: 15,000 nm
Flight deck (minimum): 550'0" x 75' 0"
Elevators: 2 (45'0" x 34'0" rated at 15,000 pounds)
Arrester wires: 6
Barriers: 2
Aviation fuel stowage: 75,000 gallons
Aircraft: 25 (hangar stowage for 16)
Armament: 2 x twin 4" DP, 4 x four-barrel 2-pdr AA, additional
    20mm AA
Escort Carrier Type B
Maximum speed: 18 knots
Endurance: 15,000 nm
Flight deck (minimum): 500'0" x 70' 0"
Elevators: 1 (45'0" x 34'0" rated at 15,000 pounds)
Arrester wires: 6
Barriers: 2
Aviation fuel stowage: 50,000 gallons
Aircraft: 15 (hangar stowage for 12)
Armament: 2 x twin 4" DP, 4 x four-barrel 2-pdr AA, additional
    20mm AA
Escort Carrier Type C
Maximum speed: 16.5 knots
Endurance: as great as possible
Flight deck (minimum): 450'0" x 60' 0"
Elevators: 1 (42'0" x 20'0" rated at 10,000 pounds)
Arrester wires: 4–5
Barriers: 1
Aviation fuel stowage: 33,000 gallons
Aircraft: 10 (hangar stowage for 4)
Armament: 1 x twin 4" DP, 4 x four-barrel 2-pdr AA, additional
    20mm AA

Shortages of suitable vessels for conversion and the exigencies of
the wartime situation effectively blocked concrete action on these
plans.

After the fall of France in June 1940 the North Atlantic convoy
protection situation seriously worsened, since bases on the French
Atlantic coast gave German U-boats and long-range bombers greatly
enhanced access to assail British sea lanes. In January 1941 the Admiralty ordered a very basic conversion of the captured German

merchantman *Hannover* into an escort carrier. The superstructure was stripped to the upper deck, a flight deck with arresting gear and crash barriers fitted atop accommodation and aviation stowage spaces, the diesel exhausts rerouted clear of the sides, a basic navigation platform added to starboard, and a limited antiaircraft battery installed. There was no hangar (and therefore no elevator), so all aircraft were carried on deck at all times. Renamed the *Audacity,* it commissioned in June 1941 and, during a brief six-month career before its loss to a U-boat torpedo on December 20, thoroughly demonstrated the potential utility of small slow auxiliary carriers in escorting convoys.

The Royal Navy ordered four later escort carrier conversions from incomplete mercantile hulls and also converted the liner *Pretoria Castle,* but relied primarily on large numbers of American-built escort carriers to fulfill its requirements in this category of warship. After the shocks of the loss of the *Avenger* to explosions after a single torpedo hit on December 15, 1942, and the accidental destruction of the *Dasher* by aviation gas explosion on March 27, 1943, the Admiralty ordered substantial changes to aviation fuel and ordnance stowage arrangements, internal subdivision, and hangar integrity in American-built escort carriers before their entry into service to improve survivability. This provoked serious complaints from the United States Navy that the modification program substantially delayed their entry into service and contributed to the decision to hold back the *Casablanca* class escort carriers slated for transfer to the Royal Navy. Interestingly enough, despite the modification program the working-up period for both American and British escort carriers actually was virtually identical at the time, though it probably was fortunate that no further vessels were transferred, since the Royal Navy was suffering from acute shortages of manpower by mid 1944 and would have been extremely hard pressed to put them into service.

In addition to modifications to improve survivability, the British-operated escort carriers received specialized outfits to optimize them for one of three different roles: antisubmarine warfare, fighter operation, or assault missions. In large part this reflected the shortage of British fleet carriers to provide fighter cover and fighter-bomber support for landing operations or to conduct strike operations against enemy shipping. Several escort carriers also were fitted out to provide night-fighter cover for the British Pacific Fleet, reflecting the impact of such specialized aircraft on the limited air groups of the Royal Navy's fleet carriers.

In view of the urgency of the situation during mid-1942 in the North Atlantic Gap, the area then beyond the range of shore-based aircraft coverage, the Royal Navy also began deploying Merchant Aircraft Carriers (MAC-ships) to compensate for shortages of full-fledged escort carriers. The initial MAC-ship design simply added a flight deck atop a grain carrier hull, because this type's cargo-handling gear was unaffected by the change. There was a small hangar aft served by an elevator, and each ship could carrier three or four obsolescent Swordfish biplanes, whose exceptional slow-speed handling characteristics allowed safe operation from a flight deck just over 400 feet long. Tankers also were suitable candidates for conversion, but their cargo-discharging pipework precluded the erection of a hangar, so their aircraft at all times were carried on the flight deck, which consequently was extended by some 100 feet. It was planned to convert thirty grain carriers and tankers into MAC-ships, but the arrival of quantities of far superior escort carriers cut short the program in May 1944 after six grain ships and thirteen tankers had been converted. Unlike escort carriers, MAC-ships retained most of their cargo-carrying capacity and operated as normal merchant vessels with merchant service commanders and crews. Only the aircrews and necessary aviation maintenance staff were naval personnel.

All the large British carriers that entered service during World War II were ordered prior to the conflict's start. They represented the Admiralty's thinking on carrier design and operation immediately before the war elevated aircraft carriers to capital ship status. It is clear from their designs that the Royal Navy already was moving beyond its concept of hangar space determining aircraft capacity toward the United States Navy's ideas of permanent large-scale deck parks. Shortages of both aircraft and aircrew delayed full implementation of this change until well into the conflict, but the design features of the *Malta* class in particular clearly demonstrate the Admiralty's acceptance of this more effective and powerful operational paradigm.

The British approach to light carriers, exemplified by the *Colossus* class, was remarkably effective. There is no disputing that the American decision to deploy conversions of existing hulls as light carriers enabled the United States Navy to bring more carriers on line much earlier than the British, but the Royal Navy's light carriers proved vastly more capable and adaptable, as demonstrated by their very long and varied careers over more than sixty years since they first entered service.

British wartime escort carriers derived from prewar appreciation of the potential of small carriers as valuable participants in the trade protection campaign. Their deployment as front-line assault and fighter defense vessels reflects the shortages of more effective large units resulting from limited resources and the overarching priority of warship construction for trade protection and antisubmarine duties.

GERMAN CARRIER DEVELOPMENTS DURING WORLD WAR II

The Seekriegsleitung (Naval War Staff) began exploring aircraft carrier requirements in early 1934. It suggested a 15,000-ton vessel capable of 33 knots with a cruising range of 12,000 nautical miles to be armed with either nine 6-inch or six 8-inch guns in triple mountings, armored on the cruiser scale, carrying 60 aircraft and fitted with 2 catapults. In April 1934 it was decided to proceed with a carrier in the 1935 construction program and design work was entrusted to a team led by Wilhelm Hadeler. In view of the novelty of this type of vessel in the German Navy, Hadeler started from the design of the British *Courageous*. He also was able to obtain useful input from Japanese experience, sending a team of investigators to Japan in 1936.

The final construction design featured two hangars linked to the flight deck by three electrically powered elevators. The flight deck carried transverse-wire arresting gear and two compressed-air powered catapults forward that each could launch nine aircraft in four minutes, after which it would take almost an hour to recharge the compressed air reservoirs. The starboard island was long and low, and incorporated a large part of the antiaircraft battery either on or fore and aft of it. Four high-angle directors were provided to control the heavy antiaircraft weapons. The main antisurface battery was disposed in casemates along the sides of the hull, where its position made it likely to be of limited efficacy at sea. Fitting separate antiship and antiaircraft batteries, although typical of German practice on heavy ships at this time, was very wasteful of tonnage and space. During World War II the design was modified to incorporate large bulges, mainly to offset light antiaircraft battery additions and some stability problems that had emerged. These bulges stowed additional fuel, raising the total bunkerage to 6,740 tons.

Two ships were ordered, "Carrier B" on February 11, 1935, from Krupp Germania Werft at Kiel, and "Carrier A" on November 16, 1935, from Deutsche Werke at Kiel. Only "Carrier A" was launched, on December 8, 1938, and christened the *Graf Zeppelin* by the

Gräfin Hella von Brandenstein-Zeppelin, the famous airship designer's daughter. Construction of "Carrier B" was stopped on September 19, 1939, after World War II began and the incomplete hull was broken up in February 1940. Work on the *Graf Zeppelin* also ceased until greater appreciation of the value of carriers made its addition to the fleet more important and the ship was dry-docked for completion to a slightly revised design in December 1942. The debacle of the German heavy ships' excursion into the Barents Sea (Operation Regenbögen) later the same month, however, put an end to serious consideration of deploying long-distance raiding squadrons, and work ceased once again on January 30, 1943. The abandoned hull was scuttled at Stettin on April 25, 1945. It was raised by Soviet Union forces and renamed *PO-101* on February 3, 1947, then used as a target for bombs and torpedoes. The hulk finally was sunk on August 16, 1947, off Swinemunde.

In the late summer of 1942 the Seekriegsleitung came to the conclusion that future fleet construction should center on aircraft carriers, although building battleships should continue, so that the Kriegsmarine could operate balanced carrier-battleship task forces. Initial sketch designs envisaged two different types of carriers: a 15,000-ton vessel suitable for series production, carrying 4.9-inch guns and about twenty aircraft, and a large unit of 58,000 tons carrying 100 aircraft, armed with twenty 5-inch dual-purpose guns, and featuring a 4-inch armored flight deck. Further elaboration of these concepts resulted in two more refined sketch designs for a *grosse-flugzeugträger* and an *Atlantikflugzeugträger*. The smaller *grosse-flugzeugträger* displaced 40,000 tons at full load, was 820 feet long with a beam of 105 feet and drew 28 feet 9 inches. A three-shaft 280,000 shaft horsepower plant gave it a top speed of 34 knots and a range of 18,000 miles at 15 knots. The single hangar, 689 feet long and 69 feet wide, accommodated 26 bombers and 12 fighters. Protection included a 6-inch belt, 4-inch hangar deck and 2-inch flight deck, and the antiaircraft battery comprised 8 twin 4.1-inch and 10 twin 37mm guns. The larger *Atlantikflugzeugträger* displaced 67,500 tons at full load, was 919 feet long with a beam of 125 feet and drew 36 feet. A 4-shaft 280,000 shaft horsepower plant gave it a top speed of 34 knots and a range of 20,000 miles at 15 knots. The single hangar, 820 feet long and 85 feet wide, accommodated 38 bombers and 12 fighters. Protection included a 9-3/4-inch belt, 6-inch hangar deck and 2-inch flight deck, and the battery comprised 8 twin 5.9-inch surface guns and 8 twin 4.1-inch and 10 twin 37mm antiaircraft guns.

There also was much discussion of cruiser-carriers, vessels combining aviation facilities with a powerful gun armament and primarily intended for the guerre de course against merchant shipping. Two equivalent sketch designs were prepared for a *grosseflugzeugkreuzer* and an *Atlantikflugzeugkreuzer*. The former corresponded to the *grosseflugzeugträger*, but had a smaller 525-foot long hangar accommodating ten fewer bombers and added eight twin 5.9-inch surface guns to its armament. The *Atlantikflugzeugkreuzer* matched the *Atlantikflugzeugträger*'s dimensions, except that displacement rose to 71,500 tons as a result of fitting two triple 11-inch turrets, while the smaller 623-foot long hangar accommodated twelve fewer bombers. Both these designs incorporated full flight decks that were supported above the antisurface ship weapons.

Several other sketches were worked out at this time for three much smaller carrier-cruisers and two tenders (*flugbootträger*) intended to support oceanic operation of large flying boats. None of these projects, however, moved further toward fruition because German dreams of powerful surface forces were shattered by the reality of British naval power and, in particular, its carrier strength, as demonstrated only a few months later. In March 1944 there were some discussions about converting small merchant ships into emergency carriers, but these were clearly unrealistic in view of the military situation at the time.

Simultaneous with its approval of the resumption of work on the *Graf Zeppelin*, the Seekriegsleitung also took some concrete action to address the perceived need for additional carriers. The incomplete hull of the heavy cruiser *Seydlitz*, on which there had been little progress since late 1940, was selected for conversion into a carrier. The superstructure was razed to the upper deck in preparation for erecting a hangar and flight deck but, as with the *Graf Zeppelin*, all work ceased at the end of January 1943. The hulk was towed to Königsberg and scuttled there in April 1945. The Kriegsmarine never commissioned a carrier.

ITALIAN CARRIER DEVELOPMENT DURING WORLD WAR II

The Regia Marina (Royal Italian Navy) explored various projects for adding one or more aircraft carriers to the fleet in the 1930s but took no action beyond developing a basic design for constructing a new vessel and identifying suitable candidate merchant ships for conversion. In mid-1940, as Italy prepared to enter the war as an ally of Germany, a design was prepared for a simple conversion of the fast liner *Roma* into an aircraft carrier, but again was deemed less of a priority than other construction and set aside in January 1941.

It took the shock of defeat at Cape Matapan (March 28, 1941), which the Italians largely attributed to effective British deployment of its carrier *Formidable,* to revive demands for a carrier as an urgent requirement. In July 1941 the Undersecretary of the Navy authorized the conversion of the *Roma* into a carrier, using the design studies of the previous year as a basis. In the event, the project became much more ambitious and required a major transformation of the relatively elderly liner into the carrier *Aquila.*

Displacement: 23,350 tons (standard), 27,800 tons (full load)
Dimensions: 759'2" (oa) x 96'6" x 24'0"
Flight deck: 700'0" x 83'0"
Machinery: Belluzzo geared turbines, 8 Thornycroft boilers,
    4 shafts, 140,000 shp = 30 knots
Bunkerage: 2,800 tons = 4,000 nm @ 18 knots
Aircraft: 36
Armament: 8 x 5.3", 12 x 65mm AA, 22 x 6-barrel 20mm AA
Complement: 1,420

The superstructure was razed completely and a large hangar 525 feet long and 59 feet wide was erected beneath the steel flight deck. The *Roma*'s original power plant was replaced completely with two sets of machinery originally intended for light cruisers of the Capitani Romani class, raising the carrier's speed from 21 knots to 30 knots. The furnace uptakes were trunked to starboard into a very large stack that was incorporated into a substantial island structure. Two elevators connected the hangar and flight deck, which carried two catapults and full arresting gear. All armament was fitted on platforms sponsoned out from the ship's side. Magazines and aviation fuel stowage were created and protected by 3-inch armor decks. To ensure stability and provide effective defense against torpedo attack, the hull was fitted with deep bulges on each side.

When Italy surrendered on September 8, 1943, the *Aquila* was virtually complete. The Germans seized the ship but it was heavily damaged by United States Army Air Force bombing on June 16, 1944 and a human torpedo attack on April 19, 1945. On April 24, 1945, the ship was scuttled at Genoa. After World War II the ship was raised and taken to La Spezia in 1949. Initially the Italian Navy considered refitting the *Aquila* for service as a carrier but this plan was abandoned and the ship broken up in 1952.

In late 1942 the Regia Marina decided to add a second carrier to the fleet and began a simple conversion of the liner *Augustus* along the lines originally proposed for the *Roma*. When the ship, by then renamed the *Sparviero*, was seized by Germany after Italy surrendered only the superstructure had been razed. The hulk was scuttled on April 24, 1945, in an attempt to block the entrance to the harbor at Genoa. It was raised in 1947 and scrapped.

SOVIET UNION CARRIER DEVELOPMENT DURING WORLD WAR II

The Soviet Navy explored designs for two different types of small carriers in the years immediately before World War II whose construction was included in the 1938–1942 Five-Year Plan. Since its designers realized the extent of their ignorance of carrier design, immediately after the conclusion of the German-Soviet Non-Aggression Pact on August 23, 1939, the Soviet Union requested assistance from Germany, offering to purchase either the unfinished carrier *Graf Zeppelin* or design plans for the ship. Germany rebuffed both offers, eventually leading Josef Stalin to delete the two projected carriers from the construction plan.

More carrier design work began in November 1943, under Project 72, that generated draft designs by November 1944, again not translated into shipyard steel. In January 1945 the central government set up a commission to examine existing warship designs in light of wartime experience and develop fresh concepts. Its carrier branch developed a huge array of sketch proposals: two for heavy carriers, four for fleet carriers, three for light carriers, and no less than twenty-four for escort carriers. Given the complete absence of suitable aircraft and the lack of appropriate design experience, these concepts tended toward the fanciful. One heavy carrier was 1,148 feet long, 134 feet in beam, drew 35 feet, and displaced 82,379 tons, requiring 384,000 shaft horsepower to attain a top speed of 34 knots. Its air group comprised 24 fighters, 24 light attack aircraft, and 40 medium attack aircraft. A fleet carrier proposal was more realistic: it was to be 899 feet in length with a beam of 106 feet and a draft of 34 feet, displace 35,270 tons, and attain 34 knots on

277,000 shaft horsepower. 24 fighters, 24 light attack aircraft, and 24 medium attack aircraft made up its air group. Another sketch design, for a light carrier, again envisaged very powerful machinery developing 242,000 shaft horsepower to drive the 30,560-ton ship at 34 knots. It was 794 feet long, 97 feet in beam with a draft of 27 feet, and could embark 36 fighters and 27 torpedo bombers. Finally, one of the escort carrier concepts was for an 18,410-ton vessel capable of 20 knots on 33,500 shaft horsepower and carrying 24 fighters and 18 antisubmarine aircraft. None of these design efforts resulted in serious plans to construct aircraft carriers and it was to be more than twenty years before the Soviet navy took delivery of its first air-capable warship.

JAPANESE CARRIER DEVELOPMENT DURING WORLD WAR II

The final fleet carriers completed before Japan entered World War II represented a great advance on earlier vessels while retaining many similar features from the *Soryu* class. The hull again was long and narrow but its much greater size allowed the designers to incorporate much enhanced passive armor protection and a larger antiaircraft battery. Belt armor increased to 6.5 inches along the machinery spaces and 8.3 inches beside the magazines, while deck armor was 3.9 inches thick except over the magazines, where it was strengthened to 5.1 inches. The bulbous bow form below the waterline that featured in the contemporary *Yamato*-class battleship design also appeared in the new carrier and contributed to its ability to attain very high speed. Hangar arrangements replicated those of the earlier *Soryu* design but on a larger scale, with the lower hangar built into the hull itself and the longer upper hangar forming the superstructure. The elevators were much larger than in the earlier pair of ships. The *Shokaku* and the *Zuikaku* were unique among Japanese carriers in carrying a pair of catapults, derived from units developed for use on the *Yamato*-class battleships, on the flight deck. As originally designed the two ships were to have islands on opposite sides, one to starboard and the other to port, as with earlier pairs of vessels operating in *koku-sentai* formation. By the time construction reached the point of fitting islands the disadvantages of the port side island amidships had made themselves apparent, so both vessels received islands forward of amidships on the starboard side.

The largest fleet carrier to enter Japanese service during World War II, the *Taiho,* combined the basic features of the preceding *Shokaku* class with several innovations: a 3-inch armored flight deck, a greatly enlarged island that accommodated the stack within its structure, and an enclosed bow plated to flight deck level. The *Taiho* retained the double hangar without side protection of earlier Japanese designs and sacrificed one deck level within the hull to reduce freeboard in compensation for the topweight of the armored flight deck. It was strongly protected elsewhere with a 5-inch hangar deck and 6-inch side belt armor. Five further vessels, similar to the *Taiho* but slightly enlarged and somewhat better protected, were projected but none was ever laid down before war's end.

When it became clear in 1941 that Japan was going to war with the United States, the Imperial Japanese Navy prepared a fleet carrier design for large-scale production. Based on the successful *Hiryu* design, it differed mainly in incorporating only two elevators rather than the three of the earlier design, and in reverting to the starboard side island of the *Soryu.* Two vessels were ordered under the 1941 program, one of which was cancelled the following year and replaced by seven very slightly different ships. Finally, a further eight carriers were ordered late in 1942, again slightly enlarged, making this class the largest ever envisaged by the Imperial Japanese Navy. Ultimately, the realities of Japan's material shortages caused only six units to be laid down, of which only three were completed (one of which, the *Katsuragi,* did not commission), and none saw front-line service.

To address the shortfall in carrier tonnage imposed by the Washington and London treaties, Japanese naval planners added to the fleet a number of modern auxiliaries whose design incorporated specific features allowing their relatively straightforward conversion into full-fledged aircraft carriers if required. A total of seven such vessels were ordered, three submarine depot ships (the *Taigei,* the *Tsurugisaki,* and the *Takasagi*) and four seaplane carriers (the *Chitose,* the *Chiyoda,* the *Mizuho,* and the *Nisshin*). All but two of the seaplane carriers (which were sunk while operating in their original role) were converted into carriers either before Japan's entry into World War II or during the conflict. Most of these vessels also featured somewhat unusual machinery arrangements—all three depot ships and seaplane carriers *Mizuho* and *Nisshin* (which were never converted) were diesel engined, while the seaplane carriers *Chitose* and *Chiyoda* had mixed steam turbine and diesel machinery. The depot ships' diesels, among the earliest installed in the navy's surface ships, were not very reliable, so they were replaced with destroyer-type turbine installations when the ships later were converted into aircraft carriers.

The seaplane carriers were characterized externally by very flat sheers, largely clear upper decks over two-thirds of their lengths, and minimal superstructures: features that greatly eased their conversion into aircraft carriers. Internally, their designs included foundation assemblies and pits for elevators, plus spaces appropriate for use as magazines and aviation fuel stowage. The depot ships were similar, although they had large midship superstructures, much of which was designed for simple conversion to form the hangars of the new carriers. Conversion involved razing superstructure as required, erecting a long hangar over the midship three-quarters of the hull's length, installing elevators at each end of the hangar, constructing a wooden full-length flight deck over the hangar complete with arresting gear, fitting antiaircraft batteries sponsored along the flight deck edge, and trunking furnace gases to starboard. The converted carriers embarked about 30 aircraft and carried 4 twin 5-inch mountings, plus varying numbers of lighter weapons for self-defense. Within the limitations of their small size, restricted air groups, and minimal protection, these "shadow" carriers were useful, though clearly they were much less effective than purpose-built vessels.

The Imperial Japanese Navy also established a further "shadow" carrier program based on subsidized liners suitable for conversion. The construction of the three 21-knot 17,000-ton liners of the *Asama Maru* class that entered service on the trans-Pacific routes of the Nippon Yusen Kaisha (NYK–Japan Mail Steamship Company) between September 1929 and March 1930 was subsidized by the Ministry of Transportation with the proviso that their design incorporate features specifically intended to allow their conversion into aircraft carriers within three months. In 1933 and in 1935 NYK and Osaka Shoshen Kaisha (OSK–Osaka Merchant Ship Company) planned to build further subsidized 24-knot 20,000 ton vessels, also suitable for conversion into carriers, for their North American, European, and South American services, but financial constraints forced the abandonment of these projects. Subsidies allowed NYK to build the three smaller 21-knot 17,000-ton *Nitta Maru* class liners for its European routes in 1937, and also aided OSK in constructing two 21-knot ships of the still smaller 13,000-ton *Argentina Maru* class for service to South America in 1938. Finally, in late 1938 NYK ordered a pair of large 24-knot 27,700-ton subsidized liners of the *Kashiwara Maru* class for its trans-Pacific routes. All seven of these ships incorporated substantial provisions for rapid conversion into carriers into their design.

As war with the United States became increasingly probable, the Imperial Japanese Navy began to convert much of this "shadow" carrier fleet. It took over the *Kashiwara Maru* and its sister, the *Izumo Maru,* in October 1941 while they still were incomplete and converted them into the fleet carriers *Junyo* and *Hiyo* respectively. Since they had been completed only to the main deck, conversion work was rapid because there was little superstructure requiring prior removal, and both vessels commissioned within eight months. As front line units their principal deficiencies were slow speed, limited internal subdivision, and the absence of armor protection, but they otherwise compared quite favorably with purpose-built Japanese carriers.

The *Kasuga Maru* of the *Nitta Maru* class was still under construction when it was taken over on May 1, 1941, for conversion into the prototype Japanese escort carrier at Sasebo Navy Yard. This was a limited conversion involving clearing the hull to the upper deck, erecting a 300-foot long hangar topped by a 492-foot long flight deck, fitting two elevators, trunking the furnace uptakes to exhaust on the starboard side, and adding an antiaircraft battery. It commissioned some four months later as the *Taiyo,* and was followed by its two sisters the *Yawata Maru* and the *Nitta Maru,* which became the *Unyo* and the *Chuyo* respectively after six-month conversions at Kure Navy Yard. The two smaller OSK liners *Argentina Maru* and *Brazil Maru* also were slated for similar conversions in late 1942 but in the event only the former commissioned as the escort carrier *Taiyo* because the *Brazil Maru* was sunk while serving as a troopship before conversion could begin. In its place the ex-German Norddeutscher Line liner *Scharnhorst,* which had been trapped at Kobe by the outbreak of war in Europe and taken over by Japan in early 1942, was similarly converted into the escort carrier *Shinyo* during 1943. The three *Asama Maru* class liners, the original group of subsidized "shadow" carriers, never converted into aircraft carriers because all were sunk while serving as naval transports.

The original intent of the subsidy program was to expedite expansion of the front-line carrier fleet. Although the Japanese escort carriers were much larger than their British and American counterparts, they were too slow, small, and weakly-armed for front-line operations. Within Japanese fleet doctrine there was no real place for the escort carriers either, since the Imperial Japanese Navy did not develop a coherent policy for deploying antisubmarine forces until very late in the war. Consequently, the escort carrier conversions spent almost their entire careers operating as aircraft transports and training carriers. Only the larger, faster, and very much more sophisticated conversions *Hiyo* and *Junyo* fulfilled the promise of the "shadow" program.

The impact of Japan's carrier losses in 1942 and the realization of the limitations of the nation's shipbuilding capacity led to the decision to undertake conversions of other warship types on an emergency basis in an attempt to rebuild the carrier fleet. Nevertheless, shortages of suitable candidates for conversion, raw materials, shipways, shipyard equipment, and labor all combined to limit severely Japan's ability to follow this course successfully. Just two warship conversions were initiated, and only one ever put to sea. The *Ibuki*, the first of a pair of improved *Tone* class heavy cruisers, was laid down at Kure Navy Yard on April 24, 1942, and launched May 21, 1943. Construction of both cruisers was suspended in midsummer 1943, and conversion of the *Ibuki* into an aircraft carrier was initiated at Sasebo Navy Yard in November 1943.

> Displacement: 12,500 tons (standard)
> Dimensions: 672'7" (oa) x 69'7" x 20'8" (mean)
> Flight deck: 660'0" x 75'6"
> Machinery: Geared turbines, 4 boilers, 2 shafts, 72,000 shp = 29 knots
> Aircraft: 27
> Armament: 2 x twin 3" DP, 8 x triple 25mm AA, 6 x 28-barrelled 120mm AA rocket launchers
> Complement: 1,105

The superstructure was razed to the upper deck and replaced with a single-level hangar under a full-length flight deck served by two elevators. Internally, four boilers were removed to provide space for additional fuel and stores stowage and the furnace uptakes trunked to starboard. A typical Japanese-style island was to be fitted and the armament installed in sponsons at flight deck level. Very large bulges were fitted to the hull as compensation for the added topweight and to improve stability. Conversion work proceeded slowly, largely because of material and labor shortages, and was abandoned in March 1945. The incomplete hull was scrapped in 1947.

The second warship conversion was of the incomplete *Yamato* class battleship *Shinano*. When the decision was made, the hull was complete only to the upper deck, simplifying the project. A large hangar supporting an armored flight deck served by two elevators was constructed on the upper deck, the uptakes trunked to a single very large stack incorporated into an island that was an enlarged version of that fitted on the *Hiyo* class, and an extensive antiaircraft battery installed in sponsons at flight deck level. The *Shinano* was conceived as a floating support platform for carrier task forces rather than an operational front-line combat unit, but never entered service. While sailing from Yokosuka to Kure for final fitting out, the carrier was torpedoed by the submarine *Archerfish* on November 29, 1944, and sank as a result of uncontrolled flooding, since the watertight doors had yet to be installed.

Japanese carrier development during World War II in large part continued the two central themes of prewar design efforts: a search for both qualitative excellence in individual vessels and for quantitative equality or superiority relative to the United States Navy. The search for qualitative excellence was demonstrated by the *Taiho*, which combined the performance and aircraft capacity of the *Shokaku* class (the epitome of Japanese prewar design) with greatly enhanced protection, while the demand for quantity production was exemplified by the *Unryu* class and the Imperial Japanese Navy's very extensive "shadow" carrier fleet. The limitations of Japan's industrial base made this an impossible task. Most of the "shadow" carrier designs required major qualitative concessions of speed, aircraft capacity, or protection that limited their contribution to carrier task force capabilities, the *Unryu* class represented a step back in Japanese carrier quality, and the Imperial Japanese Navy abandoned its hopes of producing further carriers of the *Taiho*'s excellence.

UNITED STATES CARRIER DEVELOPMENT DURING WORLD WAR II

The end of treaty restrictions on the individual size and overall numbers of carriers presented the United States Navy with the opportunity to construct a carrier force incorporating all the lessons and experience from the fleet's experiments and operations since the 1920s. The new *Essex* class design, derived from the earlier successful *Yorktown* class, featured a 25 percent larger air group, a 50 percent increase in defensive armament, machinery rearranged for better survivability, and substantially improved armor protection, most notably the addition of a 3-inch armored hangar deck. All these improvements came at a price. Overall dimensions increased by some 10 percent to meet requirements for more accommodation space, stowage for bunker and aviation fuel and munitions, and 25 percent more powerful machinery to maintain speed, while displacement rose by 37 percent.

The *Essex* class was a highly successful design. Improved passive protection demonstrated its value, especially in the face of kamikaze strikes that caused very serious damage to four of the class, all of which survived. The larger flight deck and deck-edge elevator greatly facilitated large-scale rapid aircraft operations. The design was large enough to accommodate bigger air groups of larger machines than envisaged originally (late war examples operated as many as 103 aircraft rather than the 91 as designed). As the war progressed, the light antiaircraft battery of *Essex* class carriers more than doubled in size and there was a major expansion of the radar suite. Nevertheless, by war's end the class was very crowded, since complements had grown by 50 percent to serve the larger air groups and enhanced batteries and equipment suites.

The succeeding *Midway* class was the ultimate development of the characteristic American open-hangar type of carrier that first appeared as the *Ranger* in 1934. The design was very unusual in that its size was driven primarily by a demand for enhanced protection rather than by requests for greater aircraft capacity and aviation features. British and American operational experience appeared to demonstrate both the vulnerability of carriers to relatively modest bombs and shells and the effectiveness of armor protection. The Bureau of Ordnance's development of super-heavy shells and the more general deployment of heavy bombs led to the decision to upgrade protection to defend against an 8-inch shell rather than a 6-inch shell (the previous standard) and also to add substantial armor protection to the flight deck. This increased scale of protection required greater power to maintain speed and more power necessitated a larger hull to accommodate the machinery, initiating a growth spiral that resulted in a 45,000-ton design.

The great size of this design endowed it with an air group 50 percent larger than that of the previous *Essex* class. Standard World War II-era operating procedures meant that the *Midway* class air group was too large for effective deployment, since the time required to launch and recover multiple complete deck load strikes plus aircraft for combat air patrol and anti submarine patrol exceeded one-half of normal daylight hours. Nevertheless the large size of both the hull and the flight deck proved very useful after the war when larger thirstier jet aircraft, that demanded more space and fuel to operate, entered service. The class really came into its own after major postwar reconstructions that incorporated significant advances in design.

During World War II the United States Navy developed three additional series of carriers, all originally extemporized in response to concerns about carrier shortages or to fulfill unanticipated roles. Concern that the United States faced an impending short-term carrier deficiency in the event of war with Japan led President Franklin D. Roosevelt to press for more carriers as a matter of urgency, for which he suggested conversion of some of the large *Cleveland* class light cruiser hulls already under construction. The navy demurred, since it considered such conversion would be entirely inadequate compared to carriers designed and built as such, especially as the light cruiser hull would be too narrow to carry a useful hangar and flight deck or provide sufficient stability in service. The outbreak of war strengthened Roosevelt's case and he eventually prevailed, leading to the conversion of nine incomplete *Cleveland* class hulls as light fleet carriers.

The conversion was very basic, requiring large side bulges to provide stability and allow fitting a 320-foot long hangar supporting a 544-foot long wooden flight deck served by elevators at each end of the hangar. The individual furnace flues were trunked to starboard and a small bridge derived from the units fitted to escort carriers was installed, supported by braces so that it was clear of the flight deck. In service they proved cramped with minimal potential for upgrade and much less capable than the big carriers of absorbing combat damage, as the loss of the *Princeton* on October 24, 1944, demonstrated. Nevertheless all nine units commissioned between January and December 1943, providing an important boost to American carrier strength at a crucial moment in the Pacific War.

Somewhat surprisingly, the navy decided it needed to make up for anticipated combat losses of light fleet carriers, and ordered two units designed and built as such, using the hull of the *Baltimore* class heavy cruiser as a basis. The new ships were essentially enlarged *Independence* class light carriers with a much larger air group, but the *Saipan* and the *Wright*, both commissioned after the war's end, saw little useful service and represented a dead end in American carrier development.

During 1940 the British convoy situation in the North Atlantic and the clear threat of a Pacific war that would require small carriers for support duties led the United States Navy to consider acquiring several type C3 diesel-engined merchantmen for conversion into auxiliary aircraft carriers. The first, the *Mormacmail,* was taken over in March 1941 and converted as the *Long Island* by stripping most of the superstructure, fitting a small hangar aft, served by a single elevator, supporting a wooden flight deck, and adding basic armament for self defense. The *Long Island*'s success led to further similar conversions and the construction of almost identical escort carriers from the keel up, the majority of which were rather more sophisticated, with longer hangars served by two elevators and small island superstructures for navigation and control. The great majority of the first fifty escort carriers based on the type C3 hull design was delivered to the Royal Navy under Lend-Lease, while the balance mainly served on antisubmarine warfare and aircraft transportation duties with the United States Navy.

Mass production of escort carriers exclusively for United States Navy service began with the *Casablanca* class. The design was based on a modified Maritime Commission type S4 hull design with hangar and flight deck arrangements similar to earlier escort carriers. The design differed markedly in its propulsion, however, since it employed a pair of triple-expansion reciprocating engines driving twin screws. All fifty ships of the class were ordered from Kaiser Shipbuilding by the Maritime Commission and commissioned within twelve months from July 8, 1943. These escort carriers were a very successful design, though rather cramped and with limited survivability in the event of significant combat damage.

The third series of extemporized carriers emerged from the pressing need for additional escort carriers in early 1942. Four large type T3 tankers serving with the United States Navy as replenishment oilers were converted into escort carriers as the *Sangamon* class, which entered service in the early fall of 1942. They were similar to earlier conversions, though their greater length allowed for a much longer hangar and flight deck, and their configuration allowed for some continued limited service in a replenishment role. Their greater size and speed also led to their occasional deployment as front-line units and they proved very popular in service. Consequently, when the navy itself set out to design an escort carrier, it used the *Sangamon* class design as its basis. The resulting *Commencement Bay* class was very similar in layout and size but better armed and carried two catapults. It is significant that only this class remained in commission after the war's end and formed the core of the United States Navy's antisubmarine warfare fleet until the late 1950s.

The large American carriers developed or delivered during World War II represented the ultimate expression of their central design concept: launching the maximum number of aircraft in the shortest possible time. Freedom from limitations of size allowed American designers to add greater armor protection, improved machinery layouts and internal subdivision, enhanced antiaircraft batteries, and ever more sophisticated electronics, all of which endowed these designs with greater survivability. Their larger size endowed them with a remarkable capacity for modification and improvement, which allowed them long and successful post-war careers. Nevertheless, they also represented the end of the line for that particular approach to carrier design, as the *Midway* class's limitations on effective aircraft operation demonstrated. The extemporized carriers also represented evolutionary dead ends. Both the *Saipan* and the *Commencement Bay* classes were fine designs but they were incapable of further useful development and, especially in the case of the light fleet carriers, lacked the flexibility and adaptability of both their larger sisters and their British equivalents. Having pushed their fundamental design to its limits, American carrier designers had to start afresh after World War II.

CARRIER AIRCRAFT DEVELOPMENT DURING WORLD WAR II

In 1939 a major transition in the design of naval aircraft was underway. All metal monoplane machines of stressed skin construction were in front-line service with all the world's carrier operating navies, but they also still operated large numbers of fabric-covered biplanes. The war years would see the biplanes virtually vanish from the scene and a great leap in aircraft performance, in large part a result of a doubling of engine power outputs. Aircraft became larger, faster, very much tougher (thanks to armor protection and self-sealing fuel tanks), and capable of carrying heavier loads of ordnance over longer distances. By the end of World War II the final generation of piston engined naval aircraft was on the horizon.

Operating these larger faster aircraft imposed a penalty. Even before the war, efficient use of the restricted space aboard carriers (both for stowage and for operation) led navies to deploy aircraft capable of undertaking multiple missions. This tendency accelerated during the war, although a simultaneous demand to embark aircraft for specialized missions arose late in the conflict. Thus, while fighters increasingly took on a large part of the strike role, air groups came to include additional specialized aircraft to fulfill the demands of electronic warfare.

When World War II began all navies assigned the reconnaissance mission to strike aircraft: scout bombers (SB) in the United States Navy, torpedo strike reconnaissance (TSR) aircraft in the Royal Navy, and attack bombers in the Imperial Japanese Navy. The Japanese found that this was not an entirely satisfactory situation, in large part because attack bomber units did not place sufficient emphasis on thorough training in reconnaissance techniques. The Imperial Japanese Navy therefore decided to reintroduce specialized carrier reconnaissance aircraft into its air groups. In response Nakajima's Fukuda Yasua and Yamamoto Yoshizo designed a very clean three-seat monoplane that entered service in the spring of 1944 as the Carrier Reconnaissance Plane Saiun (C6N). Powered by a 1,990 horsepower Nakajima NK9H Homare 21 18-cylinder radial engine, it attained a top speed of 397 miles per hour at 20,000 feet, cruised at 242 miles per hour and had a range of 1,914 miles on internal fuel or 3,300 miles with a 200-gallon drop tank. The Saiun's performance closely matched that of contemporary United States Navy fighters, rendering it close to immune to interception.

In all navies, however, the majority of carrier reconnaissance missions were undertaken by less specialized machines. The Royal Navy initially used its venerable Fairey Swordfish torpedo bombers. From early 1941 they were supplanted by the Fairey Albacore, an all-metal biplane with fabric covered wings, a monocoque fuselage, and enclosed cockpit. Powered by a 1,085 horsepower Bristol Taurus 14-cylinder radial engine, it reached 159 miles per hour at 4,500 feet, cruised at 113 miles per hour, and had a maximum range of 930 miles. It could carry one 18-inch torpedo or up to three 500-pound bombs and was equipped with air brakes for dive-bombing attacks. Its successor was the Fairey Barracuda, which entered front-line service in early 1943. This all-metal monoplane was powered by a 1,640 horsepower Rolls-Royce Merlin 323 V-12 engine, giving it a top speed of 235 miles per hour at 5,000 feet, a cruising speed of 170 miles per hour, and a maximum range of 1,150 miles. It could carry one 18-inch torpedo or up to four 500-pound bombs. Its Fowler flaps made the Barracuda a very effective dive-bomber, which became its principal role.

In 1939 Japanese carriers deployed Nakajima B5N attack bombers, probably the best of their kind at the time, for strike and reconnaissance missions. In mid-1943 another Nakajima product, the Carrier Attack Bomber Tenzan (B6N) began replacing the earlier type. Its improved performance resulted from the substantially greater power of its Nakajima NK7A Mamoru 11 14-cylinder radial engine that produced 1,750 horsepower and gave the B6N a top speed of 289 miles per hour at 15,000 feet, a cruising speed of 207 miles per hour, and a maximum range of 2,142 miles. It could carry one torpedo or up to 1,800 pounds of bombs.

The Imperial Japanese Navy deployed its first monoplane dive-bomber aboard carriers in 1940. In order to save weight, the Aichi design team, led by Goake Tokuhishiro, used a fixed undercarriage, but otherwise its Type 99 Carrier Bomber (D3A) was a thoroughly modern machine. Powered by a 1,070 horsepower Mitsubishi Kinsei 14-cylinder radial engine, it attained 240 miles per hour at 10,000 feet, cruised at 184 miles per hour, and had a maximum range of 915 miles with up to 800 pounds of bombs. Its successor, the Yoko-suka Carrier Bomber Suisei (D4Y) that entered service in mid-1943 was the fastest of its class in the world, thanks to its 1,280 horse-power Aichi AE1P Atsuta V-12 liquid cooled engine, which endowed it with a top speed of 360 miles per hour at 16,000 feet, a cruising speed of 260 miles per hour, and a range of 910 miles carrying up to 1,200 pounds of bombs, or 2,240 miles with maximum fuel. This performance came at a severe price, however, for the D4Y had nei-ther armor nor fuel protection and proved terribly vulnerable to American fighters.

The United States Navy began replacing its earlier scout bombers with the excellent Douglas SBD in mid-1941. It used a 1,000 horse-power Wright R-1820 Cyclone 9-cylinder radial engine, giving it a top speed of 245 miles per hour at 16,000 feet, a cruising speed of 144 miles per hour, and a range of 1,100 miles. The SBD could carry up to 1,600 pounds of bombs and all operational versions ex-cept the very earliest were equipped with armor protection and self-sealing fuel tanks. In mid-1943 the Curtiss SB2C Helldiver began replacing the SBD. This large scout bomber was powered by a 1,900 horsepower Wright R-2600 Double Cyclone 14-cylinder radial en-gine, with which it reached a top speed of 295 miles per hour at 16,500 feet, cruised at 158 miles per hour, and had a range of 1,165 miles with a 1,000 pound bomb load.

Grumman's TBF Avenger began replacing the earlier Douglas TBD in United States Navy torpedo squadrons in mid-1942 and continued in service until war's end. A 1,700 horsepower Wright R-2600 Double Cyclone 14-cylinder radial engine powered the TBF, giving it a top speed of 271 miles per hour at 12,000 feet, a cruising speed of 145 miles per hour, and a range of 1,215 miles. It could carry a single torpedo or up to 1,600 pounds of bombs in its enclosed bomb bay. Unlike contemporary United States Navy dive bombers, very large numbers of Avengers were transferred under Lend-Lease to the Royal Navy, in which they came to equip a majority of that service's strike squadrons.

The Royal Navy's fighter squadrons began World War II equipped with either the Blackburn Skua, a monoplane designed primarily as a dive-bomber, or the Sea Gladiator, a fabric-covered biplane adapted from a Royal Air Force fighter type. From mid-1940 both types were replaced by the Fairey Fulmar, a two-seater all metal low-wing monoplane. The Fulmar, powered by a 1,080 horsepower Rolls-Royce Merlin V-12 engine, reached a top speed of 246 miles per hour, cruised at 160 miles per hour, and had a range of 830 miles. It was armed with eight 0.303-inch machine guns in its wings and was equipped with pilot armor protection and self-sealing fuel tanks. Its principal deficiency was that it simply was not fast enough to be an effective fighter, a consequence of the decision to include a navigator in its crew. The Fulmar's lineal successor, the Fairey Firefly, entered front-line service in mid-1944, but was tasked primarily with strike and reconnaissance missions. Its 1,990 horsepower Rolls-Royce Griffon V-12 engine gave it a top speed of 319 miles per hour at 17,000 feet, a cruising speed of 200 miles per hour, and a range of 1,088 miles. The Firefly was armed with four 20mm cannons in its wings and could carry either eight 60-pound rocket projectiles of two 1,000-pound bombs under its wings.

The Royal Navy followed two separate tracks toward deploying effective fighters aboard its carriers thereafter. The first was to purchase or obtain via Lend-Lease sufficient numbers of American carrier fighters. The second was to adapt existing British single-seat landplane fighters for naval service. Consequently, both the Royal Air Force's Hurricane and Spitfire fighters served extensively aboard British carriers. The Hawker Sea Hurricane began deploying in early 1942. Most were powered by 1,030 Rolls-Royce Merlin V-12 engines that gave them a top speed of 315 miles per hour, a cruising speed of 208 miles per hour, and a range of 500 miles. They were armed with eight 0.303-inch machine guns in their wings and were equipped with pilot armor protection and self-sealing fuel tanks. Sea Hurricanes were not fitted with folding wings which restricted the number that could be embarked. The naval Spitfire, the Supermarine Seafire, began its service in the spring of 1942. Early aircraft had fixed wings but a version with folding wings began deployments in late 1943. These later versions used a 1,585 horsepower Rolls-Royce Merlin V-12 engine, giving a top speed of 352 miles per hour, a cruising speed of 250 miles per hour, and a range of 400 miles with a 90 Imperial gallon drop tank. They were armed with two 20mm cannons and four 0.303 machine guns in the wings and were equipped with pilot armor protection and self-sealing fuel tanks.

The Imperial Japanese Navy began replacing its successful Mitsubishi A5M fighters with the even more successful Mitsubishi Type 0 Carrier Fighter (A6M2) in the summer of 1941. Powered by a 950 horsepower Nakajima NK1C Sakae 14-cylinder radial engine, the A6M2 reached 331 miles per hour at 15,000 feet, cruised at 207 miles per hour, and had a maximum range of 1,930 miles with a 90 gallon drop tank. It was armed with two 20mm wing-mounted cannons and a pair of 7.7mm machine guns in the fuselage. Popularly know as the Zero, it was very maneuverable and had an astonishing range for the period, but was slow in a dive and very fragile in combat, both because of its light structure and its lack of pilot protection and self-sealing tanks. Japan also never succeeded in developing a replacement for the Zero, so it continued in service until the end of the war. Later model Zeros (A6M5) used a 1,100 horsepower Sakae engine, which increased performance to 351 miles per hour, with a cruising speed of 230 miles per hour, but reduced range to 1,194 miles. Armament was increased by replacing one of the 7.7mm machine guns with a 13.2mm machine gun. The wings were given thicker skins to permit faster dives, limited pilot protection was added, and automatic fire extinguishers for the fuel tanks were fitted. Nevertheless, the Zero's light structure placed it at a severe disadvantage in combat with United States Navy carrier fighters.

The United States Navy began deploying Grumman F4F-3 fighters aboard its carriers in January 1941. Powered by a 1,200 horsepower Pratt & Whitney R-1830 Twin Wasp 14-cylinder radial engine, it could reach 328 miles per hour at 21,000 feet, cruise at 155 miles per hour, had a range of 845 miles, and was armed with four 0.5-inch wing machine guns. Pilot armor, self-sealing fuel tanks, and robust construction made the F4F a tough opponent. A version with folding wings and six machine guns entered service in mid-1942. Speed fell to 315 miles per hour and range dropped to 770 miles. The Royal Navy acquired large numbers of F4Fs as Grumman Martlets and made extensive use of the type. The F4F's successor was the Grumman F6F Hellcat, designed as a private initiative in response to feedback from fleet aviators, which entered front-line service in mid-1943. It was powered by a 2,000 horsepower Pratt & Whitney R-2800 18-cylinder radial engine, giving it a maximum speed of 376 miles per hour, a cruising speed of 168 miles per hour, and a range of 1,090 miles on internal fuel or 1,590 miles with a 150-gallon drop tank. The F6F was armed with six 0.5-inch machine guns and also could carry rockets or bombs. The Royal Navy also operated substantial numbers of F6Fs as the Grumman Hellcat. The United States Navy's chosen successor to the Grumman F4F was the Vought F4U Corsair. With a 2,000 horsepower Pratt & Whitney R-2800 18-cylinder radial engine, it reached 417 miles per hour at 19,000 feet, cruised at 182 miles per hour, and had a maximum range of 1,015 miles. It was armed with six 0.5-inch machine guns and most versions also could carry rockets or bombs. The F4U's deck landing characteristics, however, were judged unsatisfactory. So, from February 1943, it was issued for front-line service only with shore-based United States Navy and Marine Corps squadrons. The Royal Navy also received large numbers which, since it needed every modern carrier fighter possible, successfully undertook an urgent modification and trials program to suit the Corsair for carrier operation. Corsairs began front-line operations aboard British carriers in the spring of 1944 and were in action by the beginning of April. As a result, the United States Navy conducted new carrier trials the same month and Corsair began operations from American carriers in the late summer of 1944, going on to become probably the most successful carrier fighter of the entire war.

NAVAL AVIATORS DURING WORLD WAR II

While constructing carriers and producing aircraft to operate from them required great effort and investment, the biggest single challenge the carrier-operating navies had to meet was recruiting and training the huge numbers of competent naval aviators needed to fulfill the demands of a global war. Both warships and aircraft became more technologically sophisticated and operationally effective, but most often it was the training and skill of their operators, especially the naval aircrews that determined the outcome.

Although Japan was engaged in a major conflict from the fall of 1937, its training program for naval aviators did not accelerate very substantially to cope with more extended operations and combat losses. In November 1940 the flight training components of all the various enlisted entry programs were made uniform and the number of units enlarged (the old program for direct entry from the fleet also was renamed the *heisu hikoyoka renshusei* (Class-C flight reserve trainee program and integrated more completely with the other reserve trainee programs). Selection standards remained high, training continued to be rigorous, and consequently relatively few new aviators graduated. It was not until April 1943 that there was any substantial change in the system. The need for more aircrew by then had become so pressing that it was decided to significantly reduce entry standards and cut the standard flight training period by six months. The *heisu hikoyoka renshusei* was terminated and the *toku otsushi hikoyoka renshusei* (special class-B flight reserve trainee program) took its place. It established an accelerated five to seven-month training regimen for more mature entrants into the regular *otsushi hikoyoka renshusei*. There was a parallel expansion of the *koku yobi gakusei* (air reserve student program) to encompass young men completing high school (the equivalent of the second year of undergraduate college in the United States), who received commissions on completing the course. The net result was a tenfold increase in the number of graduating pilots. The following year saw a lowering of the educational requirements for enlistees and a further massive increase in the number of pilots graduated, but fuel shortages put an end to all training programs on March 1, 1945, when all supplies were reserved for combat operations or defense against an anticipated American invasion of Japan itself. During the period from 1937 to 1945 the Imperial Japanese Navy graduated over 50,000 pilots from its various courses.

Until the end of 1942 the quality of new arrivals at front-line units remained high but aircrew losses in the great carrier battles in the summer of 1942 and during the Guadalcanal campaign began to have a disastrous impact on the quality of Japanese aviation units. Before the Pacific War began, the Imperial Japanese Navy relied on front-line units for the operational training of new aircrew. Heavy losses of experienced aviators and the retention of units on the front line rapidly diminished the quality of operational training. The dilution of unit quality accelerated after the fall of 1943 as the few surviving veterans could no longer compensate for the reduced skills of less well trained replacements. The disastrous outcome of the Battle of the Philippine Sea in June 1944 demonstrated the failure of the Imperial Japanese Navy's flight training programs to adapt to the demands of a major war.

Unlike the Imperial Japanese Navy, the United States Navy made major efforts to increase the numbers of its pilots and establish training programs that would meet the requirements of a major war well before the conflict came. In 1939, as a massive expansion of naval aviation began and war in Europe loomed, Congress passed the Naval Aviation Cadet Act. Aviation cadets henceforth were commissioned as reserve ensigns on completing basic training, their active term of duty expanded to seven years, and they became eligible for promotion to lieutenant (junior grade) after three years of service. The Civil Aeronautics Authority Civilian Pilot Training Program also started in 1939, offering very low cost basic training leading to a private pilot's license. This program generated a very large pool of young men with basic flying skills that all the armed services could tap as their air forces expanded.

The basic curriculum established in October 1939 served the United States Navy well throughout World War II. Aspiring aviators first spent one month at a naval reserve air base for elimination flying training, by the end of which they made their first solo flights. Those who successfully completed this indoctrination period became aviation cadets and proceeded to one of several training bases. Primary training required three months flying biplane trainers, combined with ground school. Successful cadets then moved onto intermediate training, learning basic formation flying and instrument and blind flying using obsolete front-line types and monoplane advanced trainers. Finally, cadets went to advanced training, where they practiced formation flying, aerobatics, night flying, gunnery and dive bombing, and simulated carrier landings. The total training period, including indoctrination, was seven months, after which graduates received commissions as reserve ensigns with about 200 hours of flying time in their log books. Between 1941 and 1945 the United States Navy trained over 65,000 pilots.

Until mid-1941 newly commissioned ensigns completed their operational training with front-line fleet squadrons that were shore based for routine refresher training. This was very inefficient and, as a result, the navy created advanced carrier training groups, initially one for each coast, that could undertake this task. The curriculum for newly-minted aviators devoted seventy-five hours to teaching navigation, advanced gunnery, dive and torpedo bombing, and night and instrument flying, culminating in carrier landing qualification (eight successful landings) after extensive practice on dummy flight decks ashore. From mid-1942 further advanced carrier training groups were created to accommodate the rapidly growing number of new aviators. Several escort carriers spent much of their careers serving as deck landing training vessels and two Great Lakes paddle steamers were fitted with flight decks for the same purpose.

As the United States Navy's ambitious program of carrier construction hit its stride, it needed to create new air groups for the new carriers. The navy also adopted a policy of withdrawing existing air groups from carriers and replacing them with new groups rather than allowing them to be ground down completely in combat. These new groups coalesced around a core of combat-experienced squadron and flight leaders with the balance of their complements made up of new graduates from the advanced carrier training groups. Before embarking on their first cruise, these new groups spent several weeks "working up," so that the novices could start to learn all they could from the veterans.

The Royal Navy was still in the process of establishing its own aircrew training system when war began in 1939. Aircrew candidates spent seven weeks at an induction center, usually H.M.S. *St. Vincent* at Gosport near Portsmouth, where they learned naval discipline, routines, customs, basic navigation, meteorology, and signalling. Next was flying training. Early in the war all Fleet Air Arm basic flying training was handled by the Royal Air Force in the United Kingdom, but as the war continued, training naval pilots also took place within the United States Navy's program at Pensacola (even before the United States entered the war), or within the British Commonwealth Air Training Program in Canada or Empire Air Training Scheme in New Zealand. Royal Navy aircrew trained in the United States followed the same curriculum as their American counterparts. Those trained in Britain, Canada, or New Zealand spent eight weeks at elementary flying school, graduating after successfully soloing. Then followed ten to sixteen weeks of service flying training, using more advanced aircraft to study navigation, communications, gunnery, bombing, and night, instrument, and formation flying. Graduates, who by then had accumulated about 150 flying hours, received their commissions and then returned to the Royal Navy's charge.

The newly commissioned aircrew then began operational training. Those trained in Britain went to operational training units, designated second-line squadrons by the Fleet Air Arm, which provided intensive instruction in bombing, reconnaissance, or fighter operations, depending on their specializations. They also practiced deck landing on dummy decks ashore and on carriers at sea. Initially, those trained in the United States and Canada also returned to

Britain for operational training but from early 1942 the Royal Navy set up operational training units in the United States that provided these services for those graduates and took advantage of American training carriers for deck landing practice.

At the end of their operational training period, with up to 100 flying hours added to their logbooks, pilots went to operational squadrons. Very early in World War II the Royal Navy began the practice of forming new squadrons or re-forming old units around a nucleus of experienced aircrew as squadron and flight commanders, thus ensuring that the new squadrons worked up as effective frontline units. From early 1943, the Royal Navy also began forming new squadrons that were to equip with Lend-Lease aircraft in the United States itself. These squadrons completed all their operational training in the United States before moving to the operational zones in Europe or, later, the Far East and Pacific.

A fundamental organizational difference between the American and British naval air services, on the one hand, and that of Japan, on the other, had a major impact on aircrews' operational experience and wartime careers. Both the United States and Royal navies adhered to a squadron-based organizational pattern. The overwhelming majority of squadrons were established to operate a single aircraft type, usually between 12 and 24 machines but sometimes, especially late in the war among fighter units, with as many as 30 or more. Squadron rosters often included more aircrews than aircraft, and also included the all-important maintenance personnel: mechanics, airframe repairmen, electricians, armorers, and so on. Essentially, each squadron was self-sufficient from an operational perspective. Almost invariably, new squadrons formed or older units returning from combat re-formed around a nucleus of combat-experienced aircrew amidst a larger number of freshly-trained personnel, so that the veterans could impart their hard-won skills to the new crews.

Each British or American carrier embarked a number of squadrons to endow it with an air group made up of the appropriate mix of aircraft types to suit operational requirements. By the later stages of the war, most air groups undertook some coordinated training prior to embarking on their carriers, but the bulk of such training still took place afterwards. After an extended period of combat or heavy losses, it was straightforward to replace a carrier's air group without withdrawing the ship itself from operations, thus maintaining a high level of operational tempo and also ensuring that the aviators could recuperate from combat stress and also prepare for a return to action as the core leadership of fresh squadrons and air groups. Furthermore, an individual squadron that suffered disproportionately high losses could be replaced very simply by an available fresh unit.

The Imperial Japanese Navy followed a very different pattern. From the early days of naval aviation, the basic unit was the *hikokitai* (basically equivalent to an air group), but there was a very important difference: the aircrews and the maintenance personnel formed an integral part of the parent ship's crew and had no separate identity. As a result the *hikokitai* could not operate apart from the parent carrier, it could not transfer readily to another carrier or to shore operations. The only option for replacing combat losses was to post individual replacements to the *hikokitai* and, as long as the carrier remained in commission, it was difficult to transfer experienced aircrews to form the nucleus of new units. Consequently, experienced aircrews tended to remain in the front line for extended periods, operating amid increasingly inexperienced replacement crews.

The *hikokitai* was commanded by a *hikotaicho* (air group leader). Each *hikokitai* contained a mix of fighters, torpedo bombers, and dive-bombers organized into *buntai* (flying units), but again these *buntai* were not autonomous. The *buntai* were divided into two or more *chutai* (divisions), led by *buntaicho* (division leaders), with the senior *buntaicho* also commanding the *buntai*. The *chutai* were divided into *shotai* (sections), usually of three aircraft, commanded by a *shotaicho* (section leader), who was almost invariably a noncommissioned officer.

By the late 1930s the Japanese fleet had taken its organization a step further by undertaking intensive group training for the two *hikokitai* of a *koku sentai* (a two-carrier division). Each *koku sentai* contained two or more *hikotaicho* who were qualified to lead strikes of aircraft from not only their own *hikokitai* but also from aircraft from other carriers both within their *koku sentai* and outside it. This arrangement gave the Japanese carrier fleet a powerful advantage during the early part of the Pacific War in competence to launch coordinated mass strike operations.

CARRIER OPERATIONS DURING WORLD WAR II

During the first two years of World War II carriers operated in an asymmetrical environment. No carriers engaged fleets that themselves operated carriers: they operated against surface warships, submarines, or land-based installations or aircraft only.

Japan's carriers, in particular, found themselves embroiled in a very different war from that for which they were designed. Within a very few months of the beginning of the conflict in China on July 7, 1937, most of the Chinese fleet was either sunk by Japanese naval aircraft or captured by Japanese forces. Thereafter, the carriers' air groups were engaged almost continuously in long-range operations in support of Japan's land forces against terrestrial targets until the end of 1939. In the fall of 1940, Japan's carriers returned to the front line to provide similar support for a renewed offensive in China and the occupation of French Indo-China.

The greatest problems Japan's naval aviators had to overcome were those related to long-range operations (accurate navigation, cohesive formation flying, and careful fuel economy) and contending with land-based defenses over their targets (fighters and antiaircraft artillery). These were very valuable skills for a future conflict in the Pacific but, since Japanese carriers were effectively immune to attack by Chinese land-based aircraft, the war in China did not provide lessons in defending a fleet against air attack. Consequently, Japanese naval aviation tacticians came to emphasize the importance of fighter escort for strike aircraft over the deployment of fighters in defense of the carriers against attack.

The Royal Navy faced a very different situation when World War II began in Europe. Its carriers were largely immune to the threat of German shore-based aircraft, but were very vulnerable to German U-boats, as a near-miss attack against the *Ark Royal* on September 14, 1939 by the *U-39* and the sinking of the *Courageous* by the *U-29* on September 17, 1939 demonstrated. The carriers were deployed with fast heavy surface warships to hunt German raiders until February 1940, without significant success. During the campaign in Norway three carriers, the *Ark Royal,* the *Furious,* and the *Glorious,* provided much of the British army's air cover and close support. The *Glorious,* however, succumbed to the German battleships *Scharnhorst* and *Gneisenau* on June 8, 1940, while its flight deck was filled with Royal Air Force aircraft evacuated from Bardufoss that prevented it from flying off its own aircraft.

Events in June 1940 radically changed the situation. Italy's entry into the war on June 10 presented the Royal Navy with an opponent with a powerful surface fleet and large air force with a strong dedicated antishipping component. France's surrender on June 25 not only allowed Germany to deploy aircraft and warships so they had direct access to the Atlantic but also raised the specter of the French fleet becoming an enemy force. The Royal Navy scrambled to deploy its three remaining large carriers, retaining the *Furious* in the Atlantic, sending the *Eagle* to join the Mediterranean Fleet, and forming Force H at Gibraltar around the *Ark Royal* and the fast battle cruiser *Hood* (later replaced by the *Renown*). Its two smaller carriers also moved closer to home, the *Argus* covering convoys in the North Atlantic and the *Hermes* patrolling West African waters.

The carriers played key roles in addressing these threats. The Royal Navy launched a series of attacks to neutralize the French fleet. Carrier aircraft from Force H spotted for a battleship bombardment of Oran on July 3 that destroyed the battleship *Bretagne* and severely damaged the fast battleship *Dunkerque*. Several follow-up daylight torpedo strikes inflicted more damage on the *Dunkerque*, and another on July 8 by aircraft from the *Hermes* immobilized the battleship *Richelieu* at Dakar. In September Force H covered an abortive landing operation by Free French forces at Dakar, the first occasion that carrier aircraft provided all air support for an amphibious landing. Meanwhile the *Eagle*'s aircraft provided fighter defense for Mediterranean Fleet sorties and conducted concentrated strikes against Italian naval and merchant shipping in North Africa and the Aegean. When the new carrier *Illustrious* joined the Mediterranean Fleet on September 1, these raids increased in intensity, culminating in the strike against the main Italian fleet at Taranto on the night of November 11–12 that sank two battleships and crippled a third, putting half the Italian battlefleet out of action for the loss of two aircraft. In reaction, the Italian main body withdrew to its northern bases and thereafter proceeded with great caution at sea whenever British carriers were found to be operating within their vicinity.

While the strike at Taranto and similar raids on Italian warships and merchantmen in port made real the visions of prewar carrier proponents such as Admiral R. G. H. Henderson, who had planned such an attack on the Italian fleet in harbor (in the event of war) while he was commanding the Mediterranean Fleet's carriers in the 1930s, two carrier operations in 1941 conformed very closely with mainstream prewar British concepts. Albacore aircraft from the *Formidable* torpedoed and immobilized the Italian heavy cruiser *Pola* and damaged the battleship *Vittorio Veneto* on March 27 off Matapan, allowing the Mediterranean Fleet's battleships to surprise the cruiser, the ship's two sisters *Fiume* and *Zara*, and two escorting destroyers, and sink all five warships in a night surface action. Two months later, Swordfish aircraft from the *Victorious* and the *Ark Royal* torpedoed the German battleship *Bismarck,* one hit wrecking its steering gear and rudders and leading to its destruction by British battleships on May 27.

The vast majority of carrier operations in the Atlantic and Mediterranean area after the summer of 1941 encompassed either distant or close cover of convoys, strikes against coastal shipping either in the littoral or in port, and support of amphibious operations. The big fleet carriers conducted distant cover operations for convoys to Malta, from April 1941 until August 1942, and to Russia, starting in August. Two carriers, the *Ark Royal* and the *Eagle,* were lost while covering Malta convoys, both to submarine torpedoes. Twenty merchant ships of the 45 that sailed also were lost, the majority after the carriers had left the convoys as they entered confined waters. Distant cover of Russian convoys was much more effective, even when the debacle of convoy PQ17 in June 1942 is taken into account. Prior to PQ17, 194 merchants ships sailed for Russia of which 29 were sunk while in convoy. 24 of 39 ships sailing in PQ17 were lost, all but 3 after the Admiralty ordered the convoy to scatter and deployed the covering force to block an expected attack by the battleship *Tirpitz* (which itself had returned to port because of the threat of the British carrier *Victorious*'s aircraft). Starting with convoy PQ18 in September 1942, the Royal Navy provided close escort carrier support for about half of the Russian convoys in addition to distant cover by the Home Fleet. PQ18 lost 11 ships while accompanied by the escort carrier *Avenger* and 5 more after it was withdrawn. Of 44 subsequent convoys, escort carriers provided close cover for 25, losing a total of only 8 out of 705 merchant ships, while the 19 convoys without close carrier support lost 21 out of 376 merchantmen.

Close carrier support of Atlantic convoys began in September 1941 when the *Audacity,* the first British escort carrier, sailed with convoy OG74 from Liverpool to Gibraltar. The *Audacity* was torpedoed and sunk by the *U-751* on December 21, 1941, while escorting convoy HG76 but its value had been demonstrated: of the 98 merchantmen in the 4 convoys it escorted, only 5 were lost. Although American-built escort carriers commissioned in both the Royal and United States navies during the summer of 1942, they were employed for training and preparation for amphibious landings in North Africa later in the year and did not begin convoy support operations until the spring of 1943. They were joined very quickly by the first MAC-ships (merchant aircraft carriers), converted from tankers and grain ships. By late summer 1943, carriers operating in support of convoys succeeded in slashing losses in the North Atlantic and Bay of Biscay, not only by driving off or sinking U-boats but also by inducing Admiral Dönitz, commander of Germany's submarine forces, to redeploy his boats to areas where shipping was less well protected and they could achieve their successes with less risk of losses. As the British and American escort carrier forces expanded, they were able to follow the U-boats into zones outside the North Atlantic, especially the Arctic and South Atlantic. Between March 1943 and September 1944, Allied escort carrier aircraft participated in the destruction of over 40 U-boats in the Atlantic and their success was such that it was no longer necessary to provide escort carrier support for North Atlantic convoys thereafter.

Royal Navy carriers conducted a few largely inconclusive strike operations against coastal shipping in Norway in the summer of 1941 and again two years later, when they were joined on the final mission by the American carrier *Ranger*. From April 1944 until the end of the war in Europe the Royal Navy greatly increased the intensity of its attacks on shipping in the Norwegian littoral, undertaking over 30 such operations. During 1944, four of the big fleet carriers conducted strikes but the bulk of these missions were the work of aircraft from assault escort carriers, no less than twelve participating at various times. Escort carrier aircraft also laid mines along the coast and in total this campaign sank close to 200,000 gross register tons of shipping plus numerous small warships. Seven escort carriers also carried out an intensive antishipping operation against vessels that were undertaking the withdrawal of German forces from the Aegean in September and October 1944.

Closely related to the antishipping campaign in Norwegian waters was a series of three attacks on the German battleship *Tirpitz* at its anchorage in Kaafjord in April, July, and August 1944. The first, which achieved surprise, scored fourteen direct hits on the battleship and inflicted sufficient damage to put it out of action for three months. The subsequent attacks, absent the element of surprise, were much less successful.

Aircraft carriers played a vital role in providing air cover and support for a series of major amphibious operations between November 1942 and August 1944. For Operation Torch, the Allied invasion of French North Africa in November 1942, four fleet carriers, three British and one American, the old British carrier *Argus*, and seven escort carriers, four American and three British, deployed 240 fighters and 103 attack aircraft in support of landings at Oran, Algiers, Port Lyautey, and Safi for three days until the ground forces had consolidated their positions and air force aircraft could take over, flying from captured airfields. British fleet carriers provided distant support to block interference by the Italian Navy with the invasion of Sicily in July 1943 (Operation Husky) but did not participate in close cover operations, since Sicily was within range of land-based aircraft in North Africa. The landing at Salerno in September (Operation Avalanche), however, required close carrier support, since it was the extreme limit of range for aircraft from Sicily. The Royal Navy deployed two fleet carriers, the light fleet carrier *Unicorn*, and four escort carriers both to block any attack by the Italian Navy and to provide close air support for the invasion. German resistance proved much tougher than expected, so for four days the carriers mounted operations that provided over 50 percent of all air support over the beachhead until land-based aircraft could begin operating ashore. The final European amphibious assault, the invasion of the south of France in August 1944 (Operation Dragoon) again relied heavily on naval air support from the outset. Nine escort carriers, seven British and two American, deployed 216 fighters for six days, providing close support over the beachhead, conducting interdiction missions against German attempts to bring reinforcements into action, and covering the Allied advance up the River Rhône.

A revolution in naval combat organization occurred when the Imperial Japanese Navy created the 1st *Koku Kantai* (Air Fleet) that brought together all the navy's six carriers, joined by four seaplane carriers and ten destroyers, under unified command. This formation grew out of an ongoing debate within the navy that began early in the China conflict about the best organization of the fleet's carriers. Operational experience in China quickly demonstrated that small numbers of strike aircraft had low capabilities both in attack and in self-defense, so the navy quickly moved to using large formations and, as soon as possible, heavy fighter escort, both of which had obvious lessons for carrier deployment at sea. Simultaneously, Captain Onishi Takajiro urged the need for operational research on carrier doctrine, leading to the formation of the *kucho heiryoku iryoku kenkyukai* (Air Power Research Committee) that generated considerable data on the effectiveness of aircraft operations in various scenarios. These trends led Commander Genda Minoru, in 1940, to urge very strongly the concentration of Japanese carriers, since this would greatly enhance the massed striking power of carrier aircraft, allow launching and maintaining much stronger combat air patrols over the carrier fleet, and concentrate its antiaircraft firepower for self-defense. The commander of the 1st *koku sentai* (air or carrier division), Rear-Admiral Ozawa Jisaburo, also realized the revolutionary impact of carrier concentration, in part as a result of the constant urgings of Lieutenant-Commander Fuchida Mitsuo. Ozawa urged Admiral Yamamoto Isoroku, commander of the Combined Fleet, to bring all its front-line land and carrier based air units under unified command. His efforts ultimately led Yamamoto to authorize the change in December 1940.

The navy began experimenting, initially with the *Kaga*, the *Soryu*, and the *Hiryu*, in early 1941. The first land-based *koku kantai*, the Eleventh, was formed with three *koku sentai* in January 1941. In April, the 1st *koku kantai* brought together the Combined Fleet's carriers in a single operational units, still organized as three *koku sentai*. When the new carriers *Shokaku* and *Zuikaku* commissioned in the fall of 1941, they replaced the older carriers *Hosho* and *Ryujo*, and created the most powerful unified naval air force in the world that became Japan's principal striking force for the Pacific war it saw looming.

Operations during the Pacific war rapidly elevated the aircraft carrier to capital ship status. The conflict opened with a massed attack by aircraft from the six carriers of the 1st *koku kantai* against the United States Pacific Fleet in Pearl Harbor on December 7, 1941, and concluded with an even larger offensive sweep over Tokyo Bay on August 15, 1945, by aircraft from the United States Navy's Task Force 38, at that time made up of eight large and six light carriers plus a British fleet carrier. During the intervening period American, Japanese, and, later, British carriers raided enemy shipping, conducted strikes against shore installations, escorted convoys, supported amphibious landing operations, and engaged surface vessels and their opposite numbers in full-scale fleet actions.

The Japanese attack on Pearl Harbor was a great tactical victory, an immediate strategic success, but in many ways a failure in the longer term. The carriers launched 360 aircraft in two waves that arrived over Hawaii a little over an hour apart. For the loss of 29 aircraft and fewer than 100 aircrew, they sank 4 of the Pacific Fleet's 8 battleships, badly damaged the other 4, sank or wrecked 7 smaller vessels and seriously damaged 4 others. The attackers also largely eliminated existing American land-based air power on the island. Nevertheless, the assault left intact almost the entire base infrastructure at Pearl Harbor and missed the Pacific Fleet's carriers, because they were at sea. Vice Admiral Nagumo Chuichi, commanding the 1st *koku kantai*, declined to launch a third strike directed at shore installations, since he judged the risk of further losses not commensurate with the potential gains in what was, in the broad scheme of Japan's strategy of conquest and consolidation, a subsidiary operation.

Despite their successful deployment in the Hawaiian Operation, its carriers played a relatively minor role in Japan's rapid conquests in Malaya, the East Indies, and South West Pacific. Nagumo detached the *Soryu* and the *Hiryu* from his force while en route back to Japan to assist the Wake Island attacking force on December 21–23, while the *Akagi* and the *Kaga* provided air cover for operations to seize the Bismarck Archipelago in January. The *Ryujo,* operating independent of the 1st *koku kantai,* was the sole carrier supporting the invasion of the Philippines and, after its successful conclusion, provided further support for operations in the East Indies. Nevertheless, the Japanese invasion forces relied overwhelmingly on surface warships and land-based aircraft to provide cover for their operations.

Probably the Japanese fleet's most devastating demonstration of the capabilities of a fast carrier force was the series of operations undertaken by the 1st *koku kantai* between February and April 1942. Nagumo, with the *Akagi,* the *Kaga,* the *Soryu,* and the *Hiryu,* led off with a powerful raid on Darwin on February 19 that wrecked port and shore installations, sank or severely damaged 17 warships and merchantmen, and at least temporarily eliminated local enemy air forces, all for the loss of 10 aircraft. The *Shokaku* and the *Zuikaku* then joined the force, replacing the *Kaga,* which returned to Japan for overhaul and replenishment. The five carriers then sortied into the Indian Ocean in late March after Japanese forces seized the Andaman Islands on March 23. They struck Colombo on April 7 with devastating force, wrecking shore installations, workshops, repair yards, railroads, and the airfield, and sinking shipping in port. On their withdrawal, the carriers' aircraft located the British heavy cruisers *Cornwall* and *Dorsetshire,* part of Vice Admiral James Somerville's Eastern Fleet, and overwhelmed them. A further massive raid on Trincomalee two days later wrought similar havoc there, and again the carriers' aircraft caught part of Somerville's fleet at sea and rapidly sank the carrier *Hermes* and its escort, the destroyer *Vampire.* The carrier *Ryujo* also deployed simultaneously off the east coast of India and, accompanied by a strong cruiser-destroyer force, undertook a powerful sweep against merchant shipping. By April 10, Japanese forces dominated the Indian Ocean and Somerville was forced to withdraw his fleet to East African ports.

The outcome of the Japanese attack on Pearl Harbor generated a resolution of the argument within the United States Navy between proponents of carrier air power and supporters of the continued dominance of battleships. The elimination of the Pacific Fleet's battle line left carriers, by default, as the most powerful warships available and drove the fleet's commanders to explore and exploit the capabilities of carrier aviation in order to carry the war to Japan and bring about its defeat. During February, March, and April 1942, the carriers *Yorktown, Enterprise, Lexington,* and *Hornet* conducted a series of raids against Japanese positions in the Marshall Islands, the Bismarck Archipelago, Wake and Marcus islands, New Guinea, and finally, on April 18, against Tokyo itself using Army Air Force B-25 bombers. Carriers participated in these raids either singly or in pairs, so the American carriers were never able to conduct strikes on the same scale as their Japanese counterparts but these operations were very valuable in developing American carrier doctrine and especially methods for combining information from the basic search radar available with fighters on combat air patrol to develop an effective self-defense system for carrier forces.

In May 1942 the clash, long-anticipated by advocates of carrier aviation, between two fleets centered on their aircraft carriers finally occurred. The Japanese decided to consolidate their position in New Guinea by launching a seaborne assault on Port Moresby in the south of the island. Aircraft from the light carrier *Shoho* provided direct support for the invasion force and Vice Admiral Nagumo detached two large carriers, the *Shokaku* and the *Zuikaku,* from the 1st *koku kantai* for distant cover. Signals intelligence caused Admiral Chester W. Nimitz, commander in chief of the Pacific Fleet, to send two task forces built around the carriers *Lexington* and *Yorktown* into the Coral Sea to intercept a Japanese invasion force. The American and Japanese carrier forces met on May 7 and a two-day battle ensued. United States Navy aviators sank the *Shoho* on May 7 and heavily damaged the *Shokaku* the next day, while Japanese forces sank the *Lexington* and badly damaged the *Yorktown.* Both navies' damaged carriers had to withdraw for repairs and Japanese aircraft losses had been sufficient to cripple the *Zuikaku* as a combat unit. The Japanese invasion force, bereft of air support, turned back.

Despite its setback in the Coral Sea, Japan continued its efforts to extend its defensive perimeter further east by seizing Midway Island. Admiral Yamamoto saw the invasion operation, in addition to accomplishing this larger strategic goal, as an opportunity to draw out the Pacific Fleet's carriers and destroy them in a decisive battle. He was correct in anticipating that the Midway attack would force a response from the United States Navy but his plan was undone in large part because American cryptographers had broken the Japanese naval codes and Admiral Nimitz was able to use the knowledge to surprise Yamamoto's fleet with a carrier force led by Rear Admiral Raymond Spruance. American land-based aircraft sighted the Japanese fleet on June 3. Still unaware that the *Enterprise*, the *Hornet*, and the *Yorktown* were in the vicinity, Nagumo launched his assault on Midway Island on the morning of June 4 and then received reports of the presence of enemy carriers. Amid the chaos of switching missions, dive bombers from the *Enterprise* and the *Yorktown* struck the Japanese carriers and shattered the *Akagi*, the *Kaga*, and the *Soryu*. The lone survivor, the *Hiryu*, succeeded in launching a counterstrike that wrecked the *Yorktown* but was itself devastated by a second American attack. By the evening of June 6 the battle was over. The Pacific Fleet lost the crippled *Yorktown* and the destroyer *Hammann* to torpedoes from the Japanese submarine *I-168*, while all four Japanese carriers and the heavy cruiser *Mikuma* were sunk. Even though Yamamoto's fleet still vastly outnumbered Spruance's force, his only remaining carriers were the old and small *Hosho* and *Ryujo*, and he was forced to withdraw and abandon the Midway operation in the face of the Pacific Fleet's still substantial air power.

The Battle of Midway was a crushing blow to the Imperial Japanese Navy. The destruction of the fleet's four finest carriers was in itself a major setback but even more devastating was the loss of over 330 aircraft and a very large percentage of their highly experienced aircrew. The Japanese training system and its integrated air group organization made it all but impossible for the fleet to reconstitute its carrier force at a level of skill anything like that of the 1st *koku kantai* at the start of the Pacific War. As the number of highly skilled and experienced naval aviators diminished, the quality of the carrier *hikotai* fell dramatically. Their losses rose rapidly while their effectiveness plummeted. The Imperial Japanese Navy, already in difficulties facing American wartime production of materiel, was further hampered by its own organizational system in competing on a qualitative level with American aviation personnel.

Victory at Midway enabled the United States to go on the offensive in the Pacific. During the Guadalcanal campaign, which began with a landing on the island by United States Marines on August 7, 1942, and concluded with the night evacuation of Japanese forces between February 1 and February 7, 1943, air power played a crucial role and the contribution of carrier aviation was vital. A carrier task force, consisting of the *Enterprise,* the *Saratoga,* and the *Wasp* and commanded by Vice Admiral Frank Jack Fletcher, covered the landings and provided distant cover against Japanese attempts to reinforce the island. The Japanese dispatched a major reinforcement convoy from Rabaul on August 20, covered by a task force commanded by Vice Admiral Kondo Nobutake centered on the carriers *Ryujo, Shokaku,* and *Zuikaku.* American reconnaissance aircraft located the Japanese carriers on August 24. Fletcher's two carriers (the *Wasp* was absent for refueling) attacked and sank the *Ryujo* but aircraft from the big Japanese carriers severely damaged the *Enterprise,* forcing its return to Pearl Harbor for repairs, and the Japanese convoy successfully landed its reinforcements. To add to American woes, the submarine *I-26* torpedoed and heavily damaged the *Saratoga* on August 31, putting it out of action for three months, and the *Wasp* was torpedoed and sunk by the *I-19* on September 15, leaving only one carrier, the *Hornet* (which had arrived in late August), in the South Pacific until the *Enterprise* returned in mid-October.

By this time Kondo's force had received reinforcements with the arrival of the carriers *Junyo* and *Zuiho,* so he set out to break American air superiority over Guadalcanal. American naval forces, now led by Vice Admiral William F. Halsey, intercepted Kondo's force. In the ensuing Battle of the Santa Cruz Islands, both fleets launched a series of near-simultaneous strikes on October 26. Halsey's force lost the *Hornet,* the *Enterprise* suffered sufficient damage to put it out of action temporarily, while two of Kondo's carriers, the *Zuiho* and *Zuikaku,* also suffered substantial damage and he called off the pursuit of the American fleet on the morning of October 27, allowing Halsey to withdraw. The *Enterprise* was repaired locally and continued to operate in the South Pacific until May 1943, participating in the Naval Battle of Guadalcanal (November 12–15) and the Battle of Rennell Island (January 30, 1943), and then supporting further operations after the Japanese evacuated Guadalcanal.

The *Saratoga* returned to the South Pacific in December 1942 and became the mainstay of American naval forces in the region until November 1943. It was reinforced by the British carrier *Victorious* from May to July and then by the light carrier *Princeton* in October. Land-based aircraft provided much of American air support for the advance in the Southwest Pacific, but the carriers played an important role in covering the major landings at Bougainville on

November 1, 1943, including a very successful major strike against the Japanese stronghold at Rabaul on November 5.

By mid-1943 new *Essex* class fleet carriers and *Independence* class light carriers were commissioning in the United States Navy, providing resources for a second thrust against Japan through the Central Pacific. Supported by the new fast battleships of the *North Carolina* and *South Dakota* classes, valuable for their very powerful antiaircraft batteries and the shore bombardment capabilities of their main guns, these new fast carriers constituted a naval force that could generate overwhelming air cover and firepower for amphibious operations. The Central Pacific campaign began with Operation Galvanic, landings on Tarawa and Makin atolls in the Gilbert Islands. Operations lasted from November 20 to 24, 1943, and relied primarily on six fleet and five light carriers for air support. The assault on the Marshall Islands, Japanese-held since the end of World War I, began with operations Flintlock and Catchpole, intended to capture the Kwajalein and Eniwetok atolls. Two days of bombardment from both the sea and the air began on January 31, 1944, with the fast carriers and their fast battleship escorts again providing the lion's share of the attackers' firepower. Troops landed on February 1 and both atolls were subdued completely by February 6.

These successes encouraged American commanders to accelerate the timetable for the Central Pacific campaign. Operation Forager to capture the Marianas Islands of Guam, Saipan, and Tinian began on June 13, 1944, with a heavy preliminary naval and air bombardment of Saipan, spearheaded by the fast carriers and battleships of Admiral Raymond Spruance's Fifth Fleet. Landings began on June 15 and ran into heavy opposition. The landing also induced the main Japanese fleet, commanded by Vice Admiral Ozawa Jisaburo, to sortie and launch an attack on Spruance's force. The ensuing Battle of the Philippine Sea, fought from June 19 to June 21, was the largest carrier combat of the war, pitting Ozawa's five fleet carriers and four light carriers, embarking 473 aircraft, against Vice Admiral Marc Mitscher's force of seven fleet carriers and eight light carriers with 956 aircraft. On the morning of June 19, Ozawa launched a series of four attacks against the American carriers but lost almost 75 percent of his aircraft to skillfully-directed United States Navy fighters. The same day Ozawa also lost two big carriers, the *Taiho* and the *Shokaku*, to the American submarines *Albacore* and *Cavalla*. On the afternoon of June 20 Mitscher's search aircraft finally located Ozawa's fleet and he launched his assault, accepting the risk of heavy losses caused by the returning strike aircraft having to land on his carriers after dark. The attackers sank the Japanese carrier *Hiyo,* severely damaged the *Junyo* and the *Zuikaku,* and reduced Ozawa'a air strength to 35 aircraft. Mitscher's strike lost 20 aircraft to Japanese defenses but another 80 either ditched before reaching his carriers or crash landed, though all but 49 aircrew were recovered. The Battle of the Philippines Sea, also known as the "Great Marianas Turkey Shoot," marked the effective destruction of Japanese carrier air power, both because of the destruction of their ships and as a result of the wholesale losses of aircrew. With the elimination of any chance of relief, the Marianas fell in quick succession. Saipan was overrun by July 13, Tinian was seized in an operation lasting from July 24 to August 2, and Guam was taken in an assault that began on July 21 and was completed on August 10.

The two American axes of assault came together in an invasion of the Philippines that began with landings at Leyte on October 20, 1944, and ended only with General Yamashita Tomoyuki's surrender on August 15, 1945. The landings provoked a large-scale response from Japan's Combined Fleet, commanded by Admiral Toyoda Soemu. He dispatched his force divided into four groups, with the carriers again concentrated under the command of Vice Admiral Ozawa. Opposing these attackers were two American fleets: Vice Admiral Thomas C. Kinkaid's Seventh Fleet, tasked with amphibious assault and including old refurbished battleships, heavy and light cruisers, escorting destroyers and destroyer escorts, and a strong contingent of sixteen escort carriers, all assigned to close support and protection of the invasion forces, and Admiral William F. Halsey's Third Fleet, whose main strength lay in Vice Admiral Marc Mitscher's fourteen fast carriers. The ensuing Battle of Leyte Gulf, from October 23 to October 26, 1944, incorporated a series of actions fought as American forces attacked or encountered the four thrusts of the Japanese riposte to the invasion. The battle was a true combined arms operation, including submarine attack, surface combat between battleships and other heavy warships, destroyer torpedo assaults, and large scale air strikes. Mitscher's carriers sank the huge Japanese battleship *Musashi* on October 24 in the Battle of the Sibuyan Sea, along with two heavy cruisers, and annihilated Ozawa's carrier force at the Battle of Cape Engaño, sinking four carriers (the *Chitose,* the *Chiyoda,* the *Zuiho,* and the *Zuikaku*) and five escorting warships. Mitscher lost the light carrier *Princeton* to land-based air attack on October 25, while Kinkaid's fleet lost two escort carriers during the battle: the *Gambier Bay* sunk by Japanese heavy ships during the action off Samar on October 24 and the *St. Lo,* the first victim of a kamikaze attack, later the same day. The Battle of Leyte Gulf marked the effective end of the Imperial Japanese Navy as a capable fighting force since, although several battleships and other heavy vessels remained in service, the navy's carrier fleet had been all but eliminated and virtually no trained aircrew existed.

The two final major operations in the Pacific War were the assaults on Iwo Jima and Okinawa. In these operations the primary mission of the United States Navy's carriers was to provide both direct support for the landing forces and cover to protect the invasion fleets from attack by the remaining Japanese heavy ships and land-based aviation units. The operation against Iwo Jima lasted from February 19 to March 26, 1945. The assault on Okinawa, long a part of Japan and only 350 miles south of the Japanese mainland island of Kyushu, began in March with preliminary landings on the Kerama Islets on March 16 and on Keise-jima on March 21. A full scale assault on Okinawa itself began on April 1 and, although American troops reached most of their objectives within four days, bitter fighting continued until well into June and the island was finally declared secured only on July 2. The Imperial Japanese Navy launched a one-way attack (there was insufficient fuel available for them to return to base) on the invasion force, centered on the battleship *Yamato* but it was defeated by carrier aircraft on April 7 and the battleship sunk by multiple bomb and torpedo hits. The principal enemy the American carriers faced at Iwo Jima and especially at Okinawa was kamikaze attacks that severely damaged six fleet units and less seriously injured five others, although none of the fleet carriers engaged in either operation was sunk.

Once airfields were established to provide land-based air support and cover on Okinawa, Pacific Fleet carriers began a near-continuous campaign against Japanese ports and the littoral, interdicting shipping, assailing the Imperial Japanese Navy's remaining warships, and striking shore installations and facilities. By the time of Japan's surrender on August 15, 1945, a mere handful of Japanese warships remained afloat and United States Navy aircraft roamed largely at will over the mainland islands and their coasts.

NAVAL AVIATION IN 1945

During the course of World War II the aircraft carrier demonstrated its unrivalled flexibility and effectiveness in combat. In addition to engaging other carriers and major fleet units in full scale naval battles, aircraft carriers supported major landing operations; raided and interdicted warship and shipping movement on the high seas and in the littoral; attacked and destroyed shore installations and facilities; protected merchant shipping against submarine, surface, and air attack; and hunted submarine and surface raiders. This great flexibility sprang from the relative ease with which carriers could both upgrade their capabilities through embarking superior aircraft and change missions by taking aboard air groups with varying compositions of aircraft types. Carriers attained capital ship status not only because of their flexibility but also because, especially from 1941 onward, they could deploy both long-range power and overwhelming local force. This combination of capabilities reduced battleships, previously the arbiters of naval power, to a subsidiary role.

The wartime combat experience of the United States and Royal navies, the only fleets still operating carriers by the end of the war, profoundly influenced their approaches to carrier aviation in the postwar era. The dominant mission of carriers during the war, combat against their cohorts, became irrelevant with the dominance of the United States Navy and the disappearance of carrier-operating potential enemies. In its place, the projection of power from the sea against an enemy homeland and the protection of naval and mercantile assets, mainly against submarine and air attack, took center stage. As carrier-operating navies and those with ambitions to join their ranks entered this new environment, the role of carriers shifted subtly away from the traditional mission of capital ships, like on like combat, into this less clear-cut realm.

CHAPTER FOUR

The Cold War and After

WORLD WAR II DRAMATICALLY ALTERED the world's naval situation. Thanks to the realization of its immediate prewar building plans and an additional massive wartime construction program, the United States Navy's fleet enjoyed an overwhelming preponderance in both numbers and overall quality relative to any other individual navy or combination, either friendly or potentially hostile. Nowhere was this more apparent than in comparing strengths of carrier fleets: by December 1945 the United States Navy possessed twenty-one modern fleet carriers and eight light carriers, while the Royal Navy, the only other carrier operator, had but six fleet carriers and six light carriers.

After the virtual elimination of the Imperial Japanese Navy as a surface fighting force, the American (and British) experience of carrier warfare during the final six months of World War II comprised operations in support of large-scale amphibious invasions, antishipping strikes, and raids on ports and shore installations and facilities. In a postwar environment of massive naval superiority, the United States Navy found this experience to be the most relevant in planning for its future. Both American and British planners therefore envisaged the primary offensive role of carriers as an assault on targets on land. The United States Navy was particularly concerned: that its experience of such operations during World War II demonstrated that success in this would require employing much heavier weapons over longer ranges, both beyond the capabilities of its existing attack aircraft. This concern was highlighted by the one immediate major threat both navies recognized as threatening their naval hegemony: the Soviet Union's acquisition and deployment of submarines using captured German advanced technologies endowing them with high submerged speed over extended ranges, which would require their destruction in port before reaching the open sea where they would be extremely difficult to locate and destroy.

Three elements dominated carrier design and operation during this post–World War II era. The first was the requirement to deploy long-range attack aircraft capable of lifting heavy weapon loads and surviving in a hostile environment, all of which necessitated large fast airframes. Size became a dominant feature of new carrier design, so that such large aircraft could be accommodated and operated. The second was the need to operate high-performance jet aircraft. When the primary role of carriers was combat with other carriers, the aircraft needed to have a performance matching that of other carrier machines. When land attacks came to dominate the carrier mission, the performance of carrier aircraft needed to match that of contemporary land-based machines if they were to succeed. This situation prevailed at the end of World War II but the arrival of high-performance land-based jet aircraft required carriers to deploy comparable machines. Jets required long flight decks, because they landed at high speeds; new launching and safety arrangements, because they accelerated slowly; and greatly increased fuel stowage capacity, because they were extremely thirsty. Finally, there was the influence of atomic and nuclear weapons, which raised problems of both the role of carriers in delivering them against an opponent, and the survivability of the ships themselves in the face of an attack with such weapons.

Three British inventions were crucial in enabling jet aircraft carrier operation: the steam catapult, the angled flight deck, and the mirror landing aid. The longer takeoff runs and slower accelerations of early jet aircraft made launching without a catapult a marginal affair. Jet aircraft also were heavier and the older hydraulic catapult designs were approaching the limits of their potential for producing greater power. The slotted tube steam catapult, in which the propulsion force was transmitted directly to a piston, was substantially more powerful than the older types that relied on a system of wires and sheaves to transfer hydraulic impulsive forces to the shuttle. C. C. Mitchell, an employee of MacTaggart, Scott & Company, Ltd., that manufactured catapults for the Royal Navy, first conceived the idea of a slotted tube catapult in 1936 and obtained a patent for his concept in 1938. By late 1944 he had tested a prototype powered by an explosive charge. In 1946 the Admiralty, because of the design advantages of relative simplicity and greater potential power, determined to adopt slotted tube catapults for all its carriers. The first prototype powered directly by boiler steam was tested extensively in 1951 to 1952 and its success led to immediate adoption of steam catapults aboard British carriers, with American carriers following shortly afterwards.

Operating jet aircraft on conventional axial decked carriers presented several substantial problems. Jet aircraft landed faster and at flatter angles than earlier types, so they tended to land further along the deck and pull out the arresting wires more extensively. This greatly increased the chances of hitting the barrier, placing the deck park forward of the barrier at grave risk. During a conference on flight deck designs on August 7, 1951, Captain Dennis Campbell, the assistant chief naval representative to the Air Ministry, and Lewis Boddington, a scientist at the Royal Aircraft Establishment, Farnborough, came up with the idea of angling the landing path to one side so that the deck park forward would be completely clear of the flight path. This arrangement had the added advantages of allowing an aircraft that missed the arresting wires to accelerate off the deck and make another landing attempt and of permitting catapulting and landing aircraft simultaneously. The Royal Navy undertook trials aboard the carrier *Triumph* in 1952 and their success led to the immediate adoption of the arrangement in all design studies (and suitable modifications to incorporate an angle deck on the *Ark Royal* then under construction) and further trials by the United States Navy aboard the carrier *Antietam* between April and August 1953.

The higher landing speeds of jet aircraft rapidly pushed beyond the limits of landing signals officers' ability to appreciate the aircrafts' motions and make signals to which the pilots could respond. Captain Campbell's assistant, Lieutenant Commander Nick Goodhart, initially proposed an optical landing control system in a paper he wrote in 1951. A gyro-stabilized mirror, surrounded by red and green illuminated datum lines, reflected a fixed light back to the pilot's eyes so that he could tell his position relative to the optimum glide approach path, while an audio tone indicated his airspeed. Goodhart formally presented his concept, which he had tested on a small scale using his secretary's pocket make-up mirror with datum lines drawn on with her lipstick, in January 1952. The first very successful full-scale trials took place in November 1953 aboard the carrier *Illustrious,* leading to the adoption of the mirror landing aid on British and American carriers within less than two years. The later Fresnel lens system replaced the mirror with a lens and moved the light source forward of the unit but operates identically.

UNITED STATES CARRIER DEVELOPMENT
IN THE COLD WAR ERA

Even before the end of hostilities, the United States Navy's designers began exploring a new generation of carriers that would incorporate features suiting them for the land attack mission requiring the operation of large strike aircraft over an extended period of time. The navy recognized that the large number of new carriers delivered by the wartime construction program made it most improbable that new vessels would materialize from these studies, but made the decision to proceed both to keep together the experienced carrier design team and to explore the ramifications of this shift in mission emphasis. To enhance the flight deck operating cycle even with larger aircraft, these studies incorporated two basic changes: all elevators were removed from within the flight deck to the deck edges and one or two additional more powerful catapults were added to launch aircraft simultaneously from the waist and the bow of the ship (adding two waist catapults required either a flush deck arrangement or fitting a catapult atop the island structure, neither of which was explored seriously in this series of designs). To support extended operational periods aviation fuel capacity rose to 500,000 gallons and bomb magazines were enlarged, simultaneously allowing for stowage of heavier weapons that, in turn, required stronger bomb elevators. The result of these studies was a design (C2) that incorporated four deck edge elevators, two on each side, and three catapults. The hull was the same length as an *Essex* class carrier but substantially beamier, requiring an increase in power output to 220,000 shaft horsepower and boosting standard displacement to 40,400 tons.

Since it was clear no funds would become available for constructing new fleet carriers, the navy turned to upgrading its large fleet of *Essex* class carriers to correct deficiencies revealed or created during wartime operation and to suit them for jet aircraft operation. The addition to these ships of a heavier and more extensive suite of radar sets and antennae and the very substantial enhancement of their light antiaircraft batteries significantly reduced their margins of stability. Action damage, especially from the kamikaze strikes on the *Franklin* and the *Bunker Hill,* demonstrated the need for greater protection of the crew ready rooms and the combat information centers, and improved fire fighting arrangements. The fleet's experience at Okinawa in particular showed the need for a heavier automatic antiaircraft weapon that, because of its greater range and larger shell, could destroy guided missiles (kamikazes) and attacking warplanes further from the ship and more easily.

Although intended as a limited reconstruction, the SCB27A upgrade project replaced approximately 40 percent of the original structure of an *Essex* class carrier. The *Oriskany,* still incomplete at the end of the war, was selected as the prototype of nine similar conversions. Stability was improved by removing the belt armor and replacing it with a deep bulge that reached to the hangar deck and faired cleanly into the existing hull structure fore and aft. The crew ready rooms and the combat information center were relocated under the armored hangar deck and connected to the flight deck and island by an external escalator. New foam firefighting equipment, additional firefighting stations, and fire curtains dividing the hangar into three sections greatly improved fire protection. The antiaircraft battery was enhanced by removing the 5-inch turrets from the flight deck, fitting single 5-inch weapons on starboard side sponsons that matched those on the port side, and replacing the quadruple 40mm mounts with new 3-inch automatic twin mounts. New aircraft entering service were heavier and faster, so the elevators were enlarged and the elevators and the flight deck were strengthened, more powerful catapults fitted, and the arresting gear was also made stronger. The converted carriers also received greater stowage for aviation fuel to suit them for operating thirstier jet aircraft. The new smaller island and heavy pole mast supported an enhanced radar suite and the stack was raked aft to minimize the corrosive effect of furnace gases on the antennae.

Six further *Essex* class carriers received improved SCB27C conversions. A starboard side deck edge elevator took the place of the aft inboard unit and new steam catapults replaced the original hydraulic items. The flight deck acquired jet blast deflectors behind the catapults, deck cooling equipment, strengthened arresting gear, and a new nylon crash barrier designed to trap safely the streamlined noses of jet aircraft. Jets had proved to need even more fuel than expected, so these conversions received fuel blending equipment that allowed much greater flexibility in fuel stowage and boosted total aviation fuel capacity to close to four times as much as the *Essex* class originally boasted. Three of these vessels received further enhancements in the form of an angled flight deck and enclosed "hurricane" bows to improve their sea-keeping, changes applied retrospectively to the other three carriers in this group. The navy also decided to upgrade the earlier SCB27A ships to the same standard as the angle deck SCB27C vessels. As a cost-cutting measure, however, only the

Oriskany received new steam catapults, the others retained their hydraulic units, while the *Lake Champlain*'s conversion was cancelled.

The *Franklin D. Roosevelt* and the *Midway* underwent a conversion (SCB110) similar to the SCB27C *Essex* class modification but their larger sizes allowed installing a third catapult in the waist on the port side. The *Coral Sea*'s somewhat later conversion (SCB110A) included replacing the forward inboard elevator with a further deck edge unit on the starboard side ahead of the island.

While the postwar C2 design remained a useful paper study, the slightly later series of studies for a much larger "strategic" carrier led to the contract to build the *United States*, the direct ancestor of all the large American carriers built since the end of World War II. In the design process itself, the navy was somewhat ambivalent. Some within the fleet sought a very large and powerful attack carrier, the ultimate expression of the concepts embodied in the earlier C2 design. Others envisaged the new carrier as a platform for strategic nuclear attack, enabling long-range bombers launched from off the coast to strike deeper within enemy territory. Both tracks were driven by the requirements for operating very large notional heavy attack bombers (ADR-42) weighing 100,000 pounds with a combat radius of 2,000 nautical miles at 500 knots while carrying a 10,000-pound bomb load. Initially the design concentrated on the strategic strike aspect, eschewing a hangar in favor of stowing all the attack aircraft on the flight deck and relying on a pair of very powerful catapults to launch them. Although the naval aviators demanded a completely flush deck, the designers, citing problems of smoke disposal that were impossible to solve otherwise, insisted on incorporating a very much reduced island structure. The resulting single-purpose design with an air group of twenty-four ADR-42s was a vessel displacing 69,000 tons standard (82,000 tons in trials condition), 1,190 feet long, 130 feet in beam (154 feet over the gun sponsons), with a flight deck 1,120 feet long and 132 feet wide.

Two factors led the designers to move toward a multipurpose vessel. First, serious concerns soon arose about the survivability of the ADR-42 in the face of enemy interceptors, requiring the addition of long-range escort fighters to the carrier's air group. Second, the proposed carrier was too large for existing dry dock facilities to accommodate. Modifying the design to include hangar stowage for at least a substantial part of the air group would permit a reduction in flight deck dimensions and bring the carrier's dimensions within the limits of dry dock facilities. The evolved design (SCB6A) reverted to the flush deck arrangement demanded by the aviators, while the need for rapidly launching both the attack planes and large numbers of jet fighters for strike escort and carrier self-defense led to the decision to install four catapults, two in the bow and two on sponsons on either side of the ship. Three deck edge elevators positioned one behind each forward catapult and the third behind the starboard midship unit allowed rapid launching, while positioning the midship catapults on sponsons kept the flight deck clear for aircraft to land simultaneous with catapult launches. A fourth elevator at the extreme stern facilitated rapid ranging of a deck-load strike. The catapults were to be a new design: a direct acting slotted cylinder type powered by an explosive charge. The hull was designed with the flight deck as the strength deck for the first time in American carrier design. It received 2-inch armor and there was a further 1-inch of armor on the gallery deck and 1-1/2-inches on the hangar deck. Especially heavy armor was necessary for the aviation ordnance magazines, since they were to contain atomic or nuclear weapons. As a consequence, to save weight the magazines for the gun batteries had to be left unprotected. A new high-powered steam plant was required to achieve speed requirements and this design was among the first to take advantage of the new boiler technology that supplied 950° steam at 1,200 pounds per square inch. Furnace gases were to be exhausted through a crossover arrangement (to allow venting on the leeward side to avoid smoke fouling clear vision of the flight deck) via stacks that could be raised and lowered. The radar masts also swiveled downward to clear the flight deck during flying operations and the ship was to be conned from a retractable bridge structure. The air group was to consist of either twelve ADR-42s (now weighing only 89,000 pounds) or eighteen ADR-45As (a 45,700-pound design with a 750 nautical mile combat radius of action) and fifty-four fighters (McDonnell F2H Banshees).

Displacement: 79,000 tons (standard), 83,249 tons (full load)
Dimensions: 1,088'0" (oa) x 130'0" x 34'6" (mean)
Flight deck: 1,034'0" x 190'0"
Machinery: Geared turbines, 8 boilers, 4 shafts, 280,000 shp = 33 knots
Bunkerage and range: 8,126 tons = 12,000 nm @ 20 knots
Aircraft: 72
Armament: 8 x 5" DP, 8 x twin 3" AA, 20 x 20mm
Complement: 4,127

Funds for constructing supercarriers were provided in the Naval Appropriations Act. The navy looked forward to building four such vessels as the basis for four nuclear weapons strike groups, and President Harry S Truman approved construction of the supercarrier *United States* on July 29, 1948. Its keel was laid down on April 18, 1949 at the Newport News Shipbuilding and Dry Dock Corporation's yard but only five days later construction was cancelled by Secretary of Defense Louis A. Johnson in favor of additional intercontinental heavy bombers for the United States Air Force.

The decision was very controversial, leading to the immediate resignation of Secretary of the Navy John L. Sullivan in protest and the "Revolt of the Admirals" that summer which cost Admiral Louis Denfield, the Chief of Naval Operations, and several other senior naval officers their jobs. It seemed to end the navy's hopes of developing a powerful force to undertake the land attack mission it recognized to be its future central role. The invasion of South Korea by North Korean forces on June 25, 1950, provided the opportunity for the United States Navy to demonstrate the value, efficacy, and speed of response of tactical carrier air power when, just over a week later, aircraft from the *Valley Forge* and the Royal Navy's carrier *Triumph* launched air strikes against North Korean airfields and its capital, Pyongyang, on July 3. The ensuing build-up of American forces in support of the United Nations operation in Korea supported the navy's drive to add new large carriers to its fleet.

The design of the new attack carriers of the *Forrestal* class owed much to that of the unbuilt *United States*. Congressman Carl Vinson, a long-time supporter of the navy, made it known soon after the *United States*'s cancellation that Congress might well support construction of a new large carrier of no more than 60,000 tons. The final design was again a flush decked carrier, essentially a slightly reduced version of the earlier project. Significant changes included fitting a "hurricane" bow plated all the way to the flight deck, moving the stern elevator to the port side to serve the port waist catapult, and changing the catapults to a newly-designed slotted tube type powered by an explosive charge. The first two ships of the class, the *Forrestal* and the *Saratoga*, were laid down to this design but altered while under construction to incorporate an angled flight deck, a conventional starboard side island and stack, and steam catapults (the explosive charge design having failed to materialize). The angled deck arrangement required relocating the aft port side deck edge elevator to the starboard side and also moved the starboard waist catapult to the port side. The second pair of ships in the class, the *Ranger* and the *Independence,* were built to the modified design from the keel up.

Operational experience with the *Forrestal* class prompted modifications to the design for the follow-on ships of the *Kitty Hawk* class. The most significant was a rearrangement of the flight deck layout. The island and the middle starboard side elevator changed places, creating an enlarged deck park ahead of the island that was served by two elevators and fed aircraft directly to the two forward catapults. The single port side elevator moved aft toward the after end of the flight deck, clearing the forward end of the angled deck and also enhancing the utility of the two waist catapults. The large forward 5-inch gun sponsons were deleted because they limited speed and were vulnerable to damage in heavy North Atlantic weather. This amended general configuration proved so successful that it has served as a pattern for all subsequent United States Navy carriers.

The ultimate alteration to the design of large American attack carriers was the installation of a nuclear power plant. There was considerable debate about the wisdom of the nuclear power option for aircraft carriers, since the ships themselves were so large and capacious that it was not at all clear that there would be substantial benefits in terms of higher sustained speeds or extended operational range commensurate with the very appreciable additional costs of construction. The very large power plant initially required was not in itself substantially bigger than a conventional installation, though it was much more expensive. The liquid loading required for underwater protection that usually would have comprised the necessary fuel oil for a conventional plant was translated into additional aviation fuel, 2,720,000 gallons versus 1,186,000 gallons in the earlier classes. Consequently, the nuclear carrier *Enterprise* could operate a larger air group than usual for a longer period and was enlarged to take advantage of this fact, increasing the ship's aviation ordnance capacity to 2,520 tons instead of the 2,000 tons of its conventionally-powered precursors. The *Enterprise* also carried a much smaller island, since there was no need for a stack. The island's faces mounted the flat panel arrays for advanced electronically scanning radars.

The combination of greater size, a larger air group, advanced electronics, and nuclear power made the *Enterprise* very expensive, costing some 40 percent more than the earlier carriers, and leading to the decision to omit all defensive armament in a cost cutting endeavor. In reaction, instead of a new carrier ordered every fiscal year from 1952 to 1958, for two years not one carrier was included in the naval appropriations and Defense Secretary Robert S. McNamara imposed a schedule of one carrier every two years from 1961.

Furthermore, the next two carriers ordered, the *America* and the *John F. Kennedy,* both were conventionally powered, and largely repeated the *Kitty Hawk* design, although the *John F. Kennedy* introduced a new narrower side protection scheme designed for use in future nuclear powered carriers in an attempt to reduce the space it consumed and thus prevent the escalation in size that occurred with the *Enterprise.* Reflecting the increased threat that Soviet submarines posed to American carrier task forces, both ships also received large forefoot domes for sonar apparatus, although only the *America* actually carried its SQS-23 set since the *John F. Kennedy's* was omitted to save money.

The final design to date is that of the *Nimitz* class. The main changes from the *Enterprise* design flowed from the availability of much more powerful individual reactors that allowed the use of only two units rather than the eight of the first nuclear powered carrier. Internally, this also allowed concentrating the ordnance magazines and reducing their number from three to two. Unlike the earlier ship, this class also reverted to dividing the hangar into three bays with fire curtains, as in the conventionally powered ships, rather than the two bays of the *Enterprise,* thus improving fire protection and providing additional support for the flight deck. Flight deck arrangements were modified slightly by decreasing the angle of the landing area to improve air flow abaft the ship and fitting four very long C-13 catapults to cope with ever heavier aircraft (the power of a steam catapult is directly proportional to its length). The use of the narrow side protection system first applied in the *John F. Kennedy* allowed aviation fuel capacity to rise to 2,600,000 gallons.

Secretary McNamara, as a result of the navy's demonstration of the effectiveness of carrier strikes in Vietnam, in February 1966 determined that the fleet should maintain a force of fifteen carriers: three of the *Midway* class, eight of the *Forrestal* type, the *Enterprise,* and three new nuclear powered ships to be built to a common design at two years intervals starting with the *Nimitz* in fiscal year 1967 with the goal of completing all three by 1975. This program was disrupted by two factors: disputes over funding that delayed authorization for the *Dwight D. Eisenhower* until fiscal year 1970 and for the *Carl Vinson* until fiscal year 1974, and slow construction rates that delayed the commissioning of the *Nimitz* until 1975, of the *Dwight D. Eisenhower* until 1977, and of the *Carl Vinson* until 1982. When the Reagan administration decided to resume large carrier construction in 1980, the delay that creating a new design would have entailed was unacceptable. The five new ships authorized between fiscal years 1980 and 1988 therefore were repeats of the *Nimitz* design with some enhancements, most notably the use of Kevlar armor to save weight, new catapults that operated with lower pressure steam thus reducing the drain on the main propulsion supply, and more modern electronics.

The *Ronald Reagan*, the most recent United States Navy carrier to commission, also uses the same basic design as the *Nimitz* (for the same reasons as before), but has a large bow bulb to improve performance and the island is one level lower than on earlier ships. Internal rearrangement allows an increased aviation fuel capacity of 3,400,000 gallons, and the angled flight deck is extended further forward, which permits simultaneous landing and launching operations on the port side. The *George H. W. Bush*, scheduled to enter service in 2008, will have similar hull and flight deck arrangements but will incorporate integrated information systems, open-system computer and combat systems architecture, and cabling using fiber optics and arranged zonally. The island will be a new design using composite materials for its construction and incorporating embedded antennae. Internal arrangements will be changed substantially and designed to reduce lifetime operating costs by 20 percent and also cut 500 personnel from the crew.

The United States Navy envisages an ongoing program of large nuclear powered carrier construction and proposes to lay down two new ships in 2007 and 2011. Design concepts are still in a state of flux but are based on the hull form and flight deck arrangements of the *Ronald Reagan*, perhaps somewhat enlarged (although that would make the hull too big to fit any existing military or commercial building dock or dry dock). A new reactor design, possibly supplying power for electric drive, and all-electric auxiliary services are envisaged. Plans are to fit newly-designed 300-foot long linear electromagnetic motor driven catapults able to launch 90,000 pound aircraft at over 150 miles per hour and a new design of arresting gear.

In 1957–1958, while the large carriers of the *Forrestal* type were entering service, the navy undertook a series of studies for small attack carriers with both nuclear and conventional power but the necessary sacrifices of capability and flexibility were deemed unacceptable. Interest in smaller carriers revived in 1972, resulting in a long-running series of design studies for ships of no more than 60,000 tons fully loaded. The advent of viable VSTOL (Vertical or Short Take Off and Landing) aircraft in particular seemed to offer the chance to reduce both the size and the cost of carriers. Nevertheless, it still was necessary to design a smaller carrier to operate conventional aircraft, since VSTOL machines could not fulfill all mission requirements and insurance was important should they not live up to expectations. Once again, the sacrifices entailed by reducing a carrier's size were substantial: only two elevators and two catapults were possible, ordnance and aviation fuel supply dramatically reduced the number of strike days the air group could generate, and the ship's speed was marginally acceptable. Furthermore, planners soon realized that many of the costs of a carrier were unrelated to its size, including electronics, self-defense armament, vital auxiliary machinery, and protection. By the end of 1978 the effort to produce a viable design for a small carrier was abandoned.

Antisubmarine warfare was a major concern of the United States Navy immediately after World War II, since the design elements (readily available to the Soviet Union) of the radical German Type XXI U-boats suggested that countering such vessels operating in large numbers would be very challenging. Only the larger escort carriers of the *Commencement Bay* class and light carriers of the *Independence* class were suitable for modernization to operate modern large antisubmarine aircraft. The escort carriers were only marginally capable of operating the new fixed wing aircraft (Grumman AF Guardian or Grumman A2F Tracker), so upgrades were limited to a redesigned island and removal of antiaircraft weapons as weight compensation. Two light carriers, the *Bataan* and the *Cabot*, received major modifications as dedicated fast antisubmarine warfare carriers. Their flight decks and elevators were strengthened and a more powerful catapult fitted, the same redesigned island was installed, and the stacks trunked together into two units. Torpedo detection sonar and homing torpedo countermeasures equipment also were added and magazines rearranged to stow antisubmarine munitions and sonobuoys. To compensate for the added weight, both ships received enlarged blisters.

The cost of conversions and the potential expense of correcting the deficiencies of the escort carriers led the navy to look into the alternative of new construction of dedicated antisubmarine warfare carriers. Design studies began in 1950 but the price for a new-construction vessel proved to be a major obstacle, since it was well over twice as expensive as the escort carrier conversion. The navy then looked at converting a Maritime Commission hull, both a Mariner-type cargo ship or a fleet oiler being options, but again the cost of conversions was excessive and approached two-thirds of that of a new carrier. By April 1954 planning for both new construction and merchant ship conversions was abandoned.

In the meantime an experiment in late 1952 using the uncon-verted *Essex* class carrier *Valley Forge* as an antisubmarine warfare ship proved very successful. All the other unmodernized *Essex* class ships transferred to antisubmarine warfare duties and they were joined by all the reconstructed ships except the *Ticonderoga*, the *Hancock*, the *Bon Homme Richard*, the *Oriskany*, and the *Shangri-La* by 1962. Eight of the converted *Essex* class antisubmarine war-fare carriers received fleet rehabilitation and modernization refits in the mid-1960s. These refits upgraded their accommodations, mod-ernized their electronics fits, and added a large bow sonar dome for SQS-23 equipment, primarily intended for detecting incoming tor-pedo attacks but found in service to be very useful for amplifying an antisubmarine hunter-killer force's capabilities.

By the early 1960s it was clear that the converted *Essex* class car-riers, even after a major overhaul, would soon come to the end of their useful service lives and would require replacement. A long se-ries of studies pursued over an eight year period failed to produce a satisfactory design that was economical enough to build in large numbers, could meet existing antisubmarine warfare requirements, and incorporated sufficient "stretch" to cope with future needs. The alternative was a more thorough reconstruction of the existing ships to allow them to operate into the 1980s, but this was sidelined by the budgetary stress of the Vietnam War. Instead, from 1972 anti-submarine warfare became an added mission of the big attack carri-ers as they were refitted to operate up to half the air group of the smaller specialized carriers without imposing a substantial reduc-tion in the size or capabilities of their usual air wing.

This solution provided the level of antisubmarine warfare capabil-ity necessary for the protection of the carrier task forces themselves but would not address the needs of sea-lane protection. The sug-gested solution was to take advantage of the advent of viable VSTOL aircraft (embodied in the AV-8A Harrier) and deploy a cheap special-ized carrier, the Sea Control Ship, to support existing helicopter-equipped escorts. It would carry a complement of twelve or more large antisubmarine helicopters backed by three or four VSTOL fighters for self-defense and provide air cover over convoys against bombers equipped with antishipping weapons in areas where there was a low threat of encountering high performance enemy fighters. The concept was tested by modifying the amphibious assault heli-copter carrier *Guam*, which, in early 1972, began generally success-ful trials that continued for some two years until April 1974. Several concept designs were developed between 1974 and 1978 but no construction followed, largely because of the type's limited capabilities and concerns within the navy that small carriers might dilute support for the big ships. The final design, however, with the addition of a ski-jump forward for accelerated takeoff by VSTOL aircraft was constructed in Spain as the *Principe de Asturias,* which entered service in the Spanish Navy in 1988, while the same yard later also built a slightly smaller version, the *Chakri Nareubet,* for the Royal Thai Navy.

The United States Navy's approach to carrier design during the Cold War era was marked by a consistent insistence on generating vessels capable of operating aircraft on the cutting edge of technology that were in no way inferior to their land-based counterparts. The navy quickly realized that this required very large carriers and that the sacrifices in capability attendant on smaller ships were not commensurate with the potential for less expensive vessels. As a result, it fought hard to maintain its fleet of very large carriers, realizing that the political and institutional effort required to gain Congressional approval for each vessel was largely unrelated to its size. Thus, while the navy explored the design of smaller carriers quite often, its analysis always concluded that only the very large type adequately met its operational requirements.

BRITISH CARRIER DEVELOPMENT
IN THE COLD WAR ERA

The Royal Navy was the only fleet other than the United States Navy that operated a carrier force immediately after World War II. With six fleet carriers and six light carriers in commission in December 1945 it possessed a much smaller force than the United States Navy. It also had a large wartime carrier construction program that was as yet incomplete. Although much of this program was cancelled with the war's end, the Admiralty decided to continue building many of the unfinished carriers, ultimately completing two further fleet carriers and twelve light carriers, although many of the light carriers quickly transferred to the service of other navies both within the Commonwealth and elsewhere.

The problems associated with jet aircraft operation loomed large in the Royal Navy, especially because its carriers were smaller than those of the United States Navy, exacerbating the difficulties. Solutions were found in the steam catapult, angled flight deck, and mirror landing aid, but on the way a number of more radical options were explored, including landing aircraft without undercarriages on flexible rubber decks, which was tested on the light carrier *Warrior* in 1948. Steam catapult trials took place aboard the *Perseus* beginning in 1951 and the angle deck concept was tested aboard the *Triumph* the following year.

The only large carriers to enter Royal Navy service after World War II were the *Eagle* and the *Ark Royal*, the two carriers of the *Audacious* class at the most advanced stage of construction at war's end. As designed, they essentially were substantially enlarged versions of the *Implacable* class. The *Eagle*, when completed in 1951, did not differ substantially from the original design but the *Ark Royal* commissioned in 1955 with a 5-1/2-degree angled deck, steam catapults, a mirror landing aid, and a deck edge elevator on the port side, which did not prove very satisfactory since it served only the upper hangar. The *Eagle* refitted in 1954–1955 to a similar standard but without the steam catapults or deck-edge lift and then underwent a major reconstruction from 1959 to 1964, emerging as the Royal Navy's most modern carrier with an 8-1/2-degree angled deck, steam catapults, an advanced radar suite, upgraded machinery and auxiliary systems, and an all-missile antiaircraft battery. The *Ark Royal*, too, underwent modernization refits in the early 1960s and again later in the decade, though it never quite matched its sister's standard of equipment.

Unlike the United States Navy, the Royal Navy did not embark on a wholesale reconstruction program for its wartime carriers to make them suitable for jet aircraft operation. Only one ship, the *Victorious*, was reconstructed. The project amounted to a virtual rebuild, since the hull was lengthened, widened, and deepened, the machinery replaced, the flight deck rebuilt with an 8-degree angled landing zone, steam catapults, and a mirror landing aid, the superstructure replaced, and a modern radar suite installed. This seven-year project proved so expensive that plans for reconstructing the other five wartime carriers were abandoned and the *Victorious* remained a prototype.

The Royal Navy found its light carriers very suitable for peacetime operation. They were economical, both in terms of operating costs and as far as crew requirements were concerned, and proved most appropriate for service policing the still extensive British Empire. In the mid-1950s the first generation of light carriers gave way to newer ships of the *Centaur* class that had been laid down late in World War II and were completed over an extended period to an improved design with an angled flight deck and, via a refit in the late

1950s, steam catapults and mirror landing aids. By the 1960s, however, these light carriers were too small to operate an adequate air group of large modern aircraft and two, the *Bulwark* and the *Albion,* became helicopter assault ships. The final ship of the class to complete, the *Hermes,* was very different from its sisters. It had a bigger angled flight deck, more powerful steam catapults, a much updated radar suite, and a deck edge elevator to port. The *Hermes,* too, transferred to assault duties in 1971, became an antisubmarine warfare ship in 1977, and then was refitted to operate Sea Harrier VSTOL aircraft, using a ski-jump ramp at the forward end of the flight deck to launch these aircraft.

In 1959 the Admiralty began planning for new carriers since the late war generation of ships that formed the carrier force would need replacing by the early 1970s. This process took place in a rather unfavorable climate: there were very stringent fiscal constraints from the Treasury, the Royal Air Force was opposed to the emergence of a powerful attack carrier, and there was strong political pressure to minimize the carrier's size. These constraints forced some unusual approaches to the design of what became known as CVA-01. The flight deck was offset to port and incorporated only a shallow angle for the landing area. There was a wide passageway to starboard outside the island to allow movement of aircraft without interfering with the deck park. The hangar had an opening at its after end to allow aircraft to run up their engines inside the hangar. Two elevators (of a novel "scissors" type) linked the hangar to the flight deck, which carried two steam catapults and had water-spray cooled arresting gear. The power plant was sufficient only for 28 knots and used a three-shaft arrangement, similar to that seen in the *Illustrious* class of 1940.

Displacement: 53,000 tons (standard), 63,000 tons (full load)
Dimensions: 925'0" (oa) x 122'0" x 32'0" (full load)
Flight deck: 884'0" x 184'0"
Machinery: Geared turbines, 6 Foster-Wheeler boilers, 4 shafts, 135,000 shp = 28 knots
Aircraft: 45
Armament: 1 twin Sea Dart SAM launcher, 2 quadruple Sea Cat SAM launchers.
Complement: 3,230

Detail design work began in July 1963 but the entire project was cancelled in February 1966 when Secretary of Defence Denis

Healey's Defence Review determined that the Royal Navy should give up its fixed wing carriers and transfer the aircraft to the Royal Air Force. This decision not only ended plans for new carriers (two were envisaged) but also led to a rapid run down of existing carrier strength.

The Royal Navy continued to require a seaborne aviation capability and, in 1967, began design work on a helicopter-carrying command cruiser using a gas turbine power plant. This was essentially an updated version of the *Tiger* class cruisers with missile and gun armaments forward and hangar and flight deck facilities for helicopters aft. It soon became apparent that a more efficient vessel would result from moving the superstructure to the starboard side and constructing a through flight deck from end to end of the ship over greatly enlarged hangar and workshop spaces. The design of the resulting through-deck cruiser was unusual in its capacious internal volume, a result of extensive use of alloys for construction and the elimination of most armor protection. This large internal volume allowed the incorporation of extensive modularity into the arrangements of machinery and workshop spaces. Almost all machinery and auxiliary equipment was designed to be maintained on an exchange basis, with modules being removed for repair and maintenance and replaced by new units. The modular arrangement of workshops also allowed great flexibility in operation, since new workshop blocks could be embarked to suit different air groups.

The through deck cruiser received an additional boost with the advent of effective VSTOL fighters in the form of Sea Harriers. Operations with these aircraft did not require catapults and, as a result of experiments at the Royal Aircraft Establishment in Farnborough, the design also received a 7-degree ski lift jump at the forward end of the flight deck, which allowed launching Sea Harriers with a short takeoff run with much heavier payloads. Just as these ships entered service they were officially reclassified as support carriers, and proved very useful in operations in the South Atlantic, Adriatic, and Persian Gulf.

In July 1998 the Defence Review included provision for the addition of two conventional aircraft carriers to the Royal Navy. Details of the design are still unclear but best estimates are that the new carrier will be 945 feet long with a beam of 125 feet and a flight deck width, depending on whether it features an angled deck or not, of 210 or 270 feet. The power plant is to be four Rolls-Royce WR21 intercooled recuperative gas turbines driving shaft-mounted electric generators for both ship propulsion and service power. At present, the navy anticipates operating an air group primarily of American F-35 Joint Strike Fighters along with large antisubmarine helicopters as yet undefined Maritime Airborne Surveillance and Control platforms, for a total of about forty-eight aircraft. This air group would not require catapults or arresting gear but provision for this equipment is to be incorporated and a contract has been assigned for design of a novel electromagnetic drive catapult. These two 60,000-ton ships are programmed to enter service between 2012 and 2015.

Although the Royal Navy's aircraft carriers were equipped with reasonably modern aircraft, it was not until the early 1960s that they deployed an effective strike aircraft, the Buccaneer. This was a reflection of the primary mission of British carriers in the early Cold War era, imperial policing. By 1966, as Britain's imperial commitments contracted, it was clear that its finances would not allow the deployment of large attack carriers analogous to those of the United States Navy, not least because of the costs entailed for their air groups. The primary roles of British carriers became operations in the littoral and antisubmarine warfare, requiring rather different vessels. The Royal Navy's adoption of VSTOL technology endowed its carriers with greater flexibility and operational effectiveness within the limits of its mission profiles so, despite the British origins of the angle flight deck, steam catapults, and mirror landing aids, its new Cold War-era carrier designs have been somewhat outside the mainstream represented by the big American ships.

FRENCH CARRIER DEVELOPMENT
IN THE COLD WAR ERA

During the course of World War II designers in unoccupied France continued to work on aircraft carrier projects, though without any real hope of seeing them come to fruition. Their efforts, however, allowed the French government to approve construction of a new carrier, to design PA28, in 1947. The ship was similar in size and aviation facilities to the late-war British light carriers but also incorporated the offset flight deck of the prewar *Joffre* design and had an exceptionally heavy antiaircraft battery. Budgetary constraints, however, led to the cancellation of this ship, by then named the *Clémenceau,* in 1950.

Like the British, the French quickly realized the value of aircraft carriers in maintaining their far-flung empire. The French Navy first

operated the escort carrier *Dixmunde,* originally the *Biter* in the
Royal Navy, then added three light carriers between 1946 and 1953,
the *Arromanches* (previously the British *Colossus*), and the *Lafayette*
and the *Bois Belleau* (originally the United States Navy's the *Langley*
and the *Belleau Wood*). The two American carriers were returned in
the early 1960s, while the *Arromanches* became an antisubmarine
warfare and amphibious assault ship.

The first French carriers built as such from the keel up were to
project PA54, developed in the early 1950s from PA28 but incorporating all the advances in design that had evolved to facilitate jet aircraft operations. Consequently, the *Clémenceau* and the *Foch* were
considerably larger than PA28. The design incorporated an 8-degree
angled flight deck, two 170-foot long steam catapults, one at the
bow and the other in the waist to port, and a mirror landing aid. The
after elevator was a deck edge unit, while the forward elevator was
set in the deck. The flight deck had 1-3/4-inch armor and a 1 to 2-
inch armor box enclosed the machinery and magazines. The French
Navy, in the interest of making the machinery as compact as possible inside a limited hull volume, was forced to use a two-shaft
arrangement and to accept unusually high individual shaft power
loads. The ships also were constructed rather more lightly than
usual, in order to improve their performance, which had a significant influence on the French Navy's inability to upgrade the ships to
operate heavier aircraft without very major reconstruction.

In 1958 a third new French carrier was approved under project
PA58. This ship was considerably larger than its precursors to enable it to operate larger strike aircraft.

> Displacement: 35,000 tons (standard), 45,000 tons (full load)
> Dimensions: 939'0" (oa) x 112'0" x 32'0" (full load)
> Flight deck: 920'0" x 190'0"
> Machinery: Geared turbines, 8 boilers, 4 shafts, 200,000 shp =
>   33 knots
> Armament: 2 x twin Masurca SAM launchers, 8 x 3.9" DP

It featured a wider flight deck supported by large sponsons, similar
to contemporary American carriers, two deck edge elevators on the
starboard side, and two very much more powerful 245-foot long
steam catapults disposed as in the earlier ships. In addition to the
forty fighter-bombers and antisubmarine aircraft embarked on its
precursors, it was also to include a dozen naval derivatives of the
French supersonic nuclear bomber, designated the Mirage IVM, in

its air group. There was much concern about the cost of the projected construction of the new carrier, tentatively named the *Verdun,* leading to its cancellation in 1961.

By 1970 the antisubmarine and amphibious assault carrier *Arromanches* was ready for replacement. A series of designs was prepared for a new helicopter carrier to take up the *Arromanches*'s missions. The first was 610 feet long with a beam of 91 feet and incorporated a docking well aft that was 130 feet long and 46 feet wide. The flight deck, similar in style to that of the American *Iwo Jima* class, was served by two deck-edge elevators staggered on either beam. The second design was 40 feet longer with a 30-foot longer docking well and featured large flight deck overhangs amidships with both deck-edge elevators on the starboard side, while the third in the series was almost identical but deleted the docking well. All designs could accommodate eight heavy assault helicopters and up to eighteen light helicopters, plus 600 troops and their equipment. A smaller design, 550 feet long with a beam of 81 feet, could carry only seven large and sixteen small helicopters plus 450 troops.

In 1975 a more ambitious vessel, similar to the third design but with nuclear power, superceded the earlier projects.

> Displacement: 16,400 tons (standard), 18,400 tons (full load)
> Dimensions: 682'0" (oa) x 87'0" x 21'0" (full load)
> Flight deck: 640'0" x 157'0"
> Machinery: Geared turbines, 1 CAS-230 reactor, 2 shafts,
>   65,000 shp = 28 knots
> Armament: 2 x octuple Crotale SAM launchers, 2 x 3.9" DP
> Aircraft: 26 helicopters
> Complement: 890 + 1,000 troops

The PH75 design was a dual-purpose antisubmarine warfare or amphibious assault ship and could accommodate a further 500 troops when configured for assault operations. It included very extensive medical facilities for disaster relief missions. Again, financial problems, this time a result of French efforts to develop an independent nuclear deterrent, delayed progress. The design was modified to reconfigure it to operate VSTOL aircraft in addition to helicopters and became the basis for a series of four carrier projects but ultimately it was abandoned in favor of an improved design for a nuclear carrier, the PAN.

In 1980 the Conseil Supérieure determined that the future needs of the fleet included two nuclear-powered 35,000-ton carriers of which the first should enter service in 1992. Financial constraints led to serious delays in obtaining authorization for the project, designated PAN, and it was not until 1986 that an order was placed for the first ship, the *Charles de Gaulle,* while the second ship was deleted from the plan shortly afterwards. The basic hull is very similar to that of the *Clémenceau* class but it supports a very wide flight deck with the large overhangs supported by massive sponsons. Two deck-edge elevators to starboard link the 450-foot long hangar (divided into two bays by fire doors) to the flight deck, which carries two American C-13 steam catapults arranged in a similar fashion to the layout on other French carriers. The speed is limited to 27 knots by the decision to use only two reactors due to lack of space within the hull. Construction of the *Charles de Gaulle* was very protracted, taking over twelve years, and the ship did not commission until May 2001.

The French Navy demonstrated a consistent commitment to operating conventional aircraft carriers throughout the Cold War era, although its aspirations during the 1970s and 1980s were aborted as the government devoted an exorbitant percentage of the national defense budget to developing and deploying France's nuclear attack forces, especially its submarine-borne ballistic missile deterrent. The navy remains eager to replace its second carrier and has expressed an interest in acquiring a third example of the British gas turbine powered carrier design currently projected to enter service in 2012.

SOVIET UNION CARRIER DEVELOPMENT IN THE COLD WAR ERA

Although Soviet designers expended much effort on developing carrier concepts, particularly late in World War II, none of their sketch designs led to construction of new warships. Admiral Nikolai Kuznetsov gained Josef Stalin's approval for the inclusion of two light carriers in the postwar Soviet fleet but they were deleted from the 1946 ten-year plan. When Kuznetsov became Navy Minister in 1951, he and his deputy, Admiral Arseni Golovko, succeeded in reinstating the two carriers, though no design work began until after Stalin's death in 1953 and the whole project died when Kuznetsov was dismissed by Nikita Kruschev in 1955. The carriers were conceived as very similar to the sketch designs for light carriers prepared by the Warship Evaluation Commission in 1945 but added a pair of steam catapults.

The threat of American nuclear-powered submarines armed with Polaris ballistic missiles led to the development of a design for an antisubmarine ship that could support operations by large numbers of helicopters for a sustained period in the open ocean. The resulting Project 1123 was initiated on January 31, 1959, and the design was completed on January 25, 1962. It combined a heavy ship-based antisubmarine battery forward with a large flight deck and stowage for up to fourteen antisubmarine helicopters aft. The ship also carried a powerful sonar system that proved to be the most successful element of the design that otherwise was not entirely satisfactory in service. The *Moskva* at least had considerable trouble with its machinery, and both ships were disappointing sea boats, trimming by the bow, pitching badly in heavy seas, and carrying an ineffective stabilizer system. Furthermore, the air group was found to be too small for sustained operations.

The succeeding Project 1143 was initiated on October 16, 1968, as an enlarged version of the Project 1123 type. Its principal mission was defense of the operating areas for Soviet ballistic missile submarines against an assault by NATO (North Atlantic Treaty Organization) surface ships or aircraft. The Project 1123's antisubmarine armament was enhanced with a powerful antiship missile battery, while the need to correct the earlier type's aviation deficiencies led to extending the flight deck forward as an angled deck alongside the superstructure, which was moved to starboard. The powerplant was created by installing two Project 1123 plants. The most significant change in NATO eyes was the addition of VSTOL fixed wing jet fighters but it appears that this was serendipitous and resulted from the coincidental maturing of the Yakovlev Yak-38 at the time the new vessels prepared to commission. The two later units of the class, the *Minsk* and the *Novorossiysk,* completed to Project 1143M with upgraded sonar and electronic warfare suites and a 50 percent increase in aircraft accommodation. The final ship of the class, laid down as the *Baku* but renamed the *Admiral Flota Sovetskogo Soyuza Gorshkov,* was completed to yet another variant, Project 1143.4, with an extended flight deck, modified armament, and much improved electronics.

Early in the 1970s the Soviet Navy formulated a requirement for a conventional carrier, and a design bureau was assigned to the project in 1973. The initial sketch suggested a nuclear powered vessel of 75,000 to 80,000 tons equipped with four steam catapults and embarking an air group of seventy or more aircraft: fighters, attack aircraft, and aircraft for antisubmarine warfare and airborne early warning. By June 1974 this was revised downward to about 60,000 tons, still with nuclear power, and a fifty-plane air group. Two vessels were included in the 1976 five-year plan but the design parameters again were revised downward by 1979 and finally emerged as the *Kuznetsov* class, classified as Project 1143.5 although there was little similarity between these ships and the earlier type.

The *Kuznetsov* class was the first Soviet full decked carrier. Initially they were intended to carry a pair of steam catapults but the designers encountered considerable difficulties in developing a reliable unit, so the carriers were modified to feature a 12-degree ski jump that could launch current jet aircraft using a rolling takeoff into a moderate wind. Otherwise, the design was quite conventional, except that it included a large antiship and antisubmarine missile battery in addition to the usual antiaircraft weapons. The lead ship's naming history reflects the turmoil inside the Soviet Union during its construction. It was laid down as the *Tbilisi*, renamed the *Leonid Brezhnev* on November 18, 1982, and finally, after President Mikhail Gorbachev denounced the former Soviet leader in November 1988, again renamed the *Admiral Flota Sovetskogo Soyuza Kuznetsov*. The second unit of the class, the *Varyag*, was incomplete when the Soviet Union broke up and was sold to Chinese investors who propose to convert the ship into a floating casino.

The Soviet Navy's plans for a very large conventional carrier finally became real with the inclusion of two such nuclear-powered vessels in the 1986 five-year plan. The design was derived from the concepts developed for the 1973 project. The ships were to be 1,089 feet long and 125 feet in beam with a draft of 38 feet and displace 85,000 tons fully loaded. Power came from four nuclear reactors generating steam for four geared turbines producing 200,000 shaft horsepower, sufficient to give them a speed of 30 knots. The flight deck was 246 feet wide across the angled deck and was to carry either two steam catapults in the waist and a 12-degree ski jump forward, or a total of four catapults on a conventional flat flight deck. The air group was seventy to eighty aircraft including antisubmarine helicopters and fixed wing airborne early warning aircraft. Like earlier Soviet carriers, these ships carried powerful antiship and antisubmarine missile batteries in addition to more conventional antiaircraft weapons. The first ship was laid down at the Chernomorskiy Shipyard 444 in Nikolayev on November 25, 1988, as the *Kremlin* but renamed the *Ulyanovsk* shortly afterwards. It was 40 percent complete when the Soviet Union broke up. Construction was terminated on November 1, 1991, and the ship was ordered to be scrapped on February 4, 1992, because the Ukraine, where the shipyard was located, and Russia could not agree on how to proceed. A sister ship was due to commence construction on the same slip once the *Ulyanovsk* was launched.

The Soviet Union's development of aviation-capable ships followed a logical progression as the navy moved from defending against American ballistic missile submarines to protecting its own strategic submarines and finally projecting its strength against the United States Navy on the open ocean. Since the navy was very much a subordinate service to the army and the strategic rocket forces, it is not surprising that this progression was slow and sometimes tentative, since both political and financial support was limited. Nevertheless, the fleet's designers demonstrated a clear understanding of the potential of naval aviation in the context of contemporary Soviet strategy and demonstrated themselves capable of producing very effective warships.

OTHER CARRIER DEVELOPMENTS
IN THE COLD WAR ERA

In the aftermath of World War II several of the world's smaller navies found aircraft carriers to be very attractive prospects as capital ships since, at first sight, they seemed to be relatively inexpensive to acquire and operate. Ultimately, the overhead expenses of maintaining and upgrading air groups, specialized aircrew training, and the upkeep and improvement of the ships themselves became more apparent and induced many of these fleets to give up aircraft carrier operation. Very few moved beyond their first generation of ships or their second generation of aircraft.

Britain was the biggest single source of ships for these navies. As British Commonwealth fleets rebuilt after the war and the Royal Navy began replacing its first generation of light carriers with later vessels, these original vessels dispersed around the world. Of the sixteen first generation light carriers, no less than nine were sold or transferred on loan, some more than once. Within the Commonwealth, the Royal Australian Navy used three light carriers, one on a temporary basis awaiting the arrival of the final unit, the *Melbourne,* which was being upgraded with an angled deck, steam catapult, and mirror landing aid. The Royal Canadian Navy, too, operated three in succession, each representing an improvement in specifications that culminated in the *Bonaventure,* which also featured an angled deck, steam catapult, and mirror landing aid. India purchased one of the *Majestic* class carriers, configured in very similar fashion to the *Bonaventure,* which entered service as the *Vikrant.* India later replaced the *Vikrant* with the Royal Navy's second-generation light carrier *Hermes,* renamed the *Viraat.*

France took one unmodified light carrier but the other ships sold elsewhere were upgraded with angled flight decks and steam catapults. Two went to South America: the *Independencia* to Argentina and the *Minas Gerais* to Brazil. The Royal Netherlands Navy purchased one modified light carrier that entered its service as the *Karel Doorman,* and subsequently sold it to Argentina as the *Veinticinco de Mayo.*

The United States was much less involved in supplying carriers to the world's navies. Two *Independence* class carriers were loaned to France in the 1950s and a third example joined the Spanish fleet as the *Dédalo.* Spain later built a carrier using the United States Navy's Sea Control Ship design for its own service as the *Principe de Asturias* and a second example that entered the Royal Thai Navy as the *Chakri Nareubet.*

The Italian Navy contemplated overhauling and completing its salvaged carrier *Aquila* after World War II but abandoned the project because of its cost. Nevertheless, the navy continued its interest in taking aircraft to sea, since many naval officers attributed the fleet's defeats during the war to a lack of integral aviation. During the 1960s this interest finally manifested itself in the commissioning of three helicopter cruisers, two ships of the *Doria* class and the much more satisfactory *Vittorio Veneto.* When it became time to start planning for replacing the two earlier ships, the navy decided essentially to combine the aviation facilities of the *Doria* class cruisers into a single ship and designed a small helicopter carrier that entered service as the *Giuseppe Garibaldi* in 1985. Although the carrier was intended to embark only antisubmarine helicopters, in 1992 the navy was able to have repealed a long-standing law prohibiting it from operating combat aircraft from ships. This allowed the *Giuseppe Garibaldi* to operate either helicopters or VSTOL Harriers, or a mixed air group, and endowed the navy with a much enhanced strike potential within the Mediterranean Sea.

Of all the smaller navies that adopted aircraft carriers in the 1940s and 1950s, only Brazil and India remain committed to their operation. Brazil purchased the French carrier *Foch* in 2000 and, after refitting it, commissioned the ship as the *Sao Paulo* the following year. India, in addition to replacing its original carrier with a later British light carrier, purchased the *Admiral Flota Sovetskogo Soyuza Gorshkov* from Russia in January 2004 after prolonged negotiations. The vessel is to undergo a very major reconstruction and is due to enter Indian service in 2008 as the *Vikramaditya*. In addition, India laid down an indigenously-designed (though with much foreign assistance) 37,500-ton carrier at the state-run Cochin Shipyard on April 12, 2005. It is to be 831 feet long and will be powered by four license-built LM-2500 gas turbines. It has an angled flight deck but uses a 14-degree ski-jump ramp for launching aircraft, though there is arresting gear to catch landing aircraft. The air group will be a mixture of fighter-bombers, antisubmarine helicopters, and airborne early warning aircraft for a total of approximately thirty-six machines. The carrier, currently to be named the *Vikrant,* is scheduled for completion in 2012.

As the cost of effective air groups and specialized training for their crews became greater, the ranks of carrier operating navies contracted. Unlike battleships, which retained a measure of effectiveness even when obsolescent, aircraft carriers largely became powerless once they no longer operated up-to-date aircraft. For navies unable to fund either research and development of their own combat aircraft or the purchase of modern machines abroad, this made carriers hard to support even as status symbols, rapidly reducing the number of their operators to those nations that could both afford their real costs and had a compelling operational requirement for their deployment.

CARRIER AIRCRAFT DEVELOPMENTS
IN THE COLD WAR ERA

There were several very striking features of aircraft development in the Cold War era. The first was a dramatic increase in aircraft performance, measured in terms of speed, load-carrying ability, and electronic sophistication, largely enabled by the transition to jet engines. A second was the proliferation of aircraft configured for specialized support missions, such as airborne early warning and electronic warfare. Both these trends in general manifested themselves in the form of larger, heavier airframes. The combination led to demands for larger carriers to accommodate both bigger aircraft and the burden of specialized "overhead" without excessive reductions in strike and self-defense capabilities. It also led eventually to a search for multirole airframes, either the same basic aircraft configured permanently for one of several missions or, preferably, readily adapted for different roles by packaging the necessary specialized equipment in modules, to be either attached externally or fitted into easily accessible internal bays within the airframe, thus enhancing flexibility in air group assignments.

Long distance strategic atomic or nuclear attack was viewed as the preeminent carrier strike mission until the early 1960s. The United States Navy formulated general requirements for suitable aircraft very shortly after World War II that envisaged two developmental steps, an interim machine and the ideal platform. The interim aircraft materialized as the North American AJ Savage that began entering service late in 1949. This large aircraft (it had a wingspan of 75 feet, a length of 63 feet, and a gross weight of 54,000 pounds) reflected the state of the art at the time it was designed; it featured a mixed power plant of two 2,400 horsepower Pratt & Whitney Double Wasp radial engines for long range cruising and a single 4,600 pounds static thrust Allison J33 turbojet for a high speed dash at the target. Top speed was 471 miles per hour and its range with a 7,600-pound Mk.15 nuclear weapon was 1,730 miles. These aircraft were deployed in detachments aboard attack carriers and at least one such unit was operational (with its nuclear weapons) off Korea in 1953. The AJ's replacement, the definitive long-range attack bomber, was the Douglas A3D Skywarrior that began entering service in 1956. The Skywarrior (with a wingspan of 72 feet, a length of 76 feet, and a gross weight of 82,000 pounds) was the largest and heaviest aircraft ever to operate on a regular basis from aircraft carriers. Its twin 12,400 pounds static thrust Pratt & Whitney J57 turbojets gave it a top speed of 610 miles per hour and a combat radius of 1,050 miles carrying a 7,600-pound Mk.15 nuclear weapon. The United States Navy's final long-range nuclear attack bomber was the North American A3J Vigilante, which began entering service in late 1961. The Vigilante, powered by two General Electric J79 turbojets rated at 10,800 pounds static thrust (16,500 pounds with afterburning), could attain Mach 2 at 40,000 feet, cruised at 1,254 miles per hour, and had a combat radius of 1,290 miles with a single Mk.27 nuclear weapon. It also represented the swan song for the long-range nuclear attack mission, since the navy gave up its aspirations of participating in manned strategic strikes in 1963 in favor of concentrating on nuclear powered ballistic missile submarines, and the Vigilante and Skywarrior heavy attack aircraft were adapted for other missions, including strategic reconnaissance, electronic warfare, and in-flight refueling.

By the late 1940s the Royal Navy, too, was working toward deploying long-range nuclear attack aircraft aboard carriers but found itself limited by the small size of its available ships and the eventually insuperable obstacles, both fiscal and political, to the procurement of large new vessels. The reduction in size of nuclear weapons (from the 7,600 pounds of early shipboard bombs to 2,000 pounds by the mid-1950s) allowed the Royal Navy to proceed, first by adapting an existing design and then by introducing a purpose-built type. The Supermarine Scimitar, already well along in the design process, was selected for adaptation as a heavy strike aircraft, carrying a 2,000-pound nuclear weapon externally. Its two 11,250 pounds static thrust Rolls-Royce Avon turbojets gave it a top speed of Mach 0.97 at 40,000 feet and an armed range of 1,422 miles. It also demonstrated the extreme difficulties of operating large high-performance aircraft from small flight decks, since the Scimitar suffered an alarming attrition rate in excess of 50 percent from all causes during its brief front line career from 1958 to 1966. Its purpose-built successor, the Blackburn Buccaneer, was designed for low-level high-speed penetration beneath opposing radar cover and began entering service in 1962. Initial versions used two 7,100 pounds static thrust de Havilland Gyron Junior turbojets, while later versions were powered by a pair of 11,100 pounds static thrust Rolls-Royce Spey turbofans. At sea level, the Buccaneer could attain 720 miles per hour. The early models had a range of 1,100 miles while the later versions reached 2,300 miles, both carrying a 2,000-pound nuclear weapon. The departure of the Royal Navy's large flight deck carriers in the 1970s finally ended its involvement in long-range nuclear attack.

The development of tactical strike aircraft in the Cold War era illustrates the convergence of multiple mission capabilities within single airframes. At the end of World War II, two very different types of aircraft undertook tactical strike operations: large, relatively slow, single-engine, multiplace aircraft with internal weapons bays were responsible for long range missions while smaller, faster, single-seat fighter bombers carrying their weapons on external racks took on closer targets. Immediately after the war the United States Navy moved to a single-seat type, the Douglas AD Skyraider, for the long-range mission. It entered service in 1947 and was powered by a

2,700 horsepower Wright Cyclone radial engine, giving it a top speed of 343 miles per hours, a range of 1,300 miles. The Skyraider was armed with four 20mm wing cannon and could carry up to 8,000 pounds of external weapons such as bombs and rockets.

The navy, as it had with the long-range nuclear attack category, then sought to replace the Skyraider with a jet-powered successor. Douglas's designer, Ed Heinemann, and his team, reacting vigorously to the ever-increasing complexity and weight of contemporary combat aircraft, responded with the A4D Skyhawk, a lightweight specialized attack and ground support machine that was barely half the weight anticipated in the navy's specification. The first versions, entering service in 1956, were powered by a single 7,800 pounds static thrust Wright J65 turbojet, could attain a top speed of 677 miles per hour, and had a range of 1,000 miles with up to 5,000 pounds of ordnance carried externally. Later versions were powered by a 8,500 pounds static thrust Pratt & Whitney J52 turbojet, giving a similar performance but increasing the ordnance load to as much as 9,000 pounds. The Skyhawk's successor was the Vought A-7 Corsair, which began entering service in 1967. it was powered by a 11,350 pounds static thrust Pratt & Whitney TF30 turbofan which gave it a top speed of 680 miles per hour and the ability to carry up to 15,000 pounds of ordnance over a range of 700 miles. Later versions received 14,250 pounds static thrust Allison TF41 turbofans, boosting top speed to 693 miles per hour and increasing range to 900 miles.

The aircraft that more closely resembled the United States Navy's concept of a jet-powered replacement for the Skyraider was the Grumman A-6 Intruder. This large two-seat all-weather attack aircraft, which began entering frontline service in 1965, was powered by twin 9,300 pounds static thrust Pratt & Whitney J52 turbojets, giving it a top speed of 644 miles per hour and a range of 1,010 miles with 18,000 pounds of external ordnance. The sophisticated electronics suite of the Intruder gave it the ability to strike very small targets with great accuracy in all weather conditions, which represented a quantum leap in efficiency for navy attack squadrons.

The first dedicated carrier strike aircraft to enter Royal Navy service after World War II were designs under development before the war's end. The Blackburn Firebrand originated as a carrier fighter but, after a very protracted development process, emerged as a single-seat strike aircraft, entering service in 1945. Its 2,520 horsepower Bristol Centaurus radial engine gave it a top speed of 340 miles per hour and a range of 740 miles. It was armed with four 20mm cannon in the wings and could carry up to 2,000 pounds of external ordnance. Its successor, the Westland Wyvern, was another large single-seat machine and joined the fleet in 1954. It was powered by a 4,110 shaft horsepower Armstrong Siddeley Python turboprop engine driving two large four-bladed contra-rotating propellers that gave the Wyvern a top speed of 383 miles per hour and a range of 904 miles. It was armed with four wing-mounted 20mm cannon and could carry up to 3,000 pounds of ordnance on external pylons.

The French Navy initially employed American equipment of World War II vintage as its carrier strike aircraft: successively Douglas SBD Dauntlesses, Curtiss SB2C Helldivers, and Vought F4U Corsairs. The impending commissioning of the new carriers *Clémenceau* and *Foch* created a requirement for more modern equipment, leading to the adoption of the Dassault Etendard IVM as the French Navy's standard strike aircraft. The single-seat Etendard, powered by a 9,700 pounds static thrust SNECMA Atar turbojet, had a top speed of 683 miles per hour, a range of 1,000 miles, and was armed with two 30mm cannon and up to 3,000 pounds of ordnance carried externally. By the early 1970s it was clear that a replacement was needed, so Dassault upgraded the existing design, creating the Super Etendard, which entered service in 1978. The principal changes were the use of a SNECMA Atar uprated to 11,000 pounds static thrust and the installation of sea search and weapons control radar. The Super Etendard was faster, capable of 733 miles per hour, and could carry up to 4,600 pounds of ordnance. More important was the fact that it was specifically configured to launch the Aérospatiale AM39 Exocet air-to-surface missile, which had a stand-off range of 40 miles, or the Aérospatiale ASMP missile, with a stand-off range of 60 miles, armed with a nuclear warhead.

Carrier fighter aircraft constituted the other developmental track that converged toward the multimission concept. Given the limited numbers of aircraft embarked on carriers, all fighters had some degree of strike capability. Nevertheless, this was to become more and more important as time went on. The United States Navy immediately after World War II standardized on the new Grumman F8F Bearcat (one 2,100 horsepower Pratt & Whitney Double Wasp with a 421 miles per hour maximum speed and a range of 1,105 miles) or improved versions of the wartime Vought Corsair for its fighter and fighter-bomber units. The semi-experimental squadron deployments of the McDonnell FH-1 Phantom and the North American FJ-1 Fury in 1948 gave the navy a foretaste of the difficulties of operating jet aircraft from axial deck carriers. The navy's first jet fighter to see large-scale service was the Grumman F9F Panther that began deploying in 1949 and operated extensively during the Korean War. Most used a 5,000 pounds static thrust Pratt & Whitney J42 turbojet (a license-built Rolls-Royce Nene engine), giving them a top speed of 579 miles per hour, a range of 1,175 miles, and the ability to carry up to 2,000 pounds of external ordnance in addition to the built-in armament of four 20mm cannon in the nose. Larger, longer-ranged McDonnell F2H Banshees began supplementing the Panthers in 1952. Their twin 3,250 pounds static thrust Westinghouse J34 turbojets gave them a top speed of 532 miles per hour and a range of 1,475 miles. They also were armed with four 20mm cannon and could carry 1,000 pounds of external ordnance. Later versions of the Banshee were fitted with search radar and could operate in the all-weather interceptor role.

Swept wing jet fighters appeared in United States Navy service immediately after the Korean War. First there was the Grumman F9F Cougar, essentially a Panther with swept wings. With more powerful 7,250 pounds static thrust Pratt & Whitney J48 turbojets, they reached 647 miles per hour and had a range of 1,200 miles. They were armed with four 20mm cannon and could carry up to 2,000 pounds of external ordnance. Later versions were equipped to carry four AIM-9B Sidewinder air-to-air missiles. Within a year North American FJ-3 Furies joined the Cougars aboard carriers. These aircraft, basically naval versions of North American's famous F-86 Sabre fighter, were powered by 6,000 pounds static thrust General Electric J47 turbojets, giving them a top speed of 676 miles per hours and a range of 990 miles. They also were armed with four 20mm cannon and later versions also carried Sidewinders. Almost simultaneously the radical tail-less Vought F7U Cutlass entered limited service. Its twin 4,600 pounds static thrust Westinghouse J46 turbojets gave it a maximum speed of 680 miles per hour and a range of 660 miles. Armament was identical to that of its missile-armed contemporaries from Grumman and North American.

The arrival of the final generation of United States Navy day fighters came in 1957. The Grumman F11F-1 Tiger was the ultimate refinement of the Panther design. It used a single 7,450 pounds static thrust Wright J65 turbojet to reach 750 miles per hour. Its range was 1,270 miles and its armament was the standard four 20mm cannon and four Sidewinders. The Tiger was phased out of service within two years but its contemporary, the Vought F8U Crusader, enjoyed a very long career. Its 10,000 pounds static thrust (16,200 pounds static thrust with afterburner) Pratt & Whitney J57 turbojet gave it a top speed of Mach 1.53 at 35,000 feet and a range of 1,474 miles. It was armed with four 20mm cannon and two Sidewinders. Later versions used uprated engines generating 10,700 pounds static thrust (18,000 pounds with afterburner). They attained Mach 1.72 at 35,000 feet and had a 1,425-mile range. In addition to four 20mm cannon, they could carry four Sidewinders and up to 5,000 pounds of external ordnance. The later versions also had limited all-weather capabilities.

The United States Navy began its acquisition of a jet-powered all-weather fighter force with the delivery of the Douglas F3D Skyknight, though it saw only very limited service on carriers. Interim radar-equipped versions of the Banshee were replaced beginning in 1957 by two new types, the McDonnell F3H Demon and the Douglas F4D Skyray, both with limited all-weather capability. The Demon was powered by a 9,700 pounds static thrust Allison J71 turbojet to reach a top speed of 647 miles per hour. Its range was 1,370 miles and armament was the usual four 20mm cannon, supplemented on later models by four Sidewinders or four AIM-7C Sparrows. The Skyray used a 10,500 pounds static thrust Pratt & Whitney J57 turbojet. Its maximum speed was 695 miles per hour and its range was 1,200 miles. It too was armed with four 20mm cannon. Both types were supplanted, beginning in 1962, by the McDonnell F-4 Phantom II, destined to become one of the most successful naval aircraft ever deployed. It was a large, two-seat, twin-engined aircraft powered by two 10,900 pounds static thrust (17,000 pounds static thrust with afterburner) General Electric J79 turbojets, giving it a top speed of 1,485 miles per hour and a combat radius of 600 miles. It was armed with missiles exclusively, carrying up to six Sparrows or a mix of four Sparrows and four Sidewinders. It also could carry up to 16,000 pounds of external ordnance. The combination of powerful radar, efficient long-range missiles, and great load-carrying capacity made the Phantom II the first effective multirole carrier aircraft, successful both as an interceptor or strike package escort and a tactical strike platform.

The Phantom II's successor as an air-superiority fighter was the Grumman F-14 Tomcat that began its service career in 1974. The Tomcat was a very large two-seat twin-engined swing-wing fighter, initially powered by two 12,350 pounds static thrust (20,900 pounds static thrust with afterburner) Pratt & Whitney TF30 turbofans, giving it a top speed of Mach 2.23 at 40,000 feet and a combat radius of 766 miles. Its most important feature was its very advanced AWG-9 radar combined with very long range AIM-54

Phoenix air-to-air missiles that made it a potent fleet defense asset. The Tomcat had a built-in multibarreled 20mm cannon and could carry various combinations of Phoenix, Sparrow, and Sidewinder missiles. Later versions of the Tomcat were powered by two 14,000 pounds static thrust (27,000 pounds static thrust with afterburner) General Electric F110 turbofan that boosted its performance to Mach 2.34 at 40,000 feet (many earlier airframes also were upgraded retroactively). They also received much upgraded digital avionics, centered on the new APG-71 radar. As the press for more mission flexibility became stronger, it was decided to equip the Tomcat for both tactical reconnaissance and later for tactical strike using laser-guided munitions. The solution was to fit it with appropriate equipment carried externally; the TARPS (Tactical Air Reconnaissance Pod System) introduced in 1980, or LANTIRN (Low Altitude Navigation and Targeting Infra-Red for Night) pod, first used in 1996.

In the mid-1970s the United States Navy put forward a requirement for a lightweight, low cost, multimission fighter, initially to replace the A-7 light attack aircraft. This produced the McDonnell Douglas F/A-18 Hornet, delivered in both single-seat and two-seat forms. Powered by two 10,600 pounds static thrust (15,800 pound static thrust with afterburner) General Electric F404 turbofans, it could reach Mach 1.8 at 35,000 feet and had a combat radius of 460 miles. Armament was one built-in multibarreled 20mm cannon and up to six air-to-air missiles or a mix of air-to-surface missiles, "smart" weapons, or iron bombs totaling 17,000 pounds. Later versions had uprated engines, upgraded avionics suites, and were equipped with FLIR (Forward Looking Infra Red) equipment and provision for pilot night vision goggles, giving them all-weather night attack capability. Some two-seaters also were configured for reconnaissance, using externally-mounted ATARS (Advanced Tactical Airborne Reconnaissance System) pods.

By the late 1980s the navy saw an impending need to replace both the Intruder and the Tomcat. McDonnell Douglas put forward a substantially modified version of the Hornet as its candidate. Although it is essentially a new aircraft, the F/A-18 designation was retained, implying it was only a later model of an existing aircraft. Both single and two-seat models are in production, the single-seaters destined to replace the earlier Hornets in the attack role and the two-seaters intended to take over from the Tomcat in the fleet defense role. The Super Hornet is powered by two 21,890 pounds static thrust (with afterburner) General Electric F414 turbofans.

Top speed remains Mach 1.8 at 35,000 feet but the Super Hornet's combat radius has increased to 760 miles and it can carry up to 17,750 pounds of ordnance, thanks to two additional hard points. It also features very substantially improved avionics. The Super Hornet entered frontline service in 1999 and is planned to remain in production until 2014.

The Royal Navy initially deployed improved versions of its wartime Seafire fighters before replacing them with its final piston-engined day fighter, the Hawker Sea Fury, beginning in 1947. The Sea Fury was powered by a 2,480 horsepower Bristol Centaurus radial engine that gave it a maximum speed of 460 miles per hour and a range of 680 miles. It was armed with four wing-mounted 20mm cannon and could carry up to 2,000 pounds of bombs or rockets for ground attack missions. The navy's first jet day fighter, the Supermarine Attacker, saw relatively limited frontline service between 1951 and 1954 only. It used a single 5,100 pounds static thrust Rolls-Royce Nene turbojet to reach 590 miles per hour and had a range of 590 miles. The Attacker was armed with four 20mm cannon and most could also carry rockets or bombs. Its replacement, the Hawker Sea Hawk, offered an almost identical performance from the same power plant but possessed far superior handling both in the air and onto the flight deck. Later models were configured primarily as fighter-bombers, carrying up to 2,000 pounds of ordnance under the wings.

The Sea Hawk was the Royal Navy's last day fighter. Its first postwar all-weather fighter was the de Havilland Sea Hornet, which entered service in 1951. This two-seater was powered by two 2,030 horsepower Rolls-Royce Merlin liquid-cooled engines that gave it a top speed of 430 miles per hour and a range of 1,500 miles. Its replacement, the de Havilland Sea Venom, went to sea in 1954 and was a two-seater powered by a single 5,300 pounds static thrust de Havilland Ghost turbojet that endowed it with a maximum speed of 575 miles per hour and a range of 950 miles. Both the Sea Hornet and the Sea Venom had the standard British armament of four 20mm cannon and could carry bombs or rockets for ground attack missions. The final British-designed all-weather fighter for the Royal Navy was the de Havilland Sea Vixen, which replaced the Sea Venom. It was a two-seater powered by two 11,230 pounds static thrust Rolls-Royce Avon turbojets, allowing it to reach Mach 0.95 at 40,000 feet and giving it a range of 1,950 miles. The Sea Vixen was exclusively missile armed, carrying four Firestreak or Red Top air-to-air missiles plus two retractable packs for unguided rockets. It entered frontline service in 1959 and was replaced, beginning in 1970, by the Royal Navy's final fighter, a modified version of the McDonnell Phantom II using two 12,250 pounds static thrust (20,515 pounds static thrust with afterburner) Rolls-Royce Spey turbofans in place of the original American engines.

The French Navy used no indigenous fighters from its carriers until 2001. After World War II it first deployed Supermarine Seafires, followed by Grumman F6F Hellcats and Vought F4U Corsairs. In 1955 the navy's first jet fighters began to enter service in the form of the Sud-Est Aquilon, a license-built version of the de Havilland Sea Venom. In 1965 these were replaced by a unique variant of the Vought F-8 Crusader, modified to suit it for operations from the relatively small French flight decks. With periodic upgrades, these Crusaders remained in service until the arrival of the Dassault Rafale in 2001. The Rafale is a single-seat aircraft powered by two 11,240 pounds static thrust (16,860 pounds static thrust with afterburner) SNECMA M88 turbofans, giving it a maximum speed of Mach 2 and a combat radius of 680 miles. It is armed with a built-in 30mm cannon and can carry up to 20,925 pounds of ordnance, including MICA air-to-air missiles, "smart" weapons, Exocet air-to-surface missiles, and the nuclear warhead equipped ASMP stand-off missile. The French Navy still remains undecided about acquiring the two-seat version of the Rafale to more effectively fulfill the strike role.

When the carrier *Admiral Flota Sovetskogo Soyuza Kuznetsov* commissioned it became necessary to put frontline strike and interceptor aircraft into production for the air group. In keeping with a policy of minimizing the number of different airframes in production, especially in view of the fiscal difficulties attendant to the realignment of the Soviet Union into the Russian Confederation, it was decided to pursue a variant of the successful Sukhoi Su-27 (NATO designation Flanker). The Sukhoi Su-33 (NATO designation Flanker-D) has folding wings and nose radome to ease stowage aboard carriers. It is powered by two 16,720 pounds static thrust (27,500 pounds static thrust with afterburner) Lyulka AL-31F turbofan engines, giving it a maximum speed of Mach 2.35 at 40,000 feet and a combat radius of 940 miles. It has a built in 30mm multi-barreled cannon and can carry up to ten R-27 (NATO designation AA-10 Alamo) or R-73 (NATO designation AA-11 Archer) air-to-air missiles, or several Kh-41 (NATO designation ASM-MSS) air-to-surface missiles. Its radar, the Fazotron N-014, has a range of 80 miles with track-while-scan and look-down/shoot-down capabilities.

Photographic reconnaissance was an early substantial component of the "overhead" that became such a feature of carrier air groups after World War II. The United States Navy has consistently deployed detachments, usually of four to six aircraft, to almost all its attack carriers for pre- and post-mission reconnaissance. Many of these aircraft were specialized variants of standard frontline fighters, including Bearcats, Corsairs, Panthers, Banshees, Cougars, Cutlasses, and Crusaders. There was also a photoreconnaissance version of the Phantom II but only the Marine Corps received it and very few ever deployed aboard carriers. There also were long-range reconnaissance versions of the Savage, Skywarrior, and, most important, the Vigilante, the bulk of whose naval service was as a reconnaissance platform. Changes for the smaller fighter types usually were limited to fitting new noses carrying suitable outfits of cameras but the larger attack aircraft also carried equipment for electronic reconnaissance and radar search, as do the recent generations of reconnaissance aircraft, Tomcats and Hornets, which carry their equipment externally in detachable pods.

After World War II the Royal Navy made extensive use of piston-engined fighter-reconnaissance types, aircraft that retained their armament and offensive capabilities while also being equipped with cameras for photographic reconnaissance. After jet fighters entered service, the navy continued to prefer this type of solution and made much use of pods incorporating appropriate reconnaissance equipment, a practice that continues to this day. The French Navy also preferred the fighter-reconnaissance solution but, in the early 1960s, it started to embark the dedicated photoreconnaissance Etendard IVP, a version of the contemporary strike aircraft with a camera nose and facilities to also attach an additional camera pod beneath the fuselage. This version of the Etendard proved so useful that it remained in service long after the strike aircraft had been replaced by the later Super Etendard and was not withdrawn until 1998. The new Dassault Rafale aircraft in service now use podded reconnaissance equipment for such missions.

The second great consumer of space was provision for airborne early warning. The United States Navy began deploying aircraft for early warning late in World War II, using aircraft fitted with existing airborne surface search radar sets. Immediately after the war, the navy put the large APS-20 search radar into service, using first Grumman Avenger torpedo bombers and then Douglas Skyraiders modified as platforms with radomes beneath the fuselage and accommodation space arranged within the fuselage for the operators.

In 1958 the navy began receiving Grumman WF Tracers, very highly modified versions of the existing Grumman S2F Tracker antisubmarine aircraft with a massive fixed dish radome above the fuselage to house its APS-82 radar set and accommodation for the equipment operators within the fuselage. The Tracker began to be replaced by the Grumman E-2 Hawkeye in 1964. The Hawkeye was designed for the airborne early warning mission from the outset. It was powered by two 4,590 shaft horsepower Allison T56 turboprop engines that gave it a top speed of 372 miles per hour and a maximum range of 1,605 miles. The search radar, the APS-120 (later replaced by the improved APS-125) was housed in a huge circular rotating dome above the fuselage, which also contained large working spaces for the operators. The Hawkeye remains in service, although the radar, avionics, and power plants have undergone continuous upgrading and it currently deploys the APS-145 search set.

The Royal Navy initially deployed Fairey Firefly strike aircraft to provide limited airborne early warning capabilities aboard its carriers immediately after World War II. In 1952 it began receiving ex-United States Navy airborne early warning Skyraiders under the Mutual Defense Assistance Program (MDAP). Several saw action during the Suez operation in 1956, where resourceful naval aviators discovered that, among its other operational advantages, the radar operators' compartment provided much useful space to accommodate substantial quantities of beer for transport to thirsty troops ashore. The Skyraiders were replaced in 1960 by a specialized version of the Fairey Gannet that used the same APS-20 radar. This airborne early warning Gannet remained in service until the *Ark Royal* decommissioned in 1978, leaving the navy without any early warning coverage. This proved very dangerous during the 1981 Falklands/Malvinas operation and led to the hurried development of an airborne early warning system suitable for operation from the very small flight decks of British support carriers. The solution was to use a Westland Sea King helicopter as a platform for a compact long-range search radar set and accommodation for its operators. This combination entered service within a very few months of the end of the campaign and continues in operation today, albeit after substantial systems upgrades.

The French Navy's first airborne early warning aircraft were ex-United States Navy Grumman Avengers delivered under MDAP that served from 1950 until the early 1960s. After the Avengers departed, French carriers operated without their own airborne early warning systems and had to rely on cover provided by shore-based aircraft.

The impending commissioning of the *Charles de Gaulle* prompted a reassessment of this situation and led to the decision to order Grumman Hawkeye aircraft from the United States to provide the carrier with its own airborne early warning system.

The Russian fleet took a similar approach to that of the Royal Navy when the time arrived to design a suitable airborne early warning aircraft for its new carriers. The Kamov Ka-29RLD (NATO designation Helix-B) flew in prototype form in 1993 and has entered limited production, mainly for export to India. It is a variant of the Ka-27 antisubmarine helicopter (though using the same basic fuselage as the specialized Ka-29TB assault helicopter), fitted with a large E-801 search radar with its retractable rotating antenna beneath the fuselage.

Electronic warfare aircraft constituted a third component of an air group's "overhead." The United States Navy again led the way in this, deploying small numbers of Douglas Skyraider aircraft carrying electronic countermeasure equipment and its operators from late 1948. Various models of electronic countermeasure Skyraiders continued to serve aboard the *Essex* class carriers until their withdrawal and aboard the larger carriers until the early 1960s when they were first supplemented and then supplanted by Douglas Skywarrior aircraft modified for this mission. The navy's experience of operations over Vietnam and the good results obtained by modified Grumman Intruder aircraft deployed by the Marine Corps from 1964 led to the decision to develop a dedicated electronic warfare aircraft for carrier operation. Using the Intruder as a basis, Grumman produced the EA-6B Prowler, which had an extended forward fuselage to accommodate a crew of four and extensive specialized electronic warfare equipment carried both internally and in external pods. The Prowler entered frontline service in 1971 and remains fully operational today, having gone through four major upgrades of both its avionics and its structure to keep it at the cutting edge of electronic warfare. It is planned to replace it with a variant of the two-seater Super Hornet, the F/A-18G Growler, by 2010.

The Royal Navy began adding electronic warfare aircraft to its carrier air groups in the mid-1950s, using extensively modified Grumman Avengers as platforms. Their replacements were de Havilland Sea Venoms modified as two-seat electronic countermeasures aircraft after the type was withdrawn from frontline service as an all-weather fighter. After the withdrawal of the Fairey Gannets from carrier antisubmarine squadrons in 1960 some of these low-hour airframes were modified for the electronic warfare mission and remained operational in small numbers until the *Ark Royal* left service. Aircraft aboard the smaller support carriers subsequently had to rely exclusively on small electronic countermeasures pods for self-defense until the mid-1980s, when more intensive electronic warfare missions were added to the task load of the airborne early warning Sea Kings.

French carriers deployed small numbers of Grumman Avengers modified for electronic countermeasures work during the 1950s and early 1960s. Breguet Alizé antisubmarine aircraft took over this mission thereafter, initially relying on existing avionics. In the early 1980s a large batch of Alizé aircraft received substantial electronic upgrades, including dedicated countermeasures equipment and, after a further upgrade ten years later, served aboard French carriers until withdrawn in 2000. The new Rafales now rely wholly on their own internal and supplementary podded external electronic countermeasures gear.

Ultimately, one of the largest contributors to the growth of air group "overhead" was provision for antisubmarine warfare. The United States Navy was able to finesse the problem for many years by operating dedicated antisubmarine warfare carriers, converted from existing war-built vessels, within carrier task groups. At first these ships operated modified Grumman Avenger aircraft but these were replaced by new fixed-wing and rotary-wing aircraft from 1950. The fixed wing aircraft were Grumman AF Guardians, large single-engined machines powered by 2,400 horsepower Pratt & Whitney Double Wasp engines that gave them a top speed of 317 miles per hour and a range of 1,500 miles. Because of the weight of equipment deployed, these aircraft had to operate in teams, one aircraft carrying the large APS-20 search radar and the other carrying the antisubmarine weapons and a smaller APS-30 radar for attack purposes only. The rotary-wing component was the Sikorsky HO4S, whose 350-horsepower Pratt & Whitney Wasp engines provided insufficient power to carry adequate equipment. This initial combination clearly was less than entirely satisfactory and quickly was replaced by new equipment. The Grumman S2F Tracker began entering service in 1954. It was a large aircraft powered by two 1,525 horsepower Wright Cyclone radial engines, giving it a top speed of 253 miles per hour and a range of 1,150 miles. It carried radar for search and attack, bays for sonobuoys, and a full load of antisubmarine weapons in a single airframe, vastly improving efficiency. Its rotary-winged partner, the Sikorsky HSS Seabat, followed a year later. Although an improvement over the earlier HO4S, it still was not entirely satisfactory because its 1,525 horsepower Wright Cyclone engine sufficed only to lift either dipping sonar equipment or antisubmarine weaponry, so these helicopters had to operate as hunter-killer teams. The solution was a larger helicopter that materialized as the Sikorsky SH-3 Sea King in 1961. Power from two 1,400 shaft horsepower General Electric T58 turboshaft engines gave it a top speed of 166 miles per hour, a range of 625 miles, and the ability to carry both dipping sonar and a full array of antisubmarine weapons. With periodic upgrades in power plants and equipment, the Sea King remained in frontline antisubmarine warfare service until replaced by more up-to-date Sikorsky SH-60F Seahawks beginning in 1990. The Seahawk uses two 1,543 shaft horsepower General Electric T700 turboshaft engines to attain a maximum speed of 182 miles per hour and a range of 373 miles. It carries dipping sonar, sonobuoys, magnetic anomaly detection equipment for detection, and an array of antisubmarine weaponry. A substantial upgrade program for the navy's Seahawks commenced in 2004.

Real problems arose for the United States Navy in providing antisubmarine coverage for carrier groups in the late 1960s. The converted war-built *Essex* class ships were wearing out and the cost of constructing replacement vessels was prohibitive, given the expense of conducting the war in Vietnam. The navy therefore was driven to transfer antisubmarine warfare assets to the attack carriers, creating general purpose air groups and adding greatly to the "overhead" size. Initially, only the Sea Kings embarked on the carriers but they were joined by new fixed-wing antisubmarine warfare aircraft in 1975, when the Lockheed S-3 Viking entered frontline service. The Viking was powered by two 9,275 pounds static thrust General Electric TF34 turbofan engines, giving it a top speed of 518 miles per hour and a range of 2,300 miles. It was equipped with a full array of sensors: search radar, sonobuoys, and forward looking infrared and magnetic anomaly detection equipment. Its offensive weapons included bombs, mines, homing torpedoes, and depth charges, all carried in an internal weapons bay. The Viking is still in service thanks to several upgrade programs.

The Royal Navy began embarking antisubmarine warfare versions of its existing Fairey Firefly very shortly after World War II and supplemented them with American Grumman Avengers from early 1955. The navy's carriers then began receiving new Fairey Gannet antisubmarine warfare aircraft in 1955. The Gannet was a large three-seater powered by a 2,950 shaft horsepower Armstrong Siddeley Double Mamba turboshaft engine driving twin four-bladed contra-props, giving it a maximum speed of 299 miles per hour and a range of 662 miles. It was equipped with search radar in a retractable radome and could carry a wide array of antisubmarine weaponry in an internal weapons bay.

The Gannet did not remain in service long because the Royal Navy had determined to concentrate its antisubmarine warfare assets in helicopters. Westland Whirlwinds became operational in 1957 and started to replace the Gannets. The Whirlwind was a license-built version of the Sikorsky S-55, powered by a 750 horsepower Alvis Leonides Major radial engine, giving it a top speed of 106 miles per hour, a range of 290 miles, and the ability to lift search radar, dipping sonar, and a homing torpedo or depth charges. A license-built variant of Sikorsky's S-58, the Westland Wessex, followed and entered service beginning in 1961. A 1,450 shaft horsepower Napier Gazelle turboshaft engine replaced the piston radial engine of the American machine, giving the Wessex a top speed of 135 miles per hour, a range of 390 miles, and the ability to lift search radar, dipping sonar, and multiple combinations of homing torpedoes or depth charges. It was superceded by yet another license-built Sikorsky airframe, the Westland Sea King that started entering service in 1970. This was powered by two 1,600 shaft horsepower Rolls-Royce Gnome turboshaft engines, giving it a maximum speed of 161 miles per hour and a range of 598 miles. Early models were equipped in similar fashion to the later Wessex helicopters but the later models, with more powerful 1,660 shaft horsepower engines, carried much more sophisticated electronics, magnetic anomaly detection equipment, multiple search radar systems, sonobuoys, and a more extensive array of weaponry, including Sea Eagle antishipping missiles, yet also boasted a range of 764 miles. In 2000 a new helicopter, the Agusta-Westland Merlin, began replacing the Sea King. It uses three 2,312 shaft horsepower Rolls-Royce/Turbomeca RTM322 turboshaft engines to attain a speed of 193 miles per hour and has a maximum range of 1,150 miles and is equipped with a more advanced version of the late model Sea King's array.

American Grumman Avengers also formed the initial inventory of antisubmarine warfare aircraft aboard French carriers, starting in 1950. They were replaced by an indigenous design, the Breguet Alizé, that entered service in 1959. A 2,100 shaft horsepower Rolls-Royce Dart turboshaft engine powered the Alizé, giving it a maximum speed of 295 miles per hour and a range of 750 miles. A CSF radar set in a retractable dome and sonobuoys in fairings under the wings provided search capabilities, while the large internal weapons bay and underwing pylons were used for offensive weaponry. The Alizés received a major upgrade in the early 1980s and another ten years later. The French Navy made extensive use of helicopters for antisubmarine warfare missions, but did not deploy them aboard aircraft carriers and confined them to smaller surface warships. The bigger Super Frelons and American S-58 machines had some useful antisubmarine warfare capabilities but were used primarily as assault transports. The first helicopter type to deploy aboard French carriers for antisubmarine warfare duties was the Aérospatiale-MBB-Agusta-Westland NH-90, which began entering service in 2005. Two 2,120 shaft horsepower Rolls-Royce/Turbomeca RTM322 turboshaft engines give it a top speed of 180 miles per hour and a range of 715 miles. It carries dipping sonar and magnetic anomaly detection equipment and is armed with a mix of homing torpedoes, depth charges, and air-to-surface missiles.

The Soviet Navy concentrated on the use of helicopters for antisubmarine warfare. The Kamov Ka-25BSh (NATO designation Hormone-A) entered service in 1964. It used Nikolai I. Kamov's unique contra-rotating rotor design that eliminated the need for a tail rotor and created a very compact machine. Two 900 shaft horsepower Glushnekov GTD-3 turboshaft engines gave it a top speed of 137 miles per hour and a range of 248 miles. Its search radar was in a chin radome, and it also carried sonobuoy dispensers, dipping sonar, and magnetic anomaly detection equipment in an external pod. Its weapons bay could accommodate wire-guided torpedoes or depth charges. The Kamov KA-27PL (NATO designation Helix-A) began replacing the Ka-25 in 1976. It was powered by two 2,205 shaft horsepower Isotov TV3-117V turboshaft engines, giving it a maximum speed of 155 miles per hour and a range of 497 miles. Its search suite matched that of the earlier type, though it was much more modern, and armament included up to four wire-guided torpedoes, four guided antisubmarine bombs, nuclear or conventional depth charges, or other bombs. The Ka-27 remains in frontline service with the Russian fleet.

One of the most significant developments for most carrier operators was the advent of practical VSTOL aircraft. The first to enter service was the McDonnell Douglas/Hawker Siddeley AV-8A Harrier, a navalized variant of the Royal Air Force's Harrier that was deployed by United States Marine Corps squadrons aboard assault ships beginning in 1971. It used a 21,500 pounds static thrust

Rolls-Royce Pegasus vectored-thrust turbofan engine to reach Mach 0.98 at 35,000 feet and had a combat radius of 400 miles. It was armed with two 30mm cannon gun packs and could carry up to 5,000 pounds of ordnance externally. In 1984 these aircraft began to be replaced by improved AV-8B Harrier IIs, which had a larger wing to improve their load-carrying capacity. Maximum speed fell slightly, to Mach 0.91 at altitude, but combat radius increased to 553 miles and the ordnance load rose to almost 10,000 pounds in addition to two 25mm cannon gun packs. Later versions have added FLIR and advanced APG-65 radar to endow them with all-weather attack capabilities and they also are wired to accept guidance pods to control "smart" munitions.

The Royal Navy did not adopt the attack version of the Harrier but instead received the Sea Harrier, configured primarily as a carrier fighter. It featured a modified nose that raised the pilot's cockpit for better visibility and carried Blue Fox intercept radar. The Sea Harrier had a similar performance to the AV-8A and could carry Sidewinder or Sky Flash air-to-air missiles or alternative ground attack munitions, plus two 30mm cannon gun packs. The Sea Harrier entered frontline service in 1980 and distinguished itself during the Falklands/Malvinas operation. They were upgraded, beginning in 1990, with new Blue Vixen radar and the capability of using the advanced AMRAAM air-to-air missile. In 2000 the Royal Navy and the Royal Air Force formed the Joint Harrier Force that combined the navy's Sea Harrier fighters and the air force's Harrier ground attack aircraft (similar in specification to the AV-8B Harrier II) into a single organization that could deploy both ashore and afloat. Consequently, British carriers now embark air groups that contain both types, depending on the operational requirements.

The Soviet Navy also adopted VSTOL aircraft as the initial fixed wing component of its carrier air groups. The Yakovlev Yak-38 (NATO designation Forger-A) entered service in 1976. It used a combination of two 6,400 pounds static thrust Kolesov RD36V-35FV lift jets for takeoff and landing and a single 13,000 pounds static thrust (14,550 pounds static thrust with afterburner) Tumansky R27V-300 main engine featuring twin hydraulically-actuated vectored thrust nozzles at the rear. The Yak-38 could attain 650 miles per hour, had a combat radius of 62 miles, and could carry up to 1,325 pounds of external ordnance, including air-to-air and air-to-surface missiles. Plans for a more capable successor to the Yak-38 never materialized in a production aircraft.

NAVAL AVIATORS DURING THE COLD WAR ERA

The United States Navy found the fundamentals of its wartime training program very successful, but made changes to suit it better for a peacetime situation and also the more complex aircraft that it was operating in frontline service. Aviation candidates first completed pre-flight training. Naval Academy graduates, whose coursework already had given them much of the required technical grounding, spent only five weeks at preflight school at Pensacola. Direct entry aviation cadets first underwent two weeks of indoctrination into navy ways, then studied technical subjects (navigation, engines, principles of flight, and aerial meteorology) plus military drill and physical education for an additional fourteen weeks. All those who successfully completed preflight school then began basic flying training. This program combined the elements of the wartime elimination, primary, and intermediate training courses into a single course. During the nine-month program, in addition to 180 hours of flying training that climaxed with six carrier qualification landings on a training carrier, students also enhanced their technical knowledge with 240 hours of ground school that expanded on the topics covered during preflight school.

Successful graduates of basic flying training received their wings and proceeded to advanced flying training. This varied in content depending on the pilot's aviation specialty: fighter, attack, antisubmarine, or multiengined patrol. Initially, all courses lasted about five months and included about 150 hours of flying training and about 200 hours of ground school. In 1953 the course for prospective fighter pilots was extended in duration by two weeks to provide time for transition training from piston-engined aircraft to jet-propelled equipment. Completion of advanced training led pilots to operational training with appropriate units within either the east or west coast training air groups. Until 1953 it was within these air groups that fighter pilots underwent transition training if they were to fly jets and a similar position prevailed within the attack aircraft community until the early 1960s.

The success of the carrier task force concept in the Pacific War led the United States Navy to make such formations the centerpiece of its worldwide fleet structure. This structure in itself was a new feature of American naval dispositions. It contrasted with the prewar focus on concentrating the main body of the fleet in the Pacific and maintaining only limited forces in other areas and reflected the ascendancy of the United States Navy over all other nation's naval forces. Carriers were ideally adapted to the needs of American strategic dispositions because of their efficacy in power projection and the flexibility and rapidity of response conferred by their mobility. The United States Navy found that the carrier task force structure (one or more aircraft carriers supported by surface warship escorts and auxiliaries) was ideally suited to conduct operations in keeping with the nation's commitments and goals, and it retained it consistently to the present, although now under the title of "carrier battle groups."

Within the United States Navy the ascension of carriers to a dominant position within the warship hierarchy had a parallel impact on the position of aviators within the officer corps. After World War II the core elements of the various American fleets in the Atlantic, Mediterranean, and Pacific became carrier task forces. Command of these carrier task forces became the principal avenue to fleet command and, ultimately, the highest echelons of the navy's command structure. Since it had long been mandated, the command of individual aircraft carriers was reserved for naval aviators. These officers naturally tended to be more likely candidates for selection for task force or fleet commands and to figure prominently among those chosen to serve with the Joint Chiefs of Staff as the professional leaders of the navy. Although surface warfare officers and, more significantly, submariners received appointments both as fleet commanders and among the ranks of the chiefs of naval operations, aviators came to receive the lion's share of these positions, largely by virtue of their prior command experience as task force commanders. Just as prior to World War II battleship command was the springboard to the top, carrier command became the most important factor in joining the navy's leadership, and this, unlike battleship command, was reserved by law for aviators.

This phenomenon of the dominance of aviators of the upper echelons of command was much less prevalent within the other carrier-operating navies of the world. This reflected both the lesser number of carriers these fleets operated, meaning that many of these navies relied more on surface warships or submarines to form much of their striking force, and that aviators in these navies did not have a legal "lock" on carrier command, but often were required to undertake tours of duty as surface warfare officers prior to gaining command of their own ships. Since World War II, the highest command in the British and, to a somewhat lesser extent, the French navies has gone more often to submariners than any other warfare specialty, perhaps reflecting an unwritten bias toward giving submarine officers preference for command of submarine forces and thus creating for them a more dominant career track than other specialists.

The end of World War II led to an immediate dramatic reduction in the size of the Royal Navy and its Fleet Air Arm. It started to grow again in the late 1940s in response to the tense international situation, whose most obvious social manifestation in the United Kingdom was the passage of the National Service Act in 1948 that mandated eighteen months of military service, followed by four years in the reserves, for all males aged eighteen or older. Two years later it was amended to extend enlisted service to two years followed by a commensurate six-month reduction in reserve obligation. The Royal Navy, however, made little use of National Service conscripts to fill its ranks, since it realized very quickly that adequate training would consume too much of the conscript's active service obligation, and generally only accepted those who had already joined the Royal Naval Volunteer Reserve (RNVR), including RNVR air squadrons, prior to their call-up. The Royal Navy therefore essentially phased out conscript intake from 1950 in favor of accepting those who volunteered and agreed to fulfill a longer service commitment

The vast majority of the Royal Navy's aircrew entered the service as aspirants for short service commissions. They spent nine months at the Royal Naval College, Dartmouth, during which time they spent three weeks in grading flying school to determine their aptitude for flying. Successful pilot candidates did their elementary flying training with the Royal Air Force, and then returned to the Royal Navy for basic flying training, either as fixed-wing or rotary-wing pilots, at the end of which they received their wings. They then went to training squadrons for advanced and operational training before joining their first frontline squadron after eighteen months of flying training. Observers (antisubmarine warfare officers, navigators, etc.) underwent twelve months of training with the Royal Navy before rejoining their pilot colleagues in advanced and operational training squadrons, then also joining their first frontline units.

In 1993, after the break-up of the Soviet Union and the contraction of British military commitments, a substantial reorganization of military flying training took place. The Ministry of Defence created a unified system for all the armed services in which the Royal Air Force took the lead. For Royal Navy aviators this meant that, after their time at Dartmouth, those who demonstrated their aptitude in the grading course then went on to a short survival course before beginning an eight-month course at the Defence Elementary Flying

Training School at RAF (Royal Air Force Station) Cranwell. Rotary-wing pilots then spent six months at the Defence Helicopter Flying School at RAF Shawbury, while fast jet pilots went to the Basic Fast Jet Training course at RAF Linton-on-Ouse for nine months. After receiving their wings at this point, all pilots received further training, the helicopter crews taking advanced and operational training courses specialized for the types they would be flying, while the fast jet crews went to RAF Valley for advanced training and RAF Wittering for operational training. Observers continued to receive all their training within the navy, first an extended twelve-month course at RNAS (Royal Naval Air Station) Culdrose, then advanced and operational training with their colleagues flying helicopters (since the Royal Navy no longer operated any two-seat fixed-wing front-line aircraft).

The growing seniority of some individual Royal Navy aircrew officers meant that by late in World War II some carriers were commanded by such officers. This became even more common into the 1950s, and the transition was marked most obviously by the promotion of Admiral Caspar John to the post of First Sea Lord and Chief of Naval Staff in 1960, the first naval aviator to become the professional head of the Royal Navy. The process that allowed naval aviators to rise to the upper ranks of the navy was selection to join the General List (those officers eligible to become ship commanders), which involved spending time at sea in surface ships to allow them to gain their watchkeeping and ocean navigation certificates. This was encouraged among officers who indicated their intention of remaining in the navy beyond the limit of their short-service commission, leading to greater prospects for promotion and stability within the naval aviation community.

At the end of World War II the French Navy had to recreate its training system from scratch. In January 1946 it adopted a system similar to that of the Royal Navy and established a series of training squadrons for the various phases of the process, but with the important distinction that the entire process was conducted "in house." Flying orientation, a four-week program for all potential aircrew, both pilots and non-pilots, was conducted by Escadrille 50S at BAN (base d'aéronautique navale) Lanvéoc-Poulmic. Those selected to become pilots then proceeded to Escadrille 51S at BAN Khouribga for elementary flying training, while other aircrew candidates went to Escadrille 52S (Escadrille 56S from 1948) at BAN Agadir, both in Morocco. Basic flying training followed in the new Escadrille 52S at

BAN Khouribga. Both pilots and non-pilots came together again (if on track for carrier aviation) in Escadrille 54S at BAN Hyères for operational flying training and carrier qualification.

France's signature of the North Atlantic Treaty on April 4, 1949, which created NATO, led to some significant changes. The United States Navy, in February 1950, agreed to make its facilities available to train French naval aircrew under MDAP. Between April 1950 and September 1957 over 500 student pilots qualified for their wings and received further advanced flying training in the United States. As a result the French Navy made some changes to its domestic training system. Escadrille 58S was established in 1951 at BAN Saint-Mandrier to train helicopter pilots who had completed the elementary flying course at BAN Khouribga. It moved to BAN Fréjus-Saint Raphäel in 1954. In 1953 a specialized fighter training school was established as Escadrille 57S at BAN Lartigue. It moved to BAN Khouribga the following year and again to BAN Port-Lyautey in 1960. In 1956, an all-weather fighter training school was created (Escadrille 59S) at BAN Hyères. In 1957 it additionally took over the training obligations of Escadrille 54S, which disbanded.

Big changes came as a result of France's departure from its former possessions in North Africa. The elimination of the navy's North African air training facilities led to the decision to turn over elementary and basic pilot training to l'Armée de l'Air in 1961. In 1960 basic helicopter pilot training became the responsibility of l'Aviation Légere de l'Armée de Terre (ALAT) at Dax and l'Armée de l'Air undertook advanced helicopter pilot training at Chambéry. In 1962 Escadrille 57S disbanded and its operational fighter training mission was undertaken by l'Armée de l'Air's Ecole de Chasse at Tours. Non-pilot aircrews continued to receive their training with Escadrille 56S, relocated first to BAN Lann-Bihoué and then, in 1964, to BAN Nîmes-Garons, while Escadrille 59S at BAN Hyères remained responsible for final operational training and carrier qualification.

National defense reorganizations continued to cause changes in the training system. L'Armée de l'Air ceased operations at Chambéry in 1975, leading to the creation of Escadrille 22S at BAN Lanvéoc-Poulmic for advanced training of helicopter pilots. Then, in 1993, the navy's deck landing trainer, the Fouga Zéphyr, was withdrawn from service without a replacement, leading to Escadrille 59S disbanding and an arrangement with the United States Navy for it to take over carrier qualification training for the French fleet. Currently, ALAT provides basic helicopter training and the French Navy handles their advanced training, while l'Armée de l'Air conducts elementary and basic fixed-wing training, the United States Navy covers advanced flying and carrier qualification, and the navy's Escadrille 57S at BAN Landivisiau addresses operational training.

CARRIER OPERATIONS DURING
THE COLD WAR ERA

The overwhelming majority of carrier operations after the end of World War II entailed the actual or threatened use of embarked aviation against targets on land or shore-based opponents. This very much aligned with late-war experience, though the carriers never faced any significant credible threat of attacks against their own security. Carriers became very important instruments for projecting power, either actual or potential, toward the attainment of national policy goals, whether by diplomatic means or the use of force.

France's ultimately failed efforts to retain its colonial hold on Indochina embroiled its carriers in a six-year campaign off the Vietnamese coast that presaged, on a much more limited scale, the operations of the United States fleet in the same waters that began a decade later. France's first postwar carrier, the escort carrier *Dixmunde* (previously the *Biter* in the Royal Navy), began operations in the Tonkin Gulf in March 1947, using SBD dive-bombers for ground attack missions against the Viet-Minh guerillas. The *Dixmunde* was too small to mount effective operations and served subsequently as an aircraft transport, its operational duties passing to the *Arromanches*, a larger ex-British light carrier, which undertook its first missions in September 1948 using SBDs and Seafires before returning to France to reequip its squadrons. It returned to the line with new aircraft, Hellcats and Helldivers, in August 1951. The French acquisition of the American light carrier *Langley*, renamed *Lafayette*, enabled the navy to maintain a carrier off the Indochina coast almost continually, a task eased greatly by the arrival of another ex-American light carrier, the *Bois Belleau*, on the line in July 1954. The three ships convincingly demonstrated the value of carriers for close support operations, since their mobility made it easier for them to apply their force over an extended area at closer range and at short notice. The navy's final carrier deployment during the French war in Indochina was that of the *Bois Belleau*, from January to June 1956, marking the end of a long campaign that was French carrier aviation's baptism of fire.

While the colonial war in Indochina was in full swing, a fresh conflict broke out in the Far East with the invasion of South Korea by North Korean troops on June 25, 1950. Two carriers, the United States Navy's *Valley Forge* and the Royal Navy's *Triumph,* constituted the striking arm of the only United Nations force immediately available to intervene. They were in action by July 3, when the *Triumph* launched a strike against the North Korean airfield at Haeju, while the *Valley Forge* struck Pyongyang, some sixty miles further north. This marked the beginning of the struggle to halt the advancing North Korean forces that relied very heavily on effective air support for the efforts of ground troops. The two existing carriers, joined by the *Philippine Sea* and two escort carriers, the *Badoeng Strait* and the *Sicily* (embarking Marine Corps Corsair fighter bomber squadrons), contributed a major part of the tonnage delivered, largely because their close proximity enabled their aircraft to trade fuel for ordnance, and the combined efforts succeeded in halting the enemy advance at the Naktong River on August 18.

These same carriers, reinforced by the arrival of another *Essex* class ship, the *Boxer,* provided air cover for General Douglas MacArthur's bold stroke, the landings at Inchon in the rear of the North Korean forces on September 15, 1950, and the advance that drove them back to the border at the 38th Parallel by September 27. The United States Joint Chiefs of Staff authorized General MacArthur's forces to press on across the border and United Nations forces reached the Yalu River by November, provoking a massive counterstroke by Chinese troops that began on November 25. During the retreat of United Nations forces that ensued, United States Navy and British Commonwealth carriers conducted very intensive ground attack operations in their support, especially in covering the fighting retreat of the 1st Marine Division from the Chosin reservoir to the port of Hungnam. This intense activity continued as Chinese and North Korean forces drove south and retook Seoul, only to be driven back by a counteroffensive that stabilized the front virtually along the 38th Parallel once more. During the two years of stalemate that ensued until the eventual signing of a cease-fire on July 27, 1953, carriers of the British Commonwealth and United States navies continued to provide close support for United Nations ground forces but also engaged in a prolonged aerial campaign against North Korean strategic targets, such as dams, power generating facilities, industrial plants, and transportation infrastructure and systems, with the objective of applying pressure to bring an end to the conflict. Alone, carrier air power was insufficient to accomplish the goal of achieving victory, but together with other arms it enabled the United Nations to attain an uneasy peace in Korea.

United States Navy carriers returned to South-East Asia in force to engage in their longest and most intensive continuous operation, the war in Vietnam. Between August 2, 1964 and August 15, 1973, twenty-one carriers (sixteen attack carriers and five antisubmarine warfare carriers) deployed to Yankee Station in the Gulf of Tonkin, most of them more than once as they made a total of eighty-six war cruises. The material and human costs of this nine-year campaign were very great: 530 aircraft and helicopters were lost in action and a further 329 destroyed in accidents, 377 aircrew were killed in action, 179 became prisoners of war, and 64 were listed as missing in action. The conflict began with action against North Vietnamese motor torpedo boats on August 2 and escalated into strikes against their bases three days later in retaliation for what was thought to be further attacks but now almost certainly can be determined to be mistaken identification of radar returns in poor weather conditions. Nevertheless, reaction in the United States was sufficient to cause Congress to pass the Gulf of Tonkin Resolution on August 10 that gave President Lyndon B. Johnson the authority to commit United States forces to a full-scale war in Vietnam.

The initial phase of the aerial campaign entailed interdiction operations against lines of communication from North Vietnam to the Viet Cong guerillas in the south. Early in 1965 it expanded into a protracted large-scale offensive against North Vietnamese infrastructure that continued until late 1968, when it was suspended until late 1971, in the hope that a peace might be negotiated. During the lull in offensive operations over North Vietnam, the navy committed its air groups to operations against the Ho Chi Minh Trail along the Laotian border and ground support missions over South Vietnam. In an effort to restart peace negotiations and force a resolution, the navy returned to a full scale offensive over North Vietnam in late 1971 that lasted until the January 23, 1973, peace agreement was signed in Paris, although operations over Laos and Cambodia continued until the United States Congress ordered an end to all combat operations in South-East Asia by August 15.

On April 2, 1982, Argentinian forces landed on the Falkland Islands and South Georgia in an attempt to solve by force a long-running dispute with Britain over their ownership. They rapidly overran the tiny British forces stationed there but this initial success provoked a substantial reaction from Britain in the form of an expeditionary force sent to retake these South Atlantic islands. The operation depended virtually entirely on air support provided by two carriers, the *Hermes* and the *Invincible,* and their embarked Sea Harrier fighters and Sea King helicopters, enhanced by additional Royal Air Force Harriers operating from aircraft carriers for the first time.

The Royal Navy's carrier aircraft went into action against Argentinian forces on the Falklands on May 1. The British had anticipated that they would encounter Argentinian naval and aerial opposition but, in fact, the threat of Royal Navy submarines sufficed to keep surface ships away after the sinking of the cruiser *General Belgrano* on May 2, and the prime threat to the British invasion force came from aircraft operating from the Argentinian mainland. The Sea Harriers proved more successful as interceptor fighters than prewar pundits had anticipated, but the Royal Navy's complete lack of airborne early warning equipment proved a major handicap and enabled the Argentinians to strike significant blows to the ships carrying the landing force and their escorting destroyers and frigates, sinking two destroyers, two frigates, two landing ships, and an auxiliary merchant ship, and damaging eleven other warships. Nevertheless, the carriers were able to remain on station to defend the invasion fleet, support substantial ground attack missions, and cover the landings of troops on May 21 and their subsequent advance to recapture Port Stanley and receive the Argentinian surrender on June 14.

The Iraqi invasion of Kuwait on August 2, 1990, led to a major international operation to expel the invaders that began the counterattack, operation Desert Storm (for United States forces) on January 17, 1991. Eight American carriers and seven helicopter assault ships plus the French carrier *Clémenceau* formed the air striking force of the international fleet that took part in this operation. The ground assault began on February 24 after an intensive air campaign using substantial quantities of precision strike ordnance against the Iraqi forces. It led to the expulsion of the Iraqis within four days and the negotiation of a cease-fire on March 1. Similarly massive carrier forces were assembled for the United States assault on the Taliban in Afghanistan after the suicide airliner attacks on the World Trade Center in New York and the Pentagon in Washington on September 11, 2001. Operation Enduring Freedom was launched on October 7, 2001. No less than ten United States Navy carriers and four helicopter assault ships took part and demonstrated the extended reach of naval aviation, for Afghanistan is totally land-locked. The later invasion of Iraq (operation Iraqi Freedom to United States forces) involved yet another large concentration of carrier air power: one British and eight American carriers plus one British and six Ameri-

can helicopter assault ships took a major role in the assault that began on March 19, 2003, and was declared complete on April 14. In
both these later operations the most notable feature of the aerial assault was its almost exclusive reliance on the use of "smart"
weapons, precision guided bombs and missiles, to achieve incompa-
rably greater accuracy and economy of operation than was possible
in earlier conflicts.

In addition to their deployment for full-scale combat operations,
aircraft carriers also took part in many missions short of war. Aircraft carriers from the United States Navy's Seventh Fleet were deployed to the Taiwan Strait in 1955 and again in 1958 during two
confrontations between China and the Chinese Nationalists over
the ownership of strategically important islands of Quemoy and
Matsu in the Strait. Their presence sufficed to cause the Chinese to
back away from outright assaults on the islands and stabilized the
situation, at least temporarily. In the summer of 1962, tension flared
in the Persian Gulf when newly-independent Kuwait was threatened
with invasion and annexation by Iraq. The British government re-
acted quickly, sending the *Bulwark,* a commando carrier, from Sin-
gapore to the Gulf with Royal Marine assault troops and their associated helicopters, and the fleet carriers *Victorious* and *Centaur* to
provide air cover and fighter defense. This rapid reaction had the effect of stopping the Iraqi intervention in its tracks and all British
forces departed the region within three months. The United States
also deployed attack carriers and helicopter assault ships in the
Caribbean to enforce a naval blockade of Cuba during the 1961
missile crisis and the Royal Navy similarly deployed carriers off
Mozambique to enforce a blockade of trade with Rhodesia after that
country's unilateral declaration of independence in November 1965.

The Mediterranean Sea became the arena for much action short
of war during the 1980s. American confrontation of Libya in the
Gulf of Sidra led to incidents on August 19, 1981, and January 4,
1989, during which aircraft from United States Navy Sixth Fleet
carriers engaged with Libyan aircraft. In the earlier incident, two F-
14A Tomcats from the *Nimitz* were fired on by a pair of Libyan Su-
22 fighters and destroyed them, while in the later incident, Tomcats
from the *John F. Kennedy* engaged and shot down two MiG-23 aircraft. The civil war in Lebanon that began in 1975 also led to outside intervention at various stages as it unfolded. United States
Marines, together with French and Italian forces, landed in Beirut
on August 20, 1982, in an attempt to stabilize the situation in the
country. Both American and French carriers provided cover for this

operation and maintained a strong presence off the Lebanese coast thereafter. On April 18, 1983, the American Embassy was struck by a suicide attack that killed sixty-three people, leading President Ronald Reagan to order retaliatory attacks. The French Embassy was bombarded on September 9, to which the French carrier *Foch* responded with air strikes against the presumed artillery positions responsible. Then, on October 23, the barracks housing both the United States Marines and French paratroopers were attacked with massive suicide truck bombs that killed 241 Marines and 58 para-troopers. Aircraft from the *Clémenceau,* the *John F. Kennedy,* and the *Independence* undertook retaliatory raids against targets in the Bekaa Valley, as well as undertaking evacuations of troops from Beirut. Both navies continued to operate carriers off the Lebanese coast for some considerable time after the withdrawal of French and American troops.

The prolonged war between Iran and Iraq that raged from 1980 to 1988 led to substantial carrier deployments to the Persian Gulf, especially after the Iranians initiated their campaign against neutral tankers transporting crude oil from the Iraqi terminal at Khargh Is-land. During the so-called "tanker war" from 1984 to 1987 both American and French carriers operated in the Gulf, providing air cover for tankers and their own surface forces. American carriers also remained in the Persian Gulf after the end of the war to liberate Kuwait, participating in the enforcement of the "no-fly" zone over southern Iraq until 2002. British, French, and American carriers also operated regularly in the Adriatic Sea during the various stages of the conflicts within the former Yugoslavia from 1993 to 2000.

The French, the British, and especially the American experience of carrier operations off Indo-China and Korea after World War II wrought a profound change in their navies' perception of the opera-tional parameters within which carriers would operate in the future. During World War II, carriers became the primary striking arm of oceanic fleets, launching concentrated forces to attack and sink en-emy warships and surface vessels across distances greatly amplified above those possible with surface weaponry. The Indo-Chinese and Korean experience rendered this paradigm obsolete. Instead, carrier air power became the supreme manifestation of the potential for mobile force projection against an enemy's heartland, especially as the unrefueled range of large carrier strike aircraft expanded. Rather than being an aberration, as some observers and even some partici-pants considered it, this experience presaged the maturation of car-rier air power as the preeminent quick-reaction force capable of rapidly bringing devastating concentrated firepower against significant national assets. Even today, despite the great advances in aerial refueling that have enabled land-base aircraft to range around the globe, aircraft carriers consistently demonstrate the economical, flexible, and effective projection of overwhelming force throughout the world.

CHAPTER FIVE

Joint Operations

ONE OF THE MOST IMPORTANT ASSETS of aircraft carriers that has made them such strikingly effective warships is their flexibility. Since their striking and self-defense powers reside in their air groups, changes in the composition or types of aircraft embarked can suit carriers for very different missions and endow them with very varied capabilities. Such modifications are relatively simple to complete on a temporary basis and do not require drastic changes to accomplish a more permanent conversion. Nowhere is this more apparent than in the adaptation of aircraft carriers for direct participation in amphibious operations as transports for large numbers of troops and platforms for assault helicopters transporting the troops ashore. Navies operating such helicopter assault ships have found that the same carriers are readily adaptable for service in antisubmarine warfare operations or as sea control vessels with little or no structural changes simply by altering the composition or types of aircraft on board. This great flexibility suits aircraft carriers very well for operations in the world's littorals that seem likely to become ever more the dominant environment for future conflicts.

UNITED STATES AMPHIBIOUS ASSAULT
CARRIER DEVELOPMENT

As early as 1946 the United States Marine Corps concluded that, in the face of the threat from atomic weapons, amphibious landing operations as conducted during World War II would be prohibitively dangerous, since just a few bombs could wipe out the concentrations of shipping and the beachheads that characterized such assaults, while dispersing shipping and troops risked a defeat in detail. Further analysis suggested alternative approaches: parachuting infantry and support weapons from large transport aircraft, gliderborne assaults, attacking from specialized transport submarines, or landing troops and equipment via helicopter from dispersed surface transports. Of these options only helicopter assault was attractive and became the main focus of the Marine Corps' efforts.

The major problem facing the concept was the limited load-carrying capacity of existing helicopters. A study in early 1951 determined that a divisional assault would require twenty small assault carriers (escort carrier conversions each carrying twenty helicopters) to accomplish. A number of exercises demonstrated the basic soundness of helicopter assault but the constraints of the shipbuilding budget prevented quick or extensive action to accommodate the Marines' needs and it was not until July 20, 1956, that the first escort carrier conversion, the *Thetis Bay,* commissioned. It accommodated 938 troops in berthing spaces created at the forward end of the hangar and had its after elevator enlarged and the end of the flight deck cut away to enable operation of larger helicopters. Weight compensation required landing all guns except eight twin 40mm mounts.

The *Thetis Bay* was an experimental project to further validate the concept. Meanwhile, the Marine Corps continued to press for the ships it needed for operational deployment. The cost of the numbers of ships required led to a dual track approach that developed a purpose-built ship while simultaneously exploring options for conversions of suitable existing warships. Eventually it became clear that the only suitable vessels available in adequate numbers, escort carriers of the *Commencement Bay* class, were too expensive to convert and had too little remaining service life and the choice was made for new construction. As an interim measure, four *Essex* class carriers, the *Boxer,* the *Lake Champlain,* the *Princeton,* and the *Valley Forge,* that had been replaced by more sophisticated *Essex* class ships for antisubmarine warfare duties were selected for conversion into assault ships. In the event, the *Lake Champlain* was not converted, largely because of a shortage of seamen to man it. The other three ships received austere conversions that deleted all guns except two twin and two single 5-inch mounts and removed four of eight boilers, cutting speed to 25 knots. They could accommodate thirty helicopters and 3,000 troops.

The purpose-built ships of the *Iwo Jima* class were smaller, much more economical to operate, and far better arranged internally for troop comfort and cohesion. They could operate twenty helicopters and embarked 2,000 troops and soon demonstrated their ability to undertake extended deployments. Amphibious force commanders appreciated the substantial advance the *Iwo Jima* class ships represented but were critical of their limitations, particularly their lack of any facilities for landing craft which made them wholly reliant on their helicopters to land or disembark their troops.

It was suggested that an *Iwo Jima* class hull lengthened by 52 feet could carry twelve LCVPs (Landing Craft Vehicle and Personnel) and two LCPLs (Landing Craft Personnel Light), but the combination of unacceptable instability problems and concerns for delays in delivery put the idea to rest. Instead, a new design emerged that combined the helicopter assault capabilities of the *Iwo Jima* class with the integral wet dock and assault craft launching facilities of a landing ship dock. The price for this very capable design was a vessel of more than double the tonnage of the previous *Iwo Jima* class ships. Nine ships of the *Tarawa* class were ordered on May 28, 1968, all from the Ingalls Shipbuilding Corporation in Pascagoula in conformity with Secretary of Defense Robert S. McNamara's single-source policy, which he believed would provide substantial cost savings in shipbuilding programs. In fact four ships had to be cancelled on January 20, 1971, due to massive cost overruns, so only five ships of the *Tarawa* class were delivered.

As the *Tarawa* class entered service the Marine Corps was gaining experience operating its VSTOL (Vertical or Short Take Off and Landing) Harrier aircraft and began deploying them aboard these vessels. The following group of assault ships, the *Wasp* class, therefore had improved facilities for operating Harriers, as well as upgraded self-defense armament and a modified wet dock configured to handle air cushion landing craft (LCAC) in addition to conventional assault craft. They also received improved facilities to suit them for deployment in the sea control carrier role. Seven ships of this type were funded between 1984 and 1996. An eighth vessel, the *Makin Island*, is under construction. It is a unique modified version, powered by gas turbine engines, and incorporating all electric auxiliary machinery, an advanced machinery control system, water-mist fire protection arrangements, and upgraded command, communications, and control systems.

Nowhere is the Marine Corps's commitment to vertical envelopment more obvious than in the assault ships of the *Wasp* class, which are larger than the World War II–era *Essex* class carriers. From the beginning, the Marine Corps envisaged deploying carrier-like vessels, whose attraction lies in their inherent flexibility to accommodate different configurations of air group and troop equipment. This flexibility also greatly assisted the Marine Corps in gaining acceptance for their requirements within the United States Navy, since the vessels they envisaged could also undertake other missions, such as sea control. In many ways this multimission capability is central to the arrangements currently envisaged for future assault ships (planned to enter service beginning in 2014), for which aircraft facilities are to be further emphasized at the expense of the wet dock feature of current vessels. Some design concepts even incorporate a "twin-track" arrangement: a central superstructure flanked by two parallel flight decks that will permit simultaneous operation of helicopters and VSTOL aircraft.

BRITISH AMPHIBIOUS ASSAULT CARRIER DEVELOPMENT

The Royal Navy was an early enthusiast of helicopter operation at sea and, as early as 1953, envisaged completely replacing fixed-wing antisubmarine warfare aircraft with large helicopters. It followed United States Marine Corps's progress with helicopter assault landing experiments with keen interest. By 1955 the Royal Navy had employed light aircraft carriers as troop transports on a number of occasions and its chief of amphibious warfare, Major General C. F. Phillips, Royal Marines, requested development of both large and small troop carrying helicopters. The Admiralty responded by approving the start of work on designing a conversion of a light fleet carrier into an amphibious assault ship, termed a commando carrier in the Royal Navy, in July 1956.

Almost immediately, before work on a full-scale conversion had begun, the concept was tested in action. The British government decided to intervene in response to Egyptian Premier Gamal Abdul Nasser's decision on July 26, 1956, to nationalize the Suez Canal. French and British officials drew up plans to launch a joint amphibious invasion to take over the Canal. As part of the invasion task force, two British light carriers, the *Ocean* and the *Theseus*, were hastily modified (in four days) to carry a full commando of 450 troops and twenty-two helicopters to transport them ashore. The mass helicopter assault concept was tested in a successful exercise just prior to their departure for Suez on October 12. Three weeks later the two carriers launched the first such assault against enemy opposition with complete success.

The success of the operation and the obvious utility of such techniques for imperial policing duties led to the permanent conversion of two later light carriers of the *Centaur* class, the *Albion* and the *Bulwark,* into commando carriers. They were stripped of most guns and fitted with accommodations for 900 troops. Sixteen helicopters provided troop lift, and four landing craft suspended from davits, transported heavy equipment ashore. Both ships were in service by 1962. A decade later their more modern semi-sister, the *Hermes,* was similarly converted when it was withdrawn from frontline carrier service as part of the run-down of Royal Navy fixed wing operation mandated by the 1966 Defence Review.

All the converted commando carriers were out of service by the early 1980s without direct replacements, although the support carriers of the *Invincible* class could readily convert to the commando role by embarking up to 1,000 troops and the assault helicopters to transport them. On September 1, 1993, however, the Royal Navy ordered a new helicopter assault ship, the *Ocean,* to compensate finally for the decommissioning of the dedicated commando carriers. The hull design was based on that of the *Invincible* class but the ship itself was constructed to Lloyd's Register specifications for similar size merchant vessels except for those features specifically military in nature, a decision that substantially reduced the cost of construction. The *Ocean* is smaller and slower than its American contemporaries and, unlike them does not have a wet dock for launching its landing craft.

OTHER AMPHIBIOUS ASSAULT
CARRIER DEVELOPMENTS

No other navies have deployed dedicated helicopter assault ships similar to those of the United States and Royal navies. Nevertheless, some navies have incorporated troop accommodations and facilities for operating assault helicopters into the designs of aviation vessels intended to fulfill other primary roles, illustrating once again the mission flexibility of carriers that makes them such effective warships.

The French *Jeanne d'Arc* was constructed primarily as a cadet training ship to replace the prewar training light cruiser of the same name. From the outset it was decided it would have a dual role and be equipped as an antisubmarine warfare helicopter carrier with a large flight deck aft and the superstructure concentrated forward. As the process continued the designers quickly realized that with minor adjustments to internal arrangements the accommodation spaces intended for cadets could be adapted for troops. As finally commissioned in 1964 the *Jeanne d'Arc* could accommodate up to 700 troops as an amphibious assault ship. It also was equipped to operate up to eight of the French Navy's standard Super Frelon heavy assault helicopters. In addition, it incorporated dedicated amphibious assault and antisubmarine warfare combat information center spaces and a helicopter flight deck operations control bridge in the forward superstructure.

In the 1990s the French Navy began planning to generate a replacement for the *Jeanne d'Arc*. The initial concept envisaged an improved version of the existing dock landing ships of the *Foudre* class but further discussion led to the decision to design a larger type of landing ship with a full length flight deck and hangar accommodation for assault helicopters. The final design is very similar in size to the British landing ship, the *Ocean*, but more capable in that it incorporates the well dock that is a feature of similar, though much larger, American helicopter assault ships. The two ships of the *Mistral* class are unusual in employing diesel-electric propulsion. The diesels generate electricity to drive podded thruster units and a bow thruster, giving the ships the potential for remarkable maneuverability and the ability to maintain fixed positions for extended periods.

The Italian Navy's new carrier the *Conte di Cavour* was originally conceived as an amphibious assault ship along the lines of the United States Navy's *Tarawa* class, though somewhat smaller. As the design evolved, carrier features suiting the ship for strike and sea control missions came to predominate. The wet dock for landing craft was eliminated and replaced by two 60-ton capacity ramps for vehicles. As finally configured, the *Conte di Cavour* will operate primarily in the sea control role with a mixed VSTOL fighter-bomber and antisubmarine helicopter air group, but will be readily adaptable to operate as a strike carrier with fighter-bombers only or as an amphibious assault ship, carrying up to 450 troops and assault helicopters to land them.

The use of carrier-type vessels as amphibious assault ships is a particularly powerful reflection of the inherent mission flexibility of such warships. The operations of the *Ocean* and the *Theseus* at Suez in November 1956 (and the United States Navy's LANTPHIPEX 1-58 fourteen months later in which helicopters from the antisubmarine warfare carriers *Tarawa* and *Valley Forge* and the attack carrier *Forrestal* transported a complete United States Marine Corps regimental landing team ashore) illustrated that carriers could undertake successful amphibious assault missions with very limited alterations other than embarking appropriate aircraft. Specialized ships certainly simplified such missions but were not a prerequisite for success.

AMPHIBIOUS ASSAULT SHIP AIRCRAFT

The United States Marine Corps first used Sikorsky HRS helicopters as its assault aircraft, operating them from land bases in Korea during the conflict there and also for trials of the vertical envelopment concept from escort carriers. Their payload of eight full-armed Marines, top speed of 101 miles per hour, and range of 370 miles made this strictly a temporary measure pending the arrival of purpose-designed assault helicopters. These were Sikorsky's HR2S helicopters, powered by twin 1,900 horsepower Pratt & Whitney Double Wasp radial engines that gave them a top speed of 130 miles per hour, and range of 147 miles, and a payload of 20 fully-armed troops. The HR2Ss were not entirely satisfactory and were soon supplemented by smaller single-engined Sikorsky HUS machines. Their 1,525 horsepower Wright Cyclone radial engines gave them a top speed of 123 miles per hour, a range of 182 miles, and a payload of up to 12 fully-armed troops.

The second generation of Marine Corps assault helicopters began entering service in 1965 to 1966, with the arrival of the Boeing Vertol CH-46 Sea Knght and Sikorsky CH-53 Sea Stallion. Both were fitted with twin turboshaft engines that endowed them with much improved speed, range, and payload. The CH-46 used 1,400 shaft horsepower General Electric T-58 engines to attain a top speed of 166 miles per hour and a range of 230 miles, and could carry up to 16 assault troops, while the CH-53, with 3,925 shaft horsepower General Electric T-64 turboshaft engines, reached 196 miles per hour, had a range of 257 miles, and could carry up to 38 troops. The CH-53 was supplanted by a three-engined version, the CH-53E Super Stallion, which entered service in 1981. Its 4,380 shaft horsepower General Electric T-64 turboshaft engines gave it a top speed of 196 miles per hour, a range of 621 miles, and a maximum capacity of 55 troops. The planned replacement for the CH-46 is the Boeing-Bell MV-22 Osprey tilt-rotor machine, which is still in development but will probably enter service in 2007. It uses two 6,150 shaft horsepower Allison T-406 turboshaft engines to drive swiveling tilt-rotors at the wing tips. Cruising speed will be 250 miles per hour, range will be 550 miles, and payload up to 24 fully armed troops.

Operations in Vietnam quickly demonstrated the need for escorting attack helicopters to provide close support during and after an assault. The Marine Corps therefore adopted a version of the United States Army's AH-1 Cobra to fulfill this mission requirement. The AH-1J was armed with a multibarreled 20mm cannon in a chin turret and could carry a variety of ground attack weapons on the stub wings. Its successor, the AH-1T could carry TOW antitank missiles and incorporated several airframe improvements, and was followed by the AH-1W, which featured twin engines to compensate for the weight gains of the earlier model and also improve survivability. These machines are now being upgraded to AH-1Z standard with four-bladed rotors and a night targeting system.

The Royal Navy initially operated a license-built version of Sikorsky's S-55, the Westland Whirlwind, which was used at Suez and aboard the *Bulwark* when the ship first commissioned. Their 750-horsepower Alvis Leonides Major radial engines gave them a top speed of 109 miles per hour, a range of 335 miles, and the capacity to carry 8 fully armed troops. These aircraft quickly were replaced with the Westland Wessex Commando, a licensed variant of the Sikorsky S-58 that was powered by a 1,450 shaft horsepower Napier Gazelle turboshaft engine instead of the American machine's Wright Cyclone radial engine. By 1964 a dedicated assault version, the Wessex HU.5 with twin 1,350 shaft horsepower Bristol Siddeley Gnome turboshaft engines was in service. These Wessex machines could carry up to 16 fully-armed troops at a top speed of 135 miles per hour. Additional fuel and more efficient engines endowed the later version with a range of 478 miles compared with the 390-mile range of the earlier Wessex version. The Westland Sea King HC.4 Commando, a specialized variant of the license-built Sikorsky S-61, entered service in 1980. Its twin 1,400 shaft horsepower Bristol Siddeley Gnome turboshaft engines gave it a top speed of 140 miles per hour, a range of 400 miles, and a troop carrying capacity of 28 fully-armed Marines. The Royal Marines also have used smaller

Westland Scout and Lynx helicopters as antitank missile platforms and gunships to support heliborne assault landings.

The principal French assault helicopter since the 1960s has been the Aérospatiale SA.321 Super Frelon. This large machine, powered by three 1,200 shaft horsepower Turboméca 3C turboshaft engines, attains a top speed of 170 miles per hour, has a range of 440 miles, and can carry up to 38 fully-equipped troops. Its replacement, the Aérospatiale-MBB-Agusta NH-90, is powered by two Rolls-Royce/Turboméca 322 turboshaft engines, giving it a top speed of 180 miles per hour, a range of 420 miles, and capacity for 20 fully-armed assault troops. The Italian Navy is introducing an armed assault transport version of the European EH.101 for service aboard the *Conte di Cavour*. It is powered by three 2,050 shaft horsepower General Electric T700 turboshaft engines, giving it a cruising speed of 170 miles per hour and a range of 625 miles, and accommodation for up to 24 fully-equipped troops.

AMPHIBIOUS ASSAULT SHIP AVIATORS

From the outset, the air groups aboard United States Navy amphibious assault carriers have comprised Marine Corps squadrons, either helicopter units or attack squadrons equipped with VSTOL fighter-bombers. Marine Corps aviators followed the same flying training program as their United States Navy counterparts with two important exceptions: regardless of their avenue of entry, all passed through the Basic School at Quantico, Virginia, where they underwent indoctrination in Marine Corps leadership skills, and their operational training was also within dedicated Marine Corps training squadrons. This system created a powerful cohesion between the aviators and the troops they delivered to the beach.

The arrangements aboard British amphibious assault ships were rather different. All the assault helicopter units were squadrons of the Royal Navy's Fleet Air Arm though, in general, a bare majority of their aviators were officers in the Royal Marines. Since 1995, one of the Royal Navy's specialized assault helicopter units, 847 Squadron, has been wholly crewed by Royal Marines. Both Royal Navy and Royal Marines aviators went through the same training system. Again, there was an important difference for Royal Marines, who were required to complete the regular commando officer's training program and spend twelve months commanding a troop (a unit equivalent to a platoon) before becoming eligible for flying aptitude assessment prior to beginning flight training.

AMPHIBIOUS ASSAULT SHIP OPERATIONS

Although the United States Navy had conducted some experimental exercises earlier, the first use of helicopters from carriers to conduct an amphibious assault against opposition was by the Royal Navy at Suez in 1956. Two light carriers, the *Ocean* and the *Theseus,* were rapidly converted between September 25 and September 29 to accommodate a complete 450-man Royal Marine commando and to operate 22 helicopters, a joint force of Royal Navy, Royal Air Force, and Army machines, to land them. After validating the concept during a successful exercise in the United Kingdom, the two carriers joined the Anglo-French fleet assembled for the operation against Egyptian forces around the Suez Canal. On November 6, 1956, helicopters aboard the carriers landed all 450 troops from 45 Commandos in the city center of Port Said within ninety minutes. The commandos successfully linked up that afternoon with paratroops who had been dropped alongside the Suez Canal itself, consolidating their position there prior to the cease-fire that went into effect at midnight the same day.

The success of these extemporized assault carriers led to the Admiralty's decision to undertake permanent conversions of two later light carriers, the *Albion* and the *Bulwark,* into commando carriers. Both ships operated extensively "east of Suez" in support of British efforts to hold on to its empire. The *Bulwark* formed part of the British force deployed to the Persian Gulf in a successful operation to deter an attempt by Iraq to invade Kuwait in the summer of 1961 (operation Vantage) then, together with its sister the *Albion,* participated in the extended British campaign confronting Indonesian efforts to take over Brunei and Borneo between late 1962 and 1966. The *Albion* also covered the British withdrawal from Aden in late 1967 while the *Bulwark* was deploying its commandos to prevent infiltration into eastern Malaysia. Britain's withdrawal from its Far Eastern imperial holdings brought the two commando carriers back to European waters, where they engaged primarily in exercises to prepare for a potential conflict with the Soviet Union fought in the Norwegian littoral.

Shortly after the British commando carriers began their operations in the South China Sea, the United States Navy commenced deploying its helicopter assault ships further north in the same sea, carrying Marine Corps amphibious forces to conduct operations along the coast of South Vietnam. Initially, these were converted *Essex* class carriers but soon the new purpose-built ships of the *Iwo Jima* class supplemented and later replaced the earlier vessels. Between 1964 and 1973 the United States Navy's Seventh Fleet almost continuously maintained two or more Amphibious Ready Groups, each built around one or more helicopter assault ships, off the Vietnamese coast. During this period the Marine Corps undertook several hundred amphibious operations against Vietcong guerilla concentrations and regular North Vietnamese Army forces in South Vietnam, using combined assaults by marines transported by assault helicopters and landing craft and, often, other marines advancing overland.

American helicopter assault ships have been very active participants in the United States' major and lesser conflicts since 1990. No less than five of the *Iwo Jima* class and two of the *Tarawa* class took part in operations Desert Shield and Desert Storm in 1990 to 1991 that first protected the Arabian Peninsula states against further threats from Iraq and then expelled Iraq from Kuwait. Others operated extensively in the Red and Adriatic seas between 1993 and 2000, conducting missions in Somalia and the former Yugoslavia. Operation Enduring Freedom between October 2001 and March 2002 against the Taliban in Afghanistan saw four helicopter assault ships, the *Nassau* of the *Tarawa* class and the *Bataan*, the *Bon Homme Richard*, and the *Kearsarge* of the *Wasp* class, participating, demonstrating the reach of Marine Corps heliborne attack forces, since Afghanistan is entirely land-locked. During the subsequent invasion of Iraq (operation Iraqi Freedom) that began on March 19, 2003, one British (the *Ocean*) and six American helicopter assault ships (the *Nassau* of the *Tarawa* class and the *Bataan*, the *Bon Homme Richard*, the *Boxer*, the *Iwo Jima*, and the *Kearsarge* of the *Wasp* class) formed part of the Coalition invasion force, the largest such concentration to date, and several have continued to maintain a regular presence in the Persian Gulf to provide quick reaction support for ongoing land operations in Iraq.

The promise of aircraft carriers in joint operations has been amply fulfilled by their successful conduct of such missions during the past fifty years. Helicopter assault ships have demonstrated their flexibility both in combat and in strenuous exercises. This flexibility is very attractive to a broad spectrum of navies, as the spurt of construction during the past decade in Britain, France, and Italy demonstrates, and is such that even a nation like Belgium, with no tradition of carrier operation, is seriously contemplating the prospect of purchasing a helicopter assault ship of the French *Mistral* class. Clearly, these smaller ships cannot project the sheer striking power of big fleet carriers, but they are extremely well suited for operations in the littorals, where so many of the world's conflicts have occurred during the past half-century, and which seem most likely to remain the primary environment for future wars.

Aircraft Carriers
of the World

ORIGINS AND EARLY DEVELOPMENT
OF THE AIRCRAFT CARRIER

France	*Foudre* (1912)
France	Converted Cross-Channel Packets (1915)
	Nord
	Pas-de-Calais
Germany	*Stuttgart* (1918)
Russia	*Almaz* (1915)
Russia	Converted Merchantmen (1915)
	Imperator Nikolai I
	Imperator Alexandr I
United Kingdom	*Hermes* (1913)
United Kingdom	*Ark Royal* (1914)
United Kingdom	Converted Cross-Channel and Isle of Man Packets (1914)
	Empress
	Riviera
	Engadine
	Ben-My-Chree
	Vindex
	Manxman
	Campania (1915)
United Kingdom	Converted Mail Steamers (1917)
	Nairana
	Pegasus
	Furious (1917)

| United Kingdom | *Argus* (1918) |
| United Kingdom | *Vindictive* (1918) |

THE AIRCRAFT CARRIER MATURES

France	*Béarn* (1917)
Japan	*Hosho* (1922)
Japan	*Akagi* (1927)
Japan	*Kaga* (1928)
Japan	*Ryujo* (1933)
Japan	*Soryu* Class (1937)
United Kingdom	*Hermes* (1923)
United Kingdom	*Eagle* (1924)
United Kingdom	*Courageous* Class (1928)
United Kingdom	*Ark Royal* (1938)
United Kingdom	*Illustrious* Class (1940)
United States	*Langley* 1922)
United States	*Lexington* Class (1927)
United States	*Ranger* (1934)
United States	*Yorktown* Class (1937)
United States	*Wasp* (1940)

CAPITAL SHIPS

Germany	*Graf Zeppelin* Class
Japan	Converted Fleet Auxiliaries (1940)
	Shoho Class
	Chitose Class
	Riyuho
Japan	*Shokaku* Class (1941)
Japan	*Hiyo* Class (1942)
Japan	*Taiho* (1944)
Japan	*Unryu* Class (1944)
Japan	*Shinano* (1944)
Japan	Merchantmen Converted to Escort Carriers (1941)
	Taiyo Class
	Kaiyo
	Shinyo

United Kingdom	*Indomitable* (1941)
United Kingdom	*Unicorn* (1943)
United Kingdom	*Implacable* Class (1944)
United Kingdom	*Colossus* Class (1944)
United Kingdom	Merchantmen Converted to Escort Carriers (1941)
	Audacity
	Activity
	Pretoria Castle
	Nairana Class
	Campania
United Kingdom	Merchant Aircraft Carriers (1943)
	Empire MacAlpine Class
	Rapana Class
	Empire MacAndrew Class
	Empire MacRae Class
	Empire Mackay
	Empire MacColl
	Empire MacMahon
	Empire MacCabe
United States	*Essex* Class (1942)
United States	*Independence* Class (1943)
United States	*Midway* Class (1945)
United States	*Saipan* Class (1946)
United States	C3-type Merchantmen Converted to Escort Carriers (1941)
	Long Island
	Archer Class
	Bogue Class
	Charger Class
United States	*Sangamon* Class (1942)
United States	*Prince William* Class (1943)
United States	*Casablanca* Class (1943)
United States	*Commencement Bay* Class (1944)

COLD WAR

France	*Clémenceau* Class (1961)
France	*Jeanne d'Arc* (1964)
France	*Charles de Gaulle* (2000)

Italy	*Giuseppe Garibaldi* 1985)
Soviet Union	*Moskva* Class (1967)
Soviet Union	*Kiev* Class (1975)
Soviet Union	*Admiral Flota Sovetskogo Soyuza Gorshkov* (1987)
Soviet Union	*Kuznetsov* Class (1991)
Spain	*Principe de Asturias* (1988)
Thailand	*Chakri Nareubet* (1997)
United Kingdom	*Eagle* Class (1951)
United Kingdom	*Centaur* Class (1953)
United Kingdom	*Victorious* (1958)
United Kingdom	*Hermes* (1959)
United Kingdom	*Invincible* Class (1980)
United States	*Essex* Class Reconstructions (1955)
United States	*Midway* Class Reconstructions (1958)
United States	*Forrestal* Class (1955)
United States	*Kitty Hawk* Class (1961)
United States	*Enterprise* (1961)
United States	*Nimitz* Class (1975)
Various nations	*Majestic* Class Carriers
Australia	*Sydney*
Australia	*Melbourne*
Canada	*Magnificent*
Canada	*Bonaventure*
India	*Vikrant*
United Kingdom	*Leviathan*

JOINT OPERATIONS

France	*Mistral* Class (2005)
Italy	*Cavour* (2007)
United Kingdom	*Ocean* (1999)
United States	*Iwo Jima* Class (1961)
United States	*Tarawa* Class (1975)
United States	*Wasp* Class (1989)

DATA TABLES EXPLANATORY NOTE

Displacement: "full load" tonnage is the ship's displacement with a full crew and all stores, fuel, water, and ammunition embarked. "Standard" tonnage excludes fuel and boiler feed water. "Gross" tonnage measures the ship's total internal volume, and usually appears when the vessel was originally in merchant service.

Dimensions: overall length, beam, and draft. "Mean" draft is the immersion of the hull in normal service conditions (usually with two-thirds of fuel loaded).

Machinery: for explanation of types, please refer to the glossary.

Bunkerage & Range: where known this shows fuel capacity in tons and range at economical cruising speed in nautical miles (6,080 feet rather than 5,280 feet).

Armament: all weapons are low-angle guns capable of engaging surface targets only unless specifically shown as antiaircraft (AA) or dual-purpose (DP) types. All are single mounts unless otherwise indicated.

ORIGINS AND
EARLY DEVELOPMENT OF
THE AIRCRAFT CARRIER

FRANCE: *FOUDRE* (1912)
Courtesy of Art-Tech

BUILDER: Forges et Chantiers de la Gironde, Bordeaux

LAID DOWN: June 9, 1892. Launched: October 20, 1895. Commissioned: 1912

DISPLACEMENT: 5,972 tons (standard), 6,089 tons (full load)

DIMENSIONS: 389'5" (oa) x 51'2" x 17'9" (mean), 23'8" (full load)

MACHINERY: Triple expansion engines, 24 Lagrafel d'Allest boilers, 2 shafts, 11,500 ihp = 19 knots

BUNKERAGE & RANGE: 787 tons coal = 7,500 nm @ 10 knots

AIRCRAFT: 8

ARMAMENT: 8 x 3.9", 4 x 65mm, 4 x 47mm

COMPLEMENT: 430

DESIGN: The *Foudre* was originally a specialized torpedo boat carrier-cruiser and was converted to a repair ship in 1907. It was converted to op-
erate seaplanes in 1912. A permanent hangar was fitted amidships abaft the stacks. The *Foudre* embarked its first aircraft on May 27. A flying-off platform, 114 feet by 26 feet, was fitted on the forecastle in early 1914 and used for several experimental flights, but was replaced by a seaplane-handling platform later in the year.

SERVICE: The *Foudre* served with the main French fleet in the Mediterranean prior to World War I, participating in many fleet exercises. After the outbreak of war it served in the Adriatic, the Suez Canal zone, and the Dardanelles. After a refit from May to August 1915, the *Foudre* operated primarily as a seagoing depot ship in the eastern Mediterranean. It was sold for scrapping on May 27, 1922.

FRANCE: CONVERTED CROSS-CHANNEL PACKETS (1915)/*NORD/PAS-DE-CALAIS*
Courtesy of Art-Tech

BUILDER: Chantiers de la Loire, St. Nazaire

LAID DOWN: 1897. Launched: 1898. Commissioned: July 1, 1915 (*Pas-de-Calais*); June 26, 1916 (*Nord*)

DISPLACEMENT: 1,541 tons (gross)

DIMENSIONS: 338'6" (oa) x 35'0" x 11'0"

MACHINERY: Triple expansion engines, 2 paddle wheels, 7,800 ihp = 21 knots

AIRCRAFT: 3

ARMAMENT: 2 x 47mm

DESIGN: These two vessels were built as cross-Channel packets for Chemins de Fer du Nord and requisitioned for service as light patrol craft on the outbreak of World War I. They were converted into aircraft carriers with a permanent hangar amidships and a canvas hangar aft.

SERVICE: Both vessels served in the Channel, the *Nord* at Dunkirk and the *Pas-de-Calais* at Cherbourg. They were withdrawn from aviation duties in 1917 and returned to mercantile service in 1919.

GERMANY: *STUTTGART* (1918)
Courtesy of Art-Tech

BUILDER: Kaiserliche Werft Danzig

LAID DOWN: 1905. Launched: September 22, 1906. Commissioned: May 16, 1918

DISPLACEMENT: 3,413 tons (normal), 3,938 tons (full load)

DIMENSIONS: 386'0" (oa) x 44' x 17'7" (mean)

MACHINERY: Vertical triple-expansion engines, 11 navy boilers, 2 shafts, 12,000 ihp = 23 knots

BUNKERAGE & RANGE: 880 tons coal = 4,170 nm @ 12 knots

AIRCRAFT: 3

ARMAMENT: 4 x 4.1", 2 x 3.4" AA, 1 x 17.7" torpedo tubes

COMPLEMENT: 350

DESIGN: The *Stuttgart* was originally completed as a light cruiser of the *Königsberg* class in 1908 (the name ship was sunk in 1915 by monitor gunfire guided by carrier aircraft), and served with the High Seas Fleet during World War I. In January 1918, conversion into an aircraft carrier began at the urgent request of the fleet for a fast aircraft carrier to work with the scouting force. Six 4.1-inch guns were removed and replaced by a pair of 3.4-inch AA guns on the forecastle. A steel-frame canvas-covered hangar was fitted abaft the aftermost stack, and cranes were installed to handle aircraft on the cleared quarterdeck.

SERVICE: The *Stuttgart* commissioned as the flagship of the admiral commanding North Sea Aerial Forces, a component of Admiral Franz von Hipper's Scouting Force. It covered minesweeping operations until rendered inactive by the High Seas Fleet mutiny at Kiel on October 30, 1918. The carrier was stricken from the German fleet on November 5, 1919, surrendered to Britain on July 20, 1920, and sold for scrapping in 1921.

RUSSIA: *ALMAZ*(1915)
Courtesy of Art-Tech

BUILDER: Baltic Works, St. Petersburg

LAID DOWN: September 25, 1902. Launched: June 2, 1903. Commissioned: 1915

DISPLACEMENT: 3,285 tons (normal)

DIMENSIONS: 363'0" (oa) x 43'6" x 17'6" (mean)

MACHINERY: Vertical triple-expansion engines, Belleville boilers, 2 shafts, 7,500 ihp = 19 knots

AIRCRAFT: 4

ARMAMENT: 7 x 4.7", 4 x 12 pdr AA

COMPLEMENT: 340

DESIGN: Originally completed as an armed yacht rated as a third-class cruiser, the *Almaz* served as the viceregal yacht in the Far East and was the largest Russian survivor of the Battle of Tsushima (May 27–29, 1905). The *Almaz* was transferred to the Black Sea Fleet in 1911 and refitted as a seaplane carrier early in 1915. Seaplane handling platforms were fitted behind the mainmast and additional booms were rigged for lifting aircraft.

SERVICE: The *Almaz* formed part of the Hydro-Cruiser Division of the Black Sea Fleet from 1915 to 1917. As the fastest of the fleet's seaplane carriers, it often undertook independent missions, including raids on Varna in Bulgaria in October 1915 and June 1916. After the popular revolution in 1917 the *Almaz* became a Bolshevik headquarters ship but was seized by French forces at Odessa in December 1918 and turned over to White Russian forces. It sailed to Algiers in 1920 with other White Russian vessels, was taken over there by the French in 1928, and scrapped in 1934.

RUSSIA: CONVERTED MERCHANTMEN (1915)
Courtesy of Art-Tech

BUILDER:
Imperator Nikolai I: John Brown & Company Ltd., Clydebank
Imperator Alexandr I: William Denny & Brothers Ltd., Dumbarton

DISPLACEMENT: 9,230–9,240 tons (normal)

DIMENSIONS: 381'0" (oa) x 52'0" x 26'0" (mean)

MACHINERY: Vertical triple-expansion engines, 4 boilers, 2 shafts, 5,100 ihp = 13.5 knots

AIRCRAFT: 8

ARMAMENT: 6 x 4.7", 4 x 12 pdr AA

COMPLEMENT: Unknown

DESIGN: These two vessels were built as fast cargo liners for the Russian Steam Navigation Trading Company and completed in 1913 and 1914, respectively. They were requisitioned as naval auxiliaries after the outbreak of World War I and converted into seaplane carriers in early 1915. The conversion was minimal, involving fitting additional booms for aircraft handling and clearing after superstructure space to make room for aircraft stowage on the upper deck.

SERVICE: These vessels formed the core of the Black Sea Fleet's Hydro-Cruiser Division and were very active against Turkish and Bulgarian coastal targets from March 1915 to February 1917. After the popular revolution they were renamed the *Aviator* and the *Respublikanetz,* but were laid up from April 1917 until they were taken over by French forces in December 1918. Both vessels entered French commercial service after World War I, serving with the Compagnie des Messageries Maritimes as the *Pierre Loti* and the *Lamartine.* The *Pierre Loti* was wrecked in the Gabon River estuary in 1943 and the *Lamartine,* by then renamed the *Khaidinh,* was sunk by United States Navy aircraft in Along Bay in 1942.

UNITED KINGDOM: *HERMES* (1913)
Courtesy of Art-Tech

BUILDER: Fairfield Shipbuilding & Engineering Company, Govan

LAID DOWN: April 30, 1897. Launched: April 7, 1898. Commissioned: May 7, 1913

DISPLACEMENT: 5,650 tons (standard)

DIMENSIONS: 373'0" (oa) x 54'0" x 20'0" (mean)

MACHINERY: Vertical triple-expansion engines, 18 Babcock small-tube boilers, 2 shafts, 10,000 ihp = 20 knots

BUNKERAGE & RANGE: 1,100 tons coal

AIRCRAFT: 3

ARMAMENT: 11 x 6," 9 x 12-pdr, 6 x 3-pdr, 2 x 18" torpedo tubes

COMPLEMENT: 450

DESIGN: The *Hermes,* a 2nd-class protected cruiser of the *Highflyer* class, was selected for conversion as an aircraft carrier for the July 1913 annual fleet maneuvers, capitalizing on the success of 1912 experiments with aircraft operations from ships. Temporary canvas hangars and aircraft launching platforms were erected on the forecastle and quarterdeck and additional derricks were fitted for aircraft handling.

SERVICE: The *Hermes* conducted a series of trials of launching and recovery procedures from July to October 1913, including operations with the fleet during the maneuvers. In December 1913 it was paid off into the Reserve Fleet. The *Hermes* was reactivated and attached to the Nore Command at the outbreak of World War I. It was torpedoed and sunk by the *U-27* in the Straits of Dover on October 31, 1914.

UNITED KINGDOM: *ARK ROYAL* (1914)
Courtesy of Art-Tech

BUILDER: Blyth Shipbuilding & Dry Docks Company, Blyth

LAID DOWN: November 7, 1913. Launched: September 5, 1914. Commissioned: December 10, 1914

DISPLACEMENT: 7,450 tons (standard)

DIMENSIONS: 366'0" (oa) x 50'10" x 18'0" (mean)

FLIGHT DECK: 125'0" x 40'0"

MACHINERY: Vertical triple-expansion engines, 2 cylindrical boilers, 1 shaft, 3,000 ihp = 11 knots

BUNKERAGE & RANGE: 500 tons coal

AIRCRAFT: 7

ARMAMENT: 4 x 12-pdr

COMPLEMENT: 180

DESIGN: Laid down as a center-island collier, the *Ark Royal* was purchased by the Admiralty in May 1914 and totally redesigned. The machinery and bridge structure were moved to the stern, the sheer eliminated, and a large hold (150 feet by 40 feet) to accommodate aircraft, plus workshops, aviation bunkerage, and magazines were constructed in the forward part of the hull. Two steam cranes amidships served the hold, and the flat foredeck was kept clear for aircraft operations (landplanes or seaplanes on trolleys could take off directly from the flight deck, though more often seaplanes were hoisted over the side and took off from the water).

MODIFICATIONS: Various types of catapults were fitted on the foredeck for trials. A permanent catapult was installed in late 1940 for the ship's service as a fighter catapult ship operating three fighters (Hurricanes or Fulmars). Two 20mm AA guns were added at that time.

SERVICE: The *Ark Royal* served at the Dardanelles in 1915 and then in the eastern Mediterranean and Red Sea for the remainder of World War I and immediately postwar. In 1923 it became a depot ship at Sheerness. During the 1930s the *Ark Royal* was an aviation equipment trials ship, testing catapults and recovery systems. The ship was renamed the *Pegasus* in December 1934 when the new carrier *Ark Royal* was ordered. The *Pegasus* served briefly as a fighter catapult ship escorting convoys in 1941 before reverting to auxiliary duties. It was sold into merchant service in October 1946 as the *Anita I* and broken up in October 1950.

UNITED KINGDOM: CONVERTED CROSS-CHANNEL & ISLE OF MAN PACKETS
Courtesy of Art-Tech

LAID DOWN:

Empress: 1906. Launched: April 13, 1907. Commissioned October 1914

Riviera: 1910. Launched: April 1, 1911. Commissioned September 1914

Engadine: 1910. Launched: September 23, 1911. Commissioned September 1914

Ben-My-Chree: 1907. Launched: March 23, 1908. Commissioned: January 2, 1915

Vindex: 1904. Launched: March 7, 1905. Commissioned: March 26, 1915

Manxman: 1903. Launched: June 15, 1905. Commissioned: January 17, 1916

BUILDER:

Empress, Riviera, Engadine: William Denny & Brothers Ltd., Dumbarton

Manxman, Ben-My-Chree: Vickers (Shipbuilding) Ltd., Barrow-in-Furness

Vindex: Sir W. G. Armstrong, Whitworth & Company, Newcastle-upon-Tyne

DIMENSIONS: 316'0"–375'0" (pp), x 41'0"–46'0"

MACHINERY: Turbines, 3 shafts, 11,000–14,000 shp = 21–24 knots

AIRCRAFT: 3–8

COMPLEMENT: approximately 250

DESIGN: On the outbreak of World War I, the Admiralty took over three fast cross-Channel packets owned by the South Eastern and Chatham Railway Company for conversion into aircraft carriers. Initially, all received canvas-covered hangars at the stern and embarked three seaplanes, handled by a mainmast derrick. No armament was fitted. Early in 1915, all three received more elaborate upgrades—a permanent solid hangar aft, a pair of cranes supported by the after corners of the hangar, cut down superstructure, and mainmast removed. A sloping flying-off deck was fitted over the forecastle. Armament was four 12-pounder low-angle guns and two 3-pounder AA guns on the hangar roof. Aircraft accommodation rose to six seaplanes.

The success of the first group of conversions led the Admiralty to acquire three larger Isle of Man packets. They were converted to match the upgraded first group and could accommodate up to eight aircraft. The *Manxman* was armed with only two 12-pounder low-angle guns and two 3-pdr AA guns.

SERVICE: All but the *Ben-My-Chree* served in home waters, mainly supporting sweeps in the North Sea, until 1918 when they transferred to the Mediterranean. The *Empress*, the *Riviera*, and the *Engadine* formed the striking force for the unsuccessful raid on Cuxhaven on December 25, 1914. The *Engadine* accompanied the Battle Cruiser Force at the Battle of Jutland on May 31, 1916. A Short Type 184 seaplane crewed by Flight Lieutenant F. J. Rutland and Assistant Paymaster G. S. Trewin spotted the German battle cruisers' cruiser scouting screen, but signaling failures prevented the information from reaching Vice-Admiral Beatty on his flagship, H.M.S. *Lion*. The *Ben-My-Chree* went from the Harwich Force to the Dardanelles in June 1915, where its Short Type 184 aircraft made the first successful aerial torpedo attacks, probably sinking two small Turkish merchant vessels. It continued to serve in the eastern Mediterranean and Red Sea until it was sunk by Turkish shore batteries while anchored at Castelorizo, an island (garrisoned by French troops) close to the mainland, on January 9, 1917. The five remaining vessels returned to their original owners in late 1919 or early 1920.

BUILDER: Fairfield Shipbuilding & Engineering Company, Govan

UNITED KINGDOM: *CAMPANIA* (1915)
Courtesy of Art-Tech

LAUNCHED: September 8, 1892. Commissioned: April 17, 1915

DISPLACEMENT: 18,000 tons (standard)

DIMENSIONS: 622'0" (oa) x 65'0" x 22'0" (mean)

FLIGHT DECK: 125'0" x 35'0"

MACHINERY: Vertical triple-expansion engines, 13 boilers, 2 shafts, 30,000 ihp = 23 knots

AIRCRAFT: 6

ARMAMENT: 6 x 4.7"

COMPLEMENT: 550

DESIGN: This erstwhile record-breaking Cunard liner was scheduled for scrapping at the outbreak of World War I but was purchased by the Admiralty in November 1914 and converted into a seaplane carrier for operations with the Grand Fleet. Aircraft stowage and workshops were constructed forward, a flying-off deck installed over the forecastle, derricks were fitted on either side of the bridge, and three guns disposed along each side.

MODIFICATIONS: The *Campania*, although much larger than the short-sea conversions, could accommodate no more aircraft. In 1915–1916 the forward stack was divided into two units on either side of a new sloping 165-foot-long flying-off deck with the bridge on a gantry 15 feet above it. The superstructure was cut down, aircraft stowage moved amidships and enlarged to accommodate ten to eleven machines, and the stern cleared for aircraft or airship operations. A single 3-inch AA gun was added right aft.

SERVICE: The *Campania* served with the Grand Fleet during World War I, mainly with the Battle Cruiser Force. A signals failure caused it to miss the Battle of Jutland in May 1916. It was sunk after a collision with the large light cruiser *Glorious* and the battleship *Royal Oak* in the Firth of Forth on November 5, 1918.

UNITED KINGDOM: CONVERTED MAIL STEAMERS (1917)
Courtesy of Art-Tech

LAID DOWN:
Nairana: 1914. Launched: June 21, 1915. Commissioned: August 23, 1917

Pegasus: 1914. Launched: June 9, 1917. Commissioned: August 1917

BUILDER:
Nairana: William Denny & Brothers Ltd., Dumbarton

Pegasus: John Brown & Company Ltd., Clydebank

DISPLACEMENT: 3,070–3,300 tons (standard)

DIMENSIONS: 352'0"–332'0" (oa) x 45'6"– 44'0" x 14'0"–15'0" (mean)

MACHINERY: Geared turbines, cylindrical boilers, 2 shafts, 6,700–9,500 shp = 19–20 knots

AIRCRAFT: 7–9

ARMAMENT: 2 x 3", 2 x 12-pdr AA

COMPLEMENT: approximately 250

DESIGN: These two ships were similar to the earlier converted short-sea vessels but were based on incomplete hulls. The most significant differences were the longer flying-off deck forward with a second smaller hangar below it, served by a primitive elevator.

SERVICE: Both vessels served with the Grand Fleet during World War I. The *Nairana* went to Russia with the British Expeditionary Force in 1919 and was sold in 1921, the *Pegasus* was retained as an aircraft transport until it was sold in August 1931 and scrapped.

UNITED KINGDOM: *FURIOUS* (1917)
Courtesy of U.S. Naval Historical Museum

BUILDER: Sir W. G. Armstrong, Whitworth & Company, Newcastle-upon-Tyne

LAID DOWN: June 8, 1915. Launched: August 15, 1916. Commissioned: June 26, 1917

DISPLACEMENT: 19,100 tons (standard), 22,400 tons (full load)

DIMENSIONS: 786'3" (oa) x 88'0" x 21'6" (mean), 25'0" (full load)

FLIGHT DECK: 228'0" x 55'0"

MACHINERY: Brown-Curtis geared turbines, 18 Yarrow small-tube boilers, 4 shafts, 90,000 shp = 31.5 knots

BUNKERAGE & RANGE: 3,400 tons = 6,000 nm @ 20 knots

AIRCRAFT: 8

ARMAMENT: 1 x 18", 11 x 5.5", 4 x 3" AA, 4 x 3-pdr AA

COMPLEMENT: 880

DESIGN: The *Furious* was laid down as a large light cruiser armed with two single 18-inch gun turrets in place of the twin 15-inch gun turrets of its semi-sisters the *Courageous* and the *Glorious*. Admiral Beatty's committee to explore solutions to the Grand Fleet's aviation requirements recommended the cruiser's conversion to a large fast aircraft carrier that could work with the fleet. Conversion began in April 1917. It replaced the forward 18-inch turret with an enclosed hangar topped by a long sloping flying-off deck, fitted a pair of aircraft handling derricks, and arranged workshops, fuel stowage, and an ordnance magazine.

MODIFICATIONS: Squadron Commander Dunning's trials landing aircraft on the *Furious*'s flying-off deck demonstrated the possibilities of successfully recovering landplanes aboard the ship. It was taken in hand for further modifications in November 1917. A second hangar, surmounted by a 300-foot by 50-foot landing-on deck, replaced the after turret and one 5.5-inch mount, more than doubling the aircraft complement. The two flight decks were connected by 11-foot wide gangways on each side so that aircraft could be moved between them. Electrically operated elevators linked the hangars and flight decks. The landing deck carried arresting gear-sandbag-weighted transverse wires and longitudinal guide wires, and a rope crash barrier system was fitted at its forward end to stop aircraft from running into the superstructure.

The *Furious* returned to service on March 15, 1918. Its new configuration was not an unqualified success. Furnace gases and eddies from the superstructure made landings hazardous. In March 1921 the Admiralty decided to reconstruct the *Furious* again. The ship was razed to the hangar-deck level. A lower hangar (550 feet by 50 feet) and upper hangar (530 feet by 50 feet) were topped by a 576-foot by 90-foot flight deck. Longitudinal wires were fitted to guide landing aircraft. Two large new elevators linked the hangars and flight deck. The forward end of the upper hangar opened onto a 200-foot long secondary flight deck on the forecastle. Furnace gases were trunked aft along the sides of

the hangar and there were auxiliary ducts exhausted through the flight deck abreast the elevators. The navigation station was set into the starboard forward edge of the main flight deck, with the flying control station opposite, and there was a retractable chart house on the flight deck centerline. Bulges increased the beam to 107 feet, draft was now 24 feet (standard), and standard tonnage rose to 22,130 tons. Armament changed to ten 5.5-inch AA, six 4-inch AA, and four 2-pounder AA, with accommodation for sixty aircraft.

Shortly after the *Furious* recommissioned in 1925 the four forward 4-inch AA guns and the longitudinal landing wires were removed. During a 1931–1932 refit, the quarterdeck was raised one level and the two beam 4-inch AA mountings removed and replaced by a single centerline mounting. Two 4-inch AA guns returned forward with 8-barrelled 2-pounder mountings ahead of them. In 1936 transverse wire arresting gear was installed. A 1938–1939 refit featured a major rearmament: the 5.5-inch and single 4-inch AA guns were removed and replaced by six twin 4-inch AA mounts (two on each beam, one aft and one forward on the lower flying-off deck) and an additional 8-barrelled 2-pounder mounting fitted on the starboard side of the flight deck. A small island was fitted to starboard and it now had two high-angle directors for the 4-inch AA guns. Displacement rose to 22,450 tons (standard) and 28,500 tons (full load), draft increased to 24 feet (standard) and 27 feet 9 inches (full load), and speed dropped to 29.5 knots. During World War II the *Furious* received additional light AA weapons: a further 8-barrelled 2-pounder mounting on the forecastle and twenty-two 20mm AA guns. Type 285 gunnery radar was also added and the bulges deepened to compensate for additional topweight. The aircraft complement fell to thirty.

SERVICE: The *Furious* served with the Grand Fleet during World War I. Its aircraft destroyed the airships *L54* and *L60* at Tondern on July 19, 1918. After its major postwar reconstruction, the carrier served with the Home Fleet until mid-1941, when it operated briefly in the western Mediterranean. The *Furious* provided air cover for the landings in North Africa (Operation Torch) in November 1942, then returned to the Home Fleet in February 1943. In April, July, and August 1944, aircraft from the *Furious* participated in strikes against the *Tirpitz* in Kaafjord (operations Tungsten, Mascot, and Goodwood) that disabled the German battleship but failed to sink it. The *Furious*'s aircraft also took part in eleven strike operations against German shipping in Norwegian coastal waters between April and September 1944, after which it was placed in reserve. The *Furious* was sold for scrapping in January 1948.

UNITED KINGDOM: *ARGUS* (1918)
Courtesy of Art-Tech

BUILDER: William Beardmore & Company Ltd., Dalmuir

LAID DOWN: 1914. Launched: December 2, 1917. Commissioned: September 6, 1918

DISPLACEMENT: 14,550 tons (standard), 17,000 tons (full load)

DIMENSIONS: 565'0" (oa) x 68'6" x 21'0" (mean), 24'9" (full load)

FLIGHT DECK: 550'0" x 69'0"

MACHINERY: Parsons turbines, 12 cylindrical boilers, 4 shafts, 21,500 shp = 20.25 knots

BUNKERAGE: 2,000 tons

AIRCRAFT: 20

ARMAMENT: 4 x 4" AA, 2 x 4" LA

COMPLEMENT: 373

DESIGN: The *Argus* was laid down as the liner *Conte Rosso* for the Lloyd Sabaudo Line but construction was suspended on the outbreak of World War I. In August 1916 the Admiralty purchased the incomplete hull for conversion into an aircraft carrier. Originally there was to be a flying-off deck forward and a landing-on deck aft with a raised superstructure between them. The final design, however, provided an unobstructed full-length flight deck, its forward section sloping slightly downward above a large hangar (350 feet long by 68 feet wide and 20 feet high). Two electrically operated elevators linked hangar and flight deck. Furnace gases passed through ducts running along the sides of the hangar and venting at the stern. There were lateral navigation stations below flight deck level and a retractable charthouse on the flight deck centerline. Longitudinal wires were fitted on the flight deck to assist landing aircraft.

MODIFICATIONS: Bulges that increased the beam to 75 feet 9 inches were fitted in the 1925–1926 refit and the longitudinal wires removed. All guns were removed, the forward flight deck incline was leveled and strengthened to accommodate two catapults, transverse arresting gear was fitted, and water-tube boilers installed during a 1935 refit. During World War II some ten 20mm AA guns were added.

SERVICE: The *Argus* served in home waters, the Mediterranean, and on the China station until the 1930s. It then became a training carrier until the outbreak of World War II led it to convoy escort duty and frontline service with Force H in the Mediterranean and during Operation Torch. In 1943 it reverted to training duties, became an accommodation ship in 1944, was sold in 1946, and broken up the following year.

UNITED KINGDOM: *VINDICTIVE* (1918)
Courtesy of Art-Tech

BUILDER: Harland & Wolff Ltd., Belfast

LAID DOWN: July 1916. Launched: January 17, 1918. Commissioned: October 1918

DISPLACEMENT: 9,750 tons (standard), 11,500 tons (full load)

DIMENSIONS: 605'0" (oa) x 65'0" x 17'6" (mean), 20'0" (full load)

FLIGHT DECK: 100'0" x 55'0" (forward deck), 215'0" x 65'0" (aft deck)

MACHINERY: Parsons geared turbines, 12 Yarrow small-tube boilers, 4 shafts, 60,000 shp = 29.5 knots

BUNKERAGE & RANGE: 1,480 tons

AIRCRAFT: 8

ARMAMENT: 4 x 7.5", 4 x 3" LA, 4 x 12-pdr AA, 6 x 21" torpedo tubes

COMPLEMENT: 700

DESIGN: Laid down as a light cruiser of the *Hawkins* class, the *Vindictive* (renamed from the *Cavendish* in June 1918) was converted to work with the *Furious* and the fleet's light cruisers. Three of the cruiser's original 7.5-inch guns were removed and replaced by hangars forward and aft with flight decks above them. The forward hangar incorporated a large hatchway, served by a pair of derricks, for aircraft handling, while the after hangar and flight deck were linked with an elevator. The two flight decks were connected by narrow gangway on the port side of the superstructure. Arresting gear, guide wires, and a rope crash barrier, all similar to those fitted to the *Furious,* were installed on the landing-on deck aft.

MODIFICATIONS: The *Vindictive* suffered from the same operational problems as the *Furious* before the latter's conversion with a continuous flight deck but was too small to make a full conversion worthwhile. It therefore was reconverted into a light cruiser in a reconstruction from 1923–1925.

SERVICE: The *Vindictive* saw only limited service due to its design limitations. It operated with the British Expeditionary Force to Russia in 1919 but ran aground, necessitating very extensive repairs. It returned to fleet service in 1921 but was withdrawn in 1923 for reconstruction as a cruiser. The *Vindictive* was sold for scrapping in February 1946.

THE AIRCRAFT CARRIER MATURES

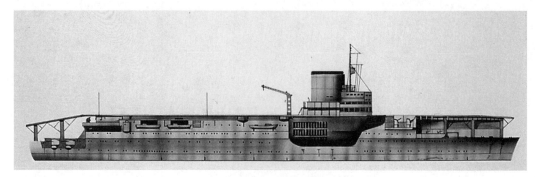

FRANCE: *BÉARN* (1927)
Courtesy of Art-Tech

BUILDER: Forges et Chantiers de la Mediterranée, La Seyne

LAID DOWN: January 10, 1914. Launched: April 1920. Commissioned: May 1927

DISPLACEMENT: 22,100 tons (standard), 28,400 tons (full load)

DIMENSIONS: 599'1" (oa) x 88'11" x 27'6" (mean), 30'6" (full load)

FLIGHT DECK: 580'0' x 70'0"

MACHINERY: Parsons turbines and triple-expansion engines, 12 du Temple small-tube boilers, 4 shafts, 40,000 shp = 21.5 knots

BUNKERAGE & RANGE: 2,165 tons = 7,000 nm @ 10 knots

AIRCRAFT: 40

ARMAMENT: 8 x 6.1", 6 x 75mm AA, 8 x 37mm AA

COMPLEMENT: 865

DESIGN: The *Béarn* was laid down as a battleship of the *Normandie* class, whose construction was suspended on the outbreak of World War I. All were due to be scrapped under the terms of the Washington Treaty but it was decided to complete the *Béarn* as an aircraft carrier. The hull essentially was unchanged but the armor belt was reduced to 3.2 inches and the upper deck armor removed. The superstructure was in two levels, a lower level with workshops and stowage for dismantled aircraft and an upper level comprising the 405-foot long hangar. Atop the hangar was the flight deck, with 1-inch armor, 600 feet long including the round downs. It was equipped with transverse wire arresting gear. Three electric elevators linked the hangar and flight deck. A very large starboard-side sponson with prominent cooling vents enclosed the furnace uptakes and supported the large stack and island.

MODIFICATIONS: Shortly after completion the forward section of the flight deck was rebuilt with a noticeable downward slope. A 1935 refit added additional cooling vents in the sponson and partially enclosed the flight deck's forward overhang. In May 1942, the entire antiaircraft battery was landed at Martinique. The ship was completely refitted at New Orleans from late 1943 as an aircraft transport. The flight deck was shortened fore and aft, all remaining original armament removed, and a new antiaircraft battery of 4 x 5"/38 DP, 24 x 40mm AA, and 26 x 20mm AA was fitted.

SERVICE: The *Béarn* served in the Mediterranean prior to World War II. After war broke out the ship was used to transport American aircraft to France and was held in Martinique, while engaged in this service, when France fell in June 1940. After its 1943–1944 refit it operated as an aircraft transport until 1948, primarily in the Pacific and Southeast Asia. The *Béarn* then became a static training ship and submarine depot until it was sold for scrapping in 1967.

JAPAN: *HOSHO* (1922)
Courtesy of Art-Tech

BUILDER: Asano Shipbuilding Company, Tsurumi

LAID DOWN: December 16, 1919. Launched: November 13, 1921. Commissioned: December 7, 1922

DISPLACEMENT: 7,470 tons (standard), 10,000 tons (full load)

DIMENSIONS: 551'6" (oa) x 59'1" x 20'3" (mean)

FLIGHT DECK: 520'0" x 70'0"

MACHINERY: Parsons geared turbines, 12 Kampon boilers, 2 shafts, 30,000 shp = 25 knots

BUNKERAGE & RANGE: 2, 695 tons oil + 940 tons coal = 8,690 nm @ 12 knots

AIRCRAFT: 26

ARMAMENT: 4 x 5.5", 2 x 3" AA

COMPLEMENT: 550

DESIGN: The *Hosho* was the first carrier designed as such to commission, although it was laid down later than the British *Hermes*. The forward end of the full-length flight deck sloped downwards and was supported by stanchions. Two elevators, one at each end of the hangar amidships, handled aircraft movement. The furnace gas flues were trunked to starboard and emerged through three hinged stacks that folded flat during flight operations. Ahead of the stacks was a small round island with a large tripod mast. Longitudinal guide wires, duplicating contemporary British practice, were fitted on the flight deck

MODIFICATIONS: The island and mast were removed in 1923, primarily to correct instability problems and the downward slope of the flight deck leveled. In 1934 the stacks were fixed in a vertical position and in 1936 twelve 13.2mm AA guns replaced the 3-inch AA weapons. In 1941 eight 25mm AA were added and the stacks altered to discharge horizontally. The following year the 5.5-inch guns were landed and replaced with a further eight 25mm AA guns. In 1944 the flight deck was extended to 593 feet 3 inches in length. The following year armament was reduced to only six 25mm.

SERVICE: The *Hosho* served with the Combined Fleet mainly in flying and aviation operations development, and took part in air operations during the Shanghai Incident in February 1932. In 1933 it was relegated to training duties but the outbreak of war with China brought the ship back into the front line. The *Hosho* served off the China coast from July to October 1937, and again from November 1940 until September 1941. It reverted to training and second-line duties thereafter, except for a short stint with the Combined Fleet during the Midway operation in May–June 1942. It was damaged in an air attack at Kure on March 19, 1945, and surrendered in August. Postwar, the ship served as a repatriation transport until August 16, 1946, and was broken up at Osaka in 1947.

JAPAN: *AKAGI* (1927)
Courtesy of Art-Tech

BUILDER: Kure Navy Yard

LAID DOWN: December 6, 1920. Launched: April 22, 1925. Commissioned: March 25, 1927

DISPLACEMENT: 29,600 tons (standard), 34,364 tons (full load)

DIMENSIONS: 857'0" (oa) x 95'0" x 26'6" (mean)

FLIGHT DECK: 624'0" x 100'0"

MACHINERY: Gijutsu-Hombu geared turbines, 19 Kampon boilers, 4 shafts, 131,000 shp = 32.5 knots

BUNKERAGE & RANGE: 3,900 tons oil + 2,100 tons coal = 8,000 nm @ 14 knots

AIRCRAFT: 60

ARMAMENT: 10 x 8", 12 x 4.7" AA

COMPLEMENT: 1,600

DESIGN: The *Akagi* was laid down as a battle cruiser of the *Amagi* class, all of which were scheduled for scrapping under the terms of the Washington Treaty. The treaty allowed Japan to convert two hulls into aircraft carriers, so the *Amagi* and the *Akagi*, the most advanced of the battle cruisers, were selected. The *Amagi*, however, was irreparably damaged by an earthquake while on the ways at the Yokosuka Naval Dockyard and scrapped; conversion proceeded on the *Akagi*. Belt armor was reduced to 6 inches and narrowed, deck armor thinned to 3.1 inches and lowered to main deck level. There were two hangars, one atop the other, each opening onto a short flying-off deck forward, the lower deck 175 feet long, the upper only 50 feet long. The main flight deck extended almost to the stern, carried longitudinal guide wires, and was supported aft by stanchions. Two elevators linked the hangars and main flight deck. Furnace gas flues were trunked to starboard and emerged through a large downward-pointing stack supplemented by a smaller vertical stack abaft it. The ship was conned from a navigation station under the forward edge of the main flight deck.

MODIFICATIONS: Soon after completion an additional navigation station was fitted on the starboard side at the front of the main flight deck. The longitudinal wires were replaced by transverse wire arresting gear in 1931. Between October 24, 1935, and August 31, 1938, the *Akagi* underwent a major reconstruction. The bulges were enlarged, bringing the beam to 102 feet 9 inches. The forward flying-off decks and two twin 8-inch gun turrets were removed, the hangars extended forward, the flight deck lengthened to the bow and strengthened, and a third elevator fitted amidships. The two stacks were consolidated into one very large unit and navigation and flying control facilities moved into a new island on the port side. New wholly oil-fired boilers replaced the old units and bunkerage rose to 5,770 tons, exclusively oil. Fourteen twin 25mm AA guns were added. Tonnage rose to 36,500 tons (standard) and 42,750 tons (full load), draft increased to 28 feet 6 inches (mean), and speed fell to 31.5 knots. Aircraft capacity increased substantially to 91 machines.

SERVICE: The *Akagi* served with the 1st *Kokutai* (Carrier Squadron) of the Combined Fleet throughout its career. In April 1941 the large carriers of the Imperial Japanese Navy were combined together as the 1st *Koku-Kantai* (Carrier Fleet) with the *Akagi* as the fleet flagship. The *Akagi* took part in all the fleet's operations: Pearl Harbor, Rabaul, Darwin, Java, Ceylon, and Midway, where it was severely damaged by aircraft from the United States Navy carrier *Enterprise* on June 4, 1942, and scuttled the following day.

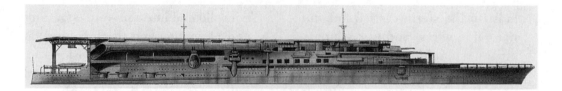

JAPAN: *KAGA* (1928)
Courtesy of Art-Tech

BUILDER: Kawasaki Dockyard Company, Kobe & Yokosuka Navy Yard

LAID DOWN: Jul 19, 1920. Launched: November 17, 1921. Commissioned: March 31, 1928

DISPLACEMENT: 29,600 tons (standard), 33,693 tons (full load)

DIMENSIONS: 782'6" (oa) x 97'0" x 26'0" (mean)

FLIGHT DECK: 560'0" x 100'0"

MACHINERY: Brown-Curtis geared turbines, 12 Kampon boilers, 4 shafts, 91,000 shp = 27.5 knots

BUNKERAGE & RANGE: 3,600 tons oil + 1,700 tons coal = 8,000 nm @ 14 knots

AIRCRAFT: 60

ARMAMENT: 10 x 8", 12 x 4.7" AA

COMPLEMENT: 1,340

DESIGN: The *Kaga* was laid down as a battleship and was one of several incomplete capital ships scheduled for scrapping under the terms of the Washington Treaty. When the hull of the *Amagi*, due to be converted into a carrier like its sister the *Akagi*, was irreparably damaged by the 1923 Kanto Earthquake, it was decided to use the extant hull of the *Kaga* as a replacement. The conversion was very similar to that of the *Akagi*, except that the furnace gases were discharged at the stern through very prominent 300-foot long external tubular ducts running just below the flight deck on each side, and transverse wire arresting gear was installed from the outset.

MODIFICATIONS: The *Kaga* underwent a major reconstruction between June 25, 1934, and June 25, 1935, very similar to that later carried out on the *Akagi*. Notable differences were that the hull was lengthened at the stern by 40 feet; new turbines and eight oil-fired boilers were installed, which produced 127,500 shaft horsepower and raised the speed by 1 knot; and enlarged bulges increased the beam to 106 feet 8 inches. Exhaust gases were ducted to a single large downward-facing stack on the starboard side and a small bridge fitted ahead of the stack. The forward 8-inch guns were retained but relocated just ahead of the existing casemated weapons aft, and a completely new antiaircraft battery was installed comprising sixteen 4-inch guns in eight twin mounts and twenty-two 25mm guns in twin mounts. Tonnage rose to 38,200 tons (standard) and 43,650 tons (full load) and its draft was increased to 31 feet 1 inch (mean). Bunkerage increased to 8,208 tons, exclusively oil, and range to 10,000 nm at 16 knots. The *Kaga*, as reconstructed, could accommodate 90 aircraft. Late in 1941, its antiaircraft battery increased by eight 25mm in twin mounts.

SERVICE: The *Kaga* served with the 1st *Kokutai* (Carrier Squadron) of the Combined Fleet throughout its career. Its aircraft were major participants in air operations during the Shanghai Incident in February 1932, and in subsequent operations off the coast of China from August 1937 to December 1938 and again from August 1939 to October 1940. In April 1941 the large carriers of the Imperial Japanese Navy were combined as the 1st *Koku-Kantai* (Carrier Fleet). The *Kaga* took part in all the fleet's operations: Pearl Harbor, Rabaul, Darwin, Java, Ceylon, and Midway, where it was sunk by aircraft from the United States Navy carrier *Enterprise* on June 4, 1942.

JAPAN: *RYUJO* (1933)
Courtesy of Art-Tech

BUILDER: Yokohama Dockyard Company, Yokohama

LAID DOWN: November 26, 1929. Launched: April 2, 1930. Commissioned: May 9, 1933

DISPLACEMENT: 8,000 tons (standard) 11,070 (full load)

DIMENSIONS: 590'3" (oa) x 66'8" x 18'3" (mean)

FLIGHT DECK: 513'6" x 75'6"

MACHINERY: Geared turbines, 6 Kampon boilers, 2 shafts, 65,000 shp = 29 knots

BUNKERAGE & RANGE: 2,490 tons = 10,000 nm @ 14 knots

AIRCRAFT: 48

ARMAMENT: 6 x twin 5" AA, 24 x 13.2 mm AA

COMPLEMENT: 600

DESIGN: The *Ryujo* was designed to fall below the limits of the Washington Treaty and thus not impinge on Japan's available carrier tonnage. The *Ryujo* had two hangars, one above the other, with a flight deck above them that extended from the stern to the forward end of the hangars. Two elevators linked the hangars and the flight deck, which carried transverse wire arresting gear. The furnace gases exhausted through two downward inclined stacks on the starboard side. The navigation bridge was immediately below the forward end of the flight deck. The antiaircraft battery was carried on sponsons just below flight deck level on each side and had excellent sky arcs.

MODIFICATIONS: The *Ryujo's* instability problems, a consequence of attempting to incorporate full carrier features on such a limited displacement, necessitated a major refit between 1934 and 1936. Four 5-inch AA were removed and replaced by four 25mm AA. The hull was strengthened, ballast loaded, and the bulges enlarged, bringing the beam to 68 feet 2 inches. Displacement rose to 10,800 tons (standard), 13,650 tons (full load). Its draft increased to 23 feet 3 inches (mean) and the loss of freeboard led to a further refit in the winter of 1939 to 1940 that raised the forecastle to compensate. In 1942 six triple 25mm AA guns were added.

SERVICE: The *Ryujo* operated off the

Chinese coast, providing air support for operations in eastern and southern China. After a period as a training carrier, it returned to the front line covering assaults on the Philippines, Dutch East Indies, and Aleutians. It was sunk on August 24, 1942, during the Battle of the Eastern Solomons by aircraft from the USS *Saratoga*.

JAPAN: *SORYU* CLASS (1937)
Courtesy of Art-Tech

BUILDER:

Soryu: Kure Navy Yard

Hiryu: Kure Navy Yard

LAID DOWN:

Soryu: November 20, 1934. Launched: December 31 1935. Commissioned: January 29, 1937

Hiryu: July 8, 1936. Launched: November 16, 1937. Commissioned: July 5, 1939

DISPLACEMENT:

Soryu: 15,900 tons (standard) 19,800 tons (full load)

Hiryu: 17,300 tons (standard) 21,900 tons (full load)

DIMENSIONS:

Soryu: 746'5" (oa) x 69'11" x 25'0" (mean)

Hiryu: 745'0" (oa) x 73'3" x 25'9" (mean)

FLIGHT DECK:

Soryu: 705'6" x 85'6"

Hiryu: 705'6" x 88'6"

MACHINERY:

Soryu: Geared turbines, 8 Kampon boilers, 4 shafts. 152,000 shp = 34.5 knots

Hiryu: Geared turbines, 8 Kampon boilers, 4 shafts. 152,000 shp = 34.5 knots

BUNKERAGE & RANGE:

Soryu: 3,670 tons = 7,750 nm @ 18 knots

Hiryu: 4,400 tons = 7,750 nm @ 18 knots

AIRCRAFT:

Soryu: 71

Hiryu: 73

ARMAMENT:

Soryu: 6 x twin 5" AA, 14 x twin 25 mm AA

Hiryu: 6 x twin 5" AA, 6 x triple 25 mm AA, 5 x twin 25 mm AA

COMPLEMENT:

Soryu: 1,100

Hiryu: 1,100

UNITED KINGDOM: *HERMES* (1923)
Courtesy of Art-Tech

BUILDER: Sir W. G. Armstrong, Whitworth & Company, Newcastle-upon-Tyne

LAID DOWN: January 15, 1918. Launched: September 11, 1919. Commissioned: July 1923

DISPLACEMENT: 10,850 tons (standard), 13,000 tons (full load)

DIMENSIONS: 600'0" (oa) x 70'3" x 18'9" (mean), 21'6" (full load)

FLIGHT DECK: 580'0" x 65'0"

MACHINERY: Parsons geared turbines, 6 Yarrow small-tube boilers, 2 shafts, 40,000 shp = 25 knots

BUNKERAGE & RANGE: 1,956 tons

AIRCRAFT: 20

ARMAMENT: 6 x 5.5", 3 x 4" AA

COMPLEMENT: 664

DESIGN: The *Hermes* was the first British carrier designed as such from the keel up. Its mission was reconnaissance in company with the light cruiser force and its hull design was derived from contemporary light cruiser practice. The hangar was 400 feet long, surmounted by a full-length flight deck that incorporated a substantial hump at its after end, a feature based on aerodynamic research at the National Physical Laboratory. An electrically operated elevator was located at the stern in the center of the hump and another just forward of the island. Longitudinal wires were fitted on the flight deck to assist landing aircraft. The island, lo-

DESIGN: While nominally sister ships, there were appreciable differences between them. The later *Hiryu,* built without regard for treaty restrictions, was more strongly constructed, beamier, had greater freeboard, and was more heavily protected. The *Soryu* carried its island to starboard, the *Hiryu* to port. The carriers had two hangars, one above the other, linked to the full-length flight deck by three elevators. Two downward angled stacks on the starboard side exhausted furnace gases.

SERVICE: The *Soryu* operated off the South China coast after commission-

ing. In
covered
Indo-Chi
formed the
Koku Kanta
fleet's opera
Rabaul, Darw
Midway, where
Soryu sunk by
American carrie
4, 1942, and the
damaged by aircra
town and the *Enter*
scuttled the following

cated slightly forward of amidships on the starboard side, was very large for such a relatively small vessel. A 3-inch side belt, 1-inch deck armor, and bulges provided passive protection. The *Hermes* was very small by later standards and its aircraft capacity dropped rapidly as aircraft size increased, to fifteen aircraft by 1934 and twelve by 1939.

MODIFICATIONS: The longitudinal wires were removed in 1926. A 1934 refit added a catapult, transverse wire arresting gear, and a pair of 4-barrelled 0.5-inch mountings. In late 1940 a single 4-barrelled 2-pounder mounting and six 20mm AA guns were added.

SERVICE: The *Hermes* served mainly on the China station until the outbreak of World War II when it was trans-ferred to the Atlantic for trade protection duties and also to act in cooperation with French naval forces. After the fall of France the *Hermes* formed part of the striking force that attacked Dakar on July 8, 1940, its Swordfish aircraft scoring one torpedo hit on the battleship *Richelieu.* After further South Atlantic service (and major repairs of damage from a collision with the armed merchant cruiser *Corfu,* at Simonstown, South Africa) the *Hermes* returned to the Indian Ocean. During the Japanese 1st *koku kantai*'s raid into the Indian Ocean the carrier, together with two tankers, a destroyer, and a corvette, was caught and sunk by dive bombers southeast of Trincomalee, Ceylon, on April 9, 1942.

UNITED KINGDOM: *EAGLE* (1924)

Courtesy of Art-Tech

BUILDER: Sir W. G. Armstrong, Whitworth & Company, Newcastle-upon-Tyne

LAID DOWN: February 20, 1913. Launched: June 8, 1918. Commissioned: February 26, 1924

DISPLACEMENT: 21,850 tons (standard), 26,800 tons (full load)

DIMENSIONS: 667'6" (oa) x 105'2" x 21'9" (mean), 26'6" (full load)

FLIGHT DECK: 652'0" x 95'0"

MACHINERY: Brown-Curtis/Parsons turbines, 32 Yarrow boilers, 4 shafts, 50,000 shp = 24 knots

BUNKERAGE: 3,750 tons oil + 1,750 tons coal

AIRCRAFT: 24

ARMAMENT: 9 x 6", 5 x 4" AA, 4 x 3 pdr AA

COMPLEMENT: 834

DESIGN: The *Eagle* was laid down as the battleship *Almirante Cochrane* for Chile but work stopped at the outbreak of World War I (its sister, the *Almirante Latorre,* served in the Grand Fleet as H.M.S. *Canada* before reverting to Chilean ownership). In January 1918 the Admiralty purchased the incomplete battleship for conversion into an aircraft carrier. The initial design envisaged two islands accommodating the stacks and cabin space on either side of the flight deck, with a navigating platform between them 20 feet above the deck. The final design included a hangar (400 feet long by 90 feet wide and 20 feet 6 inches high) with a continuous flight deck above and a single island to starboard incorporating the two stacks. Two large electrically operated elevators linked hangar and flight deck. The hull was bulged for antitorpedo protection and included much battleship protection, although the belt was reduced to 4–1/2 inches. Longitudinal wires were fitted on the flight deck to assist landing aircraft.

MODIFICATIONS: The longitudinal wires were removed in a 1926 refit and two 2-pounders added. In 1931–1932 it was reboilered and received an 8-barrelled 2-pounder mounting in place of a 4-inch AA gun on the island. A 1936 refit added a further 4-barrelled 2-pounder mounting ahead of the island and transverse wire arresting gear. Just before World War II the ship received high angle director control on the foremast. Its 1941–1942 refit added twelve 20mm AA guns, Type 290 surface warning radar and Type 285 gunnery radar.

SERVICE: The *Eagle* served in the Mediterranean and on the China station until 1940 when it returned to the Mediterranean to conduct strikes against North African coastal targets, cover convoys, and provide aircraft for the attack on the Italian fleet at Taranto on November 11–12, 1940.

In 1941 the carrier served in the South Atlantic, went home to the United Kingdom for refit, and then operated in the western Mediterranean, carrying aircraft for Malta and covering convoys to the island. It was torpedoed by the *U-73* on August 11, 1942, during Operation Pedestal, and sank within five minutes.

UNITED KINGDOM: *COURAGEOUS* CLASS (1928)
Courtesy of Art-Tech

BUILDER:
Courageous: Sir W. G. Armstrong, Whitworth & Company, Newcastle-upon-Tyne
Glorious: Harland & Wolff Ltd., Belfast

LAID DOWN:
Courageous: March 28, 1915. Launched: February 5, 1916. Commissioned: March 5, 1928
Glorious: May 1, 1915. Launched: April 20, 1916. Commissioned: March 10, 1930

DISPLACEMENT: 22,000 tons (standard), 26,100 tons (full load)

DIMENSIONS: 786'6" (oa) x 90'6" x 24'0" (mean), 27'3" (full load)

FLIGHT DECK: 530'0" x 84'6"

MACHINERY: Parsons geared turbines, 18 Yarrow small-tube boilers, 4 shafts, 90,000 shp = 30.5 knots

BUNKERAGE & RANGE: 3,800 tons = 5,860 nm @ 16 knots

AIRCRAFT: 48

ARMAMENT: 16 x 4.7" AA

COMPLEMENT: 1,200

DESIGN: These vessels, semi-sisters of the *Furious,* were commissioned as large light cruisers during World War I. The terms of the Washington Treaty required their disposal and their similarity to the *Furious* made converting them into aircraft carriers an attractive proposition. They were razed to the upper deck and rebuilt in a similar fashion to *Furious* with two superimposed hangars, the upper one opening onto a short forward flying-off deck. Unlike the *Furious*, they received full starboard islands that accommodated bridges and the boiler uptakes in a conventional stack. To improve their stability they also received enlarged bulges.

MODIFICATIONS: Both carriers were fitted with four 2-pounder AA and transverse wire arresting gear around 1932. Between 1935 and 1937 both gained a pair of hydraulic catapults and three 8-barrelled 2-pounder AA guns. The *Glorious* had its quarter-deck raised one level and the flight deck extended aft, to measure 570 feet, in 1935.

SERVICE: The *Courageous* served with the Home Fleet prior to World War

II. It was torpedoed and sunk by the *U-20* in the South-West Approaches on September 17, 1939. The *Glorious* was in the Mediterranean until the outbreak of World War II. It transferred to the Home Fleet in April 1940 and conducted strikes off Norway in support of the efforts to defeat the German invasion. On June 8, 1940, while transporting evacuated Royal Air Force aircraft that blocked the flight deck, the *Glorious* was intercepted by the German battle cruisers *Scharnhorst* and *Gneisenau* off the Norwegian coast and sunk by heavy gunfire.

UNITED KINGDOM: *ARK ROYAL* (1938)
Courtesy of Art-Tech

BUILDER: Cammell Laird & Company Ltd., Birkenhead

LAID DOWN: September 16, 1935. Launched: April 13, 1937. Commissioned: November 16, 1938

DISPLACEMENT: 22,000 tons (standard), 27,200 tons (full load)

DIMENSIONS: 800'0" (oa) x 94'9" x 22'9" (mean), 27'9" (full load)

FLIGHT DECK: 780'0" x 96'0"

MACHINERY: Parsons geared turbines, 6 Admiralty 3-drum boilers, 3 shafts, 102,000 shp = 31 knots

BUNKERAGE & RANGE: 4,600 tons = 7,600 nm @ 20 knots

AIRCRAFT: 60

ARMAMENT: 8 x twin 4.5" AA, 6 x 8-barrelled 2-pdr AA, 8 x 4-barrelled 0.5" AA

COMPLEMENT: 1,600

DESIGN: The *Ark Royal* was only the second British carrier designed from the keel up and the first to be designed within Naval Treaty limitations. In a break with previous practice, the flight deck was the principal strength deck, and consequently the elevators were very narrow and offset either side of the centerline to limit the impact of the openings on longitudinal strength. There were two hangar levels, each 60 feet wide and 16 feet high, the lower being 452 feet long and the upper 568 feet long. The three boiler and three engine rooms were arranged side by side with the furnace gases trunked low down to the starboard side and venting through a single stack in the compact island. Armor protection took the form of a 4–1/2-inch belt and 3–1/2-inch plate over the machinery spaces and magazines. The flight deck overhung the stern considerably and there were two hydraulic catapults forward and transverse wire arresting gear aft. The 4.5-inch AA guns were carried just below flight deck level, had excellent sky arcs, and were controlled by four high angle directors.

MODIFICATIONS: Two 8-barrelled 2-

pounder AA were added in May 1941.

SERVICE: The *Ark Royal* served with the Home Fleet on commissioning. It operated throughout the Norwegian campaign until June 1940, after which it formed the nucleus, with first the battle cruiser *Hood* and then the battle cruiser *Renown,* of Force H based at Gibraltar. Its first operations were against the French fleet at Oran and Dakar. Thereafter the carrier supported fleet operations and covered convoys and aircraft ferry missions in the western Mediterranean, broken by its crucial partici-pation in the hunt for the German battleship *Bismarck* in May 1941. On May 26 it launched successive Swordfish strikes. The first mistakenly attacked the British cruiser *Sheffield* and, fortunately, all torpedoes missed. The second, however, scored a single hit that destroyed the battleship's steering gear and damaged the propellers, thereby dooming it to destruction. While operating off Gibraltar the *Ark Royal* was torpedoed by the *U-81* on November 13, 1941, and lost, largely because of ineffective damage control.

UNITED KINGDOM: *ILLUSTRIOUS* CLASS (1940)
Courtesy of Art-Tech

BUILDER:

Illustrious: Vickers-Armstrong Ltd., Barrow-in-Furness

Victorious: Vickers-Armstrong Ltd., Newcastle-upon-Tyne

Formidable: Harland & Wolff Ltd., Belfast

LAID DOWN:

Illustrious: April 27, 1937. Launched: April 5, 1939. Commissioned: May 25, 1940

Victorious: May 4, 1937. Launched: September 14, 1939. Commissioned: May 15, 1941

Formidable: June 17, 1937. Launched: August 17, 1939. Commissioned: November 24, 1940

DISPLACEMENT: 23,000 tons (standard), 28,210 tons (full load)

DIMENSIONS: 743'9" (oa) x 95'9" x 24'0" (mean), 28'0" (full load)

FLIGHT DECK: 650'0" x 80'0"

MACHINERY: Parsons geared turbines, 6 Admiralty 3-drum boilers, 3 shafts, 111,000 shp = 30.5 knots

BUNKERAGE & RANGE: 4,850 tons = 11,000 nm @ 14 knots

AIRCRAFT: 36

ARMAMENT: 8 x twin 4.5" DP, 6 x 8-barrelled 2 pdr AA

COMPLEMENT: 1,200

DESIGN: The central objectives of this design were preserving the ship's strike and reconnaissance force and protecting the carrier against destruction by catastrophic explosion or fire within the hangar. These were attained by designing the hangar as an armored box, and compensating for the attendant weight penalty by reducing the hangar space to a single level. The flight deck and hangar floor received 3-inch armor, the hangar sides and ends were enclosed by 4–1/2-inch armor, and there was a 4–1/2-inch armor belt below the hangar floor. There were only two elevators, one at each end of the hangar. The hangar, which could accommodate 36 aircraft, was 458 feet long, 62 feet wide, and had an overhead clearance of 16 feet. The design's machinery was similar to *Ark Royal*'s but more widely spaced and all auxiliary machinery was outside the main compartments. Transverse-wire arresting gear and a single more powerful catapult were fitted on the flight deck, which also had long round downs to improve airflow. The starboard island also received careful streamlining. The 4.5-inch antiaircraft guns were in power-operated enclosed mountings.

MODIFICATIONS: The principal modifications during wartime involved flattening the round downs fore and aft to expand available deck length to 740 feet and augmenting the light antiaircraft battery with 20mm and 40mm weapons (the *Victorious*, for example, had forty-five 20mm and twenty-one 40mm by war's end). Elevators were enlarged and arresting gear strengthened to cope with larger, heavier aircraft. Deck park stowage increased aircraft capacity to 54. Radar was updated and expanded as the war progressed. By the end of the war, complements exceeded 2,000 officers and men and tonnage had risen to about 26,000 tons standard and as much as 31,650 tons at deep load. Postwar, the *Illustrious*

was stripped of most light AA weapons and the flight deck extended forward, while the *Victorious* was given a major reconstruction.

SERVICE: The *Illustrious* first served in the Mediterranean, covering convoys and undertaking strikes against the Italian fleet, most notably the attack on Taranto on the night of November 10–11, 1940, that sank the battleship *Conte di Cavour* and damaged the battleships *Caio Duilio* and *Littorio*. Subsequently, on January 10, 1941, it survived probably the worst damage of any carrier, when it was hit by eight 500-pound or 1,000-pound bombs off Crete, followed by several other hits while at Malta for emergency repairs. The *Illustrious* was repaired at Norfolk Navy Yard in the United States from May to November 1941 and returned to operations in May 1942, covering landings at Madagascar. It served in the Home Fleet in 1943 until it went to the Mediterranean to cover the Salerno landings in September 1943. In 1944 the *Illustrious* went to the East Indies Fleet for operations against targets in Java and Sumatra. It then formed part of the main striking force of the British Pacific Fleet for operations at Okinawa. After World War II, the *Illustrious* became a trials carrier until laid up at the end of 1954. It was sold for scrapping on November 3, 1956. The *Victorious* took part in the hunt for the battleship *Bismarck*, followed by further Home fleet service covering Russian convoys and making strikes against Norwegian targets. In 1942 it participated in a series of Malta convoy operations before a refit at Norfolk Navy Yard the following winter. The *Victorious* operated in the Solomons with the United States Pacific Fleet from May to July 1943 and returned to the Home Fleet for strikes on the *Tirpitz* in April 1944. It then went to the East Indies and British Pacific fleets until war's end, after which it was in reserve until reconstructed.

The *Formidable* served almost continuously in the Mediterranean, where it played a crucial role in the Battle of Matapan and, after a major repair and refit, covered landings in North Africa and Sicily. In the fall of 1944 it joined its sisters in the East Indies and British Pacific fleets. After World War II, the *Formidable* was in reserve from 1947 until sold in 1953 for scrapping.

UNITED STATES: *LANGLEY* (1922)
Courtesy of Art-Tech

BUILDER: Mare Island Navy Yard

LAID DOWN: October 18, 1911. Launched: August 24,1912. Commissioned: March 20, 1922

DISPLACEMENT: 11,050 tons (standard), 14,700 tons (full load)

DIMENSIONS: 542'2" (oa) x 65'3" x 20'6" (mean)

FLIGHT DECK: 523'0" x 65'0"

MACHINERY: General Electric turbo-electric drive, 3 Bureau boilers, 2 shafts, 7,152 shp = 15 knots

BUNKERAGE & RANGE: 2,003 tons = 12,260 nm @ 10 knots.

AIRCRAFT: 33

ARMAMENT: 4 x 5" AA

COMPLEMENT: 410

DESIGN: The *Langley* originally was completed as the collier *Jupiter* on April 7, 1913 and was the United States Navy's first turbo-electric drive ship. The collier was selected for conversion into an aircraft carrier because it had large holds and hatches suitable for stowing aircraft, hoisting gear was already in place, and its turbo-electric drive enabled it to back down at full power, which could be advantageous during aircraft operations. Design work for the conversion was completed in July 1919 and the project began in March 1920. The wooden flight deck was built over the upper deck and the original bridge was retained. The forward hold was converted to stow aviation fuel and the fourth hold accommodated the elevator. The remaining four holds stowed disassembled aircraft—there was no hangar or hangar deck and aircraft were made ready on the lowered elevator before being raised to the flight deck. Furnace gases were vented through a folding stack on the port side aft and cross-connected to a smoke vent on the starboard side. The flight deck carried longitudinal wire arresting gear derived from British practice and there was a single catapult forward on the flight deck.

MODIFICATIONS: Soon after completion, the single folding stack to port was replaced by a pair of folding units and the starboard smoke vent eliminated. The single catapult, similar to those used on prewar cruisers, was removed and replaced by a pair of compressed-air powered catapults set flush in the deck. The longitudinal-wire arresting system was replaced by a transverse-wire system using friction braking drums. In July 1928 the catapults were removed, and in 1936–1937 the ship was converted into a seaplane tender with the forward half of the flight deck removed.

SERVICE: The *Langley* began aircraft flying trials on October 17, 1922 and thereafter operated a wide range of both operational and experimental aircraft types in its role as an experimental carrier. Among other "firsts" was a flight by a Douglas T2D-1 in 1927, the first flight by a multiengined aircraft from a carrier, and operations by a Pitcairn XOP-1 autogyro in September 1931, the first by a rotary winged aircraft from a carrier. After conversion to a seaplane carrier, the *Langley* was assigned to the Asiatic Fleet and was sunk by Japanese naval aircraft on February 27, 1942, off the Java coast.

UNITED STATES: *LEXINGTON* CLASS (1927)
Courtesy of Art-Tech

BUILDER:

Lexington: Bethlehem Steel Company, Quincy, MA

Saratoga: New York Shipbuilding Corporation, Camden, NJ

LAID DOWN:

Lexington: January 8, 1921. Launched: October 3, 1925. Commissioned: December 14, 1927

Saratoga: September 25, 1920. Launched: April 7, 1925. Commissioned: November 16, 1927

DISPLACEMENT: 37,778 tons (standard), 43,054 tons (full load)

DIMENSIONS: 888'0" (oa) x 104'7" x 27'6" (mean), 32'6" (full load)

FLIGHT DECK: 830'0" x 105'8"

MACHINERY: General Electric turbo-electric drive, 16 water-tube boilers, 4 shafts, 180,000 shp = 33.25 knots

BUNKERAGE & RANGE: 5,400 tons = 10,000 nm @ 15 knots.

AIRCRAFT: 80

ARMAMENT: 8 x twin 8", 12 x 5" AA

COMPLEMENT: 2,122

DESIGN: These vessels were originally begun as battle cruisers but the Washington Treaty of 1922 voided their completion. The treaty instead allowed the United States to reconstruct two incomplete hulls as very large aircraft carriers. A large hangar, 440 feet long, 66 feet wide, with 21 feet of overhead clearance, was constructed on top of the original hull above the main deck and surmounted by a full-length flight deck. Below the after end of the hangar was stowage for disassembled aircraft and behind the hangar was a large aviation maintenance space. Two large elevators linked the hangar and flight deck, which also carried transverse-wire arresting gear and a 155-foot long catapult forward. The hangar was completely enclosed by hull plating to the flight deck with side openings for boat stowage. Furnace gases were evacuated via trunking through a massive stack on the starboard side. Ahead of the stack were the bridge and two of the 8-inch twin turrets with the other pair of 8-inch twin turrets abaft the stack. The 5-inch AA guns were in sponsons at gallery deck level.

MODIFICATIONS: The catapult was removed from both carriers in 1934 and the *Lexington*'s forward flight deck widened in 1936. The same year both carriers received about thirty 0.50-inch machine guns to defend them against dive-bomber attacks. In 1940 five quadruple 1.1-inch machine cannon mounts replaced some of the machine guns and the carriers gained CXAM-1 air search radar. The *Lexington* landed its 8-inch turrets in April 1942 and then carried twelve quadruple 1.1-inch machine cannon mounts, thirty-two 20mm AA, and twenty-eight 0.50-inch machine guns. The *Saratoga* at that time retained the turrets and carried nine quadruple 1.1-inch machine cannon mounts and thirty-two 20mm AA but no machine guns. The *Saratoga* was refitted between January 11 and May 22, 1942, after being torpedoed. A very large bulge on the port side was added, the 8-inch turrets and 5-inch

single AA guns removed, and eight twin 5-inch/38 caliber mounts fitted in their place. The bridge was modified and the flight deck widened forward and extended aft. Four quadruple 40mm mounts were fitted and an additional SC search radar mounted on the stack. In September and October 1942 the *Saratoga* underwent further work to repair damage from yet another torpedo attack. The remaining 1.1-inch mounts were removed and replaced with quadruple 40mm weapons, bringing the total to nine, together with fifty-two 20mm AA guns. A further refit in December 1943 added fourteen quadruple 40mm mounts, a Type SM fighter direction radar set, and two hydraulic catapults on the flight deck forward.

SERVICE: Both carriers served with the Pacific Fleet throughout the period before World War II. Their work during the annual Fleet Problems and other tactical exercises laid the foundations for the United States Navy's carrier doctrine during World War II. The *Lexington* undertook a series of raids into the Pacific after Pearl Harbor. On May 8, 1942, during the Battle of the Coral Sea aircraft from the Japanese carriers *Shokaku* and *Zuikaku* hit it with torpedoes and bombs, igniting serious fires that caused a major aviation fuel explosion. The destroyer *Phelps* scuttled it with torpedoes when it became clear it could not be saved. The *Saratoga* spent much of 1942 repairing after torpedo damage. In 1943 it operated in the southwest Pacific and Solomons. From March to May 1944 the

Saratoga joined the British East Indies Fleet in strikes against targets in Java and Sumatra and then, after a refit, it was used for pilot training. In February 1945 the *Saratoga* rejoined the Pacific Fleet as a night carrier at Iwo Jima where it was seriously damaged by bombs and kamikaze strikes. After repairs it returned to pilot training. At the end of the war, the carrier was used for troop transportation. The *Saratoga* was sunk as a target during the atomic bomb tests at Bikini on July 25, 1946.

UNITED STATES: *RANGER* (1934)
Courtesy of Art-Tech

BUILDER: Newport News Shipbuilding & Dry Dock Company, Newport News, VA

LAID DOWN: September 26, 1931. Launched: February 25, 1933. Commissioned: July 4,1934

DISPLACEMENT: 14,000 tons (standard), 17,577 tons (full load)

DIMENSIONS: 769'0" (oa) x 80'0" x 19'8" (mean), 22'6" (full load)

FLIGHT DECK: 710'0" x 87'6"

MACHINERY: Curtis/Parsons geared turbines, 6 Babcock & Wilcox boilers, 2 shafts, 53,500 shp = 29 knots

BUNKERAGE & RANGE: 2,350 tons = 10,000 nm @ 15 knots.

AIRCRAFT: 76

ARMAMENT: 8 x 5" AA, 40 x 0.50" machine guns

COMPLEMENT: 1,788

DESIGN: The *Ranger* was the first American carrier designed from the keel up. The hangar and flight deck were constructed entirely as superstructure. To maintain a clear flight deck, furnace gases were vented through three stacks on either side of the flight deck aft. To minimize the ductwork, the boiler rooms were located abaft the engine rooms. The hangar was 552 feet long and 62 feet wide, bigger than that of the *Lexington* class. It was linked to the flight deck by three elevators, the forward pair offset to starboard to ease movement of aircraft. The ship carried only antiaircraft guns and its limited tonnage precluded fitting any armor protection. Before completing, a small island was added amidships.

MODIFICATIONS: Sixteen 0.50-inch machine guns were removed in September 1941 and replaced by six quadruple 1.1-inch machine cannon mounts. In 1942 it received CXAM-1 radar and thirty 20mm AA. In January 1943 its light AA battery was six quadruple 40mm mounts and forty-six 20mm AA. In the summer of 1944, since the ship was badly overweight, all 5-inch AA guns, together with six 20mm, were landed, new radar sets installed, and a hydraulic catapult fitted forward on the flight deck.

SERVICE: The *Ranger* served with the Pacific Fleet until 1939, when it transferred to the Atlantic. It then operated as part of the Neutrality Patrol until the United States entered World War II. After a series of aircraft transportation operations the *Ranger* formed part of the force covering landings in North Africa in November 1942. It returned to aircraft transportation duties until August 1943 when it joined the British Home Fleet for operations off the coast of Norway. In January 1944 the *Ranger* returned to the United States and spent the remainder of the war on aircraft transportation and flight training duties. It was decommissioned on October 18, 1946, and sold for scrap on January 28, 1947.

UNITED STATES: *YORKTOWN* CLASS (1937)
Courtesy of Library of Congress

LAID DOWN:

Yorktown: May 21, 1934. Launched: April 4, 1936. Commissioned: September 30, 1937

Enterprise: July 16, 1934. Launched: October 3, 1936. Commissioned: 12 May 1938

Hornet: September 29, 1939. Launched: December 14, 1940. Commissioned: October 20, 1941

BUILDER: Newport News Shipbuilding & Dry Dock Company, Newport News, VA

DISPLACEMENT: 19,872 tons (standard), 25,500 tons (full load)

DIMENSIONS: 809'6" (oa) x 83'3" x 21'6" (mean), 25'11" (full load)

FLIGHT DECK: 802'0" x 86'0"

MACHINERY: Parsons geared turbines, 9 Babcock & Wilcox boilers, 4 shafts, 120,000 shp = 32.5 knots

BUNKERAGE & RANGE: 4,360 tons = 12,000 nm @ 15 knots.

AIRCRAFT: 96

ARMAMENT: 8 x 5" AA, 24 x 0.50" machine guns

COMPLEMENT: 1,890

DESIGN: The greater tonnage of this design allowed a better balance between machinery, aircraft features, and protection. The hangar (645 feet long by 68 feet wide, with 17 feet overhead clearance) and flight deck, again, were light superstructure items. The hangar had large side openings, closed by shutters in heavy weather, which eased embarkation of equipment, allowed aircraft to run up engines below deck, and naturally vented dangerous fuel vapors. It was linked to the flight deck by three elevators. The flight deck carried arresting gear both aft and forward. There were three hydraulic catapults, two on the forward flight deck and the third athwartships on the hangar deck. The machinery was arranged amidships. The furnace gases were trunked under the hangar deck and, unlike the *Ranger,* the design incorporated a conventional island that contained the large stack. The *Hornet*'s design was slightly different with a 5-foot wider flight deck. The

Hornet also came out of the yard carrying the four quadruple 1.1-inch machine cannon mounts included in the original design but not fitted because the weapons were not ready for service when the *Yorktown* and the *Enterprise* commissioned.

MODIFICATIONS: Both the *Yorktown* and the *Enterprise* received their 1.1-inch machine cannon mounts in 1940, together with CXAM radar sets. The *Hornet* initially received the then new SC set but added a CXAM set in the summer of 1942 to compensate for the newer set's disappointing performance. All three ships replaced their 0.50-inch machine guns with 20mm AA guns by June 1942, 24 weapons aboard the *Yorktown* and the *Hornet* and 32 aboard the *Enterprise*. After the Battle of Midway, the *Enterprise* and the *Hornet* received an additional quadruple 1.1-inch machine cannon mount on the bow and increased their 20mm armament to 38 and 32 mounts respectively. The *Enterprise* replaced the 1.1-inch mounts with quadruple 40mm mounts in November 1942 and added a further 8 20mm guns. In July 1943 the *Enterprise* began a major refit. The hull was bulged to 95 feet 5 inches, its light AA armament increased to a total of six quadruple 40mm, eight twin 40mm, and fifty 20mm, new Mk. 37 directors, and a new radar outfit. In addition, its aviation fuel stowage and firefighting equipment were upgraded. The *Enterprise*'s final refit, completed in September 1945, upgraded its light AA battery to a total of eleven quadruple 40mm, five twin 40mm, and sixteen twin 20mm.

SERVICE: The *Yorktown* and the *Enterprise* both served with the Pacific Fleet until April 1941, when the *Yorktown* transferred to the Atlantic Fleet for Neutrality Patrol duties. The *Yorktown* returned to the Pacific after Pearl Harbor and both carriers conducted raids into the western Pacific. The *Yorktown* then operated with the *Lexington* in the Coral Sea until the Battle of the Coral Sea, May 7–8, 1942, in which it was damaged by aircraft from the carriers *Shokaku* and *Zuikaku*. After repairs at Pearl Harbor, the *Yorktown* joined its sisters to intercept the Japanese assault on the island of Midway. Its dive-bombers devastated the carrier *Soryu* on June 4, but itself fell victim to three bombs and two torpedoes. Damage control parties seemed to be making progress in saving the ship when it was struck by two torpedoes from the submarine *I-158* on June 6 and capsized the following day. The *Hornet*'s first mission was the raid on Tokyo, launched on April 18, 1942, using United States Army Air Force B-25 bombers commanded by Colonel James H. Doolittle. It then fought in the Battle of Midway, followed by operations covering the campaign at Guadalcanal. On October 26 it and the *Enterprise* intercepted a Japanese force in the Battle of Santa Cruz, during which it was hit by numerous bombs and torpedoes, set ablaze, and sank the following day. The *Enterprise* was very heavily damaged in the Battle of the

Eastern Solomons on August 24, 1942. After the Battle of Santa Cruz, the *Enterprise* engaged in the Battle of Guadalcanal, November 13–15, and continued to operate in the Solomons area until its major refit in July 1943. From November 1943 to April 1944 the *Enterprise* conducted raids in the western Pacific with other Pacific Fleet carriers. It then covered the invasion of Saipan in June, and played a large role in the Battle of the Philippine Sea on June 19. The carrier was part of operations leading up to the invasion of the Philippines and fought again in the Battle of Leyte Gulf (October 23–26, 1944). After overhaul, the *Enterprise* covered operations at Iwo Jima and Okinawa, where it received major damage from bomb and kamikaze strikes. It did not return to operations until after the end of World War II, when it brought thousands of troops home as part of the "Magic Carpet" operation. The *Enterprise* decommissioned on February 17, 1947, and was sold for scrapping on July 1, 1958.

UNITED STATES: *WASP* (1940)
Courtesy of Art-Tech

BUILDER: Bethlehem Steel Company, Quincy, MA

LAID DOWN: April 1, 1936. Launched: April 4, 1939. Commissioned: April 25, 1940

DISPLACEMENT: 15,752 tons (standard), 19,116 tons (full load)

DIMENSIONS: 741'3" (oa) x 803'9" x 20'0" (mean), 24'6" (full load)

FLIGHT DECK: 727'6" x 93'0"

MACHINERY: Parsons geared turbines, 6 Yarrow boilers, 2 shafts, 70,000 shp = 29.5 knots

BUNKERAGE & RANGE: 2,400 tons = 12,000 nm @ 15 knots

AIRCRAFT: 84

ARMAMENT: 8 x 5" AA, 4 x quadruple 1.1" machine cannon, 16 x 0.50" machine guns

COMPLEMENT: 1,889

DESIGN: The *Wasp* was designed to use up the remaining carrier tonnage available to the United States under the Washington Treaty. Its design included several unusual features: an asymmetric hull to obviate the need for ballast to counterweight the island, a deck-edge elevator to further cut weight, and a machinery arrangement transitional between conventional and the less vulnerable unit arrangement. The hangar, 500 feet long and 75 feet wide, was a similar open-sided structure to previous carriers, topped by a wooden flight deck carrying arresting gear both fore and aft and a pair of catapults forward. Two further athwartships catapults were fitted, and the hangar was linked to the flight deck by two conventional elevators in addition to the deck-edge unit.

MODIFICATIONS: The *Wasp* received CXAM-1 search radar in 1941, and in mid-1942 its 0.50-inch machine guns were replaced by twenty 20mm AA.

SERVICE: The *Wasp* served with the Atlantic Fleet on Neutrality Patrol duties and aircraft transportation missions until the United States entered World War II. It covered major transatlantic convoys in the early part of 1942 then conducted two substantial missions to fly off Spitfire fighters for Malta in April and May. The *Wasp* transferred to the Pacific in June and provided crucial air cover for the invasion of Guadalcanal and subsequent operations to secure the island during August and September. On September 15, 1942, while operating near San Cristobal Island, the *Wasp* was torpedoed and sunk by the submarine *I-19*.

CAPITAL SHIPS

GERMANY: *GRAF ZEPPELIN* CLASS
Courtesy of Art-Tech

LAID DOWN:
Graf Zeppelin: December 28, 1936.
 Launched: December 8, 1938
Carrier "B": September 30, 1936

BUILDER:
Graf Zeppelin: Deutsche Werke, Kiel
Carrier "B": Krupp Germania Werft,
 Kiel

DISPLACEMENT: 19,250 tons (standard),
 28,100 tons (full load)

DIMENSIONS: 820'3" (oa) x 88'7" x
 24'11" (mean), 27'10" (full load)

FLIGHT DECK: 793'11" x 88'7"

MACHINERY: Brown Boverie geared turbines, 16 La Mont boilers, 4 shafts,
 200,000 shp = 36 knots

BUNKERAGE & RANGE: 5,000 tons =
 11,480 nm @ 15 knots

AIRCRAFT: 43

ARMAMENT: 16 x 5.9" LA, 6 x twin 4.1"
 AA, 11 x twin 37mm AA, 7 x 20mm
 AA

COMPLEMENT: 1,750

DESIGN: Wilhelm Hadeler's design for
 these vessels included two hangars,
 an upper 606 feet 11 inches long and
52 feet 6 inches wide and a lower
564 feet 4 inches long and 52 feet 6
inches wide, under the flight deck,
all linked together by three electrically powered elevators. The flight
deck carried transverse-wire arresting gear and two compressed-air
powered catapults forward that each
could launch nine aircraft in four
minutes, after which it would take almost an hour to recharge the compressed air reservoirs. The starboard
island was long and low, and incorporated a large part of the antiaircraft
battery either on or fore and aft of it.
Four high-angle directors were provided to control the heavy antiaircraft weapons. The main antisurface
battery was disposed in casemates
along the sides of the hull, where its
position made it likely to be of limited efficacy at sea.

MODIFICATIONS: During World War II
the design was modified to incorporate large bulges, mainly to offset
light antiaircraft battery additions

and some stability problems that had emerged. These bulges stowed additional fuel, raising the total bunkerage to 6,740 tons.

SERVICE: Construction of "Carrier B" was stopped on September 19, 1939 and the incomplete hull was broken up in February 1940. Work on the *Graf Zeppelin* also ceased. It recommenced to a slightly revised design in December 1942 but work ceased once again on January 30, 1943. The abandoned hull was scuttled at Stettin on April 25, 1945. It was raised by Soviet Union forces and renamed the *PO-101* on February 3, 1947, then used as a target for bombs and torpedoes. The hulk finally was sunk on August 16, 1947, off Swinemunde.

JAPAN: CONVERTED FLEET AUXILIARIES (1940)
Courtesy of Art-Tech

Shoho Class

Shoho
Laid down: December 3, 1934. Launched: June 1, 1935. Commissioned: January 26, 1942

Zuiho
Laid down: June 20, 1935. Launched: June 19, 1936. Commissioned: December 27, 1940
Builder: Yokosuka Navy Yard
Displacement: 11,262 tons (standard), 14,200 tons (full load)
Dimensions: 674'2" (oa) x 59'8" x 21'7" (mean)
Flight deck: 590'6" x 75'6"
Machinery: Geared turbines, 4 Kampon boilers, 2 shafts, 52,000 shp = 28 knots
Bunkerage & range: 2,600 tons = 7,800 nm @ 18 knots
Aircraft: 30
Armament: 4 x twin 5" AA, 4 x twin 25mm AA
Complement: 785

Chitose Class

Chitose
Laid down: November 26, 1934. Launched: November 29, 1936. Commissioned: January 1, 1944

Chiyoda
Laid down: December 14, 1936. Launched: November 19, 1937. Commissioned: October 31, 1943
Builder: Kure Navy Yard
Displacement: 11,190 tons (standard), 15,300 tons (full load)
Dimensions: 631'7" (oa) x 68'3" x 24'8" (mean)
Flight deck: 590'6" x 75'0"
Machinery: Geared turbines + 2 diesel engines, 4 Kampon boilers, 2 shafts, 44,000 shp + 12,800 bhp= 28.9 knots
Bunkerage & range: 3,600 tons = 11,000 nm @ 18 knots
Aircraft: 30
Armament: 4 x twin 5" AA, 10 x triple 25mm AA
Complement: 800

Ryuho

BUILDER: Yokosuka Navy Yard

LAID DOWN: April 12, 1933. Launched: November 16, 1933. Commissioned: November 28, 1942

DISPLACEMENT: 13,360 tons (standard), 16,764 tons (full load)

DIMENSIONS: 707'4" (oa) x 64'3" x 21'9" (mean)

FLIGHT DECK: 607'0" x 75'6"

MACHINERY: Geared turbines, 4 Kampon boilers, 2 shafts, 52,000 shp = 26.5 knots

BUNKERAGE & RANGE: 2,900 tons = 8,000 nm @ 18 knots

AIRCRAFT: 31

ARMAMENT: 4 x twin 5" AA, 6 x triple 25mm AA, 20 x single 25mm AA

COMPLEMENT: 989

DESIGN: Naval arms limitations treaties restricted the carrier tonnage available to Japan to a level below that considered necessary for wartime operations. The Imperial Japanese Navy, to circumvent these limitations, built a number of fast fleet auxiliaries whose designs envisaged their rapid conversion into aircraft carriers in the event of war. Five of these auxiliaries, the seaplane tenders *Chitose* and *Chiyoda,* and the submarine depot ships *Tsurugisaki* (renamed the *Shoho*), *Takasagi* (renamed the *Zuiho*), and *Taigei* (renamed the *Ryuho*), were converted between 1940 and 1944 in very similar fashion. Hangars and flight decks replaced their original superstructures, furnace gases ducted to starboard to vent through downward-inclined stacks, two elevators and arresting gear installed, and arma-ment redisposed and somewhat enhanced. The seaplane tenders received bulges to enhance their stability, while the submarine depot ships were reengined with destroyer turbines and boilers in place of their original diesel installations.

MODIFICATIONS: The *Chitose* and the *Chiyoda* received an additional six triple 25mm AA soon after completion. In 1943 the *Zuiho*'s twin 25mm mounts were replaced and supplemented by sixteen triple 25mm mounts. Twenty single 25mm weapons and six 28-barreled rocket launchers were added in 1944 and the flight deck extended forward to 632 feet overall. The *Ryuho*'s light AA battery was increased to fourteen triple 25mm and six 13.2mm weapons in 1943. In 1944 the flight deck was extended forward to 650 feet overall and a further nineteen single 25mm and fifteen 13.2mm weapons, plus six 28-barreled rocket launchers were added.

SERVICE: The *Shoho*'s first operation was to cover the proposed assault on Port Moresby, during which it was sunk by aircraft from the American carrier *Yorktown* in the Battle of the Coral Sea on May 7, 1942. The *Zuiho* covered the invasion of the Dutch East Indies and then participated in the Aleutians and Midway campaigns. During operations off Guadalcanal it participated in the Battle of Santa Cruz on October 26, 1942, during which it was damaged by aircraft from the American carrier *Enterprise.* After repairs, it returned to Guadalcanal in December 1942. It took part in operations in the Marianas in June 1943 and the Battle of the Philippine Sea in June 1944. The *Zuiho,* the *Chiyoda,* and the *Chitose,* the latter pair operating as carriers for the first time, formed part of the Japanese effort to turn back the American assault on the Philippines in Leyte Gulf, during which they were sunk at the Battle of Cape Engaño on October 25, 1944 by aircraft from Task Force 38. The *Ryuho* was damaged during the Doolittle Raid on Tokyo on April 18, 1942, and torpedoed and damaged off Tokyo on December 12, 1942, by the American submarine *Drum.* After repairs it operated mainly as a training carrier and was again torpedoed and damaged by the American submarine *Sailfish* on December 4, 1943. It formed part of the Japanese main body during the Battle of the Philippine Sea and was damaged by aircraft from the American carrier *Enterprise* on June 20, 1944. It suffered severe damage during an air raid on Kure on April 20, 1945, and did not return to service. It was broken up in 1946.

JAPAN: *SHOKAKU* CLASS (1941)
Courtesy of Art-Tech

Shokaku

BUILDER: Yokosuka Navy Yard

LAID DOWN: December 12, 1937. Launched: June 1, 1939. Commissioned: August 8, 1941

Zuikaku

BUILDER: Kawasaki Dockyard Company, Kobe

LAID DOWN: May 25, 1938. Launched: November 27, 1939. Commissioned: September 25, 1941

DISPLACEMENT: 25,675 tons (standard), 32,105 tons (full load)

DIMENSIONS: 844'10" (oa) x 85'4" x 29'0" (mean)

FLIGHT DECK: 787'0" x 95'0"

MACHINERY: Geared turbines, 8 Kampon boilers, 4 shafts, 160,000 shp = 34.25 knots

BUNKERAGE & RANGE: 5,300 tons = 10,000 nm @ 18 knots

AIRCRAFT: 84

ARMAMENT: 8 x twin 5" AA, 12 x triple 25mm AA

COMPLEMENT: 1,660

DESIGN: These two carriers were a substantial enlargement of the successful *Hiryu* design with greater protection, a more powerful antiaircraft battery, and an expanded air group. They were equipped with two catapults forward, the first aboard Japanese carriers.

MODIFICATIONS: Both carriers received substantial additions to their light antiaircraft batteries as the war progressed. Added to them were four triple 25mm mounts when combat damage was repaired in the summer of 1942 and two triple 25 mm plus sixteen single 25mm mounts at the end of the year. The *Zuikaku* received an additional two triple 25mm and twenty single 25mm weapons when repaired after the Battle of the Philippine Sea, together with six 28-barrelled rocket launchers. Both carriers also received surface and air warning radar sets in late 1943.

SERVICE: The two carriers formed the 5th *Kokutai* of the 1st *Koku-Kantai* and participated in all the fleet's operations from Pearl Harbor to the raids in the Indian Ocean. They were detached to cover the planned assault on New Guinea, aborted by the Battle of the Coral Sea May 7–8, 1942, during which the *Shokaku* was damaged. The *Zuikaku* participated in the Aleutians operation, and then both carriers reformed as the 1st *Kokutai* and took part in the series of operations around Guadalcanal between August and October 1942, including the battles of the Eastern Solomons and Santa Cruz. The *Shokaku* was heavily damaged during the Battle of Santa Cruz and re-turned to Japan for repairs. The *Zuikaku* covered the Japanese evacuation from Guadalcanal, then both carriers operated together around Truk in November 1943. Both ships refitted and trained new air groups before participating in operations leading to the Battle of the Philippine Sea, during which the *Shokaku* was torpedoed and sunk by the American submarine *Cavalla* on June 19, 1944, and the *Zuikaku* was damaged. The *Zuikaku* next took part in the Japanese assault on American operations in Leyte Gulf and was sunk by aircraft from the American carriers *Essex* and *Lexington* during the Battle of Cape Engaño on October 25, 1944.

JAPAN: *HIYO* CLASS (1942)
Courtesy of Art-Tech

Hiyo
BUILDER: Kawasaki Dockyard Company, Kobe
LAID DOWN: November 30, 1939. Launched: June 24, 1941. Commissioned: July 31, 1942

Junyo
BUILDER: Mitsubishi Shipbuilding Company, Nagasaki
LAID DOWN: March 20, 1939. Launched: June 26, 1941. Commissioned: May 5, 1942
DISPLACEMENT: 24,140 tons (standard), 29,464 tons (full load)
DIMENSIONS: 719'6" (oa) x 87'7" x 26'9" (mean)
FLIGHT DECK: 689'0" x 89'6"
MACHINERY: Geared turbines, 6 Kampon boilers, 2 shafts, 56,250 shp = 25.5 knots

BUNKERAGE & RANGE: 3,000 tons
AIRCRAFT: 53
ARMAMENT: 6 x twin 5" AA, 8 x triple 25mm AA
COMPLEMENT: 1,200
DESIGN: These vessels were part of Japan's "shadow" carrier program implemented to circumvent treaty tonnage limitations. The navy funded 60 percent of their cost when they were laid down as the fast liners *Izumo Maru* and *Kashiwara Maru* for the Nippon Yusen Kaisha (Japan Mail Steamship Company). The liner design incorporated a double hull for protection against torpedoes, extensive compartmentation, additional spaces for bunker fuel and gasoline stowage and for extra electric cabling, superstructure arrangements designed for ready modification to

incorporate hangars and elevators, and unique more powerful high-pressure steam power plants for higher service speed. All features were intended to ease conversion although, rather strangely, no foundations were prepared for armament installation nor was provision made to trunk furnace gases to one side to clear the flight deck. Both ships were complete to the main deck when conversion began in late 1940. The promenade deck was extended fore and aft to form the flight deck and fully equipped for aircraft operations with arresting gear, crash barriers, night landing lighting, a wind screen, and refueling points. The depth of the hull allowed construction of double hangars, each about 500 feet long, 49 feet wide, and 16 feet high, connected to the flight deck by two large elevators. These ships also featured the most elaborate bridge arrangements yet fitted to Japanese carriers and vented furnace gases through a large stack angled outboard at 26 degrees from the vertical to make sure they were clear of flight operations. Antiaircraft weapons were on side sponsons arranged just below the flight deck level. On commissioning both vessels also carried Type 21 radar sets.

MODIFICATIONS: The ship's antiaircraft batteries grew considerably as the war progressed. In spring 1943 each received four additional triple 25mm mounts and four more late in the year along with twelve single 25mm mounts. In August 1944 the *Junyo* added three 25mm triple mounts, two 25mm twin mounts, and eighteen 25mm single mounts, plus six 28-tube 120mm rocket launchers. The *Junyo* completed with its original wood-paneled passenger cabins for aircrew accommodations. These were stripped out and replaced with steel compartments in July–August 1944 and, at the same time, the spaces around the gasoline storage tanks were filled with concrete for protection.

SERVICE: The *Junyo* participated in operations in the Aleutians in June 1942 and then both carriers were in action throughout the Guadalcanal campaign, although machinery problems kept the *Hiyo* out of the Battle of Santa Cruz. Both carriers took part in the Battle of the Philippine Sea, during which the *Hiyo* was sunk by aircraft from the *Belleau Wood* and the *Junyo* seriously damaged. The submarines *Redfish* and *Sea Devil* hit the *Junyo* with two torpedoes on December 9, 1944. It reached Sasebo under its own power and was repaired by March 1945 but never reentered service. It was stripped of its armament between May and August 1945, stricken from the navy list on November 30, and scrapped between June and August 1946.

JAPAN: *TAIHO* (1944)

BUILDER: Kawasaki Dockyard Company, Kobe

LAID DOWN: July 10, 1941. Launched: April 7, 1943. Commissioned: March 7, 1944

DISPLACEMENT: 29,300 tons (standard), 37,270 (full load)

DIMENSIONS: 855'0" (oa) x 90'11" x 31'6" (mean)

FLIGHT DECK: 843'0" x 98'6"

MACHINERY: Geared turbines, 8 Kampon boilers, 4 shafts, 160,000 shp = 33.33 knots

BUNKERAGE & RANGE: 5,700 tons = 8,000 nm @ 18 knots

AIRCRAFT: 60

ARMAMENT: 6 x twin 100mm AA, 16 x triple 25mm AA, 23 x single 25mm AA

COMPLEMENT: 1,750

DESIGN: The *Taiho*'s design evolved from the *Shokaku*'s, eliminating one deck but adding 3-inch armor to the flight deck in addition to the 4.9 inches of armor on the hangar deck, which remained the hull's strength deck. The design also incorporated heavy 5.9-inch side armor, making the *Taiho* proportionally the most heavily protected aircraft carrier designed as such. The bow was plated to the flight deck like British carriers. The double hangars were about 500 feet long, 50 feet wide, and 16 feet 6 inches high, and the carrier actually operated an air group as large as seventy-five machines, rather than the sixty aircraft in the design. Two unarmored elevators linked the hangars to the flight deck, which was fully equipped with arresting gear, crash barriers, a wind screen, night landing lighting, and refueling points. There was a large island structure incorporating an inclined stack similar to that on the *Hiyo* class, carrying two Type 21 radar antennae.

SERVICE: The *Taiho* participated in the Battle of the Philippine Sea. On June 19, 1944, the submarine *Archerfish* hit it with a torpedo, jamming the forward elevator in the down position and rupturing gasoline lines. Gasoline vapor spread through the ship, ignited, and exploded, sinking the ship.

JAPAN: *UNRYU* CLASS (1944)
Courtesy of Art-Tech

Unryu
BUILDER: Yokosuka Navy Yard
LAID DOWN: August 1, 1942. Launched: September 25, 1943. Commissioned: August 6, 1944

Amagi
BUILDER: Mitsubishi Shipbuilding Company, Nagasaki
LAID DOWN: October 1, 1942. Launched: October 15, 1943. Commissioned: August 10, 1944

Katsuragi
BUILDER: Kure Navy Yard
LAID DOWN: December 8, 1942. Launched: January 19, 1944.

Kasagi
BUILDER: Mitsubishi Shipbuilding Company, Nagasaki
LAID DOWN: April 14, 1943. Launched: October 19, 1944.

Aso
BUILDER: Kure Navy Yard
LAID DOWN: June 8, 1943. Launched: November 1, 1944

Ikoma
BUILDER: Kawasaki Dockyard Company, Kobe
LAID DOWN: July 5, 1943. Launched: November 17, 1944
DISPLACEMENT: 17,150 tons (standard), 22,500 tons (full load)
DIMENSIONS: 745'11" (oa) x 72'2" x 25'9" (mean)
FLIGHT DECK: 712'0" x 88'6"
MACHINERY: Geared turbines, 8 Kampon boilers, 4 shafts, 152,000 shp = 34 knots
BUNKERAGE & RANGE: 3,670 tons = 8,000 miles @ 18 knots
AIRCRAFT: 65
ARMAMENT: 6 x twin 5" AA, 17 x triple 25mm AA

COMPLEMENT: 1,595

DESIGN: This design evolved from that of the *Soryu* with heavier 5.9-inch side armor protection for the magazines and only two elevators. Shortages led to the installation of 100,000 shp destroyer plants in the *Katsuragi* and the *Aso,* reducing their speed by two knots. The full Japanese carrier radar suite of two Type 21 and one Type 13 sets was installed. Two additional vessels were never laid down.

MODIFICATIONS: The light antiaircraft battery was increased to twenty-two triple 25mm mounts and twenty-three single 25mm mounts, plus six 28-tube 120mm rocket launchers.

SERVICE: The *Kasagi,* the *Aso,* and the *Ikoma* were never completed and were scrapped after World War II. The *Katsuragi* was damaged at Kure by aircraft bombs on March 19 and July 28, 1945, and never commissioned. It was used as a repatriation transport from August 1945 until November 1946, and then broken up at Osaka in 1947. The submarine *Redfish* torpedoed and sank the *Unryu* on December 19, 1944, southeast of Shanghai. Aircraft from Task Force 38 damaged the *Amagi* at Kure on March 19, 1945, and sank it on July 24. The wreck was raised and scrapped in 1947.

JAPAN: *SHINANO* (1944)
Courtesy of Art-Tech

BUILDER: Yokosuka Navy Yard

LAID DOWN: May 4, 1940. Launched: 8 October 1944

DISPLACEMENT: 64,800 tons (standard), 71,890 tons (full load)

DIMENSIONS: 872'8" (oa) x 119'1" x 33'10" (mean)

FLIGHT DECK: 827'0" x 131'0"

MACHINERY: Geared turbines, 12 Kampon boilers, 4 shafts, 150,000 shp = 27 knots

BUNKERAGE & RANGE: 8,904 tons = 10,000 nm @ 18 knots

AIRCRAFT: 120

ARMAMENT: 8 x twin 5" AA, 45 x triple 25mm AA, 12 x 28-barrel 120mm rocket launchers

COMPLEMENT: 2,400

DESIGN: The *Shinano* was laid down as a battleship of the *Yamato* class but converted, beginning in mid-1942, into an aircraft carrier. The original plan was to deploy the *Shinano* as a replenishment and support ship for carrier task forces but this was modified to include an operational air group of 40–50 aircraft in addition to large numbers of replenishment machines for other carriers. There was a single open hangar 550 feet long built over the existing battleship hull and supporting a 3.1-inch armored flight deck served by two elevators. A greatly enlarged iteration of the *Taiho*'s island structure was fitted.

SERVICE: The *Shinano* was completed for trials on November 19, 1944, but never commissioned. While in transit from Yokosuka to Kure for final fitting out it was struck by four torpedoes fired by the submarine *Archerfish* on November 29, 1944. The watertight doors for its very extensive internal subdivision and much of the pump machinery were yet to be installed so it sank within seven hours due to uncontrolled flooding.

JAPAN: MERCHANTMEN CONVERTED TO ESCORT CARRIERS (1941)
Courtesy of Art-Tech

Taiyo Class

Taiyo
LAID DOWN: January 6, 1940. Launched: October 19, 1940. Commissioned: September 15, 1941

Unyo
LAID DOWN: December 14, 1938. Launched: October 31, 1939. Commissioned: May 31, 1942

Chuyo
LAID DOWN: May 9, 1938. Launched: May 20, 1939. Commissioned: 25 November 1942
BUILDER: Mitsubishi Shipbuilding Company, Nagasaki
DISPLACEMENT: 17,830 tons (standard), 20,000 tons (full load)
DIMENSIONS: 591'4" (oa) x 73'10" x 25'5" (mean)
FLIGHT DECK: 492'0" x 75'6"
MACHINERY: Geared turbines, 4 boilers, 2 shafts, 25,200 shp = 21 knots
BUNKERAGE & RANGE: 6,500 nm @ 18 knots
AIRCRAFT: 27

ARMAMENT: 6 x 4.7" AA (*Taiyo*) or 4 x twin 5" DP, 8 x 25mm AA
COMPLEMENT: 747

Kaiyo
LAID DOWN: February 22, 1938. Launched: December 9, 1938. Commissioned: November 23, 1943
BUILDER: Mitsubishi Shipbuilding Company, Nagasaki
DISPLACEMENT: 13,600 tons (standard), 16,748 tons (full load)
DIMENSIONS: 546'5" (oa) x 71'10" x 27'0" (mean)
FLIGHT DECK: 492'0" x 72'0"
MACHINERY: Kampon geared turbines, 4 boilers, 2 shafts, 52,000 shp = 24 knots
AIRCRAFT: 24
ARMAMENT: 4 x twin 5" DP, 8 x triple 25mm AA
COMPLEMENT: 829

Shinyo
LAID DOWN: 1933. Launched: December 14, 1934. Commissioned: December 15, 1943

BUILDER: Deschimag Werke AG, Bremen

DISPLACEMENT: 17,500 tons (standard), 20,916 tons (full load)

DIMENSIONS: 621'3" (oa) x 84'0 x 26'9" (mean)

FLIGHT DECK: 553'0" x 80'0"

MACHINERY: AEG geared turbines, 4 water-tube boilers, 2 shafts, 26,000 shp = 22 knots

AIRCRAFT: 33

ARMAMENT: 4 x twin 5" DP, 10 x triple 25mm AA

COMPLEMENT: 942

DESIGN: Japanese auxiliary aircraft carriers were similar in concept to American and British escort carriers, although larger. A single hangar was constructed in place of the original superstructure, topped with a flight deck that was served by two elevators. There was neither arresting gear nor a catapult. Boiler gases vented through downward tilted stacks to starboard and sponsons on either side of the ships supported the antiaircraft battery. They were conned from bridges built under the forward end of the flight deck.

MODIFICATIONS: The light antiaircraft battery increased substantially in all ships to 40–60 25mm weapons. All ships also acquired Type 21 radar.

SERVICE: Unlike the American and British navies, the Imperial Japanese Navy employed its auxiliary carriers almost exclusively for aircraft transport and training duties. Only the *Taiyo* engaged in combat operations, supporting the battleship *Yamato* during the Eastern Solomons operation in August 1942. The *Chuyo* was sunk by torpedoes fired by the submarine *Sailfish* off Yokosuka on December 4, 1943, the *Taiyo* by the submarine *Rasher* off Luzon on August 18, 1944, the *Unyo* by the submarine *Barb* off Hong Kong on September 16, 1944, and the *Shinyo* by the submarine *Spadefish* in the Yellow Sea on November 17, 1944. The *Kaiyo* was disabled by British Pacific Fleet aircraft at Beppu on July 24, 1945, and the wreck scrapped after World War II.

UNITED KINGDOM: *INDOMITABLE* (1941)
Courtesy of Art-Tech

Builder: Vickers (Shipbuilding) Ltd., Barrow-in-Furness

Laid down: November 10, 1937. Launched: March 26, 1940. Commissioned: October 10, 1941

Displacement: 24,680 tons (standard), 29,730 tons (full load)

Dimensions: 743'9" (oa) x 95'9" x 24'0" (mean), 28'0" (full load)

Flight deck: 650'0" x 80'0"

Machinery: Parsons geared turbines, 6 Admiralty 3-drum boilers, 3 shafts, 111,000 shp = 30.5 knots

Bunkerage & range: 4,850 tons = 11,000 nm @ 14 knots.

Aircraft: 48

Armament: 8 x twin 4.5" DP, 6 x 8-barrelled 2 pdr AA, 8 x 20mm AA

Complement: 1,592

Design: The *Indomitable* was laid down as the fourth member of the *Illustrious* class but its design was altered while it was under construction to incorporate some features of the later *Implacable* class. Hull depth was increased by 6 feet and hangar side armor reduced to 1–1/2 inches to compensate for the additional top-weight. The deeper hull allowed for an additional 168-feet long lower hangar aft with 16 feet of overhead clearance, while the upper hangar was reduced to 14 feet in height. The forward elevator was enlarged and both elevators uprated to accommodate aircraft up to 20,000 pounds in weight. The deeper hull also incorporated an additional gallery deck to accommodate extra personnel and aviation equipment for an enlarged air group of 48 aircraft stowed in the hangars and a further 20 aircraft carried as a deck park.

Modifications: In April 1944 the *Indomitable* added two quadruple and two twin 40mm mounts to the light antiaircraft battery and fitted an American SM-1 fighter control radar set on the bridge. In 1945 it gained a further thirteen single 40mm mounts and thirty-six single 20mm mounts.

Service: The *Indomitable* took part in

Operation Pedestal in August 1942. On August 12 it was hit by two 1,100-pound bombs and near-missed by three others, requiring six months for repairs. While covering the invasion of Sicily the *Indomitable* was hit by a torpedo launched by a low-flying Junkers Ju 88 on July 11, 1943, and put out of action for a further eight months. It joined the British East Indies Fleet in July 1944 and participated in a series of very successful strikes during the rest of the year against targets in Sumatra. In January 1945 it transferred to the British Pacific Fleet for operations against Okinawa from March until May, during which it was hit by a kamikaze on May 4 that slid off the armored deck without causing any significant damage. After World War II the *Indomitable* served with the Mediterranean and Home fleets, was sold for scrapping in May 1953, and broken up in 1955.

UNITED KINGDOM: *UNICORN* **(1943)**
Courtesy of Art-Tech

BUILDER: Harland & Wolff Ltd., Belfast

LAID DOWN: June 29, 1939. Launched: November 20, 1941. Commissioned: March 12, 1943

DISPLACEMENT: 16,530 tons (standard), 20,300 tons (full load)

DIMENSIONS: 646'0" (oa) x 90'0" x 17'6" (mean), 20'6" (full load)

FLIGHT DECK: 610'0" x 80'0"

MACHINERY: Parsons geared turbines, 4 Admiralty 3-drum boilers, 2 shafts, 40,000 shp = 24 knots

BUNKERAGE & RANGE: 3,000 tons = 11,000 miles @ 13.5 knots

AIRCRAFT: 36

ARMAMENT: 4 x twin 4" AA, 4 x quadruple 2-pdr AA, 13 x 20mm AA

COMPLEMENT: 1,094

DESIGN: The *Unicorn* was designed as a support vessel for aircraft carrier squadrons but modified during construction to function as an effective carrier when required. The design included double hangars 16 feet 6 inches high but only 300 feet long to allow extra space for workshops. Two elevators capable of carrying aircraft up to 20,000 pounds linked the hangars to the flight deck, which had 2-inch armor, full arresting gear, and a single catapult. There was 2-inch armor around the magazines and 1.5-inch armor protecting the machinery. It also carried Type 281 air warning radar.

MODIFICATIONS: In 1943 the *Unicorn* embarked an additional quadruple 2-pdr mount and further single 40mm and 20mm mounts were added before it joined the British Pacific Fleet.

SERVICE: The *Unicorn* covered Gibraltar convoys in May and June 1943, served with the Home Fleet in July, and then went to the Mediterranean to cover the Salerno landings September 9–12, 1943, operating three squadrons of Seafire fighters. After Atlantic escort duty during 1944, the *Unicorn* joined the British Pacific Fleet in early 1945 as flagship of the aircraft service squadron, serving in its design role as a carrier support vessel. After World War II it was in reserve until 1949. It then transported aircraft and equipment from Britain to the Far East and remained there during the Korean War, again in its designed role to support British carrier operations during that conflict. It returned to reserve status in 1953 and was sold for scrapping in 1959.

UNITED KINGDOM: *IMPLACABLE* CLASS (1944)
Courtesy of Art-Tech

Indefatigable

BUILDER: John Brown & Company, Clydeside

LAID DOWN: November 3, 1939. Launched: December 8, 1942. Commissioned: May 3, 1944

Implacable

BUILDER: Fairfield Shipbuilding & Engineering Company, Govan

LAID DOWN: February 21, 1939. Launched: December 10, 1942. Commissioned: August 28, 1944

DISPLACEMENT: 23,450 tons (standard), 32,110 tons (full load)

DIMENSIONS: 766'6" (oa) x 95'9" x 26'0" (mean), 28'11" (full load)

FLIGHT DECK: 750'0" x 80'0"

MACHINERY: Parsons geared turbines, 8 Admiralty 3-drum boilers, 4 shafts, 148,000 shp = 32 knots

BUNKERAGE & RANGE: 4,690 tons = 11,000 nm @ 14 knots.

AIRCRAFT: 54

ARMAMENT: 8 x twin 4.5" DP, 6 x 8-barrelled 2 pdr AA, 37 x 20mm AA

COMPLEMENT: 1,400

DESIGN: These ships used a slightly enlarged *Illustrious* design with four-shaft machinery. The main hangar height was reduced to 14 feet, which allowed the addition of a lower hanger aft some 208 feet long. The forward elevator was enlarged and both made stronger to accommodate aircraft up to 20,000 pounds. Hangar side armor was reduced to 1.5 inches. The ships commissioned with the standard British late-war carrier radar outfit.

MODIFICATIONS: The *Implacable* added two quadruple 2-pdrs mounts, four single 40mm mounts, and fifty-one 20mm weapons to its light antiaircraft battery before deploying to the Pacific, while the *Indefatigable* gained ten single 40mm and forty 20mm weapons. The use of deck parks increased their aircraft capacity to eighty-one machines.

SERVICE: The *Implacable* joined the British Pacific Fleet in June 1945 and undertook strikes against Truk and the Japanese home islands until just before the end of World War II. It was in reserve postwar, refitted in

1948–1949, and then served as a training carrier from 1952 until 1954. The *Implacable* returned to the reserve fleet in mid-1954 and was sold for scrapping in November 1955. The *Indefatigable* participated in strikes against the German battleship *Tirpitz* (operations Mascot and Goodwood) in July and August 1944. In December 1944 it joined the British East Indies Fleet for strikes against Sumatra before transferring to the British Pacific Fleet for operations off Okinawa from March until

May 1945, being struck by a kamikaze on April 1 that put it out of action for one hour while debris was cleared from the armored flight deck. After a refit in Australia it returned to the fleet for strikes against the Japanese home islands from July until the end of the war. The *Indefatigable* was in reserve immediately after World War II. It served as a training carrier from 1950 to 1954, returned to the reserve, and was sold for scrapping in 1956.

UNITED KINGDOM: *COLOSSUS* CLASS (1944)
Courtesy of Art-Tech

Colossus
BUILDER: Vickers-Armstrong Ltd., Newcastle-upon-Tyne
LAID DOWN: June 1, 1942. Launched: September 30, 1943. Commissioned: December 16, 1944

Glory
BUILDER: Harland & Wolff Ltd., Belfast
LAID DOWN: August 27, 1942. Launched: November 27, 1943. Commissioned: April 2, 1945

Venerable
BUILDER: Cammell Laird & Company, Birkenhead
LAID DOWN: December 3, 1942. Launched: December 30,1943. Commissioned: January 17, 1944

Vengeance
BUILDER: Swan, Hunter & Wigham Richardson, Ltd., Wallsend-on-Tyne
LAID DOWN: November 16, 1942. Launched: February 23, 1944. Commissioned: January 15, 1945

Perseus
BUILDER: Vickers-Armstrong Ltd., Newcastle-upon-Tyne
LAID DOWN: June 1, 1942. Launched: March 26, 1944. Commissioned: October 19, 1945

Pioneer
BUILDER: Vickers-Armstrong Ltd., Barrow-in-Furness
LAID DOWN: December 2, 1942.

Launched: May 20, 1944. Commissioned: February 8, 1945

Warrior
BUILDER: Harland & Wolff Ltd., Belfast
LAID DOWN: December 12, 1942. Launched: May 20, 1944. Commissioned: November 1948

Theseus
BUILDER: Fairfield Shipbuilding & Engineering Company, Govan
LAID DOWN: January 6, 1943. Launched: July 6, 1944. Commissioned: February 9, 1946

Ocean
BUILDER: Alexander Stephen & Sons Ltd., Govan
LAID DOWN: November 8, 1942. Launched: July 8, 1944. Commissioned: August 8, 1945

Triumph
BUILDER: R. & W. Hawthorn Leslie & Company Ltd., Hebburn-on-Tyne
LAID DOWN: January 27, 1943. Launched: October 2, 1944. Commissioned: May 9, 1946
DISPLACEMENT: 13,190 tons (standard), 18,040 tons (full load)
DIMENSIONS: 695'0" (oa) x 80'0" x 18'6" (mean), 23'6" (full load)
FLIGHT DECK: 680'0" x 80'0"
MACHINERY: Parsons geared turbines, 4 Admiralty 3-drum boilers, 2 shafts, 40,000 shp = 25 knots
BUNKERAGE & RANGE: 3,196 tons = 12,000 nm @ 14 knots.
AIRCRAFT: 48
ARMAMENT: 6 x 4-barrelled 2 pdr AA, 16 x twin 20mm AA
COMPLEMENT: 1,300
DESIGN: These vessels were designed as

"intermediate aircraft carriers" with capabilities between those of escort carriers and the armored fleet carriers. Their hulls were built to merchant ship scantling standards to speed construction and widen the pool of potential shipyards. The final design resembled a lighter version of the armored carriers but included no armor protection, light cruiser type machinery, and a light antiaircraft battery only. There was a single hangar 445 feet long, 52 feet wide, and 17 feet 6 inches high, served by two elevators. The flight deck carried full arresting gear, crash barriers, and a single hydraulic catapult. The standard British suite of aircraft carrier radars was installed.

MODIFICATIONS: The *Perseus* and the *Pioneer* completed as maintenance carriers (similar in concept to the *Unicorn*) and could not operate aircraft. Antiaircraft batteries were upgraded during World War II and most ships eventually sported uniform batteries of 40mm weapons. In the years immediately following World War II these vessels formed the backbone of the Royal Navy's carrier force. Antiaircraft batteries were reduced to about eight 40mm weapons, improved radar sets installed, and arresting gear upgraded to operate heavier aircraft. The *Theseus* was used to test the angled flight deck concept and the *Perseus* for trials of steam catapults. The *Theseus* converted to a repair ship in 1964.

Four vessels were sold to other navies. The *Colossus* was loaned to France as the *Arromanches* in August

1946 and sold in 1951. The *Arromanches* was reconstructed in 1957–1958 with a 4-degree angled flight deck (maximum width 118 feet), a mirror landing aid, and forty-three 40mm weapons, increasing full-load displacement to 19,600 tons. The antiaircraft battery was removed by 1963, and the *Arromanches* was refitted as an antisubmarine helicopter carrier in 1968, when new French DRBV-22 air warning radar was installed. The *Venerable* was sold to the Netherlands and commissioned on May 28, 1948, as the *Karel Doorman.* The *Karel Doorman* was extensively reconstructed 1955–1958 at Scheepswerf Wilton Fijenoord, receiving a strengthened 8-degree angled flight deck with a steam catapult forward and a mirror landing aid. The elevators were upgraded and an improved antiaircraft battery of twelve new 40mm weapons was fitted. The island was enlarged and improved, with a high raking stack and a new lattice mast supporting modern Dutch radar for air and sea search, target acquisition, and height-finding. Full load displacement increased to 19,900 tons. The *Karel Doorman* suffered a boiler-room fire in April 1968, was sold to Argentina in October, and refitted at Scheepswerf Wilton Fijenoord, commissioning on March 29, 1969, as the *Veinticinco de Mayo.* The *Vengeance,* loaned to Australia from early 1953 to August 1955, was sold to Brazil in late 1956, renamed the *Minas Gerais,* and extensively modernized 1957–1960 at

Werf Verolme in Rotterdam. The *Minas Gerais* received a strengthened 8-1/2-degree angled flight deck, new elevators, a mirror landing aid, and a steam catapult. The island was upgraded with a raked stack and a large lattice mast supporting modern American radar for air and sea search, and height-finding. A new antiaircraft battery of one twin and two quadruple 40mm weapons was installed. Full load displacement increased to 19,900 tons. The *Warrior* was sold to Argentina in the summer of 1958, refitted, and commissioned as the *Independencia* on January 26, 1959. The *Independencia* carried twenty-two 40 mm antiaircraft weapons and was fitted with a 4-degree angled flight deck and a lattice mast with updated American air and sea search radar. Full load displacement rose to 19,540 tons.

SERVICE: The *Colossus,* the *Glory,* the *Venerable,* and the *Vengeance* served with the British Pacific Fleet at the end of World War II but arrived in theater too late for operations. The *Warrior* served very briefly with the Royal Canadian Navy pending the arrival of the new carrier *Bonaventure.* The *Glory,* the *Warrior,* the *Theseus,* the *Ocean,* and the *Triumph* all served during the Korean War, providing air support for ground troops and conducting strikes against shore targets. The *Pioneer* was broken up in 1954, the *Perseus* in 1958, and the *Glory* in late 1961. The *Theseus* and the *Ocean* deployed as commando carriers during the Suez operation in November–December 1956 to land assault troops via helicopter. They both were scrapped in 1962. The *Triumph* served in the Far East and Indian Ocean until placed in reserve in 1975 and was broken up in 1981.

The *Arromanches* supported French operations in Indo-China from 1949 until 1954, and then transferred to the Mediterranean. It participated in the Suez operation in November–December 1956, conducting strikes against Egyptian installations around Port Said. From 1960 to 1968 it was a training carrier, then became an antisubmarine ship, but soon reverted to training. The *Arromanches* decommissioned in 1974 and was broken up in early 1978. The *Karel Doorman* operated a mixture of jet fighters and antisubmarine aircraft and helicopters until 1964, when the fighters were withdrawn. The Argentinian *Veinticinco de Mayo* embarked A-4 Skyhawks as

fighter-bombers, replacing them with Super Etendards in 1983. It covered the initial invasion of the Falkland/Malvinas Islands in 1982 but remained in port during the remainder of the conflict. It was laid up from June 1986 with major machinery problems but the cost of a major upgrade was prohibitive and it was sold for scrapping in January 1999. The *Vengeance* was loaned to Australia from early 1953 to August 1955 pending the arrival of the carrier *Melbourne*. The *Minas Gerais* operated as an antisubmarine carrier throughout its Brazilian career, embarking a mix of fixed-wing aircraft and helicopters. It was decommissioned on October 9, 2001. The *Independencia* served as the flagship of Argentina's navy until the arrival of the *Veinticinco de Mayo* in March 1969. It was stricken in 1971 and scrapped.

UNITED KINGDOM: MERCHANTMEN CONVERTED TO ESCORT CARRIERS (1941)
Courtesy of Art-Tech

Audacity

BUILDER: Bremer Vulkan Werft, Bremen

LAID DOWN: Launched: March 29, 1939. Commissioned: June 1941

DISPLACEMENT: 10,231 tons (full load)

DIMENSIONS: 467'3" (oa) x 56'0" x 21'7" (full load)

FLIGHT DECK: 450'0" x 60'0"

MACHINERY: 7-cylinder MAN diesels, 1 shaft, 5,200 bhp = 15 knots

BUNKERAGE & RANGE: 694 tons = 12,000 nm @ 10 knots.

AIRCRAFT: 6

ARMAMENT: 1 x 4" DP, 4 x 2 pdr AA, 4 x 20mm AA

Activity

BUILDER: Caledon Shipbuilding Company Ltd., Dundee

LAID DOWN: February 1, 1940. Launched: May 30, 1942. Commissioned: September 29, 1942

DISPLACEMENT: 11,800 tons (standard), 14,300 tons (full load)

DIMENSIONS: 512'9" (oa) x 66'6" x 26'1" (full load)

FLIGHT DECK: 490'0" x 66'0"

MACHINERY: 6-cylinder Burmeister & Wain diesels, 2 shafts, 12,000 bhp = 18 knots

BUNKERAGE: 2,000 tons

AIRCRAFT: 10

ARMAMENT: 1 x twin 4" DP, 10 x twin 20mm AA, 4 x single 20mm AA

COMPLEMENT: 700

Pretoria Castle

BUILDER: Harland & Wolff Ltd., Belfast

LAID DOWN: 1936. Launched: October 12, 1938. Commissioned: April 9, 1943

DISPLACEMENT: 19,650 tons (standard), 23,450 tons (full load)

DIMENSIONS: 594'7" (oa) x 76'6" x 28'0"(full load)

FLIGHT DECK: 550'0" x 75'0"

MACHINERY: 8-cylinder Burmeister & Wain diesels, 2 shafts, 21,869 bhp = 18 knots

BUNKERAGE: 2,430 tons

AIRCRAFT: 21

ARMAMENT: 2 x twin 4" DP, 4 x 4-barrelled 2 pdr AA, 10 x twin 20mm AA

Nairana Class

Vindex

BUILDER: Swan, Hunter & Wigham Richardson, Ltd., Wallsend-on-Tyne

LAID DOWN: July 1, 1942. Launched: May 4, 1943. Commissioned: December 3, 1943

Nairana

BUILDER: John Brown & Company, Clydebank

LAID DOWN: 1942. Launched: May 20, 1943. Commissioned: December 12, 1943

DISPLACEMENT: 13,825 tons (standard), 16,980 tons (full load)

DIMENSIONS: 528'6" (oa) x 68'0" x 23'6" (mean), 25'8"(full load)

FLIGHT DECK: 495'0" x 65'0"

MACHINERY: 5-cylinder Doxford diesels, 2 shafts, 10,700 bhp = 16.5 knots

BUNKERAGE & RANGE: 1,655 tons

AIRCRAFT: 21

ARMAMENT: 1 x twin 4" DP, 4 x 4-barrelled 2 pdr AA, 8 x twin 20mm AA

COMPLEMENT: 700–728

Campania

BUILDER: Harland & Wolff Ltd., Belfast

LAID DOWN: August 12, 1941. Launched: June 17, 1943. Commissioned: March 7, 1944

DISPLACEMENT: 12,450 tons (standard), 15,970 tons (full load)

DIMENSIONS: 540'0" (oa) x 70'0" x 19'0" (mean), 22'10"(full load)

FLIGHT DECK: 510'0" x 70'0"

MACHINERY: 6-cylinder Burmeister & Wain diesels, 2 shafts, 10,700 bhp = 16 knots

BUNKERAGE & RANGE: 2,230 tons

AIRCRAFT: 18

ARMAMENT: 1 x twin 4" DP, 4 x 4-barrelled 2 pdr AA, 8 x twin 20mm AA

COMPLEMENT: 700

DESIGN: The *Audacity* was a very limited conversion from a captured German merchant ship, the *Hannover,* into a trade protection carrier. Superstructure was stripped to shelter deck level, a flight deck constructed above it, and the side plated up to the flight deck with openings for embarking stores and stowing boats. The diesel engines exhausted to starboard and platforms on either side provided space for navigation and signaling. The flight deck carried arresting gear but there was no hangar or catapult and all aircraft were parked on deck.

In 1940 the Admiralty prepared three outline designs for escort carriers, ranging from an austere 450-foot long, 16.5-knot vessel embarking ten aircraft to a 550-foot long 20-knot carrier carrying twenty-five aircraft. Only the *Activity* was converted to the austere carrier design with a small hangar (87 feet by 66 feet) aft served by a single elevator. The four other British conversions were to the intermediate standard. They incorporated long hangars (198–354 feet long, depending on the vessel), though there still was only a single elevator, which slowed aircraft operations. All these carriers had full arresting gear and crash barriers, while the *Pretoria Castle* also carried a gunpowder-operated catapult capable of launching the heaviest aircraft in service.

SERVICE: The *Audacity* exclusively escorted convoys between the United Kingdom and Gibraltar during its brief career. Its Grumman Martlet fighters saw constant action against German Focke-Wulf Fw 200 Condor long-range bombers and U-boats, destroying five Condors and contributing materially to the destruction of the *U-131* by surface escort vessels on December 17, 1941, before succumbing to two torpedoes fired by the *U-751* on December 21.

The later British escort carriers had combined Royal Navy and merchant marine crews. The *Pretoria Castle* served exclusively as a training and trials carrier throughout its career and was converted back into a liner after World War II. The *Activity* initially served in the Atlantic escorting convoys. The three other vessels all served primarily as escorts for Arctic convoys and were joined by the *Activity* in February 1944. Both the *Campania* and the *Nairana* also undertook antishipping operations along the Norwegian coast during late 1944 and early 1945. The *Activity* was sold in 1946, the *Vindex* in 1947, and the *Nairana* in 1948 (after serving with the Royal Netherlands Navy for two years). The *Campania* participated in British nuclear tests in the Pacific in 1952 and then was placed in reserve until it was broken up in November 1955.

UNITED KINGDOM: MERCHANT AIRCRAFT CARRIERS (1943)
Courtesy of Art-Tech

Empire MacAlpine Class

BUILDER: Burntisland Shipping Company, Burntisland

Empire MacAlpine
Launched: December 23, 1942. Commissioned: April 14, 1943

Empire MacKendrick
Launched: September 29, 1943. Commissioned: December 1943

Empire MacAndrew Class

BUILDER: William Denny & Brothers Ltd., Dumbarton

Empire MacAndrew
Launched: May 3, 1943. Commissioned: July 1943

Empire MacDermott
Launched: January 24, 1944 Commissioned: March 1944

Empire MacRae Class

BUILDER: Lithgow Shipbuilding, Port Glasgow

Empire MacRae
Launched: June 21, 1943. Commissioned: September 1943

Empire MacCallum
Launched: October 12, 1943. Commissioned: December 1943

Rapana Class

Ancylus
BUILDER: Swan, Hunter & Wigham Richardson, Ltd., Wallsend-on-Tyne
Launched: October 9, 1934. Commissioned: October 1943

Acavus
BUILDER: Workman Clark Ltd, Belfast

Launched: November 24, 1934. Commissioned: October 1943

Gadila
Builder: Howaldtswerke, Kiel
Launched: December 1, 1934. Commissioned: March 1944

Amastra
Builder: Lithgow Shipbuilding, Port Glasgow
Launched: December 18, 1934. Commissioned: November 1943

Alexia
Builder: Bremer Vulkan Werft, Bremen
Launched: December 20, 1934. Commissioned: December 1943

Rapana
Builder: Scheepswerf Wilton Fijenoord, Schiedam
Launched: April 1935. Commissioned: July 1943

Macoma
Builder: Nederlandse Dok, Amsterdam
Launched: December 31, 1935. Commissioned: May 1944

Miralda
Builder: Nederlandse Dok, Amsterdam
Launched: July 1936. Commissioned: January 1944

Adula
Builder: Blythswood Shipbuilding, Scotstoun
Launched: January 28, 1937. Commissioned: February 1944

Empire Mackay
Builder: Harland & Wolff Ltd., Belfast
Launched: June 17, 1943. Commissioned: October 1943

Empire MacColl
Builder: Cammell Laird & Company, Ltd., Birkenhead
Launched: July 24, 1943. Commissioned: November 1943

Empire MacCabe
Builder: Swan, Hunter & Wigham Richardson, Ltd., Wallsend-on-Tyne
Launched: May 18, 1943. Commissioned: December 1943

Empire MacMahon
Builder: Swan, Hunter & Wigham Richardson, Ltd., Wallsend-on-Tyne
Launched: July 2, 1943. Commissioned: December 1943
Displacement: 7,950 tons (gross)–12,000 tons (gross)
Dimensions: 446'6"–481'6"(oa) x 56'0"–61'0" x 24'0"–27'6" (mean)
Flight deck: 400'–460'0" x 60'0"
Machinery: Diesel engines, 1 shaft, 3,300–4,000 bhp = 11–12.5 knots
Aircraft: 4
Armament: 1 x 4" AA, 2 x 40mm AA, 4 x 20mm AA
Complement: 107–122
Design: As an emergency measure the Admiralty, in September 1942, approved fitting diesel-engined bulk cargo carriers with steel flight decks, arresting gear and crash barriers, and minimal island bridge structures supporting air warning radar so that these ships could provide air cover for North Atlantic convoys. Initially grain carriers were selected. They had minimal existing superstructures and their conversion would not affect cargo handling, since grain was handled using hoses. The grain carriers also had small hangars con-

structed below their flight decks, served by a single elevator, to accommodate their four Fairey Swordfish antisubmarine aircraft. Soon afterwards, the Admiralty also approved similar conversions using tankers. Cargo handling equipment prevented construction of hangars on these vessels, so their aircraft were parked and maintained only on the flight deck.

SERVICE: Like the British escort carrier conversions, these vessels had combined Royal Navy and merchant marine crews. The *Gadila* and the *Macoma* had Dutch crews. All the merchant aircraft carriers operated in the North Atlantic escorting convoys. At the end of World War II they were converted back into bulk carriers and returned to regular merchant service.

UNITED STATES: *ESSEX* CLASS (1942)
Courtesy of Art-Tech

Group I

Essex
BUILDER: Newport News Shipbuilding & Dry Dock Company, Newport News, VA
LAID DOWN: April 28, 1941. Launched: July 31, 1942. Commissioned: December 31, 1942

Yorktown
BUILDER: Newport News Shipbuilding & Dry Dock Company, Newport News, VA
LAID DOWN: December 1, 1941. Launched: January 31, 1943. Commissioned: April 15, 1943

Intrepid
BUILDER: Newport News Shipbuilding & Dry Dock Company, Newport News, VA

LAID DOWN: December 1, 1941. Launched: April 26, 1943. Commissioned: August 16, 1943

Hornet
BUILDER: Newport News Shipbuilding & Dry Dock Company, Newport News, VA
LAID DOWN: August 3, 1942. Launched: August 30, 1943. Commissioned: November 29, 1943

Franklin
BUILDER: Newport News Shipbuilding & Dry Dock Company, Newport News, VA
LAID DOWN: December 7, 1942. Launched: October 14, 1943. Commissioned: January 31, 1944

Lexington
BUILDER: Bethlehem Steel Company, Quincy. MA
LAID DOWN: September 15, 1941. Launched: September 26, 1942. Commissioned: February 17, 1943

Bunker Hill
BUILDER: Bethlehem Steel Company, Quincy, MA
LAID DOWN: September 15, 1941. Launched: December 7, 1942. Commissioned: May 25, 1943

Wasp
BUILDER: Bethlehem Steel Company, Quincy, MA
LAID DOWN: March 19, 1942. Launched: August 17, 1943. Commissioned: November 24, 1943

Hancock
BUILDER: Bethlehem Steel Company, Quincy, MA
LAID DOWN: January 26, 1943. Launched: January 24, 1944. Commissioned: April 15, 1944

Bennington
BUILDER: Newport News Shipbuilding & Dry Dock Company, Newport News, VA
LAID DOWN: December 15, 1942. Launched: February 26, 1944. Commissioned: August 6, 1944

Bon Homme Richard
BUILDER: New York Naval Shipyard
LAID DOWN: February 1, 1943. Launched: April 29, 1944. Commissioned: November 26, 1944

Group II

Ticonderoga
BUILDER: Newport News Shipbuilding & Dry Dock Company, Newport News, VA
LAID DOWN: February 1, 1943. Launched: February 7, 1944. Commissioned: May 8, 1944

Randolph
BUILDER: Newport News Shipbuilding & Dry Dock Company, Newport News, VA
LAID DOWN: May 10, 1943. Launched: June 29, 1944. Commissioned: October 9, 1944

Boxer
BUILDER: Newport News Shipbuilding & Dry Dock Company, Newport News, VA
LAID DOWN: September 13, 1943. Launched: December 14, 1944. Commissioned: April 16, 1945

Leyte
BUILDER: Newport News Shipbuilding & Dry Dock Company, Newport News, VA
LAID DOWN: February 21, 1944. Launched: August 23, 1945. Commissioned: April 11, 1946

Kearsarge
BUILDER: New York Navy Yard
LAID DOWN: March 1, 1944. Launched: May 5, 1945. Commissioned: March 2, 1946

Antietam
BUILDER: Philadelphia Navy Yard
LAID DOWN: March 15, 1943. Launched: August 29, 1944. Commissioned: January 28, 1945

Princeton
BUILDER: Philadelphia Naval Shipyard
LAID DOWN: September 14, 1943.

Launched: July 8, 1945. Commissioned: November 18, 1945

Shangri-La
BUILDER: Norfolk Navy Yard
LAID DOWN: January 15, 1943. Launched: February 24, 1944. Commissioned: September 15, 1944

Lake Champlain
BUILDER: Norfolk Navy Yard
LAID DOWN: March 15, 1943. Launched: November 2, 1944. Commissioned: June 3, 1945

Tarawa
BUILDER: Norfolk Navy Yard
LAID DOWN: March 1, 1944. Launched: May 12, 1945. Commissioned: December 8, 1945

Philippine Sea
BUILDER: Bethlehem Steel Company, Quincy, MA
LAID DOWN: August 19, 1944. Launched: September 5, 1945. Commissioned: May 11, 1946
DISPLACEMENT: 27,200 tons (standard), 34,880 tons (full load)
DIMENSIONS: Group I 872'0" (oa), Group II 888'0" (oa) x 93'0" x 23'0" (mean), 27'6" (full load)
FLIGHT DECK: 860'0" x 96'0"
MACHINERY: Westinghouse geared turbines, 8 Babcock & Wilcox boilers, 4 shafts, 150,000 shp = 32.7 knots
BUNKERAGE & RANGE: 6,330 tons = 15,000 nm @ 15 knots.
AIRCRAFT: 91
ARMAMENT: 4 x twin 5" DP, 4 x single 5" DP, 8 x quadruple 40mm AA, 46 x 20mm AA
COMPLEMENT: 2,682
DESIGN: The design for this class, the largest single group of fleet carriers ever constructed, was envisaged as an improved *Yorktown*, incorporating a 10 percent enlargement of the air group, improved protection, subdivision, and machinery arrangements, better flight deck layout, and an increase in the antiaircraft battery. All this was achieved, but the final design was almost 30 percent larger. The midship elevator was located at the port deck edge, while installing the starboard 5-inch guns in twin mounts fore and aft of the island not only enlarged the flight deck but also increased the heavy antiaircraft battery by 50 percent. The design called for three catapults: two on the flight deck forward and the third (a transverse unit) on the hangar deck. Production shortages meant most early units of the class completed with only one catapult, either on the flight deck or in the hangar, but eventually all carried the two flight deck catapults alone. Protection was enhanced by better subdivision, arranging the machinery on the unit system, and adding armor, principally in the form of 3-inch protection on the hangar deck. Two units, the *Reprisal* and the *Iwo Jima*, were laid down but never completed, while an additional six units were authorized but never commenced construction.
MODIFICATIONS: All ships received greatly enhanced light antiaircraft batteries as World War II progressed. The final arrangement included seventeen or eighteen quadruple 40mm mounts (the longer bow of the Group II vessels was a design change to allow fitting two mounts with enhanced sky arcs beneath the forward

end on the flight deck instead of the single mount on the earlier vessels), and up to sixty 20mm weapons in single or twin mounts. These carriers also received updated and expanded radar suites and replaced some or all of their rigid antenna masts with whip antennae. The stowage for aviation gasoline was revised for greater protection and internal subdivision improved by extending unpierced bulkheads one deck higher. Air groups expanded to as many as 103 heavier aircraft by the end of World War II, requiring additional fuel, munitions, and crew accommodations, plus stronger arresting gear. By the end of World War II the complements of the class reached 3,385 officers and men.

Most of the class received major reconstructions, described separately. Those not reconstructed were stripped of most of their light antiaircraft battery to reduce weight and crew size. The *Boxer*, the *Leyte*, the *Princeton*, the *Tarawa*, the *Valley Forge*, and the *Philippine Sea* were converted to antisubmarine carriers between 1953 and 1956. The *Boxer*, the *Princeton*, and the *Valley Forge* converted to amphibious assault ships between 1959 and 1961.

SERVICE: The *Boxer*, the *Leyte*, the *Kearsarge*, the *Antietam*, the *Princeton*, the *Lake Champlain*, the *Tarawa*, the *Valley Forge*, and the *Philippine Sea* commissioned too late for active service during World War II. The other members of the class all served in the Pacific during

World War II, forming the core of the fast carrier force. Kamikaze attacks caused very severe damage to the *Intrepid*, the *Franklin*, and the *Bunker Hill*. All were repaired but the *Franklin* never recommissioned and was sold for scrap in July 1966. The *Bunker Hill* recommissioned in July 1945, went into reserve in January 1947, and was sold for scrap in July 1973 without further service. The wartime carriers went into reserve in 1947 and did not return to service until after their reconstructions. The unreconstructed *Boxer*, *Leyte*, *Antietam*, *Princeton*, *Valley Forge*, and *Philippine Sea* all operated off Korea between 1950 and 1952, after which the *Antietam* underwent a major reconstruction as the test bed for the angled flight deck and the others were converted into antisubmarine carriers, operating a mix of helicopters and fixed-wing aircraft. The *Boxer*, the *Princeton*, and the *Valley Forge* became amphibious assault ships 1959–1961, while the *Leyte*, the *Tarawa*, and the *Philippine Sea* became aircraft transports and the *Antietam* became a training carrier. The *Tarawa* was sold for scrap in October 1968, the *Boxer*, the *Leyte*, and the *Philippine Sea* were stricken in December 1969, the *Princeton* and the *Valley Forge* were decommissioned in January 1970 and broken up in 1973, and the *Antietam* was stricken on May 1, 1973 and sold for breaking up on December 19th of the same year.

UNITED STATES: *INDEPENDENCE* CLASS (1943)
Courtesy of Art-Tech

Independence
LAID DOWN: May 1, 1941. Launched:
August 22, 1942. Commissioned:
January 1, 1943

Princeton
LAID DOWN: June 2, 1941. Launched:
October 18, 1942. Commissioned:
February 25, 1943

Belleau Wood
LAID DOWN: August 11, 1941.
Launched: December 6, 1942. Com-
missioned: March 31, 1943

Cowpens
LAID DOWN: December 17, 1941.
Launched: January 17, 1943. Com-
missioned: May 28, 1943

Monterey
LAID DOWN: December 29, 1941.
Launched: February 28, 1943. Com-
missioned: June 17, 1943

Langley
LAID DOWN: April 11, 1942. Launched:
May 22, 1943. Commissioned: Au-
gust 31, 1943

Cabot
LAID DOWN: March 13, 1942.
Launched: April 4, 1943. Commis-
sioned: July 24, 1943

Bataan
LAID DOWN: August 31, 1942.
Launched: August 1, 1943. Commis-
sioned: November 17, 1943

San Jacinto
LAID DOWN: October 16, 1942.
Launched: September 26, 1943.
Commissioned: December 15, 1943
BUILDER: New York Shipbuilding Cor-
poration, Camden, NJ
DISPLACEMENT: 10,622 tons (standard),
14,750 tons (full load)
DIMENSIONS: 622'6" (oa) x 71'6" x 21'0"
(mean), 24'3" (full load)

FLIGHT DECK: 544'0" x 73'0"

MACHINERY: General Electric geared turbines, 4 Babcock & Wilcox boilers, 4 shafts, 100,000 shp = 31 knots

BUNKERAGE & RANGE: 2,633 tons = 13,000 nm @ 15 knots.

AIRCRAFT: 30

ARMAMENT: 2 x 5" DP (*Independence* only), 2 x quadruple 40mm AA (not in *Independence*), 8 x twin 40mm AA, 10 x 20mm AA

COMPLEMENT: 1,569

DESIGN: Emergency carriers were created by converting incomplete hulls of *Cleveland* class light cruisers. The hull was bulged to compensate for added topweight, the furnace uptakes led to starboard outside the superstructure, a relatively short hangar (320 feet long and 57 feet 9 inches wide) built on top of the hull supporting a flight deck that terminated well short of the bow. Two elevators linked the hangar to the flight deck, which carried full arresting gear and two catapults. The island was sponsored outboard of the flight deck and essentially duplicated the arrangement on contemporary American escort carriers.

MODIFICATIONS: These carriers received upgraded radar suites that closely matched those of the big carriers. Most 20mm weapons were replaced one-for-one by twin or quadruple 40mm mounts as World War II progressed. In French service the *Lafayette* and the *Bois Belleau* received upgraded air warning radar and landed all their remaining 20mm weapons. The *Dédalo* received a three-dimensional search SPS52B radar in 1973 and landed all its 20mm weapons.

SERVICE: All the class served in the Pacific from their commissioning until the end of World War II. The *Princeton* was bombed on October 24, 1944, during the Leyte operation. Internal explosions wracked the ship and caused extensive damage to vessels assisting with firefighting. Less than three hours after it was hit the fires were uncontrollable and accompanying vessels sank it with torpedoes. All the survivors went into reserve immediately after World War II. The *Independence* was part of the target fleet during the Bikini Atoll atomic tests and was sunk as a target in February 1951. The *Bataan* recommissioned to serve two tours during the Korean War. The *Monterey* and the *Cabot* were training carriers between 1948 and 1955. The *Cowpens* and the *San Jacinto* saw no postwar service and were stricken in November 1959 and June 1970 respectively. The *Belleau Wood* was loaned to France as the *Bois Belleau* from 1947 to 1960, when it was stricken. The *Langley* was loaned to France as the *Lafayette* from 1951 to 1963, when it too was stricken. Both operated off Indo-China between 1953 and 1955 and the *Lafayette* also participated in the Suez operation in October to December 1956. The *Cabot* was loaned to Spain as the *Dédalo* in 1967 and sold outright in December 1973. It operated primarily as an antisubmarine carrier with twenty helicopters embarked, but also operated four to six AV-8 Matador (Harrier) aircraft from 1976. The *Dédalo* was returned to the United States in August 1989 for preserva- tion as a museum ship but this effort failed and it was scrapped in October 2000.

UNITED STATES: *MIDWAY* CLASS (1945)
Courtesy of Art-Tech

Midway

BUILDER: Newport News Shipbuilding & Dry Dock Company, Newport News, VA

LAID DOWN: October 27, 1943. Launched: March 20, 1945. Commissioned: September 10, 1945

Franklin D. Roosevelt

BUILDER: New York Navy Yard

LAID DOWN: December 1, 1943. Launched: April 29, 1945. Commissioned: October 27, 1945

Coral Sea

BUILDER: Newport News Shipbuilding & Dry Dock Company, Newport News, VA

LAID DOWN: July 10, 1944. Launched: April 2, 1946. Commissioned: October 1, 1947

DISPLACEMENT: 47,387 tons (standard), 59,901 tons (full load)

DIMENSIONS: 968'0" (oa) x 113'0" x 32'9" (mean), 34'6" (full load)

FLIGHT DECK: 932'0" x 113'0"

MACHINERY: Geared turbines, 12 Babcock & Wilcox boilers, 4 shafts, 212,000 shp = 33 knots

BUNKERAGE & RANGE: 10,000 tons = 15,000 nm @ 15 knots.

AIRCRAFT: 137

ARMAMENT: 18 x 5" DP, 21 x quadruple 40mm AA, 68 x 20mm AA

COMPLEMENT: 4,100

DESIGN: A response to both American and British operational experience in the early part of World War II, protection dominated this design. It married the basic features of the *Essex* class with an armored flight deck and heavier armor to protect the ship against 8-inch gunfire rather than the 6-inch gunfire standard of the earlier class. Side armor increased to 8 inches (7 inches on the starboard side to compensate for the weight of the island), the main and hangar decks received 2-inch armor, and there was 3–1/2 inch armor on the flight deck. The open hangar remained and its sides were protected by disposing the 5-inch weapons in single gunhouses along each side at hangar deck level. Three elevators, one a deck-edge unit, linked the hangar to the flight deck, which also carried two catapults. The great size increase necessitated by the greater level of protection allowed this class to embark a much larger air group than the *Essex* class. The air group was in fact too large for efficient operation within the deck-load-strike mode that was standard procedure when these vessels were designed and delivered, although this size proved invaluable when larger faster aircraft entered service.

MODIFICATIONS: These vessels completed with reduced 20mm batteries, while the *Coral Sea* entered service with only fourteen 5-inch guns and no 40mm weapons. In 1947–1948 their flight decks were strengthened to operate heavier aircraft and twenty twin 3-inch AA mounts replaced all 40mm weapons. They also received partially enclosed bows to improve sea keeping. All received major reconstructions, described later, in the mid to late 1950s.

SERVICE: All three carriers were very active prior to their reconstructions, mainly in developing and testing jet aircraft operation and the Regulus cruise missile.

47. UNITED STATES: *SAIPAN* CLASS (1946)
Courtesy of Art-Tech

Saipan

LAID DOWN: July 10, 1944. Launched: July 8, 1945. Commissioned: July 14, 1946

Wright

LAID DOWN: August 21, 1944. Launched: September 1, 1945. Commissioned: February 9. 1947

BUILDER: New York Shipbuilding Corporation, Camden, NJ

DISPLACEMENT: 14,500 tons (standard), 18,750 tons (full load)

DIMENSIONS: 683'7" (oa) x 76'8" x 24'6" (mean), 27'0" (full load)

FLIGHT DECK: 600'0" x 80'0"

MACHINERY: General Electric geared turbines, 4 Babcock & Wilcox boilers, 4 shafts, 120,000 shp = 33 knots

BUNKERAGE & RANGE: 2,500 tons = 10,000 nm @ 15 knots.

AIRCRAFT: 48

ARMAMENT: 10 x quadruple 40mm AA, 32 x 20mm AA

COMPLEMENT: 1,553

DESIGN: An expansion of the *Independence* class design that used the *Baltimore* class heavy cruiser hull as its starting point. Since they were built as carriers from the keel up, the hull itself was widened rather than enlarged with bulges.

MODIFICATIONS: Both ships received upgraded radar suites in the early 1950s, landed all their 20mm weapons, and carried much reduced 40mm batteries. The foremost stack was also removed. In the early 1960s the *Wright* was converted into a National Emergency Command Post Afloat and the *Saipan* into a Major Communications Relay Ship (and renamed the *Arlington*).

SERVICE: Both vessels were employed for training and development of operational systems until placed in reserve in 1956–1957. Both were stricken in 1970.

48. UNITED STATES: C3-TYPE MERCHANTMEN CONVERTED TO ESCORT CARRIERS (1941)

Courtesy of Art-Tech

Long Island

BUILDER: Sun Shipbuilding Corporation, Chester, PA

LAID DOWN: July 7, 1939. Launched: January 11, 1940. Commissioned: June 2, 1941

DISPLACEMENT: 7,886 tons (standard), 14,050 tons (full load)

DIMENSIONS: 492'0" (oa) x 69'6" x 25'6" (mean)

FLIGHT DECK: 360'0" x 78'0"

MACHINERY: 7-cylinder Sulzer diesel, 1 shaft, 8,500 bhp = 16 knots

BUNKERAGE & RANGE: 1,429 tons

AIRCRAFT: 16

ARMAMENT: 1 x 4", 2 x 3" AA, 4 x 0.5" machine guns

COMPLEMENT: 970

Archer [Royal Navy]

BUILDER: Sun Shipbuilding Corporation, Chester, PA

LAID DOWN: June 7, 1939. Launched: December 14, 1939. Commissioned: November 17, 1941

DISPLACEMENT: 10,220 tons (standard), 12,860 tons (full load)

DIMENSIONS: 492'0" (oa) x 69'6" x 22'0" (deep load)

FLIGHT DECK: 410'0" x 70'0"

MACHINERY: 7-cylinder Sulzer diesel, 1 shaft, 8,500 bhp = 16.5 knots

BUNKERAGE & RANGE: 1,400 tons

AIRCRAFT: 16

ARMAMENT: 3 x 4" AA, 15 x 20mm AA

COMPLEMENT: 555

Charger Class

Avenger [Royal Navy]

LAID DOWN: November 28, 1939. Launched: November 27, 1940. Commissioned: March 2, 1942

Biter [Royal Navy]

LAID DOWN: December 28, 1939. Launched: December 18, 1940. Commissioned: May 1, 1942

Charger

LAID DOWN: January 19, 1940. Launched: March 1, 1941. Commissioned: March 3, 1942

Dasher [Royal Navy]

LAID DOWN: March 14, 1940.

Launched: April 12, 1941. Commissioned: July 1, 1942

BUILDER: Sun Shipbuilding Corporation, Chester, PA

DISPLACEMENT: 11,800 tons (standard), 15,126 tons (full load)

DIMENSIONS: 492'0" (oa) x 69'6" x 21'6" (mean), 25'2" (full load)

FLIGHT DECK: 440'0" x 78'0"

MACHINERY: 6-cylinder Doxford diesel, 1 shaft, 8,500 bhp = 17 knots

BUNKERAGE & RANGE: 3,200 tons

AIRCRAFT: 36

ARMAMENT: 3 x 4" AA, 10 x 20mm AA

COMPLEMENT: 856

Bogue Class

Tracker [Royal Navy]

BUILDER: Seattle-Tacoma Shipbuilding Corporation, Seattle, WA

LAID DOWN: November 3, 1941. Launched: March 7, 1942. Commissioned: January 31, 1943

Battler [Royal Navy]

BUILDER: Ingalls Shipbuilding Corporation, Pascagoula, MS

LAID DOWN: April 15, 1941. Launched: April 4, 1942. Commissioned: November 15, 1942

Attacker [Royal Navy]

BUILDER: Western Pipe & Steel Corporation, San Francisco, CA

LAID DOWN: April 17, 1941. Launched: September 17, 1941. Commissioned: October 10, 1942

Hunter [Royal Navy]

BUILDER: Ingalls Shipbuilding Corporation, Pascagoula, MS

LAID DOWN: May 15, 1941. Launched:

May 22, 1942. Commissioned: January 11, 1943

Bogue

BUILDER: Seattle-Tacoma Shipbuilding Corporation, Seattle, WA

LAID DOWN: October 1, 1941. Launched: January 15, 1942. Commissioned: September 26, 1942

Chaser [Royal Navy]

BUILDER: Ingalls Shipbuilding Corporation, Pascagoula. MS

LAID DOWN: June 28, 1941. Launched: January 15, 1942. Commissioned: April 9, 1943

Card

BUILDER: Seattle-Tacoma Shipbuilding Corporation, Seattle, WA

LAID DOWN: October 27, 1941. Launched: February 21, 1942. Commissioned: November 8, 1942

Copahee

BUILDER: Seattle-Tacoma Shipbuilding Corporation, Seattle, WA

LAID DOWN: June 18, 1941. Launched: October 21, 1941. Commissioned: June 15, 1942

Core

BUILDER: Seattle-Tacoma Shipbuilding Corporation, Seattle, WA

LAID DOWN: January 2, 1942. Launched: May 15, 1942. Commissioned: December 10, 1942

Fencer [Royal Navy]

BUILDER: Western Pipe & Steel Corporation, San Francisco, CA

LAID DOWN: September 5, 1941. Launched: April 4, 1942. Commissioned: February 20, 1943

Stalker [Royal Navy]

BUILDER: Western Pipe & Steel Corporation, San Francisco, CA

LAID DOWN: October 6, 1941. Launched: March 5, 1942. Commissioned: December 30, 1942

Nassau

BUILDER: Seattle-Tacoma Shipbuilding Corporation, Seattle, WA

LAID DOWN: November 27, 1941. Launched: April 4. 1942. Commissioned: August 20, 1942

Pursuer [Royal Navy]

BUILDER: Ingalls Shipbuilding Corporation, Pascagoula, MS

LAID DOWN: July 31, 1941. Launched: July 18, 1942. Commissioned: June 14, 1943

Altamaha

BUILDER: Seattle-Tacoma Shipbuilding Corporation, Seattle, WA

LAID DOWN: December 19, 1941. Launched: May 22, 1942. Commissioned: September 15, 1942

Striker [Royal Navy]

BUILDER: Western Pipe & Steel Corporation, San Francisco, CA

LAID DOWN: December 15, 1941. Launched: May 7, 1942. Commissioned: April 29, 1943

Barnes

BUILDER: Seattle-Tacoma Shipbuilding Corporation, Seattle, WA

LAID DOWN: January 19, 1942. Launched: May 22, 1942. Commissioned: February 20, 1943

Block Island

BUILDER: Seattle-Tacoma Shipbuilding Corporation, Seattle, WA

LAID DOWN: January 19, 1942. Launched: June 6, 1942. Commissioned: March 8, 1943

Searcher [Royal Navy]

BUILDER: Seattle-Tacoma Shipbuilding Corporation, Seattle, WA

LAID DOWN: February 20, 1942. Launched: June 20, 1942. Commissioned: April 8, 1943

Breton

BUILDER: Seattle-Tacoma Shipbuilding Corporation, Seattle, WA

LAID DOWN: February 25, 1942. Launched: June 27, 1942. Commissioned: April 12, 1943

Ravager [Royal Navy]

BUILDER: Seattle-Tacoma Shipbuilding Corporation, Seattle, WA

LAID DOWN: April 11, 1942. Launched: July 16, 1942. Commissioned: April 26, 1943

Croatan

BUILDER: Seattle-Tacoma Shipbuilding Corporation, Seattle, WA

LAID DOWN: April 15, 1942. Launched: August 3, 1942. Commissioned: April 28, 1943

DISPLACEMENT: 8,390 tons [United States Navy], 10,200 tons [Royal Navy] (standard), 13,980 tons [United States Navy], 14,400 tons [Royal Navy] (full load)

DIMENSIONS: 496'0" (oa) x 69'6" x 23'3" (mean) 26'0" (deep load)

FLIGHT DECK: 440'0" x 82'0"

MACHINERY: Allis-Chalmers [United States Navy] or General Electric [Royal Navy] geared turbine, 2 Foster Wheeler boilers, 1 shaft, 8,500 shp = 18.5 knots

BUNKERAGE & RANGE: 2,400 tons [United States Navy], 3,100 tons [Royal Navy] = 26,300 nm @ 15 knots

AIRCRAFT: 28 [United States Navy], 20 [Royal Navy]

ARMAMENT: 2 x 5" DP [United States Navy], 2 x 4" AA [Royal Navy], 10 [United States Navy], 14 [Royal Navy] x 20mm AA

COMPLEMENT: 890 [United States Navy], 646 [Royal Navy]

DESIGN: Structurally all these conversions of incomplete Type C3 freighters were very similar. A hangar was erected on top of the main deck, above which was a flight deck with a single catapult. The first two conversions had very short hangars aft (only 120 feet long), the second group had hangars 190 feet long, and the *Bogue* class had full length hangers 261 feet long. In the *Long Island* and the *Archer* the hangar deck was built up above the sheer of the main deck to provide a level deck but in all the later conversions the main deck became the hangar deck and its rise fore and aft to follow the sheer caused considerable problems in handling aircraft. The first six conversions had single elevators, the remainder had an elevator at each end of the hangar. The first pair of vessels used a navigation bridge below the forward edge of the flight deck while later conversions carried an island offset to starboard. The most significant difference between the early conversions and the *Bogue* class was in machinery: the early vessels had diesel propulsion to simplify exhaust of combustion gases but the later class used steam turbines to improve speed.

MODIFICATIONS: The *Long Island*'s flight deck was extended to 420 feet in September 1941. The light antiaircraft batteries of all vessels increased greatly. British escort carriers generally replaced all single 20mm mounts with twin mounts and added small numbers of single 40mm weapons. American escort carriers increased their battery to ten twin 40mm mounts and up to twenty-eight single 20mm mounts. All these carriers also received enhanced radar suites and those primarily engaged in convoy escort also added high-frequency-direction-finding equipment. The Royal Navy's escort carriers underwent substantial changes to enhance protection and survivability, which the Admiralty considered inferior, especially for aviation fuel stowage.

SERVICE: The first two United States Navy carriers were primarily used for training duties until 1944 when they deployed as aircraft transports. The *Bogue*, the *Card*, the *Core*, the *Block Island*, and the *Croatan* served primarily in antisubmarine duties with hunter-killer units. The other United States Navy carriers mainly operated as aircraft transports in the Pacific. The British carriers mainly operated in the antisubmarine warfare role. The *Avenger*, the *Biter*, and the *Dasher* provided air cover for the North African landings in November 1942 (Operation Torch), while the *Attacker*, the *Stalker*, the *Battler*, and the *Hunter* all covered operations at

Salerno and the landings in southern France. The *Attacker,* the *Chaser,* the *Stalker,* the *Battler,* the *Fencer,* the *Striker,* and the *Hunter* all served with the British Pacific Fleet as aircraft transports and night fighter carriers. The *Avenger* was torpedoed and sunk by the *U-155* off Gibraltar on December 15, 1942, the *Dasher* was lost due to a gasoline explosion while anchored in the Firth of Clyde on March 27, 1943, and the *Block Island* was torpedoed and sunk by the *U-549* on May 29, 1944, in the Atlantic. Most of the surviving British carriers reconverted for mercantile service after World War II, while the remaining United States Navy carriers decommissioned in 1946 and saw virtually no subsequent service prior to their disposal between 1960 and 1972.

49. UNITED STATES: *SANGAMON* CLASS (1942)
Courtesy of Art-Tech

Sangamon
LAID DOWN: March 13, 1939. Launched: November 4, 1939. Commissioned: August 25, 1942

Suwanee
LAID DOWN: June 3, 1939. Launched: March 4, 1939. Commissioned: September 24, 1942
BUILDER: Federal Shipbuilding & Dry Dock Company, Kearny, NJ

Chenango
LAID DOWN: July 10, 1938. Launched: April 1, 1939. Commissioned: September 19, 1942

Santee
LAID DOWN: May 31, 1938. Launched: March 4, 1939. Commissioned: August 24, 1942

BUILDER: Sun Shipbuilding Corporation, Chester, PA
DISPLACEMENT: 10,500 tons (standard), 23,875 tons (full load)
DIMENSIONS: 553'0" (oa) x 75'0" x 30'7" (full load)
FLIGHT DECK: 495'0" x 75'6"
MACHINERY: Allis-Chalmers geared turbines, 4 Babcock & Wilcox boilers, 2 shafts, 13,500 shp = 18 knots
BUNKERAGE & RANGE: 4,780 tons = 24,000 nm @ 15 knots
AIRCRAFT: 36
ARMAMENT: 2 x 5" DP, 4 x twin 40mm AA, 12 x 20mm AA
COMPLEMENT: 1,080
DESIGN: Very similar to the *Bogue* class but constructed on the hulls of larger Type T-3 tankers, these vessels had hangars 198 feet long and 69 feet

wide. They disposed of furnace gases through short stacks on either side aft.

MODIFICATIONS: These carriers received upgraded radar suites during World War II and added a further catapult on the flight deck in 1944. Their light antiaircraft battery also increased to a final fit of two quadruple 40mm mounts, ten twin 40mm mounts, and twenty-seven single 20mm mounts.

SERVICE: All four vessels provided air cover for the North African landings in November 1942 (Operation Torch). The *Santee* remained in the Atlantic until early 1944, conducting antisubmarine operations and transporting aircraft. It then transferred to the Pacific, primarily for transport duties. The other three carriers transferred to the Pacific in 1943 and mainly operated in the antisubmarine and transport roles, and provided air cover for landing operations, notably during the Leyte operation and at Okinawa. The *Sangamon,* the *Santee,* and the *Suwanee* all were damaged during the Leyte operation in October 1944, and the *Sangamon* received further serious damage from a kamikaze strike on May 4, 1945, off Okinawa. All four carriers decommissioned in 1946 and saw no further service. The *Sangamon* was scrapped in 1948 while the other three ships were stricken in March 1959 and subsequently broken up.

50. UNITED STATES: *PRINCE WILLIAM* CLASS (1943)
Courtesy of Art-Tech

Prince William [United States Navy]
LAID DOWN: May 18, 1942. Launched: August 23, 1942. Commissioned: April 9, 1943

Slinger [Royal Navy]
LAID DOWN: May 25, 1942. Launched: December 15, 1942. Commissioned: August 11, 1943

Atheling [Royal Navy]
LAID DOWN: June 9, 1942. Launched: September 7, 1942. Commissioned: August 1, 1943

Emperor [Royal Navy]
LAID DOWN: June 23, 1942. Launched: October 7, 1942. Commissioned: August 6, 1943

Ameer [Royal Navy]
LAID DOWN: July 18, 1942. Launched: October 18, 1942. Commissioned: July 20, 1943

Begum [Royal Navy]
LAID DOWN: August 3,1942. Launched: November 11, 1942. Commissioned: August 3, 1943

Trumpeter [Royal Navy]
LAID DOWN: August 25, 1942. Launched: December 15, 1942. Commissioned: August 4, 1943

Empress [Royal Navy]
LAID DOWN: September 9, 1942. Launched: December 30, 1942. Commissioned: August 13, 1943

Khedive [Royal Navy]
LAID DOWN: September 22, 1942. Launched: December 27, 1942. Commissioned: August 23, 1943

Speaker [Royal Navy]
LAID DOWN: October 9, 1942. Launched: February 20, 1943. Commissioned: November 20, 1943

Nabob [Royal Navy]
LAID DOWN: October 20, 1942. Launched: March 9, 1943. Commissioned: September 7, 1943

Premier [Royal Navy]
LAID DOWN: October 31, 1942. Launched: March 22, 1943. Commissioned: November 3, 1943

Shah [Royal Navy]

LAID DOWN: November 13, 1942. Launched: April 21, 1943. Commissioned: September 27, 1943

Patroller [Royal Navy]

LAID DOWN: November 27, 1942. Launched: May 6, 1943. Commissioned: October 25, 1943

Rajah [Royal Navy]

LAID DOWN: December 17, 1942. Launched: May 18, 1943. Commissioned: January 17, 1944

Ranee [Royal Navy]

LAID DOWN: January 5, 1943. Launched: June 2, 1943. Commissioned: November 8, 1943

Trouncer [Royal Navy]

LAID DOWN: February 1, 1943. Launched: June 16, 1943. Commissioned: January 31, 1944

Thane [Royal Navy]

LAID DOWN: February 23, 1943. Launched: July 15, 1943. Commissioned: November 19, 1943

Queen [Royal Navy]

LAID DOWN: March 12, 1943. Launched: July 31, 1943. Commissioned: December 7, 1943

Ruler [Royal Navy]

LAID DOWN: March 25, 1943. Launched: August 21, 1943. Commissioned: December 22, 1943

Arbiter [Royal Navy]

LAID DOWN: April 26, 1943. Launched: September 9, 1943. Commissioned: December 31, 1943

Smiter [Royal Navy]

LAID DOWN: May 10, 1943. Launched: September 27, 1943. Commissioned: January 20, 1944

Puncher [Royal Navy]

LAID DOWN: May 21, 1943. Launched: November 8, 1943. Commissioned: February 5, 1944

Reaper [Royal Navy]

LAID DOWN: June 5, 1943. Launched: November 22, 1943. Commissioned: February 21, 1944

BUILDER: Seattle-Tacoma Shipbuilding Corporation, Seattle, WA

DISPLACEMENT: 11,400 tons (standard), 15,400 tons (full load)

DIMENSIONS: 494'9" (oa) x 69'6" x 23'0" (mean) 25'6" (deep load)

FLIGHT DECK: 438'0" x 88'0"

MACHINERY: General Electric geared turbine, 2 Foster Wheeler boilers, 1 shaft, 8,500 shp = 18 knots

BUNKERAGE & RANGE: 3,100 tons = 26,300 nm @ 15 knots

AIRCRAFT: 20 [Royal Navy], 28 [United States Navy]

ARMAMENT: 2 x 5" DP, 8 x twin 40mm AA, 20 x 20mm AA

COMPLEMENT: 646 [Royal Navy], 890 [United States Navy]

DESIGN: These vessels were almost identical to the *Bogue* class except that they were constructed as carriers from the keel up. All this class except the *Prince William* was transferred to the Royal Navy under Lend-Lease.

MODIFICATIONS: The British carriers received similar modifications to those of earlier vessels to enhance protection and survivability. Before commissioning they also received specialized changes to suit them for three primary roles: strike carriers (the *Emperor*, the *Ameer*, the *Empress*, the *Khedive*, the *Speaker*, and the *Ruler*), assault carriers (the *Slinger*, the *Patroller*, the *Rajah*, the *Ranee*, the *Trouncer*, the *Thane*, the *Arbiter*, and the *Reaper*), and antisubmarine warfare carriers (the *Atheling*, the *Begum*, the *Trumpeter*, the *Nabob*, the *Premier*, the *Shah*, the *Queen*, the *Smiter*, and the *Puncher*). The British carriers operating in the Pacific exchanged up to four of their 20mm mounts for single 40mm mounts.

SERVICE: The *Prince William* served as a transport in the Pacific until mid-1944, when it transferred to the Atlantic as a training carrier. It returned to the Pacific in June 1945, went into reserve in 1946, and was stricken in March 1959. The *Emperor*, the *Trumpeter*, the *Khedive*, the *Nabob*, the *Premier*, the *Thane*, the *Queen*, the *Smiter*, and the *Puncher* all served mainly in the Atlantic and European waters, although the *Emperor* transferred to the Pacific in late 1944. The remaining British carriers served exclusively in the British Eastern and Pacific fleets. The British carriers were returned to the United States after World War II, where most reverted to mercantile service in 1946.

51. UNITED STATES: *CASABLANCA* CLASS (1943)
Courtesy of Art-Tech

Casablanca
LAID DOWN: November 3, 1942. Launched: April 5, 1943. Commissioned: July 8, 1943

Liscombe Bay
LAID DOWN: December 9, 1942. Launched: April 19, 1943. Commissioned: August 7, 1943

Anzio
LAID DOWN: December 12, 1942. Launched: May 1, 1943. Commissioned: August 27, 1943

Corregidor
LAID DOWN: December 17, 1942. Launched: May 12, 1943. Commissioned: August 31, 1943

Mission Bay
LAID DOWN: December 28, 1942. Launched: May 26, 1943. Commissioned: September 13, 1943

Guadalcanal
LAID DOWN: January 5, 1943. Launched: June 5, 1943. Commissioned: September 25, 1943

Manila Bay
LAID DOWN: January 15, 1943. Launched: July 10, 1943. Commissioned: October 5, 1943

Natoma Bay
LAID DOWN: January 17, 1943. Launched: July 20, 1943. Commissioned: October 14, 1943

St Lo

LAID DOWN: January 23, 1943. Launched: August 17, 1943. Commissioned: October 23, 1943

Tripoli

LAID DOWN: February 1, 1943. Launched: September 2, 1943. Commissioned: October 31, 1943

Wake Island

LAID DOWN: February 6, 1943. Launched: September 15, 1943. Commissioned: November 7, 1943

White Plains

LAID DOWN: February 11, 1943. Launched: September 27, 1943. Commissioned: November 15, 1943

Solomons

LAID DOWN: March 19, 1943. Launched: October 6, 1943. Commissioned: November 21, 1943

Kalinin Bay

LAID DOWN: April 26, 1943. Launched: October 15, 1943. Commissioned: November 27, 1943

Kasaan Bay

LAID DOWN: May 11, 1943. Launched: October 24, 1943. Commissioned: December 4, 1943

Fanshaw Bay

LAID DOWN: May 18, 1943. Launched: November 1, 1943. Commissioned: December 9, 1943

Kitkun Bay

LAID DOWN: May 31, 1943. Launched: November 8, 1943. Commissioned: December 15, 1943

Tulagi

LAID DOWN: June 7, 1943. Launched: November 15, 1943. Commissioned: December 21, 1943

Gambier Bay

LAID DOWN: July 10, 1943. Launched: November 22, 1943. Commissioned: December 28, 1943

Nehenta Bay

LAID DOWN: July 20, 1943. Launched: November 28, 1943. Commissioned: January 3, 1944

Hoggatt Bay

LAID DOWN: August 17, 1943. Launched: December 4, 1943. Commissioned: January 11, 1944

Kadashan Bay

LAID DOWN: September 2, 1943. Launched: December 11, 1943. Commissioned: January 18, 1944

Marcus Island

LAID DOWN: September 15, 1943. Launched: December 16, 1943. Commissioned: January 26, 1944

Savo Island

LAID DOWN: September 27, 1943. Launched: December 22, 1943. Commissioned: February 3, 1944

Ommaney Bay

LAID DOWN: October 6, 1943. Launched: December 29, 1943. Commissioned: February 11, 1944

Petrof Bay

LAID DOWN: October 15, 1943. Launched: January 5, 1944. Commissioned: February 18, 1944

Rudyerd Bay

LAID DOWN: October 24, 1943. Launched: January 12, 1944. Commissioned: February 25, 1944

Saginaw Bay
LAID DOWN: November 1, 1943. Launched: January 19, 1944. Commissioned: March 2, 1944

Sargent Bay
LAID DOWN: November 8, 1943. Launched: January 31, 1944. Commissioned: March 9, 1944

Shamrock Bay
LAID DOWN: November 15, 1943. Launched: February 4, 1943. Commissioned: March 15, 1944

Shipley Bay
LAID DOWN: November 22, 1943. Launched: February 12, 1944. Commissioned: March 21, 1944

Sitkoh Bay
LAID DOWN: November 23, 1943. Launched: February 19, 1944. Commissioned: March 28, 1944

Steamer Bay
LAID DOWN: December 2, 1943. Launched: February 26, 1944. Commissioned: April 4, 1944

Cape Esperance
LAID DOWN: December 11, 1943. Launched: March 3, 1944. Commissioned: April 9, 1944

Takanis Bay
LAID DOWN: December 16, 1943. Launched: March 10, 1944. Commissioned: April 15, 1944

Thetis Bay
LAID DOWN: December 22, 1943. Launched: March 16, 1944. Commissioned: April 21, 1944

Makassar Strait
LAID DOWN: December 29, 1943. Launched: March 22, 1944. Commissioned: April 29, 1944

Windham Bay
LAID DOWN: January 5, 1944. Launched: March 29, 1944. Commissioned: May 3, 1944

Makin Island
LAID DOWN: January 12, 1944. Launched: April 5, 1944. Commissioned: May 9, 1944

Lunga Point
LAID DOWN: January 19, 1944. Launched: April 11, 1944. Commissioned: May 14, 1944

Bismark Sea
LAID DOWN: January 31, 1944. Launched: April 17, 1944. Commissioned: May 20, 1944

Salamaua
LAID DOWN: February 4, 1944. Launched: April 22, 1944. Commissioned: May 26, 1944

Hollandia
LAID DOWN: February 12, 1944. Launched: April 28, 1944. Commissioned: June 1, 1944

Kwajalein
LAID DOWN: February 19, 1944. Launched: May 4, 1944. Commissioned: June 7, 1944

Admiralty Islands
LAID DOWN: February 26, 1944. Launched: May 10, 1944. Commissioned: June 13, 1944

Bougainville
LAID DOWN: March 3, 1944. Launched: May 16, 1944. Commissioned: June 18, 1944

Matanikau

LAID DOWN: March 10, 1944. Launched: May 22, 1944. Commissioned: June 24, 1944

Attu

LAID DOWN: March 16, 1944. Launched: May 27, 1944. Commissioned: May 3, 1944

Roi

LAID DOWN: March 22, 1944. Launched: June 2, 1944. Commissioned: July 6, 1944

Munda

LAID DOWN: March 29, 1944. Launched: June 8, 1944. Commissioned: July 8, 1944

BUILDER: Henry J. Kaiser Company, Inc., Vancouver, WA

DISPLACEMENT: 8,200 tons (standard), 10,900 tons (full load)

DIMENSIONS: 512'3" (oa) x 65'2" x 20'9" (mean)

FLIGHT DECK: 475'0" x 85'0"

MACHINERY: Skinner Uniflow reciprocating engines, 4 water-tube boilers, 2 shafts, 9,000 ihp = 19 knots

BUNKERAGE & RANGE: 2,200 tons = 10,200 nm @ 15 knots

AIRCRAFT: 28

ARMAMENT: 1 x 5" DP, 4 x twin 40mm AA, 12 x 20mm AA

COMPLEMENT: 860

DESIGN: The design for this class was generated by the Maritime Commission rather than the United States Navy and was similar to the *Bogue* class. They had a noticeably lower displacement but featured a larger flight deck, comparable hangar, twin screws, and slightly greater speed, although machinery production shortages led to the use of old-fashioned reciprocating engines in place of the earlier classes' turbines. The new design featured a flat hangar deck that greatly improved aircraft movement.

MODIFICATIONS: During World War II this class received upgraded radar suites and the light antiaircraft battery increased to eight twin 40mm mounts and thirty 20mm weapons. The *Thetis Bay* underwent a major reconstruction between June 1955 and July 1956 into a helicopter assault ship. The forward elevator was removed, the after unit enlarged and the flight deck shortened aft to improve access for helicopters. Defensive armament was reduced to eight twin 40mm weapons only. The bridge was modified and new radar installed. Troop berthing was created for 938 officers and men. The ship could operate up to twenty helicopters on a displacement of 11,000 tons full load.

SERVICE: The bulk of the class served in the Pacific during World War II, although the *Mission Bay*, the *Guadalcanal*, the *Tripoli*, the *Wake Island*, the *Solomons*, the *Kasaan Bay*, the *Tulagi*, and the *Shamrock Bay* all operated in the Atlantic, the *Mission Bay*, the *Guadalcanal*, and the *Solomons* exclusively so. They undertook antisubmarine, transportation, and landing air cover duties. The *Liscombe Bay* was torpedoed and sunk by the *I-175* off the Gilbert Islands on November 24, 1943; the *St. Lo* was destroyed by a kamikaze strike off Leyte on October 25, 1944; the

Gambier Bay was sunk by Japanese surface warships off Samar on the same date; the *Ommaney Bay* was wrecked by a kamikaze in the Sulu Sea on January 3, 1945, and scuttled; and the *Bismarck Sea* was sunk by a kamikaze off Iwo Jima on February 21, 1945. All the survivors decommissioned in 1946. The *Corregidor,* the *Sitkoh Bay,* the *Cape Esperance,* and the *Windham Bay* recommissioned as aircraft transports for service during the Korean War, while the *Tripoli* recommissioned to transport aircraft to Europe between 1952 and 1958. The *Makassar Bay* was sunk as a target in 1962. The *Thetis Bay* was used for experimental work as a helicopter assault ship from 1956 until 1964. The remainder of the class saw no service after World War II and all were stricken by the early 1960s.

52. UNITED STATES: *COMMENCEMENT BAY* CLASS (1944)
Courtesy of Art-Tech

Commencement Bay
LAID DOWN: September 23, 1943. Launched: May 9, 1944. Commissioned: November 27, 1944

Block Island
LAID DOWN: October 25, 1943. Launched: June 10, 1944. Commissioned: December 30, 1944

Gilbert Islands
LAID DOWN: November 29, 1943. Launched: July 20, 1944. Commissioned: February 5, 1945

Kula Gulf
LAID DOWN: December 16, 1943. Launched: August 15, 1944. Commissioned: May 12, 1945

Cape Gloucester
LAID DOWN: January 10, 1944. Launched: September 12, 1944. Commissioned: March 5, 1945

Salerno Bay
LAID DOWN: February 7, 1944. Launched: September 26, 1944. Commissioned: May 19, 1945

Vella Gulf
LAID DOWN: March 7, 1944. Launched: October 19, 1944. Commissioned: April 9, 1945

Siboney
LAID DOWN: April 1, 1944. Launched: November 9, 1944. Commissioned: May 15, 1945

Puget Sound
LAID DOWN: May 12, 1944. Launched: November 30, 1944. Commissioned: June 18, 1945

Rendova
LAID DOWN: June 15, 1944. Launched: December 28, 1944. Commissioned: October 22, 1945

Bairoko
LAID DOWN: July 25, 1944. Launched: January 25, 1945. Commissioned: July 16, 1945

Badoeng Strait
LAID DOWN: August 18, 1944. Launched: February 15, 1945. Commissioned: November 14, 1945

Saidor
LAID DOWN: September 29, 1944. Launched: March 17, 1945. Commissioned: September 4, 1945

Sicily
LAID DOWN: October 23, 1944. Launched: April 14, 1945. Commissioned: February 27, 1946

Point Cruz
LAID DOWN: December 4, 1944. Launched: May 18, 1945. Commissioned: October 16, 1945

Mindoro
LAID DOWN: January 2, 1945. Launched: June 27, 1945. Commissioned: December 4, 1945

Rabaul
LAID DOWN: January 29, 1945. Launched: July 14, 1945. Completed: August 30, 1946

Palau
LAID DOWN: February 19, 1945. Launched: August 6, 1945. Commissioned: January 15, 1946

Tinian
LAID DOWN: March 20, 1945. Launched: September 5, 1945. Completed: July 30, 1946

BUILDER: Todd-Pacific Shipbuilding Corporation, Seattle, WA
DISPLACEMENT: 18,908 tons (standard), 21,397 tons (full load)
DIMENSIONS: 557'1" (oa) x 75'0" x 27'11" (full load)
FLIGHT DECK: 495'0" x 80'0"
MACHINERY: Allis-Chalmers geared turbines, 4 Combustion Engineering boilers, 2 shafts, 16,000 shp = 19 knots
BUNKERAGE & RANGE: 3,134 tons
AIRCRAFT: 33
ARMAMENT: 2 x 5" DP, 3 x quadruple 40mm AA, 12 x twin 40mm AA, 20 x 20mm AA
COMPLEMENT: 1,066
DESIGN: This design was based on the successful *Sangamon* class conversions. The principal changes were rearrangement of the machinery spaces to separate the engine rooms, fitting two catapults from the outset, enlarging the island, increasing the antiaircraft battery, and eliminating the tanker pumping equipment, replacing it with expanded accommodation space. These ships also were faster and better subdivided than the tanker conversions.
MODIFICATIONS: These ships received upgraded radar suites in the 1950s, together with improved and enlarged bridge arrangements and a much smaller antiaircraft battery that deleted the 5-inch and 20mm weapons entirely and reduced the number of 40mm mounts. The *Gilbert Islands* was converted into a

Major Communications Relay Ship in 1963 and renamed the *Annapolis*.

SERVICE: The *Rabaul* and the *Tinian* did not enter commissioned service, while four other units were laid down but never launched. Only the *Gilbert Islands* and the *Cape Gloucester* saw front-line service during World War II, the other vessels that commis- sioned before war's end undertaking training and transportation duties. After World War II, many recommis- sioned in the early 1950s as antisub- marine carriers, usually embarking mixed air wings of helicopters and specialized fixed wing aircraft. Most were redesignated aircraft transports by 1959 and disposed of thereafter.

COLD WAR

53. FRANCE: *CLÉMENCEAU* CLASS (1961)
Courtesy of Art-Tech

Clémenceau
BUILDER: Arsenal de Brest
LAID DOWN: May 26, 1954. Launched: December 21, 1957. Commissioned: November 22, 1961

Foch
BUILDER: Chantiers de l'Atlantique (Penhöet-Loire), St. Nazaire

LAID DOWN: February 15, 1957. Launched: July 23, 1960. Commissioned: July 15, 1963
DISPLACEMENT: 22,000 tons (standard) 31,000 tons (full load)
DIMENSIONS: 869'5" (oa) x 98'5" x 24'7" (mean), 28'3" (full load)
FLIGHT DECK: 843'10" x 150'0"
MACHINERY: Parsons geared turbines, 6

boilers, 2 shafts, 126,000 shp = 32 knots

BUNKERAGE & RANGE: 3,720 tons = 7,500 nm @ 18 knots

AIRCRAFT: 40

ARMAMENT: 8 x 3.9" DP

COMPLEMENT: 2,200

DESIGN: Immediately after World War II, French naval architects prepared a design for a 20,000-ton (full load) carrier to embark forty-five aircraft. It owed much to the prewar design for the *Joffre* class but with a single hangar and the antiaircraft armament disposed in sponsons on either side of the hull rather than fore and aft of the island. It was planned to lay down one ship to this design at the Arsenal de Brest in 1947, but France's financial condition and the obvious shortcomings of the design in an era of fast jet aircraft delayed matters. A wholesale enlargement of the design incorporated an 8-degree angled flight deck, two steam catapults (one forward and the other on the angled deck), mirror landing equipment, and much increased aviation fuel stowage. Displacement grew by 50 percent, but the antiaircraft battery still had to be cut by half, and bulges added (after completion, in the *Clémenceau*'s case), increasing the beam to 104 feet. The class carried a comprehensive radar suite of a DRBV-20 long-range air search, a DRBV-23 air search, two DRBI-10 height-finding, a DRBV-50 surface search, and a NRBA-51 carrier-controlled approach, plus sonar.

MODIFICATIONS: Both ships were upgraded to operate Super Étendard aircraft, and received an improved radar suite, completing their refits in 1978 and 1981 respectively. A DRBV-15 three-dimensional air search set replaced the DRBV-20, the DRBV-50 was removed, two DRBV-32 C fire control sets added, and a new SENIT-2 tactical data system installed in place of the original SENIT-1. The *Foch* received a further refit in 1992–1993 that overhauled the main machinery and catapults. When the *Foch* was sold to Brazil, all armament was landed, asbestos insulation removed, and the SENIT-2 system upgraded to SENIT-8 standard.

SERVICE: These carriers served primarily in the Mediterranean, including operations off Lebanon in 1982. The *Foch* was sold to Brazil on November 15, 2000, commissioning on February 20, 2001, as the *Sao Paulo*. The *Clémenceau* was retired on October 1, 1997, and sold for scrap in 2003.

54. FRANCE: *JEANNE D'ARC* (1964)
Courtesy of Art-Tech

BUILDER: Arsenal de Brest
LAID DOWN: July 7, 1960. Launched: September 30, 1961. Commissioned: January 30, 1964
DISPLACEMENT: 10,000 tons (standard) 13,000 tons (full load)
DIMENSIONS: 590'6" (oa) x 78'9" x 20'4" (mean)
FLIGHT DECK: 230'0" x 85'0"
MACHINERY: Rateau-Bretagne geared turbines, 4 multitubular boilers, 2 shafts, 40,000 shp = 26.5 knots
BUNKERAGE & RANGE: 1,360 tons = 6,000 nm @ 15 knots
AIRCRAFT: 8
ARMAMENT: 4 x 3.9" DP
COMPLEMENT: 1,050 + 700 troops
DESIGN: Originally intended as a cadet training ship but redesigned to combine antisubmarine warfare and amphibious assault roles. The superstructure incorporates dedicated amphibious assault and combat information center spaces and a helicopter control bridge. Radar comprised a DRBV-50 surface search, a DRBV-22 air search, a DRBI-10 height finder, and three DRBV-32C fire control, plus sonar.
MODIFICATIONS: The stack height was increased substantially immediately after commissioning. Six Exocet surface-to-surface missile launchers were fitted forward in 1975. A major refit in 1983–1984 replaced the DRBV-50 with DRBV-51, removed

the DRBI-10, and added two 8-round AMBL-21 Syllex decoy launchers and associated electronic warning equipment. A further refit completed in October 2000 removed all the electronic warning equipment and launchers and landed two 3.9" guns.

SERVICE: The *Jeanne d'Arc* still serves primarily as a cadet training ship embarking up to 192 cadets.

55. FRANCE: *CHARLES DE GAULLE* (2001)
Courtesy of Art-Tech

BUILDER: Arsenal de Brest

LAID DOWN: April 14, 1989. Launched: May 14, 1994. Commissioned: May 18, 2001

DISPLACEMENT: 37,085 tons (standard) 40,600 tons (full load)

DIMENSIONS: 857'11" (oa) x 103'4" x 28'6" (mean), 31'2" (full load)

FLIGHT DECK: 857'11 x 211'2"

MACHINERY: Double-reduction geared turbines, two 150 megawatt pressurized water reactors, 2 shafts, 83,000 shp = 27 knots

ENDURANCE: 45 days

AIRCRAFT: 39

ARMAMENT: 2 x 16-round Sylver A43 vertical launch SAAM systems, 2 x Sadral SAM systems, 4 x 12.7mm MG.

COMPLEMENT: 1,950

DESIGN: France's first nuclear-powered surface warship uses the same reactors as installed in the *Le Triomphant* class ballistic missile submarines. They are contained within protective structures. The hangar is 453 feet long, 95 feet wide, and 20 feet high. Two starboard side deck-edge elevators capable of handling aircraft up to 70,000 pounds link the hangar and 8.3-degree angled flight deck. There are two steam catapults, one forward and the other in the waist on the angled section of the deck, each capable of launching aircraft up to 50,000 pounds. There are three arrester wires and a deck approach and landing laser system. In designing the ship, considerable attention was paid to providing a stable platform for flying operations. A system of twelve 500-ton lead weights sliding on transverse rails (SATRAP), four pairs of fin stabilizers, a rudder roll stabilization system, and the large low-mounted sponsons on each side of the hull damp rolling to as little as one half a degree in up to sea state 6. The shape of the hull and superstructure was optimized to reduce their radar returns, the mechanical plant is sound-isolated, and the ship fitted with a comprehensive degaussing system to eliminate magnetic returns. The SENIT 8 combat data and control system can track 100 targets at once and attack 10 simultaneously. The radar suite includes two DRBN-34 navigation sets, a DRBJ-11B height finder, a DRBV-15C search set, a DRBV-26D early warning set, and an Arabel missile target designator. The ship also has a comprehensive electronic warfare suite and data links.

MODIFICATIONS: The angled deck was found to be too short for safe operation of the ship's Hawkeye early warning aircraft and was extended by 14 feet 6 inches in 2001. Propellers proved problematic, limiting speed to 25 knots, and were replaced in 2005.

SERVICE: The *Charles de Gaulle* has conducted operations in the Mediterranean, Atlantic, and West Indies since completion.

56. ITALY: *GIUSEPPE GARIBALDI* **(1985)**
Courtesy of Art-Tech

BUILDER: Italcantieri, Trieste

LAID DOWN: March 26, 1981. Launched: June 6, 1983. Commissioned: September 30, 1985

DISPLACEMENT: 10,100 tons (standard) 13,850 tons (full load)

DIMENSIONS: 590'6" (oa) x 77'1" x 22'0" (mean)

FLIGHT DECK: 570'10" x 99'9"

MACHINERY: 4 General Electric-Fiat LM-2500 gas turbines, 2 shafts, 80,000 shp = 29.5 knots

RANGE: 7,000 nm @ 20 knots

AIRCRAFT: 16

ARMAMENT: 4 x Teseo SSM, 2 x 8-round Albatros SAM launchers, 2 x twin 40mm AA, 2 x triple 12.75" ASW torpedo tubes

COMPLEMENT: 825

DESIGN: Primarily intended for antisubmarine warfare but subsequently fitted to operate Harrier VTOL aircraft for air defense and strike operations. The hangar is 361 feet long, 49 feet wide, and 20 feet high. There are two elevators and the flight deck has a slightly rising sheer forward that forms a partial ski-jump for Harrier operations. To assist flight operations in heavy weather, there are two pairs of fin stabilizers. The radar suite comprises SPN-748 navigation, SPN-702 surface search, SPS-768 air early warning, SPS-774 air search, SPS-52D three-dimensional air search, three each of SPG-74 gun and SPG-75 missile fire control, and an SPN-728 carrier controlled approach set.

MODIFICATIONS: The Mk. 1 SSM launchers were replaced by Mk. 2 launchers in 1987, doubling their capacity. A Marconi DAPS (deck approach landing sight) landing aid was added in 1994.

SERVICE: The *Giuseppe Garibaldi* serves as the flagship of the Italian fleet.

57. SOVIET UNION: *MOSKVA* CLASS (1967)
Courtesy of Art-Tech

Moskva
LAID DOWN: December 15, 1962. Launched: January 14, 1964. Commissioned: December 26, 1967

Leningrad
LAID DOWN: January 15, 1965. Launched: July 31, 1968. Commissioned: June 2, 1969

Kiev
LAID DOWN: October 1968.
BUILDER: Chernomorskiy Shipyard 444, Nikolayev
DISPLACEMENT: 14,600 tons (standard), 19,200 tons (full load)
DIMENSIONS: 620'1" (oa) x 112'0" x 24'11" (mean), 27'11" (full load)
FLIGHT DECK: 295'0" x 112'0"
MACHINERY: 2 geared turbines, 4 boilers, 2 shafts, 100,000 shp = 30 knots

BUNKERAGE & RANGE: 2,600 tons = 9,000 nm @ 18 knots
AIRCRAFT: 18
ARMAMENT: 2 x twin M-11 Shtorm (NATO SA-N-3 Goblet) SAM launchers, 1 x twin RPK-2 Vyuga (NATO SS-N-15 Starfish) ASM launcher, 2 x 12-barrel RBU-6000 rocket depth charge launchers, 2 x twin 57mm AA, 2 x quintuple 12" torpedo tubes.
COMPLEMENT: 800
DESIGN: These Project 1123 ships were intended specifically to counter Polaris-armed strategic missile submarines, so antisubmarine elements dominated. Submarine location was primarily through a huge low-frequency MG-342 Orion (NATO Horse Jaw) sonar mounted in a very

large retractable keel dome 70 feet long, 20 feet wide, and 30 feet deep, supplemented by the Soviet Navy's first variable depth sonar unit, the MG-325 Vega (NATO Mare Tail). Antisubmarine weaponry included Kamov Ka–25 helicopters, a twin antisubmarine missile launcher with eighteen rounds, two 12-barrel rocket launchers, and torpedo tubes. The radar suite comprised an MR-600 (NATO Top Sail) air search, MR-310U Angara M (NATO Head Set-C) three-dimensional air search, 2 MR-103 Bars (NATO Muff Cob) surface search, 2 Grom (NATO Head Light) missile control sets. To improve sea keeping, the ships also were fitted with stabilizers.

MODIFICATIONS: The *Moskva* at least had considerable trouble with its machinery, which had to be overhauled twice by 1973.

SERVICE: The *Kiev* was cancelled in December 1968 and the incomplete hulk scrapped the following year. Both the other ships spent their entire careers in the Black Sea Fleet. The *Leningrad* decommissioned December 15, 1991, and was scrapped, the *Moskva* decommissioned in November 1993 and was scrapped in 1997.

58. SOVIET UNION: *KIEV* CLASS (1975)
Courtesy of Art-Tech

Kiev
LAID DOWN: July 21, 1970. Launched: December 27, 1972. Commissioned: December 28, 1975

Minsk
LAID DOWN: December 29, 1972. Launched: September 30, 1975. Commissioned: September 28, 1978

Novorossiysk
LAID DOWN: September 30, 1975. Launched: December 24, 1978. Commissioned: August 14, 1982
BUILDER: Chernomorskiy Shipyard 444, Nikolayev
DISPLACEMENT: 36,000 tons (standard), 43,500 tons (full load)
DIMENSIONS: 898'11" (oa) x 150'11" x 31'2" (mean), 39'4" (full load)
FLIGHT DECK: 606'11" x 173'10"
MACHINERY: 4 geared turbines, 8 turbo-

pressurized boilers, 4 shafts, 200,000 shp = 32 knots
BUNKERAGE & RANGE: 13,000 nm @ 18 knots
AIRCRAFT: 30 (45 in *Minsk* and *Novorossiysk*)
ARMAMENT: 2 x twin M-11 Shtorm (NATO SA-N-3 Goblet) SAM launchers, 2 x twin RZ-13 (NATO SA-N-4 Gecko) SAM launchers (*Kiev* and *Minsk*), 12 x octuple Kinzhal (NATO SA-N-9 Gauntlet) SAM launchers (*Novorossiysk*), 4 x twin P-500 Bazalt (NATO SS-N-12 Sandbox) launch tubes, 1 x twin RPK-2 Vyuga (NATO SS-N-15 Starfish) ASM launcher, 2 x twin 76.2mm DP, 8 x six-barrel 30mm AK-630 gatling AA, 2 x quintuple 12" torpedo tubes.
COMPLEMENT: 1,600

Design: Project 1143 was intended to form part of a barrier force to defend Soviet ballistic missile submarines in secure holding areas from attack by NATO antisubmarine forces and United States Navy carrier task groups. Consequently, they carried a mix of antiship, antisubmarine, and antiaircraft missile launchers, supplemented by Yakovlev Yak–38 VSTOL aircraft, primarily configured for attack missions or interception attacks while under direct control from the ships. The two later ships had improved sonar outfits. The *Kiev* was fitted with MG-322 Titan–2 (NATO Bull Nose) combined active and passive bow sonar and MG-325 Vega (NATO Mare Tail) variable depth sonar. The later units received low-frequency MG-342 Orion (NATO Horse Jaw) sonar mounted in a very large retractable keel dome and MG-335 Platina (NATO Horse Tail) variable depth sonar. The radar suite comprised an MR-600 (NATO Top Sail) air search, MR-700 Fregat (NATO Top Steer) three-dimensional air search, 2 MR-320 (NATO Palm Frond) surface search, 2 Grom (NATO Head Light) missile control,

2 MR-105 Turel (NATO Owl Screech) fire control, 4 MR-123 Vympel (NATO Bass Tilt) close-in weapons control, and MPZ-301 Baza (NATO Pop Group) missile control sets.

Modifications: The flight deck edges were rounded off and wind deflectors fitted during refits in the early 1980s.

Service: All three ships initially deployed in the Black Sea but passed through the Dardanelles into the Mediterranean. The *Kiev* and the *Novorossiysk* served with the Northern Fleet, the *Minsk* with the Pacific Fleet. All three were stricken in June 1993. In 1995 the *Minsk* and the *Novorossiysk* were sold for scrapping to a South Korean firm that in turn sold the *Minsk* to a Chinese company three years later. Stripped of its armament, engines, and electronics, it opened as a floating museum in Shenzhen in September 2000. In May 2000 another Chinese company purchased the *Kiev* for conversion into a floating recreational center in Tianjin as part of the Baiyang Recreation Harbor project.

59. SOVIET UNION: *ADMIRAL FLOTA SOVETSKOGO SOYUZA GORSHKOV* 1987)

LAID DOWN: December 1978. Launched: April 1, 1982. Commissioned: December 11, 1987

BUILDER: Chernomorskiy Shipyard 444, Nikolayev

DISPLACEMENT: 38,000 tons (standard), 45,500 tons (full load)

DIMENSIONS: 898'11" (oa) x 150'11" x 31'2" (mean), 39'4" (full load)

FLIGHT DECK: 623'4" x 173'10"

MACHINERY: 4 geared turbines, 8 turbo-pressurized boilers, 4 shafts, 200,000 shp = 32 knots

BUNKERAGE & RANGE: 13,000 nm @ 18 knots

AIRCRAFT: 45

ARMAMENT: 24 x octuple Kinzhal (NATO SA-N-9 Gauntlet) SAM launchers, 6 x twin P-500 Bazalt (NATO SS-N-12 Sandbox) launch tubes, 2 x 100mm DP, 8 x six-barrel 30mm AK-630 gatling AA

COMPLEMENT: 1,600

DESIGN: A modification of the Project 1143 design, Project 1143.4 featured an extended flight deck, improved superstructure, modified armament, and much improved electronics. The radar suite comprised a Mars-Pasal (NATO Sky Watch) phased array air search, MR-750 Fregat-M (NATO Plate Steer) three-dimensional air search, 2 MR-320 Topaz (NATO Strut Pair) two-dimensional air search, 3 MR-320 (NATO Palm Frond) surface search, 4 MR-360 Podkat (NATO Cross Sword) missile control, MR218 Lev (NATO Kite Screech) and 4 MR-123 Vympel (NATO Bass Tilt) gunnery control sets. It also carried an integrated antisubmarine warfare system, Undav–1, for the Bazalt launchers.

MODIFICATIONS: Laid down as the *Baku* and renamed in 1991. Russia will undertake a major reconstruction of the ship for service in the Indian Navy, including fitting a full length flight deck with ski jump and largely reconstructing the superstructure.

SERVICE: *Admiral Flota Sovetskogo Soyuza Gorshkov* passed through the Dardanelles in 1988 and served with the Pacific Fleet. It was decommissioned in 1993 and negotiation began for its sale to India. The sale was finally agreed January 20, 2004, and the ship renamed the *Vikramaditya*. It is anticipated to complete reconstruction and join the Indian Navy in August 2008.

60. SOVIET UNION: *KUZNETSOV* CLASS (1991)
Courtesy of Art-Tech

*Admiral Flota Sovetskogo Soyuza
   Kuznetsov*

LAID DOWN: November 6, 1983.
   Launched: December 5, 1985. Commissioned: January 21, 1991

Varyag

LAID DOWN: December 6, 1985.
   Launched: December 4, 1988

BUILDER: Chernomorskiy Shipyard 444,
   Nikolayev

DISPLACEMENT: 55,000 tons (standard)
   59,100 tons (full load)

DIMENSIONS: 1,005'4" (oa) x 124'8" x
   30'0" (mean), 36'0" (full load)

FLIGHT DECK: 1,000'0" x 237'2"

MACHINERY: 4 geared turbines, 8 turbo-
   pressurized boilers, 4 shafts, 200,000
   shp = 29 knots

BUNKERAGE & RANGE: 3,100 tons =
   8,500 nm @ 18 knots

AIRCRAFT: 58

ARMAMENT: 12 x P-700 (NATO SS-N-19
   Shipwreck) cruise missile launchers,
   24 x octuple Kinzhal (NATO SA-N-9
   Gauntlet) SAM launchers, 8 x octuple Kortik (NATO SA-N-11 Grison)
   mounts (each with 2 six-barrel GSH-
   6–30L 30mm gatling weapons), 6 x
   twin P-500 Bazalt (NATO SS-N-12
   Sandbox) launch tubes, 2 x 100mm
   DP, 6 x six-barrel 30mm AK-630
   gatling AA, 2 x 10-tube RPK-5 Liven
   antitorpedo rocket launchers

COMPLEMENT: 2,626

DESIGN: This class, Project 1143.5, has
   a full length flight deck with a ski
   jump launch ramp forward rather
   than catapults, and an angled landing deck. The ship currently operates
   a mix of Sukhoi Su–27 (NATO

Flanker) fighters and Kamov Ka–29 (NATO Helix) antisubmarine and airborne early warning helicopters. The radar suite comprised a Mars-Pasal (NATO Sky Watch) phased array air search, MR-750 Fregat-M (NATO Plate Steer) three-dimensional air search, 2 MR-320 Topaz (NATO Strut Pair) two-dimensional air search, 3 MR-320 (NATO Palm Frond) surface search, 3 MR-360 Podkat (NATO Cross Sword) and 8 3P37 (NATO Hot Flash) missile control sets. Sonar comprises two Zvezda—2 low and medium frequency search and attack sets and two hull-mounted MGK-345 Bronza (NATO Ox Yoke) low frequency sets.

MODIFICATIONS: The first unit was originally named the *Tbilisi* but renamed before commissioning.

SERVICE: The *Varyag*'s construction was abandoned in 1992 and the incomplete hull sold in March 1998 to a tourist company in Macao that planned to turn it into a floating casino. The *Admiral Flota Sovetskogo Soyuza Kuznetsov* served in the Mediterranean from 1995 to 1996, then transferred to the Northern Fleet and was out of commission until November 1998, when it returned to service.

61. SPAIN: *PRINCIPE DE ASTURIAS* **(1988)**
Courtesy of Art-Tech

BUILDER: Empresa Nacional Bazan, El Ferrol

LAID DOWN: October 8, 1979. Launched: May 22, 1982. Commissioned: May 30, 1988

DISPLACEMENT: 15,912 tons (standard), 17,188 tons (full load)

DIMENSIONS: 640'0" (oa) x 80'0" x 21'8" (full load)

FLIGHT DECK: 575'0" x 105'0"

MACHINERY: 2 General Electric LM-2500 gas turbines, 1 shaft, 46,400 shp = 26 knots

BUNKERAGE & RANGE: 6,500 nm @ 20 knots

AIRCRAFT: 19

ARMAMENT: 4 x 12-barrel 20mm AA

COMPLEMENT: 774

DESIGN: The basis for the *Principe de Asturias* was the United States Navy's Sea Control Ship study that was completed in January 1972. It was modified to incorporate a second elevator forward of the island superstructure and a 12-degree ski jump bow to assist the take off of Harrier VTOL aircraft. The axial flight deck is very slightly skewed to port at its aft end. The radar suite comprises an SPS-55 for surface search, an SPS-52C three-dimensional air search, an SPN-35A for air control, an RAN-11 target designator, and a VPS-2 fire control set on each 20mm mount. Two pairs of fin stabilizers are installed and there is an American Prairie/Masker air bubble system to mask hull and propeller noise.

MODIFICATIONS: The *Principe de Asturias* underwent a substantial refit in 1990. The island superstructure was enlarged, a parallel fuel distribution system fitted, a Marconi DAPS (deck approach landing sight) landing aid added, and the SPS-52C was updated to SPS-52D. Internally, berthing was modified to accommodate mixed sex crews.

SERVICE: The *Principe de Asturias* is based at Rota and serves as the flagship of Grupo Aeronaval Alfa.

62. THAILAND: *CHAKRI NAREUBET* (1997)
Courtesy of Art-Tech

LAID DOWN: July 12, 1994. Launched: January 20, 1996. Commissioned: August 10, 1997

BUILDER: Empresa Nacional Bazan, El Ferrol

DISPLACEMENT: 11,486 tons (full load)

DIMENSIONS: 600'0" (oa) x 73'10" x 20'1" (full load)

FLIGHT DECK: 571'2" x 100'0"

MACHINERY: 2 x Bazan-MTU 16-cylinder diesels, 11,200 bhp = 17 knots; or 2 General Electric LM-2500 gas turbines, 2 shafts, 44,250 shp = 27.5 knots

BUNKERAGE & RANGE: 7,150 nm @ 16.5 knots

AIRCRAFT: 18

ARMAMENT: 3 x Sadral SAM systems, 2 x 20mm AA, 2 x 12.7mm MG

COMPLEMENT: 601

DESIGN: The *Chakri Nareubet* is essen-tially a diminutive of Spain's *Principe de Asturias* with some small changes to the aft hull form to make its oper-ation more economical. The flight deck is axial and offset slightly to port. To improve stability during fly-ing operations, two pairs of fin stabi-lizers are fitted to the hull. There is berthing for up to 675 troops in addi-tion to the normal complement, and a section of the accommodation is dedicated for use by the Thai royal family. The radar suite comprises two Kelvin-Hughes 1007 for navigation and an SPS-52C three-dimensional air search set.

SERVICE: The *Chakri Nareubet* has seen very little service (about one day per month inside the naval base at Sat-tahip) due to funding problems.

63. UNITED KINGDOM: *EAGLE* CLASS (1951)
Courtesy of Art-Tech

Eagle (ex *Audacious*)
LAID DOWN: October 24, 1942. Launched: March 19, 1946. Commissioned: October 1, 1951
BUILDER: Harland & Wolff Ltd., Belfast

Ark Royal
LAID DOWN: May 3, 1943. Launched: March 3, 1950. Commissioned: February 25, 1955

BUILDER: Cammell Laird & Company Ltd., Birkenhead

Eagle
LAID DOWN: April 19, 1944
BUILDER: Vickers-Armstrong Ltd., Newcastle-upon-Tyne
DISPLACEMENT: 36,800 tons (standard) 45,720 tons (full load)

Dimensions: 803'9" (oa) x 112'9" x 33'3" (mean), 36'0" (full load)

Flight deck: 775'0" x 105'0"

Machinery: Parsons geared turbines, 8 Admiralty 3-drum boilers, 4 shafts, 152,000 shp = 31.5 knots

Bunkerage & range: 6,500 tons = 5,000 nm @ 24 knots

Aircraft: 80

Armament: 8 x twin 4.5" DP, 8 x 6-barrel 40mm AA

Complement: 2,250

Design: These ships started as enlargements of the *Implacable* class with two full hangars but the design soon grew rapidly to accommodate larger heavier aircraft. The hangar height increased to 17 feet 6 inches, which required a greater beam for stability, and in turn provided more hangar space. The hangars and two elevators were offset slightly to port to allow passage for the furnace uptakes at a higher level. Armor protection was 4 inches on the flight deck, side belt, and over the steering gear, 1–1/2 inches on the hangar sides, and 2–1/2 inches on the hangar deck. Two catapults were fitted on the flight deck, along with arresting gear and crash barriers. The *Eagle* completed to the original design with Type 960 search radar, Type 982 fighter control radar, and Type 983 height finding radar.

Modifications: The *Eagle* received a 5–1/2-degree angled deck and mirror landing equipment in a 1954–1955 refit. A major overhaul from 1959 to 1964 included fitting an 8–1/2-degree angled deck and adding an extension to the flight deck outboard of the island to allow aircraft movement. Two steam catapults replaced the original hydraulic units and the four forward 4.5-inch mounts were removed together with all 40mm mounts and six quadruple Seacat antiaircraft missile launchers added. A Type 984 three-dimensional search radar was added above the bridge and the new lattice mast (replacing the earlier tripod) supported a large Type 965 search radar, replacing the Type 960 and Type 983 sets. At the after end of the island a Type 963 carrier-controlled approach radar was fitted. The *Eagle* displaced 44,100 tons standard (54,100 tons full load) with a mean draft of 36 feet, and the overall beam rose to 166 feet 9 inches. In 1966–1967 a further refit added a third steam catapult on the angled deck in the waist.

The *Ark Royal*'s design was modified before completion to better suit it for operating jet aircraft. It received a 5–1/2-degreee angled flight deck 800 feet long and 112 feet wide, fitted with two steam catapults and equipped with mirror landing equipment. A third deck-edge elevator was fitted to port. The ship's port forward 4.5-inch mounts were removed in 1956 and those to starboard were removed in 1959 together with the deck-edge elevator. In 1964 all remaining armament was removed, sponsons built for six quadruple Seacat antiaircraft missile launchers, though these were never fitted, and an 8–1/2-degree flight deck built. Type 965 radar replaced the Type 960 search set. Displacement rose to 43,340 tons standard (53,340 tons full load) with a draft of 36 feet and flight deck width of 160 feet 6 inches. The *Ark Royal* was refitted again 1967–1970 to operate Phantoms. Two more powerful new steam catapults replaced the earlier units, one forward and one in the waist. The island was remodeled and Type 963 carrier-controlled approach radar fitted. Displacement fell to 43,060 tons standard (50,786 tons full load).

SERVICE: The original *Eagle* of this class was cancelled in January 1946 and the name transferred to the *Audacious*. The *Eagle* participated in the Suez operation in 1956, enforced the Beira blockade against Rhodesia in 1966, covered the British withdrawal from Aden at the end of 1967, and served in the Far East until March 1969. It was stricken in January 1972 and sold for scrapping in 1978. The *Ark Royal* served primarily in the Atlantic and became the Royal Navy's last carrier for conventional aircraft. It was decommissioned in February 1979 and broken up in 1980.

64. UNITED KINGDOM: *CENTAUR* CLASS (1953)
Courtesy of Art-Tech

Centaur

LAID DOWN: May 30, 1944. Launched: April 22, 1947. Commissioned: September 1, 1953

BUILDER: Harland & Wolff Ltd., Belfast

Albion

LAID DOWN: March 23, 1944. Launched: May 6, 1947. Commissioned: May 26, 1954

BUILDER: Swan, Hunter & Wigham Richardson, Ltd., Wallsend-on-Tyne

Bulwark

LAID DOWN: May 10, 1945. Launched: June 22, 1948. Commissioned: November 4, 1954

BUILDER: Harland & Wolff Ltd., Belfast

DISPLACEMENT: 20,260 tons (standard), 26,118 tons (full load)

DIMENSIONS: 737'0" (oa) x 90'0" x 22'0" (mean), 27'0" (full load)

FLIGHT DECK: 710'0" x 120'6"

MACHINERY: Parsons geared turbines, 4 Admiralty 3-drum boilers, 2 shafts, 76,000 shp = 29 knots

BUNKERAGE & RANGE: 4,000 tons = 6,000 nm @ 20 knots

AIRCRAFT: 36

ARMAMENT: 2 x 6-barrel 40mm AA, 8 x twin 40mm AA, 4 x 40mm AA

COMPLEMENT: 1,390

DESIGN: This class was an improved light fleet carrier with greater speed, obtained by doubling the power and modifying the hull form with a transom stern, and modest armor protection, in the form of 1-inch armor over the machinery crowns and sides, magazine sides, and an internal belt, plus 2 inches armor on the magazine crowns. The flight deck and larger elevators could accommodate aircraft up to 30,000 pounds and was fitted with a single catapult. They carried Type 960 and Type 982 radar for search, Type 983 for height finding, and Type 277Q for fighter direction.

MODIFICATIONS: The *Albion* and the *Bulwark* completed with a 5–3/4-degree angled deck, increasing beam to 123 feet, and two catapults, but sacrificed three twin 40mm mounts in compensation. Both ships were converted into commando carriers (the *Bulwark* between January 1959 and January 1960, the *Albion* from February 1961 to August 1962). They landed catapults, arresting gear, and all the six-barreled 40mm mounts, added four landing craft suspended from davits, and were reconfigured internally to berth troops. They could carry 16 helicopters and up to 900 troops. Displacement increased to 22,300 tons standard (27,700 full

load). The *Centaur* refitted 1959–1960 with a 5–3/4-degree flight deck, increasing the beam to 123 feet, two steam catapults, and mirror landing equipment, sacrificing four twin 40mm mounts in compensation. Displacement rose to 22,000 tons standard (27,000 tons full load), and aircraft complement fell to 21 Sea Vixens and Scimitars.

SERVICE: The *Centaur* spent most of its career in the Mediterranean and Far East. It became a depot ship in 1966 and was stricken in 1971. The *Albion* participated in the Suez operation in 1956 and spent most of the remainder of its career in the Far East, including deploying its commandos during the Indonesian confrontation in 1966. It was stricken in 1972. The *Bulwark,* too, was at Suez in 1956. After conversion as a commando carrier it served mainly in the Mediterranean and Far East, including off Indonesia in 1966. It served briefly as an antisubmarine carrier in 1979 but was decommissioned in March 1981 and stricken in 1985.

65. UNITED KINGDOM: *VICTORIOUS* RECONSTRUCTION (1958)
Courtesy of Art-Tech

BUILDER: Portsmouth Dockyard

DISPLACEMENT: 30,530 tons (standard) 35,500 tons (full load)

DIMENSIONS: 781'0" (oa) x 103'4" x 31'0" (mean)

FLIGHT DECK: 775'0" x 157'0"

MACHINERY: Parsons geared turbines, 6 Foster-Wheeler boilers, 3 shafts, 110,000 shp = 31 knots

BUNKERAGE & RANGE: 4,850 tons = 11,000 nm @ 14 knots

AIRCRAFT: 35

ARMAMENT: 6 x twin 3" AA, 1 x 6-barrel 40mm AA

COMPLEMENT: 2,200

MODIFICATIONS: Between October 1950 and January 1958, the *Victorious* received new boilers and was rebuilt above the hangar deck almost entirely. The new hangar was 17 feet 6 inches high under the 8–3/4-degree angled flight deck stressed for aircraft up to 40,000 pounds. Two new larger elevators linked hangar and flight deck, which also carried two steam catapults, new arresting gear, and mirror landing equipment. The radar suite comprised Type 984 three-dimensional fighter control, Type 974 surface search, Type 293Q height finding, and Type 963 carrier controlled approach.

SERVICE: The *Victorious* served mainly in the Atlantic and Far East. The Admiralty decided to decommission the ship after a fire while it was under refit in 1968 and it was sold for scrapping in July 1969.

66. UNITED KINGDOM: *HERMES* (1959)
Courtesy of Art-Tech

LAID DOWN: June 21, 1944. Launched: February 16, 1953. Commissioned: November 18, 1959

BUILDER: Vickers-Armstrong Ltd., Barrow-in-Furness

DISPLACEMENT: 23,000 tons (standard), 27,800 tons (full load)

DIMENSIONS: 744'3" (oa) x 90'0" x 28'0" (mean), 27'0" (full load)

FLIGHT DECK: 710'0" x 144'6"

MACHINERY: Parsons geared turbines, 4 Admiralty 3-drum boilers, 2 shafts, 76,000 shp = 29 knots

BUNKERAGE & RANGE: 4,000 tons = 6,000 nm @ 20 knots

AIRCRAFT: 20

ARMAMENT: 5 x twin 40mm AA

COMPLEMENT: 1,834

DESIGN: Originally a member of the *Centaur* class. The modified design included automatic furnace feed, a 6–1/2-degree angled flight deck with two steam catapults forward, a forward port side deck-edge elevator in place of the centerline unit, upgraded arresting gear, and a mirror landing aid. The radar suite comprised Type 984 three-dimensional search, Type 293Q target indicator, and Type 963 carrier controlled approach sets.

MODIFICATIONS: The *Hermes* was modified to operate more modern aircraft in 1964–1966, adding a flight deck extension outboard of the island that increased overall beam to 160 feet. It was converted into an amphibious assault ship in 1971 with a strengthened flight deck, catapults and arresting gear landed, and berthing for up to 750 troops and their equipment added. In 1976–1977 the *Hermes* was again modified to operate Sea Harriers with a ski jump forward on the flight deck and two quadruple Seacat launchers added, increasing displacement to 23,900 tons standard (28,700 tons full load). After being sold to India in 1986 and re-named the *Viraat*, the carrier was re-fitted prior to delivery in 1987. The *Viraat* underwent a major overhaul between 1999 and 2001, upgrading the ship's propulsion systems, radar suite, communications systems, and elevators. Two Israeli Barak missile point defense systems replaced the Seacat launchers.

SERVICE: The *Hermes* served in the Far East and Mediterranean until 1976 and then operated in the Atlantic. The carrier was the flagship of the British task force charged with regaining the Falkland Islands/Malvinas from Argentina in 1982. It was sold in 1986 and commissioned in the Indian Navy on May 12, 1987, as the *Viraat*.

67. UNITED KINGDOM: *INVINCIBLE* CLASS (1980)
Courtesy of Art-Tech

Invincible
LAID DOWN: July 20, 1973. Launched: May 3, 1977. Commissioned: July 11, 1980
BUILDER: Vickers-Armstrong Ltd., Barrow-in-Furness

Illustrious
LAID DOWN: June 7, 1976. Launched: December 14, 1978. Commissioned: June 20, 1982
BUILDER: Swan, Hunter & Wigham Richardson, Ltd., Wallsend-on-Tyne

Ark Royal
LAID DOWN: December 14, 1978. Launched: June 4, 1981. Commissioned: November 1, 1985

BUILDER: Swan, Hunter & Wigham Richardson, Ltd., Wallsend-on-Tyne
DISPLACEMENT: 16,970 tons (standard) 20,710 tons (full load)
DIMENSIONS: 677'0" (oa) x 90'0" x 24'0" (mean)
FLIGHT DECK: 550'0" x 115'0"
MACHINERY: 4 Rolls-Royce Olympus gas turbines, 2 shafts, 112,000 shp = 28 knots
BUNKERAGE & RANGE: 7,000 nm @ 18 knots
AIRCRAFT: 20
ARMAMENT: 2 x Sea Dart SAM launchers
COMPLEMENT: 900
DESIGN: This class was originally conceived as helicopter-carrying com-

mand cruisers of about 12,500 tons with missile and gun armament forward and a hangar for six helicopters aft. It soon became apparent that more efficient operation would result from moving the superstructure to the starboard side and extending the helicopter flight deck to run from end to end of the ship, which would have the added benefit of increasing hangar and workshop space. The imminent arrival of effective VSTOL fighters in the form of the Sea Harrier led to incorporation of suitable facilities for their operation into the design, though the ships were still classified as through-deck cruisers rather than carriers until shortly before the *Invincible* entered service. The very large internal volume allows virtually all equipment to be installed on a modular basis, so that engines, control consoles, auxiliary equipment, and so on are maintained on an exchange basis rather than overhauled or repaired on board. The design includes two scissors-type elevators but no arresting gear or catapults. As completed, the first two carriers had 7-degree ski jumps to facilitate Sea Harrier operation, while the *Ark Royal* was completed with a 12-degree ski jump that extends the flight deck 40 feet further forward. The *Illustrious* and the *Ark Royal* also completed with three Mk.15 Phalanx 20mm mounts. The radar suite included Type 1022 long-range air warning, Type 992 target indicator, and Type 909 missile fire control sets.

MODIFICATIONS: The *Invincible* received three Mk.15 Phalanx 20mm mounts in 1983. It was refitted in 1999–2000, removing the Sea Dart launchers, replacing the Phalanx mounts with Goalkeeper 30mm close in weapons systems, and adding two 20mm AA mounts. The *Illustrious* was similarly refitted in 1998–1999. In addition, the space freed by removing the Sea Dart launchers and fire control radars was used to extend the flight deck outboard on the starboard side to provide additional deck park space and the ski jump was modified to match the *Ark Royal*'s. The *Ark Royal* was refitted in 1999–2001 to match the *Illustrious,* except that the Phalanx weapons were retained and not replaced by Goalkeeper mounts.

SERVICE: The *Invincible* served with the British task force charged with regaining the Falkland Islands/Malvinas from Argentina in 1982. The *Illustrious* was deployed to the South Atlantic in 1982–1983. All three carriers subsequently operated in the Atlantic and Mediterranean, including deployments to the Adriatic between 1993 and 1995 in support of NATO operations in the former Yugoslavia. The *Invincible* returned to the Adriatic in 1999 as part of Operation Allied Force in Kosovo. The *Illustrious* operated off Sierra Leone during 2000 and again in 2001 to 2002 during Operation Veritas in support of the war in Afghanistan. The *Ark Royal* formed part of the British naval force in the Persian Gulf during Operation Telic, the invasion of Iraq in 2003.

68. UNITED STATES: *ESSEX* CLASS RECONSTRUCTIONS (1950)
Courtesy of Art-Tech

SCB27A

Essex
Yorktown
Hornet
Randolph
Wasp
Bennington
Kearsarge
Oriskany
Lake Champlain
DISPLACEMENT: 40,600 tons (full load)
DIMENSIONS: 898'2" (oa) x 101'4" x 29'8" (mean)
FLIGHT DECK: 870'0" x 108'0"
MACHINERY: Westinghouse geared turbines, 8 Babcock & Wilcox boilers, 4 shafts, 150,000 shp = 31 7 knots

BUNKERAGE & RANGE: 6,330 tons = 15,000 nm @ 15 knots
AIRCRAFT: 89
ARMAMENT: 8 x 5" DP, 14 x twin 3" AA
COMPLEMENT: 3,525

SCB27C

Intrepid
Ticonderoga
Lexington
Hancock
Bon Homme Richard
Shangri-La
DISPLACEMENT: 41,944 tons (full load)
DIMENSIONS: 898'4" (oa) x 103'4" x 29'7" (mean)

FLIGHT DECK: 862'0" x 108'0" (142"0" when fitted with angled deck)

MACHINERY: Westinghouse geared turbines, 8 Babcock & Wilcox boilers, 4 shafts, 150,000 shp = 32 knots

BUNKERAGE & RANGE: 6,330 tons = 15,000 nm @ 15 knots

AIRCRAFT: 80

ARMAMENT: 8 x 5" DP, 12 (only 5 when fitted with angled deck) x twin 3" AA

COMPLEMENT: 3,525

SCB125

Essex
Yorktown
Hornet
Randolph
Wasp
Bennington
Kearsarge

DISPLACEMENT: 41,200 tons (full load)

DIMENSIONS: 890'0" (oa) x 101'4" x 30'1" (mean)

FLIGHT DECK: 861'0" x 142'0"

MACHINERY: Westinghouse geared turbines, 8 Babcock & Wilcox boilers, 4 shafts, 150,000 shp = 32 knots

BUNKERAGE & RANGE: 6,330 tons = 15,000 nm @ 15 knots

AIRCRAFT: 50

ARMAMENT: 7 x 5" DP, 4 x twin 3" AA

COMPLEMENT: 3,275

SCB125A

Oriskany

DISPLACEMENT: 44,000 tons (full load)

DIMENSIONS: 910'10" (oa) x 106'7" x 31'4" (mean)

FLIGHT DECK: 861'0" x 142'0"

MACHINERY: Westinghouse geared turbines, 8 Babcock & Wilcox boilers, 4 shafts, 150,000 shp = 32 knots

BUNKERAGE & RANGE: 6,330 tons = 15,000 nm @ 15 knots

AIRCRAFT: 50

ARMAMENT: 7 x 5" DP, 5 x twin 3" AA

COMPLEMENT: 3,275

DESIGN: SCB27A was a conversion to allow the *Essex* class carriers to operate jet fighters and the largest attack aircraft yet envisaged without requiring major structural change. In fact, approximately 40 percent of the type's original structure was replaced in this conversion. Side armor was removed and a large bulge built from 1–1/2-inch STS steel flush with the hull on each side. Hangar fire protection systems were upgraded. The island was reduced in size, the stacks raked aft, and a massive pole mast erected to support antennae for SPS-8 height finding and SPS-6 search radars. For action safety, three ready rooms were moved from the gallery deck to below the hangar deck and connected to the flight deck by a very noticeable external elevator. The stowage for aviation fuel was enlarged by 50 percent to cope with much thirstier jet aircraft. The flight deck was strengthened to support aircraft up to 52,000 pounds, and the elevators enlarged and strengthened. More powerful catapults and stronger arresting gear replaced the original outfit. As sets became available, an SPN-8 carrier controlled approach radar was fitted at the aft end of the island. The flight deck gun houses were removed and four 5-inch guns mounted to starboard in sponsons similar to those on the port side. Twin 3-inch antiaircraft mounts replaced quadruple 40mm weapons.

SCB27C was a further improvement. The bulge on each side was wider to give more stability and compensate for greater topweight. Fuel blending was introduced to almost quadruple aviation fuel capacity. The after elevator was removed and replaced with a starboard side deck edge unit, which required relocating the two aft starboard 5-inch mounts toward the stern. Two steam catapults were installed, together with upgraded arresting gear and a new nylon crash barrier specially designed for jet aircraft operation. Jet blast deflectors and a flight deck cooling system also were added. The *Lexington*, the *Bon Homme Richard*, and the *Shangri-La* in addition received angled flight decks (requiring removal of three 3-inch gun mounts), enlarged forward elevators, and enclosed "hurricane" bows.

MODIFICATIONS: In 1956–1957, the three SCB27C vessels with axial decks were reconstructed to match the other three carriers with angled decks and "hurricane" bows. SCB125 was a further reconstruction of the SCB27A ships with an angled flight deck, starboard side deck-edge elevator, and "hurricane" bow, but retaining the earlier hydraulic catapults. The *Oriskany* alone received a full reconstruction to match the SCB27C ships as SCB125A.

All the reconstructed ships except the *Ticonderoga*, the *Hancock*, the *Bon Homme Richard*, the *Oriskany*, and the *Shangri-La* became anti-

submarine warfare carriers between 1958 and 1962, and received SQS-23 sonar domes beneath the forefoot, plus internal modifications and upgraded radar suites for their new missions. The five attack carriers received upgraded radar suites in the early 1960s. The *Ticonderoga* and the *Shangri-La* also became antisubmarine warfare carriers in 1969, though they did not operate in that role. All the reconstructed *Essex* class carriers also underwent FRAM II (fleet rehabilitation and modernization) in the early 1960s. Stability concerns led to the removal of all 3-inch gun mounts and all but three or four of the remaining 5-inch mounts.

SERVICE: The *Essex*, the *Kearsarge*, the *Oriskany*, and the *Lake Champlain* all took part in operations during the Korean War. The *Yorktown*, the *Intrepid*, the *Hornet*, the *Ticonderoga*, the *Hancock*, the *Bon Homme Richard*, the *Oriskany*, and the *Shangri-La* all operated extensively off Vietnam from 1963. The remaining vessels served primarily in the Atlantic and Mediterranean. The *Lexington* became the United States Navy's training carrier in 1962, decommissioned in 1991, and became a museum ship at Corpus Christi, Texas, in 1992. The *Lake Champlain* was stricken in 1969, the *Wasp* in 1972, the *Ticonderoga*, the *Randolph*, and the *Kearsarge* in 1973, the *Essex* in 1975, the *Hancock* in 1976, the *Shangri-La* in 1982, and the *Bennington*, the *Bon Homme Richard*, and the *Oriskany* in 1989. All were scrapped. The *Hornet* decommissioned in June

1970 and eventually became a museum ship at Alameda, California, in 1998. The *Yorktown* was stricken in June 1973 and became a museum ship at Charleston, South Carolina, in 1975. The *Intrepid* decommissioned in March 1974 and became a museum ship at New York City in 1982.

69. UNITED STATES: *MIDWAY* CLASS RECONSTRUCTIONS (1956)

Courtesy of Art-Tech

SCB110

Franklin D. Roosevelt

Midway

DISPLACEMENT: 63,500 tons (full load)

DIMENSIONS: 977'2" (oa) x 121'0" x 34'6" (mean)

FLIGHT DECK: 977'2" x 192'0"

MACHINERY: Geared turbines, 12 Babcock & Wilcox boilers, 4 shafts, 212,000 shp = 30.6 knots

BUNKERAGE & RANGE: 10,000 tons = 15,000 nm @ 15 knots

AIRCRAFT: 80

ARMAMENT: 10 x 5" DP, 9 x twin 3" AA

COMPLEMENT: 4,060

SCB110A

Coral Sea

DISPLACEMENT: 62,600 tons (full load)

DIMENSIONS: 978'0" (oa) x 121'0" x 34'9" (mean)

FLIGHT DECK: 978'0" x 236'0"

MACHINERY: Geared turbines, 12 Babcock & Wilcox boilers, 4 shafts, 212,000 shp = 30.6 knots

BUNKERAGE & RANGE: 10,000 tons = 15,000 nm @ 15 knots

AIRCRAFT: 80

ARMAMENT: 6 x 5" DP

COMPLEMENT: 4,375

SCB101.66

Midway

DISPLACEMENT: 64,895 tons (full load)

DIMENSIONS: 977'0" (oa) x 121'0" x 34'9" (mean)

FLIGHT DECK: 972'2" x 258'5"

MACHINERY: Geared turbines, 12 Babcock & Wilcox boilers, 4 shafts, 212,000 shp = 31.6 knots

BUNKERAGE & RANGE: 10,000 tons = 15,000 nm @ 15 knots

AIRCRAFT: 70

ARMAMENT: 3 x 5" DP

COMPLEMENT: 4,686

DESIGN: SCB110 was a reconstruction of the *Midway* class that paralleled the SBC27C conversion of the *Essex* class. The side armor was removed and replaced with a 5-foot wide bulge from 1–1/2-inch STS steel flush with the hull. Fuel blending tripled aviation fuel capacity. An angled flight deck was fitted and the af-ter elevator relocated to the starboard deck edge. All elevators were enlarged and strengthened. Three steam catapults were fitted, two were forward and one in the waist. A "hurricane" bow was fitted and the bridge structure modified with a new mast to support antennae (SPS-12 air search, SPS-8A height finding, SC-2 long-range air search on the *Franklin D. Roosevelt,* SPS-12 air search, SPS-8A height finding, and SPS-43 long-range air search on the *Midway*), plus an SPN-8 carrier controlled approach set. As weight compensation, the gun battery was reduced substantially. The *Coral Sea* was completed to SBC110A, a modified version that entailed deleting the forward centerline elevator in favor of a starboard side deck-edge unit and cutting the gun battery to only four 5-inch mounts. The *Coral Sea*'s new pole mast carried SPS-12 air search, SPS-8A height finding, and SPS-37 air search radar.

MODIFICATIONS: The *Midway* was again reconstructed to SCB101.66 between 1966 and 1970. The forward centerline elevator was replaced with a starboard side deck-edge unit, the three steam catapults replaced with two much more powerful units on the forward flight deck, and the flight deck greatly enlarged. Arresting gear was upgraded, aviation fuel capacity almost doubled, and the gun armament slashed. An SPS-30 radar replaced the SPS-12 air search, SPS-8A height finding sets. *The Franklin D. Roosevelt* underwent a less extensive reconstruction in 1968 that removed the forward centerline elevator, replaced it with a starboard side forward deck edge unit, and reduced armament to just four 5-inch guns. New SPS-30 and SPS-43 sets replaced the earlier outfit. By 1980 the *Midway* and the *Coral Sea* had much upgraded radar suites and carried three Mk.15 Phalanx 20mm mounts. The *Midway* also carried three 8-tube Sea Sparrow launchers and landed all its guns.

SERVICE: All three carriers operated off Vietnam, the *Coral Sea* completing the most tours of any carrier in that theater. The *Franklin D. Roosevelt* served with the Atlantic Fleet until the carrier was stricken in 1977 and scrapped. The *Coral Sea* served with the Pacific Fleet until decommissioned in 1989 and scrapped. The *Midway* served with the Pacific Fleet, home ported at Yokosuka in Japan. It took part in operation Desert Storm in 1991 and decommissioned in April 1992, becoming a museum ship at San Diego, California.

70. UNITED STATES: *FORRESTAL* CLASS (1955)
Courtesy of Art-Tech

Forrestal
LAID DOWN: July 14, 1952. Launched: December 11, 1954. Commissioned: October 1, 1955
BUILDER: Newport News Shipbuilding & Dry Dock Company, Newport News, VA

Saratoga
LAID DOWN: August 2, 1954. Launched: October 8, 1955. Commissioned: April 14, 1956
BUILDER: New York Navy Yard

Ranger
LAID DOWN: July 14, 1952. Launched: September 29, 1956. Commissioned: August 10, 1957
BUILDER: Newport News Shipbuilding & Dry Dock Company, Newport News, VA

Independence
LAID DOWN: July 1, 1955. Launched: June 6, 1958. Commissioned: April 3, 1959
BUILDER: New York Navy Yard
DISPLACEMENT: 60,000 tons (standard) 78,000 tons (full load)
DIMENSIONS: 1,039'0" (oa) x 129'6" x 37'0" (full load)
FLIGHT DECK: 1,015'0" x 240'0"
MACHINERY: Geared turbines, 8 Babcock & Wilcox boilers, 4 shafts, 260,000 shp = 33 knots (*Forrestal*), 280,000 shp = 33.5 knots (others)
BUNKERAGE & RANGE: 7,800 tons = 12,000 nm @ 20 knots
AIRCRAFT: 90
ARMAMENT: 8 x 5" DP
COMPLEMENT: 4,142
DESIGN: Work on generating a smaller

version of the carrier *United States* began very shortly after its cancellation by Defense Secretary Louis Johnson on April 23, 1949. Congressman Carl Vinson suggested that the Congress might approve construction of a new carrier of no more than 60,000 tons, which became the baseline for the new design. Like *United States*, the new carrier was flush decked with large sponsons on either beam supporting a wide flight deck that carried four catapults, two forward in the bow and one on each sponson. To save weight and also because of concerns about the design capabilities of comparable hydraulic catapults, these catapults were to be a new slotted tube design powered by explosive charges. A deck-edge elevator served each catapult. Furnace gases exhausted via a crossover system venting through stacks on each side of the ship that could fold down horizontally during flying operations. The navigating bridge was retractable, and radar antennae were carried on masts that folded horizontally during flying operations. Like *United States*, the flight deck became the strength deck, but the bow was enclosed to the flight deck to improve sea keeping.

The *Forrestal* and the *Saratoga* were laid down to this design but modified extensively during construction to incorporate the latest advances in carrier design. The most important was an angled flight deck. This allowed use of a conventional island bridge structure with a large integral stack exhausting furnace

gases. The angled deck displaced the port after deck-edge elevator to the starboard side, so there were three elevators to starboard and only one, at the forward end of the angled deck, to port. The starboard sponson catapult was moved to port, oriented along the angled deck. There had been major problems in developing the explosive slotted tube catapult design, so all catapults were new steam powered units. The *Forrestal* and the *Saratoga* received two C-11 steam catapults amidships and two more powerful C-7 catapults in the bow, whereas the other ships received four C-7s. The radar suite comprised an SPS-8 height-finder and SPS-12 for air search. The two other members of the class were constructed to this same design from the outset.

MODIFICATIONS: All ships lost their forward 5-inch guns and sponsons in the 1960s and all the remaining guns by 1977. The *Saratoga*, the *Forrestal*, and the *Independence* received full Service Life Extension Program refits between 1980 and 1988, improving protection with Kevlar armor, substituting SPS-48C three-dimensional and SPS-49 two-dimensional search radars for their original fit, adding two 8-tube Sea Sparrow launchers controlled by SPS-58 sets, and gaining three Mk.15 Phalanx 20mm mounts. The *Ranger* received a major overhaul between 1984 and 1985 that brought it close to the standard of its sisters.

SERVICE: The *Forrestal* served with the Atlantic Fleet, primarily in the

Mediterranean. It deployed for operations off Vietnam in 1967 but its service was cut short by a major fire that required a major overhaul to repair. The *Forrestal* returned to the Mediterranean until decommissioning on September 11, 1993. The *Saratoga* also served in the Mediterranean until deployed to Yankee Station off Vietnam from 1972 to 1973. It returned to the Mediterranean, decommissioning August 20, 1994. The *Ranger* and the *Independence* both deployed to the Pacific Fleet and operated on Yankee Station from 1964 to 1973. The *Saratoga* and the *Independence* were active during Operation Desert Shield in 1990. The *Saratoga* and the *Ranger* took part in

Operation Desert Storm, the liberation of Kuwait in 1991, and the *Saratoga,* the *Ranger,* and the *Independence* served during Operation Southern Watch in the Persian Gulf, enforcing the "no-fly" zone over southern Iraq. The *Ranger* supported Operation Restore Hope in Somalia in 1992. The *Saratoga* also operated in the Adriatic to enforce Operation Deny Flight over Bosnia in 1994.

The *Ranger* decommissioned July 10, 1993. The *Independence* was home ported at Yokosuka in Japan from September 1991 and decommissioned on September 30, 1998. The *Forrestal,* the *Saratoga,* and the *Ranger* were all placed on hold for potential service as museum ships.

71. UNITED STATES: *KITTY HAWK* CLASS (1961)
Courtesy of Art-Tech

Kitty Hawk
LAID DOWN: December 27, 1956.
Launched: May 21, 1960. Commissioned: June 9, 1961
BUILDER: New York Shipbuilding Corporation, Camden, NJ

Constellation
LAID DOWN: September 14, 1957.
Launched: October 8, 1960. Commissioned: January 19, 1962
BUILDER: New York Navy Yard

America
LAID DOWN: January 9, 1961. Launched: February 1, 1964. Commissioned: January 23, 1965

BUILDER: Newport News Shipbuilding & Dry Dock Company, Newport News, VA

John F. Kennedy
LAID DOWN: October 22, 1964.
Launched: May 27, 1967. Commissioned: September 7, 1968
BUILDER: Newport News Shipbuilding & Dry Dock Company, Newport News, VA
DISPLACEMENT: 60,100 (61,000 *John F. Kennedy*) tons (standard), 78,250 (82,000 *John F. Kennedy*) tons (full load)
DIMENSIONS: 1,062'5" (1,052'0" *John F.*

Kennedy) (oa) x 129'4" x 35'0" (36'0" *John F. Kennedy*) (full load)

FLIGHT DECK: 1,040'0" x 252'0"

MACHINERY: Geared turbines, 8 Babcock & Wilcox (Foster-Wheeler *John F. Kennedy*) boilers, 4 shafts, 280,000 shp = 33 knots

BUNKERAGE & RANGE: 7,800 tons = 12,000 nm @ 20 knots

AIRCRAFT: 87

ARMAMENT: 2 x twin Terrier SAM launchers (3 x 8-tube Sea Sparrow launchers *John F. Kennedy*)

COMPLEMENT: 4,500

DESIGN: The flight deck arrangement of the *Forrestal* class proved unsatisfactory, since the largest deck park area was abaft the island and landing operations prevent simultaneous egress from the deck park. The revised *Kitty Hawk* flight deck arrangement reversed the positions of the central starboard elevator and the island, creating a large deck park area ahead of the island that had direct access to the forward catapults at all times. The port elevator was moved aft so that flying operations on the angled deck no longer blocked its use. More powerful C-13 catapults replaced the mix of C-7 and C-11 catapults used in the earlier class. The large forward sponsons for 5-inch weapons were deleted which much improved sea keeping and a pair of twin Terrier missile launchers aft, with forty rounds apiece, replaced all gun armament. The *America* and the *John F. Kennedy* both carried large domes at the forefoot for SQS-23 sonar, though the equipment itself was omitted from the *John F. Kennedy* to

cut costs. The *John F. Kennedy* also had a narrower underwater protection system, originally developed to save space in nuclear-powered carriers. The radar suite for the first two ships comprised SPS-37A air search, SPS-39 three-dimensional search, SPS-8B height finding, and SPG-55 missile fire control. The *America* carried SPS-43A air search, SPS-52 three-dimensional search, SPS-30 height finding, and SPG-55 missile fire control. The *John F. Kennedy* carried SPS-43A air search and SPS-48 long-range three-dimensional search.

MODIFICATIONS: The *Kitty Hawk* replaced its Terrier mounts with two 8-tube Sea Sparrow SAM launchers in 1977, and the Terriers were removed from the *Constellation* and the *America* in 1982. By 1990 all ships carried three 8-tube Sea Sparrow launchers and fitted Mk. 23 target indication radar for their control. The *America*'s SPS-52 set was replaced with an SPS-48 radar in 1982. All ships substituted SPS-49 search sets for their SPS-43A radars in 1979–1980. The *Kitty Hawk* and the *Constellation* underwent Service Life Extension Program refits in 1988–1991 and 1990–1993 respectively. The *John F. Kennedy* underwent a Comprehensive Overhaul Modernization, at about half the cost of a full SLEP refit, between 1993 and 1995.

SERVICE: The *Kitty Hawk* and the *Constellation* joined the Pacific Fleet on completion and served on Yankee Station during the Vietnam War from 1964 to 1972. The *America* joined the Atlantic Fleet on completion. It served on Yankee Station between 1968 and 1973. In the Mediterranean, it deployed off Lebanon during the crises in 1976 and 1983 and in operations in the Gulf of Sidra in 1986. The *John F. Kennedy* joined the Atlantic Fleet on commissioning and served mainly in the Mediterranean, including operations in the Gulf of Sidra during August 1988 that resulted in the destruction of two Libyan MiG-23s. In 1995 it became a reserve carrier but reverted to active status in 2000.

The *Constellation* was active during the tanker war in the Persian Gulf during 1987. Both the *John F. Kennedy* and the *America* served during the liberation of Kuwait in operations Desert Shield in 1990 and Desert Storm 1991. The *Kitty Hawk* and the *Constellation* were deployed to the Persian Gulf for Operation Southern Watch between 1992 and 2001. The *Kitty Hawk* took part in Operation Restore Hope in Somalia in 1992. The *Kitty Hawk*, the *John F. Kennedy*, and the *Constellation* formed part of the task force engaged in Operation Enduring Freedom in 2001, the attack on the Taliban in Afghanistan. The *Kitty Hawk* and the *Constellation* also took part in Iraqi Freedom, the invasion of Iraq in 2003.

The *Kitty Hawk* was home ported at Yokosuka in Japan from 1995. The *America* decommissioned in August 1996 and was scuttled in 2005.

72. UNITED STATES: *ENTERPRISE* (1961)
Courtesy of Art-Tech

LAID DOWN: February 4, 1958. Launched: September 24, 1960. Commissioned: November 25, 1961

BUILDER: Newport News Shipbuilding & Dry Dock Company, Newport News, VA

DISPLACEMENT: 75,700 tons (standard), 89,600 tons (full load)

DIMENSIONS: 1,123'0" (oa) x 133'0" x 36'0" (full load)

FLIGHT DECK: 1,100'0" x 252'0"

MACHINERY: 4 Westinghouse geared turbines, 8 Westinghouse A2W reactors, 4 shafts, 280,000 shp = 35 knots

ENDURANCE: 90 days

AIRCRAFT: 99

COMPLEMENT: 5,500

DESIGN: Although the weight of the *Enterprise*'s nuclear power plant was not very much greater than that of a fossil-fueled installation, the carrier was much larger than its conventionally powered contemporaries because of the space required for the large liquid loads needed for underwater protection. Since most of the liquid load was aviation fuel, the *Enterprise* was capable of embarking a larger than usual air group and of operating it continuously for longer. The ship's arrangement was generally similar to the earlier *Kitty Hawk*, but the island was much smaller (because it did not have to accommodate the stack) and no defensive armament was fitted to cut costs. The *Enterprise* received flat panel electronically scanning radars installed on the four faces of the island structure: SPS-32 search and SPS-33 three dimensional search.

MODIFICATIONS: In 1967 two 8-tube Sea Sparrow launchers were fitted, controlled by modified APQ-72 aircraft fire control radar sets. The following year an SPS-12 air search set was added to its suite. A refueling and refit process began in 1991 and lasted until 1994, during which three Mk.15 Phalanx 20mm mounts were added, the bridge reconstructed, and SPS-48C air search, SPS-49 long range two-dimensional air search, and SPS-65 Sea Sparrow search radars replaced the original outfit. Mk. 23 target acquisition radar, SPN-41 landing aid, and two SPN-46 air traffic control radars were added.

SERVICE: The *Enterprise* was in the Atlantic Fleet from commissioning until 1965, participating in the blockade of Cuba during the missile crisis, and then deploying to the Mediterranean. In 1965 it transferred to the Pacific Fleet and began operations on Yankee Station, flying strikes against North Vietnam until 1973. It remained in the Pacific until 1990, during which time it deployed to the Persian Gulf in 1988 in support of the tanker war. The *Enterprise* returned to the Atlantic Fleet after its refit and was engaged during Operation Southern Watch, enforcing the "no-fly" zone over southern Iraq, until 2000. In 2001 the *Enterprise* formed part of the strike force for Operation Enduring Freedom, the war against the Taliban in Afghanistan.

73. UNITED STATES: *NIMITZ* CLASS (1975)
Courtesy of Art-Tech

Nimitz
LAID DOWN: June 22, 1968. Launched: May 13, 1972. Commissioned: May 3, 1975

Dwight D. Eisenhower
LAID DOWN: August 15, 1970. Launched: October 11, 1975. Commissioned: October 18, 1977

Carl Vinson
LAID DOWN: October 11, 1975. Launched: March 18, 1980. Commissioned: March 13, 1982

Theodore Roosevelt
LAID DOWN: October 31, 1981. Launched: October 27, 1984. Commissioned: October 25, 1986

Abraham Lincoln
LAID DOWN: November 3, 1984. Launched: February 13, 1988. Commissioned: November 11, 1989

George Washington
LAID DOWN: August 25, 1986. Launched: July 21, 1990. Commissioned: July 4, 1992

John C. Stennis
LAID DOWN: March 13, 1991. Launched: October 13, 1993. Commissioned: December 9, 1995

Harry S. Truman
LAID DOWN: November 29, 1993. Launched: September 7, 1996. Commissioned: July 25, 1998

Ronald Reagan
LAID DOWN: February 12, 1998. Launched: March 4, 2001. Commissioned: July 12, 2003

George H. W. Bush

LAID DOWN: September 6, 2003. Launched: February 2006. Commissioned: Anticipated for 2008

BUILDER: Newport News Shipbuilding & Dry Dock Company (later Northrop Grumman Newport News), Newport News, VA

DISPLACEMENT: 100,020–104,581 tons (full load)

DIMENSIONS: 1,092'0" (*Dwight D. Eisenhower* and *Vinson* 1,098'0," *Nimitz* 1,115'0") (oa) x 134'0" x 37'0" (*Nimitz, Dwight D. Eisenhower,* and *Carl Vinson*), 38'6" (others) (full load)

FLIGHT DECK: 1,070'0" x 252'0"

MACHINERY: 4 General Electric geared turbines, 2 Westinghouse A4W reactors, 4 shafts, 280,000 shp = 31 knots

ENDURANCE: 90 days

AIRCRAFT: 70

ARMAMENT: 2 x 8-tube Sea Sparrow SAM launchers (all but the *Nimitz* and the *Dwight D. Eisenhower* completed with 3 mounts), 4 x Mk.15 Phalanx 20mm mounts (none in the *Nimitz* and the *Dwight D. Eisenhower* initially), 2 x 21-round RAM Mk. 49 SAM launchers (the *Ronald Reagan* and the *George H. W. Bush* only, replacing all Mk.15 Phalanx 20mm mounts)

COMPLEMENT: 6,275

DESIGN: Two substantial changes endowed this class with greater internal space for crew, munitions, and fuel. Two very compact A4W reactors, developed from a projected design intended as a single reactor installation on frigates and destroyers, replaced the eight reactors required for the *Enterprise*. The space-saving side protection system used in the *John F. Kennedy* also was applied to this class. These ships also received a more conventional island structure, since conventional antennae replaced the *Enterprise*'s flat-panel electronically scanning radars. The first three ships completed with SPS–43A air search and SPS–48 long-range three-dimensional search radars, later ships carry SPS–49 air search radar in place of the SPS–43A set. Since the class was constructed over a long period, there are many detail differences between ships. All ships now carry Mk. 23 target acquisition radar. Carrier approach is handled by SPN–42A in the *Nimitz*, the *Dwight D. Eisenhower*, the *Carl Vinson*, and the *Theodore Roosevelt*. All ships from the *Theodore Roosevelt* on carry SPN–44 landing aid radar, and the *Abraham Lincoln* and later ships all carry two SPN–46 air traffic control sets. All ships after the first three were built with extensive Kevlar armor protection installed and use new lower steam pressure catapults.

MODIFICATIONS: The first three ships received Kevlar armor protection as an upgrade in refits, the *Nimitz* in 1983–1984, the *Dwight D. Eisenhower* in 1985–1987, and the *Carl Vinson* in 1989. In 1983 the *Nimitz* and the *Carl Vinson* replaced their SPS–43A with SPS–49, The *Dwight D. Eisenhower* made the same change in 1986. All ships upgraded to SPS–48E from 1992. The *Nimitz* and the *Dwight D. Eisenhower* added an additional Sea Sparrow mount and three Mk.15 Phalanx 20mm mounts during their refits. The first seven ships began their only refueling/complex overhaul process during their careers, starting with the *Nimitz* in 1998 and scheduled to end with the *John C. Stennis* in 2018.

SERVICE: The *Nimitz* served with the Atlantic Fleet from commissioning, deploying to the Mediterranean. It provided support for the failed mission to release hostages from the United States embassy in Tehran in 1979 and participated in the first Gulf of Sidra incident on August 19, 1981, its aircraft shooting down two Libyan Su–22 fighters. In 1987 the *Nimitz* transferred to the Pacific Fleet. The *Dwight D. Eisenhower,* the *Theodore Roosevelt,* the *George Washington,* and the *Harry S. Truman* joined the Atlantic Fleet on commissioning. The *Carl Vinson,* the *Abraham Lincoln,* the *John C. Stennis,* and the *Ronald Reagan* joined the Pacific Fleet on completion.

The *Dwight D. Eisenhower,* the *Theodore Roosevelt,* and the *Abraham Lincoln* participated in Operation Desert Shield in 1990–1991, the *Nimitz,* the *Dwight D. Eisenhower,* the *Theodore Roosevelt,* and the *Abraham Lincoln* took part in Operation Desert Storm in 1991, during which the *Dwight D. Eisenhower*'s aircraft flew more missions than any other carrier. The *Nimitz,* the *Carl Vinson,* the *Theodore Roosevelt,* the *Abraham Lincoln,* and the *Harry S. Truman* participated in Operation Southern Watch between 1991 and 2003 in the Persian Gulf, enforcing the "no-fly" zone over southern Iraq. The *Theodore Roosevelt*'s air wing was very active during operations Deny Flight, Deliberate Force, and Allied Force over Bosnia and Kosovo between 1995 and 1999. The *Carl Vinson,* the *Theodore Roosevelt,* the *Abraham Lincoln,* the *George Washington,* the *John C. Stennis,* and the *Harry S. Truman* formed part of the task force engaged in Operation Enduring Freedom, the attack on the Taliban in Afghanistan, in the fall of 2001. In April 2003 the *Nimitz,* the *Abraham Lincoln,* the *Theodore Roosevelt,* and the *Harry S. Truman* formed part of the task force for Operation Iraqi Freedom, the invasion of Iraq.

74. VARIOUS NATIONS: *MAJESTIC* CLASS (1948)
Courtesy of Art-Tech

Sydney (Australia)
BUILDER: Devonport Dockyard
LAID DOWN: April 19, 1943. Launched: September 30, 1945. Commissioned: February 5, 1949

Magnificent (Canada)
BUILDER: Harland & Wolff Ltd., Belfast
LAID DOWN: July 29, 1943. Launched: November 16, 1944. Commissioned: March 21, 1948

Leviathan (United Kingdom)
BUILDER: Swan, Hunter & Wigham Richardson, Ltd., Wallsend-on-Tyne
LAID DOWN: October 18, 1943. Launched: June 7, 1945
DISPLACEMENT: 14,512 tons (standard), 19,550 tons (full load)
DIMENSIONS: 698'0" (oa) x 80'0" x 19'9" (mean), 24'6" (full load)

FLIGHT DECK: 685'0" x 75'0"
MACHINERY: Parsons geared turbines, 4 Admiralty 3-drum boilers, 2 shafts, 40,000 shp = 25 knots
BUNKERAGE & RANGE: 3,480 tons = 9,320 nm @ 12 knots
AIRCRAFT: 37
ARMAMENT: 6 x twin 40mm AA, 18 x 40mm AA
COMPLEMENT: 1,200

Melbourne (Australia)
BUILDER: Vickers-Armstrong Ltd., Barrow-in-Furness
LAID DOWN: April 15, 1943. Launched: February 28, 1945. Commissioned: October 28, 1955
DISPLACEMENT: 16,000 tons (standard), 20,320 tons (full load)
DIMENSIONS: 701'6" (oa) x 80'0" x 25'0" (full load)

FLIGHT DECK: 690'0" x 105'0"

MACHINERY: Parsons geared turbines, 4 Admiralty 3-drum boilers, 2 shafts, 40,000 shp = 24.5 knots

BUNKERAGE & RANGE: 3,000 tons = 9,320 nm @ 12 knots

AIRCRAFT: 27

ARMAMENT: 6 x twin 40mm AA, 13 x 40mm AA

COMPLEMENT: 1,210

Bonaventure (Canada)

BUILDER: Harland & Wolff Ltd., Belfast

LAID DOWN: November 27, 1943. Launched: February 27, 1945. Commissioned: January 17, 1957

DISPLACEMENT: 16,000 tons (standard), 20,000 tons (full load)

DIMENSIONS: 704'10" (oa) x 80'0" x 25'0" (full load)

FLIGHT DECK: 685'0" x 105'0"

MACHINERY: Parsons geared turbines, 4 Admiralty 3-drum boilers, 2 shafts, 40,000 shp = 24.5 knots

BUNKERAGE & RANGE: 3,000 tons = 9,320 nm @ 12 knots

AIRCRAFT: 34

ARMAMENT: 4 x twin 3" AA

COMPLEMENT: 1,200

Vikrant (India)

BUILDER: Vickers-Armstrong Ltd., Newcastle-upon-Tyne

LAID DOWN: October 14, 1943. Launched: September 22, 1945. Commissioned: March 4, 1961

DISPLACEMENT: 16,000 tons (standard), 19,550 tons (full load)

DIMENSIONS: 700'0" (oa) x 80'0" x 24'0" (full load)

FLIGHT DECK: 680'0" x 105'0"

MACHINERY: Parsons geared turbines, 4 Admiralty 3-drum boilers, 2 shafts, 40,000 shp = 24.5 knots

BUNKERAGE & RANGE: 3,000 tons = 9,320 nm @ 12 knots

AIRCRAFT: 21

ARMAMENT: 4 x twin 40mm AA, 7 x 40mm AA

COMPLEMENT: 1,343

DESIGN: An improved *Colossus* class light fleet carrier with greater subdivision and flight deck and elevators stressed to accommodate aircraft up to 30,000 pounds. Fitted with Type 277Q search radar and Type 293Q height finding and fighter direction radar.

MODIFICATIONS: The *Melbourne* completed with a 5–1/2-degree angled flight deck, uprated arresting gear, a single steam catapult, and mirror landing equipment. During a major refit between 1967–1969 new Dutch LW–01 air search, ZW surface search, and carrier controlled approach radars were added to the original suite, and in 1971 the flight deck was strengthened and the catapult upgraded. By 1976 armament was four twin 40mm and four single 40mm. The *Bonaventure* completed with an 8-degree angled flight deck, a single steam catapult, uprated arresting gear, and mirror landing equipment. American SPS–10 surface search radar, SPS–12 air search radar, and SPS–8 height finding radar was substituted for the British suite of the original design. In 1966–1967 a new Fresnel landing aid replaced the mirror and the two forward twin 3-inch mounts and their sponsors were removed. The *Vikrant* completed with an 8-degree angled flight deck, a single steam catapult, uprated arresting gear, and mirror landing equipment. It also was fully air conditioned to suit it for service in tropical seas. From 1979 to 1982 the *Vikrant* received a major refit, including new engines, and a ski jump was added in 1989 to operate Sea Harriers.

SERVICE: The *Sydney* conducted strike operations during the Korean War from 1951 to 1953. From 1957, it operated as a training carrier but became a fast transport supporting Australian operations in Malaya and Vietnam from 1962. The *Sydney* was stricken in 1973 and sold for scrapping in 1975. The *Magnificent* served in the North Atlantic until it was returned to the United Kingdom in 1957. It was placed in reserve thereafter until it was sold for scrapping in July 1965. The *Leviathan* was never completed and was sold for scrapping in May 1968. The *Melbourne* operated in Australian and Far Eastern waters, first as a strike carrier until 1963, then in the anti-submarine warfare role until June 1982, when it went into reserve. It was sold for scrapping in February 1985. The *Bonaventure* operated as an all weather carrier in the North Atlantic. From 1961 it took on a pure antisubmarine warfare role. It was decommissioned in July 1970 and sold for scrapping in 1971. The *Vikrant* participated in operations to take over Goa in December 1961. It took a very active role in operations during the second Indo-Pakistan War in December 1971, striking shore targets and shipping. By the early 1990s its poor condition kept it in port and it was decommissioned in January 1997. The *Vikrant* is maintained as a museum ship at Mumbai Naval Dockyard.

JOINT OPERATIONS

75. FRANCE: *MISTRAL* CLASS (2005)
Courtesy of Art-Tech

Mistral

LAID DOWN: July 10, 2003. Launched: October 6, 2004. Commissioned: September 2005

Tonnerre

LAID DOWN: August 26, 2003. Launched: July 26, 2005. Commissioned: Anticipated in 2006

BUILDER: Arsenal de Brest & Alstom Chantiers de l'Atlantique, St. Nazaire

DISPLACEMENT: 19,500 tons (standard), 21,500 ton (full load)

DIMENSIONS: 682'6" (oa) x 91'0" x 20'2" (full load)

FLIGHT DECK: 508'0" x 104'0"

MACHINERY: 4 Wartsilä diesel generator sets, 2 Mermaid podded azimuthal thruster units, 26,000 hp = 19 knots

RANGE: 12,000 nm @ 15 knots

AIRCRAFT: 16

ARMAMENT: 4 x 6-cell Simbad SAM system launchers, 2 x 20mm GIAT F2 AA, 4 x 12.7mm MG

COMPLEMENT: 160 + 450 troops

DESIGN: Originally to be dock landing ships, the design was changed to incorporate a full flight deck linked by two starboard side elevators to a large aircraft hangar, 210 feet long and 91 feet wide, accommodating up to 16 NH90 assault helicopters. There is also a large vehicle hangar capable of accommodating LeClerc 54-ton heavy tanks, accessed via large side-loading ramps. The well dock is 187 feet long and 50 feet wide and can handle up to four landing craft or two air-cushion assault craft. These ships have very large hospital facilities and extensive NCB (Nuclear, Chemical, Biological) protection. They are fitted with fin stabilizers for ease of helicopter operation and their unusual thruster propulsion system endows them with great maneuverability and the capability of maintaining a fixed position for an extended period. They can accommodate up to 900 troops for a short period only.

SERVICE: The *Mistral* entered service primarily to take over the cadet training role of the *Jeanne d'Arc* but will be available for amphibious missions in addition to its sister, the *Tonnerre*, which is due to enter service in 2006.

76. ITALY: *CONTE DI CAVOUR*
Courtesy of Art-Tech

BUILDER: Fincantieri, Trieste

LAID DOWN: June 2001. Launched: July 20, 2004. Commissioned: Anticipated for 2008

DISPLACEMENT: 22,130 tons (standard), 26,500 tons (full load)

DIMENSIONS: 769'0" (oa) x 96'9" x 24'3" (mean), 28'6" (full load)

FLIGHT DECK: 763'1" x 113'2"

MACHINERY: 4 General Electric-FiatAvio LM–2500 gas turbines, 2 shafts, 118,000 shp = 28 knots

BUNKERAGE & RANGE: 7,000 nm @ 16 knots

AIRCRAFT: 14

ARMAMENT: 4 x 8-cell Sylver SAM system launchers, 2 x 76.2mm OTO-Melara DP, 3 x 25mm OTO-Melara AA, 4 x 12.75" ASW torpedo tubes

COMPLEMENT: 842 + 360 troops

DESIGN: Initially conceived as an amphibious assault ship, similar to the United States Navy's *Tarawa* class though somewhat smaller, the design has evolved to emphasize aircraft carrier qualities, most notably through the deletion of the well deck. The ship has a diesel-electric drive cruise system that allows operation at 9 knots, and also has both bow and stern thrusters for maneuverability. The hull is fitted with two pairs of fin stabilizers. The hangar, 440 feet long, 69 feet wide, and 20 feet high, can also be used for vehicle stowage. It can accommodate 12 EH.101 helicopters, 8 AV–8B Harrier VTOL aircraft, 12 Ariete battle tanks, or up to

100 light trucks. The hangar connects to the flight deck via a large starboard side deck edge elevator and a smaller unit forward of the superstructure. The flight deck has spots for six helicopters. Its landing area is offset to port and terminates in a 12-degree ski jump forward. The radar suite comprises RAN–40S early warning, SPS–791 surface search, SPY–790 target designation and tracking, SPN–753 navigation, 2 SPG–76 fire control, and SPN–41 carrier controlled approach sets.

77. UNITED KINGDOM: *OCEAN* (1999)
Courtesy of Art-Tech

BUILDER: BAE Systems, Barrow-in-Furness

LAID DOWN: March 30, 1995. Launched: October 11, 1995. Commissioned: March 19, 1999

DISPLACEMENT: 21,578 tons (full load)

DIMENSIONS: 667'4" (oa) x 107'0" x 21'10" (full load)

FLIGHT DECK: 557'9" x 104'0"

MACHINERY: 2 Crossley-Pielstick 12-cylinder diesels, 2 shafts, 18,360 bhp = 19 knots

BUNKERAGE & RANGE: 1,500 tons = 8,000 nm @ 15 knots

AIRCRAFT: 18

ARMAMENT: 3 x twin 30mm AA, 3 x Mk.15 Phalanx 20mm mounts

COMPLEMENT: 461 + 500 troops

DESIGN: The design parameters for this vessel are very unusual in that it conforms to mercantile standards (Lloyd's Register specifications) except for those specific features that need to meet military requirements. This decision reduced costs considerably below that of comparable vessels. The hull form and overall layout was derived from that of the *Invincible* class. It incorporates two sets of folding fin stabilizers. The hangar can accommodate twelve large helicopters. Two elevators and a vehicle ramp connect it to the full-length flight deck (without a ski jump). Four landing craft are accommodated with openings in the hull side and there is a ramp in the stern for vehicles. The radar suite comprises Type 996(2) surface and air search, Type 1007 navigation, and 3 Mk. 90 fire control sets for the Phalanx weapons.

MODIFICATIONS: *Ocean* underwent a refit between December 2000 and May 2001 that included fitting new landing craft davits, improving replenishment-at-sea equipment, and upgrading computer systems. A 2002 refit added 165-foot long blisters aft to improve landing craft handling.

SERVICE: *Ocean* deployed for a humanitarian relief operation in Honduras in 1999, then supported operations to suppress a rebellion in Sierra Leone during 2002. In 2003 *Ocean* deployed to the Persian Gulf as part of the Royal Navy's task force for Operation Telic, the invasion of Iraq.

78. UNITED STATES: *IWO JIMA* CLASS (1961)
Courtesy of Art-Tech

Iwo Jima
BUILDER: Puget Sound Navy Yard
LAID DOWN: February 13, 1959.
Launched: September 17, 1960.
Commissioned: October 20, 1961

Okinawa
BUILDER: Philadelphia Navy Yard
LAID DOWN: April 1, 1960. Launched:
August 19, 1961. Commissioned:
April 13, 1962

Guadalcanal
BUILDER: Philadelphia Navy Yard
LAID DOWN: September 1, 1961.
Launched: August 1, 1962. Commissioned: January 25, 1963

Guam
BUILDER: Philadelphia Navy Yard
LAID DOWN: November 15, 1962.
Launched: August 22, 1964. Commissioned: January 16, 1965

Tripoli
BUILDER: Ingalls Shipbuilding Corporation, Pascagoula, MS
LAID DOWN: June 15 1964. Launched:
July 31, 1965. Commissioned: August 6, 1966

New Orleans
BUILDER: Philadelphia Navy Yard
LAID DOWN: March 1, 1966 Launched:
February 3, 1968. Commissioned:
November 16, 1968

Inchon
BUILDER: Ingalls Shipbuilding Corporation, Pascagoula, MS
LAID DOWN: April 8, 1968. Launched:
May 24, 1969. Commissioned: June 20, 1970
DISPLACEMENT: 17,000 tons (standard),
18,350 tons (full load)

DIMENSIONS: 592'0" (oa) x 84'0" x 25'0' (mean), 26'7" (full load)

FLIGHT DECK: 592'0" x 105'0"

MACHINERY: Geared turbines, 4 boilers, 1 shaft, 22,000 shp = 20 knots

AIRCRAFT: 20

ARMAMENT: 4 x twin 3" AA

COMPLEMENT: 900 + 2,000 troops

DESIGN: This class was developed specifically to meet the requirements of the United States Marine Corps for helicopter assault operations. Unlike the earlier conversions from *Essex* class carriers, this design featured berthing (complete with air conditioning) that was concentrated to maintain unit cohesion. The flight deck had spots for up to seven medium or four heavy assault helicopters, was clear from end to end, and linked to the hangar via two deck edge elevators. The hangar could accommodate up to nineteen medium or eleven heavy helicopters. The design included provision for rapid conversion for antisubmarine warfare duties but could not operate fixed wing aircraft, since there were neither catapults nor arresting gear. *Inchon* alone was fitted with davits to carry two LCVP landing craft; the other ships in the class could only use their helicopters to land troops and could not transport heavy equipment ashore. SPS–40 air search radar was fitted.

MODIFICATIONS: *Guam* was modified as a prototype Sea Control Ship in 1971, testing deployment of Harrier VTOL aircraft. It received an antisubmarine warfare sensor analysis center, additional aircraft control and direction equipment, and an upgraded aircraft maintenance shop. *Guam* reverted to amphibious assault ship status in 1974. Between 1970 and 1974 the class was refitted, replacing two 3-inch mounts with two 8-tube Sea Sparrow launchers. Ten years later the remaining 3-inch weapons were replaced with two Mk.15 Phalanx 20mm mounts. In 1991, these ships received two 25mm Bushmaster guns for close defense. *Inchon* was converted into a mine countermeasures support ship between March 1995 and May 1996, receiving major upgrades in command, control, communications, computers, and intelligence systems and in repair facilities to support embarked aircraft (eight MH–53E Sea Dragon helicopters) and other attached minecraft.

SERVICE: *Iwo Jima* deployed to the Pacific Fleet on completion. In 1962 it took part in the blockade of Cuba during the missile crisis. From 1963 to 1973 it served off Vietnam, supporting over thirty Marine Corps landings. In 1970 *Iwo Jima* was the recovery ship for the Apollo 13 mission. It transferred to the Mediterranean in 1974 and contributed substantially to operations Desert Shield and Desert Storm, the liberation of Kuwait, in 1990 to 1991. It decommissioned in July 31, 1993, and was scrapped. *Okinawa* served in the Caribbean until 1967, participating in the blockade of Cuba in 1962. It then transferred to the Pacific Fleet and operated off Vietnam until 1975. *Okinawa* took part in Operation

Desert Shield. It decommissioned November 19, 1992 and was sunk as a target in 2002. *Guadalcanal* operated in the Atlantic throughout its career and decommissioned August 31, 1994. *Guam* operated with the Atlantic Fleet throughout its career, serving in the Caribbean, Mediterranean, North Atlantic, and Red Sea. It became the first ship to deploy operationally with AV–8A Harriers in 1974. It formed part of the task force in both operations Desert Shield and Desert Storm, and supported operations in the Adriatic in 1996 and the Persian Gulf in 1997 before decommissioning August 24, 1998. *Tripoli* and *New Orleans* both joined the Pacific Fleet on commissioning and served off Vietnam until 1973. They

continued serving in the Pacific thereafter until deployed to the Persian Gulf to participate in Operation Desert Storm, during which *Tripoli* was mined and damaged on February 18, 1991. They also supported Operation Restore Hope in Somalia in 1993. *Tripoli* decommissioned September 15, 1995, and *New Orleans* on October 1, 1997. *Inchon* undertook a world cruise in 1972, and then served with the Atlantic Fleet, mainly in the Mediterranean. It supported operations in Somalia and the Adriatic during 1994 before beginning conversion to a mine countermeasures support ship in 1995–1996. *Inchon* remained with the Atlantic Fleet until decommissioning on June 20, 2002.

79. UNITED STATES: *TARAWA* CLASS (1975)
Courtesy of Art-Tech

Tarawa
LAID DOWN: November 15, 1971. Launched: December 1, 1973. Commissioned: May 29, 1975

Saipan
LAID DOWN: July 21, 1972. Launched: July 18, 1974. Commissioned: October 15, 1977

Belleau Wood
LAID DOWN: March 5, 1973. Launched: April 11, 1977. Commissioned: September 23, 1978

Nassau
LAID DOWN: August 13, 1973. Launched: January 21, 1978. Commissioned: July 28, 1979

Peleliu
LAID DOWN: November 12, 1976. Launched: November 25, 1978. Commissioned: May 3, 1980

BUILDER: Ingalls Shipbuilding Corporation, Pascagoula, MS
DISPLACEMENT: 39,300 tons (full load)
DIMENSIONS: 820'0" (oa) x 106'0" x 27'6" (full load)
FLIGHT DECK: 820'0" x 118'0"
MACHINERY: Westinghouse geared turbines, 2 Combustion Engineering boilers, 2 shafts, 77,000 shp = 24 knots
BUNKERAGE & RANGE: 5,900 tons = 10,000 nm @ 20 knots
AIRCRAFT: 43
ARMAMENT: 3 x 5" DP, 6 x 20mm AA, 2 x Mk 25 8-barrel Sea Sparrow SAM launchers.
COMPLEMENT: 901 + 1,800 troops
DESIGN: The principal deficiency of the *Iwo Jima* design was its restriction to using helicopters to land troops and its inability to transport their heavy equipment to the beach. The *Tarawa*

design combined the basic concept of the *Iwo Jima* type enlarged to incorporate a 268-foot long and 78-foot wide well deck for launching landing craft and amphibious tracked vehicles. The large flight deck has spots for twelve medium or nine heavy assault helicopters. It is linked to the full-length hangar deck (820 feet long, 78 feet wide, with a clear height of 20 feet) by a port side deck-edge elevator and another at the stern. The hangar can accommodate up to thirty medium or nineteen heavy assault helicopters. The dedicated vehicle deck can handle up to thirty-five amphibious tracked vehicles and the well deck can accommodate four LCU1610 landing craft, seven LCM(8) landing craft, seventeen LCM(6) landing craft, or forty-five amphibious tracked vehicles. The design includes sophisticated automated cargo-handling arrangements, a large space for troop acclimatization training, fully equipped medical facilities (including three operating theaters), and very elaborate command, communications, and control facilities. A powerful thruster is fitted forward for use while launching landing craft. The radar suite comprises SPS–40 air search, SPS–52 three-dimensional search and control, SPG–60 fire control, and SPQ–9 search and track weapons control sets.

MODIFICATIONS: The Sea Sparrow launcher, 5-inch guns, and 20mm mounts were removed and replaced with two 21-cell RAM launchers, two Mk.15 Phalanx 20mm mounts, and four single 25mm Bushmaster mounts in the early 1990s. The radar suite also was upgraded to SPS–40E air search, SPS–48E three-dimensional air search, SPS–67 surface search, SPS–64 navigation, and Mk. 23 target acquisition system.

SERVICE: *Tarawa* joined the Pacific Fleet on commissioning. It participated in operations Desert Shield and Desert Storm to liberate Kuwait in 1990–1991 and supported Operation Southern Watch, enforcing the "no-fly" zone over southern Iraq, in 1996. *Saipan* became part of the Atlantic fleet on commissioning and has served primarily in the Mediterranean. After commissioning in 1978, *Belleau Wood* was assigned to the Pacific Fleet. Sasebo in Japan became its home port from 1992 to 2000. *Belleau Wood* began operating in the Persian Gulf region in 2002. *Nassau* was assigned to the Atlantic Fleet after commissioning and operated primarily in the Mediterranean. It formed part of the task force for operations Desert Shield and Desert Storm in 1990–1991, and subsequently supported operations in the Adriatic off Bosnia and Kosovo. *Nassau* was engaged in Operation Iraqi Freedom, the invasion of Iraq, in 2003. *Peleliu* joined the Pacific Fleet on commissioning. In 2001 it formed part of the task force supporting Operation Enduring Freedom, the attack on the Taliban in Afghanistan, and subsequently deployed to the Persian Gulf in late 2003.

80. UNITED STATES: *WASP* CLASS (1989)
Courtesy of Art-Tech

Wasp
LAID DOWN: May 30, 1985. Launched: August 4, 1987. Commissioned: July 29, 1989

Essex
LAID DOWN: March 20, 1989. Launched: January 4, 1991. Commissioned: October 17, 1992

Kearsarge
LAID DOWN: February 6, 1990. Launched: March 26, 1992. Commissioned: September 25, 1993

Boxer
LAID DOWN: April 8, 1991. Launched: August 13, 1993. Commissioned: February 11, 1995

Bataan
LAID DOWN: June 22, 1994. Launched: March 15, 1996. Commissioned: September 20, 1997

Bonhomme Richard
LAID DOWN: April 18, 1995. Launched:

March 14, 1997. Commissioned: August 15, 1998

Iwo Jima
LAID DOWN: December 12, 1997. Launched: March 25, 2000. Commissioned: June 14, 2001

Makin Island
LAID DOWN: February 14, 2004. Launched: Anticipated for 2006. Commissioned: Anticipated by 2007
BUILDER: Ingalls Shipbuilding Corporation, Pascagoula, MS
DISPLACEMENT: 40,300 tons (full load), 41,335 tons (*Makin Island*) (full load)
DIMENSIONS: 844'2" (oa) x 140'0" x 28'0" (full load)
FLIGHT DECK: 830'0" x 140'0"
MACHINERY: Westinghouse geared turbines, 2 Combustion Engineering boilers, 2 shafts, 77,000 shp = 24 knots. 2 General Electric LM.2500 gas turbines, 2 shafts, 70,000 shp = 22 knots (*Makin Island* only)

BUNKERAGE & RANGE: 6,200 tons = 9,500 nm @ 20 knots (steam-powered vessels)

AIRCRAFT: 43

ARMAMENT: 2 x Mk 29 8-cell Sea Sparrow SAM launchers (not on *Makin Island*), 2 x 21-cell RAM launchers (*Iwo Jima* and *Makin Island* only), 3 (2 on *Iwo Jima* and *Makin Island*) x Mk.15 Phalanx 20mm mounts, 4 (3 on *Iwo Jima* and none on *Makin Island*) x 25mm Bushmaster LA, 4 x twin 0.50" machine guns.

COMPLEMENT: 1,082 + 1,900 troops

DESIGN: These ships are similar to the *Tarawa* class with improved aviation facilities. In place of the stern elevator, a starboard side deck-edge unit was fitted and more substantial support facilities for AV–8 Harrier aircraft were arranged. The well deck was modified to better suit it for air-cushion landing craft operation: it can accommodate three such craft, two LCU1610 landing craft, six LCM(8) landing craft, or twelve LCM(6) landing craft. The radar suite comprises SPS–49 air search, SPS–48E three-dimensional air search, SPS–67 surface search, SPS–64 navigation, and Mk. 23 target acquisition system. These ships carry thirty medium and heavy assault helicopters plus six AV–8B Harriers while serving in the amphibious role or about twenty AV–8B Harriers plus six antisubmarine helicopters while serving in the sea control carrier role.

The *Makin Island* is a unique modified version of the class, powered by gas turbine engines, and incorporating all electric auxiliary machinery, an advanced machinery control system, water-mist fire protection arrangements, and upgraded command, communications, and control systems.

MODIFICATIONS: The first six vessels received two 21-cell RAM launchers after completion and landed one Mk.15 Phalanx 20mm mount in compensation.

SERVICE: The *Wasp* joined the Atlantic Fleet on completion and served mainly in the Caribbean and Mediterranean. The *Essex* deployed to the Pacific Fleet and has been home ported at Sasebo, Japan, since 2002. It has undertaken several deployments to the Persian Gulf since 1995. The *Kearsarge* joined the Atlantic Fleet and operated in the Adriatic between 1995 and 2000 off Bosnia and Kosovo. It formed part of the task force for Operation Enduring Freedom, the attack on the Taliban in Afghanistan, in 2001, participated in Operation Iraqi Freedom, the invasion of Iraq, in 2003, and has deployed to the Persian Gulf since then. On commissioning, the *Boxer* joined the Pacific Fleet and supported Operation Iraqi Freedom, the invasion of Iraq, in 2003, and subsequent operations in the Persian Gulf. The *Bataan* and the *Iwo Jima* serve with the Atlantic Fleet, the *Bon Homme Richard* with the Pacific Fleet. Both the *Bataan* and the *Bon Homme Richard* formed part of the task forces for operations Enduring Freedom and Iraqi Freedom, and the *Bataan* has returned to the Persian Gulf for further operations. The *Iwo Jima* also took part in Operation Iraqi Freedom.

GLOSSARY

Admiralty: Shorthand terminology for the Royal Navy's Board of Admiralty, which heads its central administration. Unlike most such boards, it includes both the civilian political appointees and the professional heads of the fleet.

Air Group/Wing: The aircraft embarked aboard an aircraft carrier.

Airborne Early Warning: Aircraft configured to carry radar sets and operators to extend the reach of their search.

Aircraft Engine Types: *See* Liquid Cooled; Radial; Rotary; Turbofan; Turboshaft.

Aircraft Types: *See* Airborne Early Warning; Amphibian; Biplane; Flying Boat; Landplane; Monoplane; Seaplane; Triplane; VSTOL.

Amphibian: An aircraft capable of operating from both the water and the land.

Armor Belt: Vertical armor on the side of a ship's hull.

Armor Bulkhead: Vertical armor across a ship's hull.

Arresting Gear: Systems, usually of wires, designed to engage hooks attached to an aircraft to slow it as it lands on a carrier.

Battle cruiser: A battleship type that trades armor protection for higher speed.

Biplane: An aircraft with two sets of wings, one above the other.

Bridge: The ship's navigating and control station.

Brake Horsepower (bhp): The measure of the power output of internal combustion engines.

Bulge: Structures built onto a ship's side beyond the primary hull structure. Initially these were used to enhance protection against damage from a torpedo hit but they came to be employed more to enhance stability by increasing a hull's internal volume.

Catapult: A device for launching aircraft into the air. On aircraft carriers they usually were powered by hydraulic engines or steam from the boilers.

Conseil Superieur: The French Navy's professional leadership.

Crash Barrier: Usually nets or similar arrangements to prevent aircraft from striking other machines beyond the barrier.

Cruiser, Armored: A cruising warship type used until the first quarter of the twentieth century that depended on an armored belt for its main protection.

Cruiser, Heavy: A cruiser armed with 8-inch guns.

Cruiser, Light: A cruiser armed with 6-inch or smaller guns.

Cruiser, Protected: A cruising warship type used until the first quarter of the twentieth century that depended on an armored deck for its main protection.

Deck Load Strike: An attack force made up of as many aircraft as could be ranged on the flight deck with sufficient space remaining forward for the first aircraft to take off under its own power.

Deck Park: Space on the flight deck in which aircraft may be kept while other flight deck operations continue. Widely used by the United States Navy from early in its carrier operations to maximize the size of air groups, it is now a normal feature of carrier operations, with much of a carrier's air group remaining on the flight deck at all times except for overhaul and major maintenance.

Diesel: Internal combustion engines using oil fuel and compression ignition.

Dreadnought: A battleship armed primarily with eight or more very large caliber guns.

Electronic Warfare: The use of electronic jamming and distortion to protect aircraft against discovery and location by radar.

Elevator: A platform to move aircraft between the hangar and the flight deck.

Flight Deck: The deck from which aircraft take off and on which they land.

Flight Deck, Angled: A flight deck arrangement in which the landing area is angled away from the ship's centerline toward the port side to allow a longer landing zone and a clear exit in the event of not catching the arresting gear.

Flight Deck, Axial: A flight deck arrangement entirely along the centerline axis of the ship.

Flying Boat: An aircraft that operates from water, landing and taking off using the bottom of its fuselage as the interface with the water.

Gallery Deck: A deck level suspended below the flight deck.

General Board: The professional leadership of the United States Navy until 1948.

Hangar: Enclosed stowage space for aircraft.

Hangar, Closed: A hangar that is wholly enclosed and accessible only via the elevator openings.

Hangar, Open: A hangar with large openings toward the side of the ship in addition to elevator openings.

Hangar Deck: The floor of the hangar.

Horsepower (hp): A measure of work over time equal to 33,000 foot-pounds per minute or 745.7 watts per minute. *See* Brake Horsepower; Indicated Horsepower; Shaft Horsepower.

Indicated Horsepower (ihp): The measure of the power output of reciprocating steam engines.

Island: Offset superstructure containing the principal navigating and control spaces for an aircraft carrier.

Landing Signals Officer: Popularly know as "paddles" or a "batsman." A pilot trained to signal pilots of approaching aircraft to indicate their position as they come in to land on a flight deck.

Landplane: An aircraft using a wheeled undercarriage.

Liquid Cooled: Piston engines that are cooled by liquids running in jackets around the cylinders. Initially this was water but later liquids with higher boiling points came in to use.

Machinery Types: *See* Diesel; Triple Expansion; Turbine.

Magazine: Stowage space for munitions.

Monitor: A small shallow draft vessel carrying heavy guns, primarily intended for shore bombardment.

Monocoque Construction: Aircraft fuselage construction that creates an integral shell structure.

Monoplane: An aircraft with a single set of wings. They may be low or high on the fuselage (low or high-winged) or set above the fuselage on struts (parasol-winged).

Pre-Dreadnought: A battleship usually armed with four large caliber guns and a substantial secondary armament.

Radar: Electronic location equipment, initially for search only but rapidly developed to provide gunnery control and missile guidance.

Radial: Piston engines that almost always are cooled by the passage of air over fins on their cylinders, which are arranged radially around a central crankcase. Because of this configuration, there are always odd numbers of cylinders in each bank. Radial engines may have one, two, or occasionally four banks of cylinders.

Radome: A protective enclosure for a radar antenna.

Rotary: Piston engines that appear very similar to radial engines but differ in that the crankshaft is stationary and the cylinder assembly rotates around it.

Round Down: Sections of a flight deck, either forward or aft, that are shaped to improve airflow and facilitate landing.

Run Out: The extension of arresting gear wires as they are pulled by the landing aircraft.

Seaplane: Also called a floatplane, using floats suspended below the fuselage for landing and taking off from water.

Shaft Horsepower (shp): The measure of the power output of turbine engines.

Sheer: The shape of the top of a ship's hull as viewed from the side.

Sonar: Acoustic detection equipment for locating submarines.

Sonobuoy: A floating device containing a sonar set and transmitter that may be dropped from an aircraft to locate submarines and transmit the information back to the aircraft.

Sponson: A platform set outside the hull.

Stack: An enclosure for furnace flues.

Stressed Skin Construction: Aircraft construction system in which the skin itself contributes to the structural strength of the aircraft.

Superstructure: All of a ship's structure above the hull's sheer.

Topweight: The component of the ship's weight that is above its center of gravity.

Torpedo: Self-propelled underwater weapon.

Triplane: An aircraft with three sets of wings, one above the other.

Triple Expansion: Reciprocating steam engines using multiple cylinders to maximize steam usage.

Trunk: Ductwork that carries gases from the furnace to outside the ship.

Turbine: Engines that use the passage of steam or hot gases to rotate encased fan blade assemblies to generate power.

Turbofan: A jet engine in which the turbine drives powerful fans to force air behind the engine, generating thrust.

Turbojet: A jet engine that generates thrust through the rapid compression, combustion, and expulsion of the fuel-air mixture.

Turboshaft: A jet engine in which the turbine drives a shaft connected to a conventional aircraft propeller.

Uptakes: Vertical furnace gas ductwork.

Variable Pitch Propeller: A propeller whose blades may be twisted to vary their angles according to power needs.

VSTOL: Aircraft designed for Vertical or Short Take Off and Landing.

Warship Types: *See* Battle cruiser; Cruiser, Armored; Cruiser, Heavy; Cruiser, Light; Cruiser, Protected; Dreadnought; Pre-Dreadnought.

BIBLIOGRAPHY

Adcock, Al. *Escort Carriers in Action*. Carrollton: Squadron/Signal Publications, 1996.

Agawa Hiroyuki. *Reluctant Admiral: Yamamoto and the Imperial Navy*. Tokyo: Kodansha International, 1979.

Antier, Jean-Jacques. *Les Porte-Avions et la Maîtresse de la Mer*. Paris: Robert Laffont, 1966.

———. *Le Porte-Avions* Clemenceau. Brest: Ouest-France, 1984.

Arthur, Reginald Wright. *Contact: Careers of Naval Aviators Assigned Numbers 1–2000*. Washington, DC: Naval Aviation Register, 1967.

Atkinson, Scott R. *Civilian-Military Differences on Soviet Aircraft Carrier Deployment*. Alexandria, VA: Center for Naval Analyses, 1990.

Bail, René, and Jean Moulin. *Le Porte-Avions* Arromanches. Paris: Charles-Lavauzelle, 1984.

———. *Les Porte-Avions* Clemenceau *et* Foch. Paris: Charles-Lavauzelle, 1985.

Baker, A.D., III (ed.). *The Naval Institute Guide to Combat Fleets of the World*. Annapolis, MD: Naval Institute Press, various editions from 1976 to date (editions from 2005 edited by Eric Wertheim).

———. *German Naval Vessels of World War Two: Compiled by US Naval Intelligence*. Annapolis, MD: Naval Institute Press, 1993.

Baldwin, Sherman. *Ironclaw: A Navy Carrier Pilot's Gulf War Experience*. New York: William Morrow and Company, 1996.

Barjot, P. *Vers la Marine de l'Âge Atomique*. Paris: Amiot Dumont, 1951.

———. *Histoire de la Guerre Aéronavale*. Paris: Flammarion, 1961.

Barlow, Jeffrey G. *Revolt of the Admirals: The Fight for Naval Aviation, 1945–1950*. Washington, DC: Government Printing Office, 1995.

Beaver, Paul. *Carrier Air Operations since 1945*. London: Arms and Armour Press, 1983.

———. *Britain's Armed Forces Today: 2, Fleet Command*. London: Ian Allan, 1984.

———. *The British Aircraft Carrier*. Cambridge: Patrick Stephens Ltd., 1987.

Belote, James H., and William M. Belote. *Titans of the Sea: The Development and Operations of Japanese and American Carrier Task Force During World War II*. New York: Harper & Row, 1975.

Bennett, Christopher. *Supercarrier.* Osceola, WI: Motorbooks International, 1996.

Bergaust, Erik. *Aircraft Carrier in Action.* New York: Putnam, 1968.

Bergerud, Eric M. *Fire in the Sky: The Air War in the South Pacific.* Boulder: Westview Press, 1999.

Blechman, Barry M., and Stephen S. Kaplan (eds.). *Force without War: US Armed Forces as a Political Instrument.* Washington, DC: Brookings Institution, 1978.

Blundell, W. G. D. *British Aircraft Carriers.* London: Model & Allied Publications Ltd., 1969.

Bonds, Ray. *Modern Carriers.* New York: Prentice Hall Press, 1988.

Bradshaw, Thomas I. *Carrier Down: The Story of the Sinking of the USS Princeton (CVL-23).* Austin: Eakin Press, 1990.

Breyer, Siegfried. *Battleships and Battlecruisers, 1905–1970.* New York: Doubleday, 1971.

———. *The German Aircraft Carrier* Graf Zeppelin. Atglen: Schiffer Publishing, 1989.

———, and Norman Polmar. *Guide to the Soviet Navy.* Annapolis, MD: Naval Institute Press, various editions from 1970 to 1991 (later editions Norman Polmar only).

Brown, David K., (ed.). *Conway's History of the Ship: The Eclipse of the Big Gun: The Warship 1906–45.* Annapolis, MD: Naval Institute Press, 1992.

———. *The Grand Fleet: Warship Design and Development 1906–1922.* Annapolis, MD: Naval Institute Press, 1999.

———. Nelson *to* Vanguard: *Warship Design and Development 1923–1945.* Annapolis, MD: Naval Institute Press, 2000.

Brown, David K., and George Moore. *Rebuilding the Royal Navy: Warship Design since 1945.* Annapolis, MD: Naval Institute Press, 2003.

Brown, Eric. *Wings of the Navy: Flying Allied Carrier Aircraft of World War Two.* Annapolis, MD: Naval Institute Press, 1987.

———. *Duels in the Sky: World War II Naval Aircraft in Combat.* Annapolis, MD: Naval Institute Press, 1988.

Brown, (J.) David. *Carrier Operations in World War II, 2 vols.* London: Ian Allan, 1968 & 1974.

———. *HMS* Illustrious, *Part. 2.* Windsor: Profile Publications Ltd., 1971.

———. *Carrier Air Groups: HMS* Eagle. Windsor: Profile Publications Ltd., 1972.

———. *HMS* Eagle. Windsor: Profile Publications Ltd., 1973.

———. *The Seafire.* London: Ian Allan, 1973.

Cable, James. *Gunboat Diplomacy: Political Uses of Limited Force.* London: MacMillan, 1981.

————. *Britain's Naval Future*. Annapolis, MD: Naval Institute Press, 1983.

————. *Navies in a Violent Peace*. London: MacMillan, 1989.

Careley, Demetrios. *The Politics of Military Unification: A Study of Conflict and the Policy Process*. New York: Columbia University Press, 1966.

Carlin, Michael. *Trial, Ordeal of the USS* Enterprise, *14 January 1969*. West Grove, PA: Tuscarora Press, 1993.

Chesneau, Roger. *Aircraft Carriers of the World, 1914– Present*. Annapolis, MD: Naval Institute Press, 1984.

Coletta, Paolo E. *Admiral Bradley A. Fiske and the American Navy*. Lawrence: Regents Press of Kansas, 1979.

————. *Patrick N. L. Bellinger and U.S. Naval Aviation*. Lanham: University Press of America, 1987.

Condon, John Pomeroy. *Corsairs and Flattops: Marine Carrier Air Warfare, 1944–1945*. Annapolis, MD: Naval Institute Press, 1997.

Coutau-Bégarie, Hervé. *Le Probléme du Porte-Avions*. Paris: CREST-École Polytechnique/Éditions Economica, 1990.

Cracknell, William H. *USS* Hornet *(CV-8): Aircraft Carrier*. Windsor: Profile Publications Ltd., 1971.

————. *USS* Enterprise *(CVAN-65): Nuclear Attack Carrier*. Windsor: Profile Publications Ltd., 1972.

Cressman, Robert. *That Gallant Ship U.S.S.* Yorktown *(CV-5)*. Missoula: Pictorial Histories Publishing, 1985.

————, and Michael J. Wenger. *Steady Nerves and Stout Hearts: The* Enterprise *(CV-6) Air Group and Pearl Harbor, 7 December 1941*. Missoula: Pictorial Histories Publishing, 1990.

Cronin, Dick, *Royal Navy Shipboard Aircraft Developments 1912–1931*. Tunbridge Wells: Air-Britain, 1990.

Davis, Jacquelyn K. *Aircraft Carriers and the Role of Naval Power in the Twenty-first Century*. Cambridge, MA: Institute for Foreign Policy Analysis, 1993.

————. *CVX: A Smart Carrier for the New Era*. Washington, DC: Brassey's, 1998.

Dickson, W. David. *Battle of the Philippine Sea, June 1944*. London: Ian Allan, 1974.

Dousset, Francis. *Les Porte-Avions Français des Origines (1911) á nos Jours*. Brest: Éditions de la Cité, 1975.

Dresser, James. *Escort Carriers and Their Air Unit Markings during World War II in the Pacific*. Ames: J. Dresser, 1980.

Dull, Paul S. *A Battle History of the Imperial Japanese Navy (1941–1945)*. Annapolis, MD: Naval Institute Press, 1978.

Dunn, Patrick T. *The Advent of Carrier Warfare*. Ann Arbor: University of Michigan Press, 1991.

Evans, David C. *The Japanese Navy in World War in the Words of Former Japanese Naval Officers*. Annapolis, MD: Naval Institute Press, 1982.

————, and Mark R. Peattie. *Kaigun: Strategy, Tactics, and Technology in the Imperial Japanese Navy, 1887–1941*. Annapolis, MD: Naval Institute Press, 1997.

Ewing, Steve. *USS Enterprise (CV-6): The Most Decorated Ship of WW II, A Pictorial History*. Missoula: Pictorial Histories Publishing, 1982.

————. *The "Lady Lex" and the "Blue Ghost": A Pictorial History of the USS Lexingtons CV-2 and CV-16*. Missoula: Pictorial Histories Publishing, 1983.

Faltum, Andrew. *The Essex Class Carriers*. Baltimore: Nautical and Aviation Publishing, 1996.

————. *The Independence Class Light Aircraft Carriers*. Baltimore: Nautical and Aviation Publishing, 2002.

Feifer, George. *Tennozan: The Battle of Okinawa and the Atomic Bomb*. New York: Ticknor & Fields, 1992.

Foster, Wynn F. *Captain Hook: A Pilot's Tragedy and Triumph in the Vietnam War*. Annapolis, MD: Naval Institute Press, 1992.

Francillon, Rene J. *Japanese Aircraft of the Pacific War*. London: Putnam, 1987.

————. *Tonkin Gulf Yacht Club: US Carrier Operations Off Vietnam*. London: Conway Maritime Press., 1988.

Frank, Richard. *Guadalcanal*. New York: Penguin Books, 1990.

Friedman, Norman. *Carrier Air Power*. London: Conway Maritime Press, 1981.

————. *U.S. Naval Weapons: Every Gun, Missile, Mine and Torpedo Used by the U.S. Navy From 1883 to the Present Day*. Annapolis, MD: Naval Institute Press, 1982.

————. *US Aircraft Carriers: An Illustrated Design History*. Annapolis, MD: Naval Institute Press, 1983.

————. *British Carrier Aviation: The Evolution of the Ships and Their Aircraft*. Annapolis, MD: Naval Institute Press, 1988.

————. (ed.). *U.S. Army-Navy Journal Of Recognition, September 1943—February 1944, Numbers 1–6*. Annapolis, MD: Naval Institute Press, 1990.

————. (ed.). *Conway's History of the Ship: Navies in the Nuclear Age*. Annapolis, MD: Naval Institute Press, 1993.

Fry, John. *USS Saratoga CV-3: An Illustrated History of the Legendary Aircraft Carrier, 1927–1946*. Atglen: Schiffer Publishing, 1996.

Fuchida Mitsuo and Masatake Okumiya. *Midway: The Battle that Doomed Japan*. Annapolis, MD: Naval Institute Press, 1955.

Fukui Shizuo. *Nihon no gunkan: waga gijutsu no hattatsu to kantei no hensen* [Japanese warships: our development of ship construction technology and changes over time]. Tokyo: Shuppan Kyodosha, 1959.

————. *Japanese Naval Vessels at the End of the War*. Old Greenwich, CT: W.E., Inc., 1970.

————. *Shashin Nihon kaigun zen kantei shi* [A photographic history of all the ships in the Japanese Navy], 3 vols. Tokyo: Best Sellers, 1994.

Gardiner, Robert (ed.). *Conway's All the World's Fighting Ships, 1922–1946*. London: Conway Maritime Press, 1980.

————. *Conway's All the World's Fighting Ships, 1906–1921*. London: Conway Maritime Press, 1985.

————. *Conway's All The World's Fighting Ships, 1947–1995*. London: Conway Maritime Press, 1995.

Garrison, Peter, and George Hall. *CV: Carrier Aviation, Airpower No. 1001*. Novato: Presidio Press, 1987.

Genda Minoru. *Kaigun kokutai shimatsuki* [A record of the particulars of the Japanese naval air service], 2 vols. Tokyo: Bungei Shunju, 1961–1962.

————. *Shinjuwan sakusen kaikoroku* [Recollections of the Pearl Harbor operation] Tokyo: Yomiuri Shimbunsha, 1972.

Gilcrist, Paul T. *Vulture's Row: Thirty Years in Naval Aviation*. Atglen, PA: Schiffer Publishing, 1996.

————. *Feet Wet: Reflections of a Carrier Pilot*. Atglen, PA: Schiffer Publishing, 1997.

Giorgerini, Giorgio, and Augusto Nani. *Navi di Linea Italiane 1861–1961*. Rome: Ufficio Storico Marina Militare, 1966.

Goldstein, Donald M., and Katherine V. Dillon (eds.). *The Pearl Harbor Papers: Inside the Japanese Plans*. New York: Brassey's, 1993.

————, and Michael Wenger. *The Way It Was: Pearl Harbor, The Original Photographs*. Alexandria, VA: Brassey's, 1991.

Grant, Zalin. *Over the Beach: The Air War in Vietnam*. New York: W. W. Norton, 1986.

Greger, René. *The Russian Fleet 1914–1917*. London: Ian Allan, 1972.

Gröner, Erich, Dieter Jung, and Martin Maass. *German Warships 1815–1945, Vol. I: Major Surface Vessels*. Annapolis, MD: Naval Institute Press, 1990.

Grossnick, Roy A. *Dictionary of Naval Aviation Squadrons, Vol. 1, The History of VA, VAH, VAK, VAL, VAP and VFA Squadrons*. Washington, DC: Naval Historical Center, 1995.

Grove, Eric. *Vanguard to Trident: British Naval Policy since World War II*. Annapolis, MD: Naval Institute Press, 1987.

Hall, George. *Top Gun: The Navy's Fighter Weapons School*. Novato, CA: Presidio Press, 1987.

Hallion, Richard P. *The Naval Air War in Korea*. Baltimore: Nautical & Aviation Publishing, 1986.

Halpern, Paul G. *The Naval War in the Mediterranean, 1914–1918*. Annapolis, MD: Naval Institute Press, 1987.

Hammel, Eric. *Guadalcanal: The Carrier Battles*. New York: Crown Publishers, 1987.

————. *Guadalcanal: Decision at Sea*. New York: Crown Publishers, 1988.

Hanson, Norman. *Carrier Pilot*. Cambridge: Patrick Stephens, 1979.

Hargis, Robert. *US Naval Aviator 1941–45*. Oxford: Osprey Publishing, 2002.

Harper, John A. *Paddles! The Foibles and Finesse of One World War II Landing Signal Officer*. Atglen: Schiffer Publishing, 1996.

Hasegawa Toichi. *Nihon no kokubokan* [Japanese aircraft carriers]. Tokyo: Grand Prix Shuppan, 1997.

Hata Ikuhiko ,and Yasuho Izawa. *Japanese Naval Aces and Fighter Units in World War II*. Annapolis, MD: Naval Institute Press, 1989.

Herrick, Robert. *Soviet Naval Theory and Practice*. Washington, DC: Government Printing Office, 1988.

Hezlet, Sir Arthur Richard R. *Aircraft and Sea Power*. New York: Stein and Day, 1970.

Hines, Eugene G. *The "Fighting Hannah": A War History of USS* Hancock *(CV-19)*. Nashville: Battery Press, 1989.

Horikoshi Jiro. *Eagles of Mitsubishi: The Story of the Zero Fighter*. Seattle: University of Washington Press, 1981.

Hobbs, David. *Aircraft Carriers of the Royal and Commonwealth Navies*. London: Greenhill Books, 1996.

Hoehling, A. *The* Lexington *Goes Down: The Last Seven Hours of a Fighting Lady*. New York: Prentice-Hall, 1971.

Holmes, Tony. *Carriers: United States Naval Air Power in Action*. New York: Military Press, 1990.

———. *Seventh Fleet Super Carriers: US Naval Air Power in the Pacific*. London: Osprey Publishing, 1987.

———, and Jean-Pierre Montbazet. *World Super Carriers, Naval Air Power Today*. London: Osprey Publishing, 1988.

Hone, Thomas, Norman Friedman, and Mark Mandeles. *American & British Aircraft Carrier Development 1919–1941*. Annapolis, MD: Naval Institute Press, 1999.

Hoyt, Edwin P. *The Carrier War*. New York: Simon and Schuster, 1965.

———. *Carrier Wars: Naval Aviation from World War II to the Persian Gulf*. New York: McGraw-Hill, 1989.

———. *The Men of the* Gambier Bay. Middlebury, VT: P. S. Eriksson, 1979.

Humble, Richard. *Aircraft Carriers: The Illustrated History*. New York: Chartwell Books, 1982.

———. *United States Fleet Carriers of World War II in Action*. New York: Blandford Press, 1984.

Ireland, Bernard. *Warships of The World: Major Classes*. New York: Charles Scribner's Sons, 1976.

———. *The Aircraft Carrier: An Illustrated History*. New York: Chartwell Books, 1979.

Jenkins, C. A. *HMS* Furious, *Aircraft Carrier 1917–1948; 2 parts*. Windsor: Profile Publications, 1972.

Jensen, Oliver. *Carrier War*. New York: Simon &Schuster, 1945.

Jentschura, HansGeorg, Dieter Jung, and Peter Mickel. *Warships of the Imperial Japanese Navy 1869–1945*. Annapolis, MD: Naval Institute Press, 1977.

Johnson, Brian. *Fly Navy: The History of Maritime Aviation*. London: David & Charles, 1981.

Johnston, Stanley P. *Queen of the Flattops: The USS* Lexington *and Coral Sea Battle*. New York: E. P. Dutton, 1942

Jordon, John. *Illustrated Guide to Modern Naval Aviation and Aircraft Carriers*. New York: Arco, 1983.

———. *Soviet Warships: The Soviet Surface Fleet 1960 to the Present*. Annapolis, MD: Naval Institute Press, 1983.

———. *The New Illustrated Guide to the Modern US Navy*. London: Smithmark, 1992.

Joss, John. *Strike: U.S. Naval Strike Warfare School*. Novato, CA: Presidio Press, 1989.

Kaplan, Stephen S. (ed.). *Diplomacy of Power: Soviet Armed Forces as a Political Instrument*. Washington, DC: Brookings Institution, 1981.

Kaufman, R.G. *Arms Control during the Pre-Nuclear Era: The United States and Naval Limitations between the Two World Wars*. New York: Columbia University Press, 1990.

Kaufman, Yogi. *City at Sea*. Annapolis, MD: Naval Institute Press, 1995

Kemp, Paul. *The Russian Convoys 1941–45*. London: Arms & Armor Press, 1987.

———. *Malta Convoys 1940–43*. London: Arms & Armor Press, 1988.

Kenney, Douglas, and William Butler. *No Easy Days: The Incredible Drama of Naval Aviation*. Louisville, KY: Butler, Kenney, Farmer, 1995.

Kernan, Alvin. *Crossing the Line: A Bluejacket's World War II Odyssey*. Annapolis, MD: Naval Institute Press, 1994.

Kilbracken, Lord. *Bring Back My Stringbag: A Stringbag Pilot at War*. London: Pan Books, 1980.

Kilduff, Peter. *US Carriers at War*. Harrisburg, PA: Stackpole Books, 1981.

King, Brad. *Royal Naval Air Service 1912–1918*. Aldershot: Hikoki Publications, 1997.

Kinzey, Bert. *USS* Lexington *in Detail and Scale*. Blue Ridge Summit, PA: Tab Books, 1988.

———. *USS* America *in Detail and Scale*. Blue Ridge Summit, PA: Tab Books, 1989.

———. *USS* Enterprise *in Detail and Scale*. Blue Ridge Summit, PA: Tab Books, 1991.

———. *USS* Forrestal *in Detail and Scale*. Waukesha, WI: Kalmbach Books, 1993.

———. *USS* John F. Kennedy *in Detail and Scale*. Waukesha, WI: Kalmbach Books, 1993.

Knott, Richard C. *The Naval Aviation Guide*. Annapolis, MD: Naval Institute Press, 1985.

———. *A Heritage of Wings: An Illustrated History of Navy Aviation*. Annapolis, MD: Naval Institute Press, 1997.

Kuwabara Torao. *Kaigun koku kaisoroku, soso hen* [Recollections of naval aviation, the early years]. Tokyo: Koku Shimbun Sha, 1964.

Labayle-Couhat, Jean. *French Warships of World War II*. London: Ian Allan, 1971.

———. *French Warships of World War I*. London: Ian Allan, 1972.

Lawson, Robert L. *Carrier Air War in Original WWII Color*. Osceola, WI: Motorbooks International, 1996.

———. *Carrier Air Group Commanders: The Men and Their Machines*. Atglen, PA: Schiffer Publishing, 2000.

Layman, R. D. *To Ascend from a Floating Base: Shipboard Aeronautics and Aviation, 1783–1914*. Rutherford, NJ: Fairleigh Dickinson University Press, 1979.

———. *Before the Aircraft Carrier: The Development of Aviation Vessels (1849–1922)*. Annapolis, MD: Naval Institute Press, 1989.

———. *Naval Aviation in the First World War: Its Influence and Impact*. Annapolis, MD: Naval Institute Press, 1996.

———, and Stephen McLaughlin. *The Hybrid Warship: The Amalgamation of Big Guns and Aircraft*. Annapolis, MD: Naval Institute Press, 1991.

Lehman, John F. *Aircraft Carriers: The Real Choices*. Thousand Oaks, CA: Sage Publications, 1978.

———. *Command of the Seas: Building the 600 Ship Navy*. New York: Charles Scribner's Sons MacMillan Publishing, 1988.

Le Masson, Henri. *The French Navy* Vol. I. Garden City: Doubleday, 1969.

Lenton, Henry T. *American Battleships, Carriers and Cruisers*. Garden City: Doubleday, 1968.

———. *British Battleships and Aircraft Carriers*. Garden City: Doubleday, 1972.

———. *German Warships of the Second World War*. London: Macdonald & Janes, 1975.

———, and J. J. Colledge, [British & Commonwealth] *Warships of World War II*. London: Ian Allan, 1973.

Lindley, John M. *Carrier Victory: The Air War in the Pacific*. New York: Elsevier-Dutton, 1978.

Lundstrom, John. *The First South Pacific Campaign*. Annapolis, MD: Naval Institute Press, 1979.

———. *The First Team: Pacific Naval Air Combat from Pearl Harbor to Midway*. Annapolis, MD: Naval Institute Press, 1984.

———. *The First Team and the Guadalcanal Campaign: Naval Fighter Combat from August to November 1942*. Annapolis, MD: Naval Institute Press, 1994.

Lyon, D J. *HMS* Illustrious *Part.1*. Windsor: Profile Publications, 1971.

MacConnell, James, and Bradford Dismukes (eds.). *Soviet Naval Diplomacy*. New York: Pergamon Press, 1979.

MacDonald, Scot. *Evolution of Aircraft Carriers*. Washington, DC: Government Printing Office, 1964.

MacGlashing, John W. *Batmen: Night Air Group 90 in World War II*. New York: Phalanx Publishing, 1995.

MacIntyre, Donald G. F. W. *Aircraft Carrier*. New York: Ballantine Books, 1968.

Marolda, Edward J. *By Sea, Air, and Land: An Illustrated History of the U.S. Navy and the War in Southeast Asia*. Washington, DC: Government Printing Office, 1994.

Marston, Daniel (ed.). *The Pacific War Companion: From Pearl Harbor to Hiroshima*. London: Osprey Publishing, 2005.

Maru Mechanics. *Mechanism of Japanese Warships 2: Aircraft Carriers*. Tokyo: Kojinsha, 1991.

———. *Imperial Japanese Navy Photo File 5*: Akagi, Kaga, Hosho, Ryujo. Tokyo: Kojinsha, 1991.

———. *Imperial Japanese Navy Photo File 6*: Shokaku, Zuikaku, Soryu, Hiryu, Unryu *class*, Taiho. Tokyo: Kojinsha, 1991.

———. *Imperial Japanese Navy Photo File 7*: Junyo, Hiyo, Zuiho *class*, Ryuho, Chitose *class*, Shinano. Tokyo: Kojinsha, 1991.

Masters, A. O. *"Cappy," Memoirs of a Reluctant Batsman*. London: Janus, 1995.

McGwire, Michael, and John MacDonnell (eds.). *Soviet Naval Influence: Domestic and Foreign Dimensions*. New York: Praeger, 1977.

Meister, Jürg. *Soviet Warships of the Second World War*. London: Macdonald & Janes, 1977.

Melhorn, Charles M. *Two-Block Fox, the Rise of the Aircraft Carrier, 1911–1929*. Annapolis, MD: Naval Institute Press, 1974.

Mersky, Peter B., and Norman Polmar. *The Naval Air War in Vietnam*. Baltimore: Nautical & Aviation Publishing, 1986.

Messimer, Dwight R. *Pawns of War: The Loss of the USS* Langley *and the USS* Pecos. Annapolis, MD: Naval Institute Press, 1983.

Mikesh, Robert C. *Zero: Combat and Development History of Japan's Legendary Mitsubishi A6M Zero Fighter*. Osceola, WI: Motorbooks International, 1994.

———, and Shorzoe Abe, *Japanese Aircraft 1910–1941*. London: Putnam, 1990.

Miller, Edward S. *War Plan Orange: The U.S. Strategy to Defeat Japan, 1897–1945*. Annapolis, MD: Naval Institute Press, 1991.

Miller, Nathan. *The Naval Air War, 1939–1945*. Baltimore: Nautical & Aviation, 1991.

Miller, Max. *Daybreak for Our Carrier*. New York: McGraw-Hill, 1944.

Mizrahi, J. V. *Carrier Fighters*, 2 vols. Northridge, CA: Sentry Books, 1969.

Moore, John E. *Warships of the Royal Navy*. Annapolis, MD: Naval Institute Press, 1979.

Morareau, Lucien, Robert Feuilloy, Jean-Louis Courtinat, Thierry Le Roy, and Jean-Paul Rossignol. *L'Aviation Maritime Française pendant la Grande Guerre*. Paris: ARDHAN, 1999.

Morrison, Wilbur H. *Above and Beyond, 1941–1945*. New York: St. Martin's Press, 1983.

Musicant, Ivan. *U.S. Armored Cruisers: A Design and Operational History*. Annapolis, MD: Naval Institute Press, 1985.

Naval Historical Center. *Dictionary of American Naval Fighting Ships*. 9 vols. Washington, DC: Government Printing Office, 1954–1991.

Nichols, John B., and Barrett Tillman. *On Yankee Station: The Naval Air War over Vietnam*. Annapolis, MD: Naval Institute Press, 1987.

Norman, C. J. *Aircraft Carriers*. New York: F. Watts, 1986.

O'Connor, Raymond. *Perilous Equilibrium: The United States and the London Naval Conference of 1930*. Lawrence: University of Kansas Press, 1962.

O'Leary, Michael, and Eric Schulzinger. *Airwing* Enterprise. Osceola, WI: Motorbooks International, 1991.

Pavlov, A. S. *Warships of the USSR and Russia, 1945–1995*. Annapolis, MD: Naval Institute Press, 1997.

Pawlowski, Garth L. *Flat-Tops and Fledglings: A History of American Aircraft Carriers*. London: Thomas Yoseloff, 1971.

Polmar, Norman. *Aggressors, Vol. 2, Carrier Power vs. Fighting Ship*. Charlottesville, VA: Howell Press, 1990.

———. *The Naval Institute Guide to the Ships and Aircraft of the U.S. Fleet*, 12th–18th editions. Annapolis, MD: Naval Institute Press, 1981–2005.

———. *Aircraft Carriers: A History of Carrier Aviation and Its Influence on World Events, Vol. I., 1909–1945*. Alexandria, VA: Potomac Books, 2006.

Poolman, Kenneth. *Aircraft Carriers*. London: Grosset & Dunlap, 1979.

———. *Escort Carrier: HMS* Vindex *at War*. London: Secker & Warburg, 1983.

———. *Allied Escort Carriers of WW II in Action*. Annapolis, MD: Naval Institute Press, 1988.

———. *Escort Carriers of World War Two*. New York: Sterling Publishers, 1989.

Power, Hugh Irvin. *Carrier* Lexington. College Station, TX: Texas A&M University Press, 1996.

Preston, Antony. *Aircraft Carriers: An Illustrated History*. London: Hamlyn, 1979.

Quentric, Jean-Paul, and Guy Thévenin. *Aéronautique Navale: Formation des Pilotes aux États-Unis (1950–1957)*. Paris: ARDHAN, 1997.

Raven, Alan. *Essex-Class Carriers*. Annapolis, MD: Naval Institute Press, 1988.

Reese, Lee Fleming (ed). *Men of the Blue Ghost, (USS* Lexington *CV-16) 1943–1946*. San Diego, CA: Lexington Book, 1980.

Reynolds, Clark G. *The Fast Carriers: The Forging of an Air Navy.* Huntington, NY: Robert E. Krieger, 1978.

———. *The Carrier War.* Alexandria, VA: Time-Life Books, 1982.

———. *The Fighting Lady, The New* Yorktown *in the Pacific War.* Missoula: Pictorial Histories Publishing, 1986.

———. *Admiral John H. Towers: The Struggle for Naval Air Supremacy.* Annapolis, MD: Naval Institute Press, 1991.

———.*On the Warpath in the Pacific: Admiral Jocko Clark and the Fast Carriers.* Annapolis, MD: Naval Institute Press, 2005.

Roberts, John. *The Aircraft Carrier* Intrepid. Annapolis, MD: Naval Institute Press, 1982.

Rose, Lisle Abbott. *The Ship That Held the Line: The USS* Hornet *and the First Year of the Pacific War.* Annapolis, MD: Naval Institute Press, 1996.

Roskill, Stephen W. *The War at Sea, 1939–1945,* 3 vols. in 4. London: Her Majesty's Stationery Office, 1956–1961.

———. *Naval Policy between the Wars,* 2 vols. in 1. New York: Walker, 1968.

Documents Relating to the Naval Air Service. London: Naval Records Society, 1969.

Ross, Al. *The Escort Carrier* Gambier Bay. Annapolis, MD: Naval Institute Press, 1993.

Rossano, Geoffrey L. (ed). *The Price of Honor: The World War One Letters of Naval Aviator Kenneth MacLeish.* Annapolis, MD: Naval Institute Press, 1991.

Self, Chuck. *The USS* Hornet *CV-12, CVA-12, CVS-12.* Shreveport, LA: The Aircraft Carrier USS Hornet Foundation, 1995.

Sherman, Frederick C. *Combat Command: The American Aircraft Carriers in the Pacific War.* New York: E.P. Dutton, 1950.

Shirley, Noel. *United States Naval Aviation, 1910-1918.* Atglen, PA: Schiffer Publishing, 2000.

Silverstone, Paul H. *U.S. Warships of World War II,* London: Ian Allan, 1965.

———. *U.S. Warships of World War I.* London: Ian Allan, 1970.

———. *U.S. Warships Since 1945.* Annapolis, MD: Naval Institute Press, 1987.

Skiera, Joseph A. (ed.). *Aircraft Carriers in Peace and War.* New York: F. Watts, 1965.

Skwiot, Miroslaw. *Shokaku/Zuikaku.* Warsaw: AJ Press, 1994.

———, and Adam Jarski. *Akagi.* Warsaw: AJ Press, 1994.

Smith, John T. *Rolling Thunder: The Strategic Bombing Campaign – North Vietnam, 1965–1968.* New Malden: Air Research Publications, 1994.

Smith, Peter C. *The History of Dive Bombing.* Nautical & Aviation Publishing, 1982.

Sowinski, Larry. *Action in the Pacific: As Seen by US Navy Photographers during World War 2.* Annapolis, MD: Naval Institute Press, 1981.

St. John, Philip A. *USS* Yorktown: *CV-10, CVA-10, CVS-10: The Fighting Lady.* Paducah, KY: Turner Publishing, 1993.

Stafford, Edward P. *The Big E: The Story of the USS* Enterprise. New York: Random House, 1962.

Steichen, Edward. *The Blue Ghost: A Photographic Log and Personal Narrative of the Aircraft Carrier USS* Lexington *in Combat Operation.* New York: Harcourt, Brace, 1947.

Stern, Robert C. *The* Lexington-*Class Carriers.* Annapolis, MD: Naval Institute Press, 1993.

Stillwell, Paul. *Air Raid: Pearl Harbor!: Recollections of a Day of Infamy.* Annapolis, MD: Naval Institute Press, 1981.

Sturtivant, Ray. *Fleet Air Arm at War.* London: Ian Allan, 1982.

———. *Fleet Air Arm 1920–1939.* London: Arms and Armour Press, 1990.

———. *British Naval Aviation, The Fleet Air Arm, 1917–1990.* Annapolis, MD: Naval Institute Press, 1990.

———, and Gordon Page, *Royal Navy Aircraft Serials and Units 1911–1919.* Tunbridge Wells: Air-Britain, 1992.

———, and Theo Balance. *The Squadrons of the Fleet Air Arm.* Tunbridge Wells: Air-Britain, 1994.

———, and Mick Burrow. *Fleet Air Arm Aircraft 1939 to 1945.* Tunbridge Wells: Air-Britain, 1995.

———, and Dick Cronin. *Fleet Air Arm Aircraft, Units and Ships 1920 to 1939.* Tunbridge Wells: Air-Britain, 1998.

Sumrall, Robert F. (ed.). *USS* Hornet *(CV-8): Lost in Action in the Battle of Santa Cruz, 27 October 1942.* Missoula, MT: Pictorial Histories Publishing, 1985.

———. *USS* Intrepid *(CV 11).* Missoula, MT: Pictorial Histories Publishing, 1989.

Swanborough, Gordon, and Peter M. Bowers. *United States Navy Aircraft since 1911.* Annapolis, MD: Naval Institute Press, 1976.

Sweetman, Bill. *US Naval Air Power: Supercarrier in Action.* Osceola, WI: Motorbooks International, 1987.

Tagaya Osuma. *Imperial Japanese Naval Aviator 1937–1945.* Oxford: Osprey Publishing, 2002.

Tanner, Jane. *The USS* Saratoga: *Remembering One of America's Great Aircraft Carriers, 1956–1994.* Atlanta: Longstreet Press, 1994

Taylor, Theodore. *The Magnificent Mitscher.* New York: W. W. Norton, 1985.

Terzibaschitsch, Stefan. *Aircraft Carriers of the US Navy.* Annapolis, MD: Naval Institute Press, 1989.

———. *Escort Carriers and Aviation Support Ships of the US Navy.* Annapolis, MD: Naval Institute Press, 1989.

Thetford, Owen. *British Naval Aircraft since 1912.* London: Putnam, 1991.

Till, Geoffrey. *Air Power and the Royal Navy, 1914–1945.* London: Jane's Publishing, 1979.

Tillman, Barrett. *The Dauntless Dive Bomber of World War Two*. Annapolis, MD: Naval Institute Press, 1976.

———. *Hellcat: The F6F in World War II*. Annapolis, MD: Naval Institute Press, 1979.

———. *Corsair: The F4U in World War II and Korea*. Annapolis, MD: Naval Institute Press, 1979.

———. *Avenger at War*. New York: Scribner, 1980.

———. *MIG Master: The Story of the F-8 Crusader*. Baltimore: Nautical & Aviation Publishing, 1980.

———. *The Wildcat in World War II*. Baltimore: Nautical & Aviation Publishing, 1983.

Trimble, W. F. *Admiral William A. Moffett, Architect of Naval Aviation*. Washington, DC: Smithsonian Institution, 1994.

Turnbull, A. D., and C. L. Lord. *History of United States Naval Aviation*. New Haven: Yale University Press, 1949.

United States General Accounting Office. *Navy Carrier Battle Groups: The Structure and Affordability of the Future Force: Report to the Congress*. Washington, DC: Government Printing Office, 1993.

United States Navy. *Escort Carrier Force. The Escort Carriers in Action: The Story, in Pictures, of the Escort Carrier Force, U.S. Pacific Fleet, 1945*. Atlanta: Ruralist Press, 1946.

———. *Historic Ship Exhibits in the United States*. Washington, DC: Government Printing Office, 1969.

———. *United States Naval Aviation, 1910–1980*. Washington, DC: Government Printing Office, 1981.

United States Strategic Bombing Survey. *The Campaigns of the Pacific War*. Washington, DC: Government Printing Office, 1946.

Utz, Curtis Alan. *Carrier Aviation Policy and Procurement in the US Navy, 1936–1940*. Master's thesis, University of Maryland at College Park, MD, 1989.

Van Deurs, George. *Wings for the Fleet: A Narrative of Naval Aviation's Early Development, 1910–1916*. Annapolis, MD: Naval Institute Press, 1966.

———. *Anchors in the Sky: Spuds Ellyson, the First Naval Aviator*. San Rafael: Presidio Press, 1978.

Van Vleet, Clark, and William J. Armstrong. *United States Naval Aviation, 1910–1980*. Washington, DC: Government Printing Office, 1981.

Van Wyen, Adrian O. *Naval Aviation in World War I*. Washington, DC: Government Printing Office, 1969.

Vego, Milan. *The Soviet Navy Today*. London: Arms & Armour Press, 1986.

Vercken, Roger. *Histoire Succincte de l'Aéronautique Naval (1910–1998)*. Paris: ARDHAN, 1998.

Watson, Bruce W., and Peter M. Dunn (eds.). *The Future of the Soviet Navy*. Boulder: Westview Press, 1986.

Watton, Ross. *The Aircraft Carrier* Victorious. Annapolis, MD: Naval Institute Press, 1991.

Watts, A. J., and B. G. Gordon. *The Imperial Japanese Navy.* London: Macdonald, 1971.

Wellham, John. *With Naval Wings: The Autobiography of a Fleet Air Arm Pilot in World War II.* Staplehurst: Spellmount, 1995.

Whitley, M J. *German Capital Ships of World War Two.* London: Arms and Armour Press, 1989.

Wildenburg, Thomas. *Gray Steel and Black Oil: Fast Tankers and Replenishment at Sea in the U.S. Navy, 1912–1992.* Annapolis, MD: Naval Institute Press, 1996.

———. *Destined for Glory: Dive Bombing, Midway, and the Evolution of Carrier Air Power.* Annapolis, MD: Naval Institute Press, 1998.

Wilson, Eugene E. *Slipstream: The Autobiography of an Air Craftsman.* New York: McGraw-Hill, 1950.

Wilson, George C. *Supercarrier: An Inside Account of Life Aboard the World's Most Powerful Ship, the USS* John F. Kennedy. New York: MacMillan, 1986.

Winston, Robert A. *Aircraft Carrier.* New York: Harper & Brothers, 1942.

Winton, John. *The Forgotten Fleet.* London: Michael Joseph, 1960.

———. *Air Power at Sea, 1939–1945.* New York: Crowell Press, 1977.

———. *Carrier* Glorious. London: Leo Cooper, 1986.

———. *Air Power at Sea, 1945 to Present.* New York: Carroll and Graf, 1987.

Woodhouse, Henry. *Textbook of Naval Aeronautics.* New York: Century Books, 1917.

Woods, G. A. *Wings at Sea: A Fleet Air Arm Observer's War, 1940–45.* London: Conway Maritime Press, 1985.

Wooldridge, E. T. (ed.). *Carrier Warfare in the Pacific, an Oral History Collection.* Washington, DC: Smithsonian Institute Press, 1993.

———. *Into The Jet Age: Conflict and Change in Naval Aviation, 1945–1975.* Annapolis, MD: Naval Institute Press, 1995.

———. *The Golden Age Remembered: U.S. Naval Aviation, 1919–1941.* Annapolis, MD: Naval Institute Press, 1998.

Wragg, David. *Wings over the Sea: A History of Naval Aviation.* London: David & Charles, 1979.

———. *Carrier Combat.* Stroud: Sutton Publishing, 1997.

———. *Fleet Air Arm Handbook 1939–1945.* Stroud: Sutton Publishing, 2001.

Wukowvits, John F. *Devotion to Duty: A Biography of Admiral Clifton A.F. Sprague.* Annapolis, MD: Naval Institute Press, 1995.

Y'Blood, William T. *Hunter-Killer: US Escort Carriers in the Battle of the Atlantic.* Annapolis, MD: Naval Institute Press, 1983.

———. *The Little Giants.* Annapolis, MD: Naval Institute Press, 1987.

WEBSITES

Federation of American Scientists
www.fas.org
Fleet Air Arm Archive
www.fleetairarmarchive.net
GlobalSecurity.org
www.globalsecurity.org/military/index.html
Haze Gray & Under Way
www.hazegray.org
Imperial Japanese Navy Page
www.combinedfleet.com/kaigun.htm
Naval Historical Center
www.history.navy.mil

INDEX

Note: italic page numbers indicate pictures.

ABOUT THE AUTHOR

PAUL FONTENOY earned his degrees from King's College, London, East Carolina University, and London University. After a career in commercial aircraft operations, he returned to academia and taught at New York University. He is now Curator of Maritime Research and Technology at the North Carolina Maritime Museum. He is the author of four books (two as coauthor) and over 100 articles on naval, maritime, and aviation history.